CONSERVATISM, RADICALISM, AND SCIENTIFIC METHOD

THE MACMILLAN COMPANY
NEW YORK · BOSTON · CHICAGO · DALLAS
ATLANTA · SAN FRANCISCO

MACMILLAN & CO., LIMITED
LONDON · BOMBAY · CALCUTTA
MELBOURNE

THE MACMILLAN CO. OF CANADA, LTD.
TORONTO

Conservatism, Radicalism, and Scientific Method

AN ESSAY ON SOCIAL ATTITUDES

BY

A. B. WOLFE

PROFESSOR OF ECONOMICS, OHIO STATE UNIVERSITY

New York
THE MACMILLAN COMPANY
1923

PRINTED IN THE UNITED STATES OF AMERICA

FERRIS PRINTING COMPANY
NEW YORK CITY

TO
THE MOST COURAGEOUS,
AND THE GENTLEST,
PERSON I KNOW.

PREFACE

Fifteen years ago I initiated a college course in what I conceived to be the broader and basic, but concrete and specific, social problems. My students were Juniors and Seniors, supposedly in possession of a modicum of that liberal culture which the first class American college prides itself on bestowing. Nevertheless, it was quickly evident that something was wrong. The students were not ready for profitable discussion of problems involving conflict of human interest and sentiments. They lacked the essential open-mindedness and objectivity. They were, in spite of what the undergraduate curriculum had been doing for them, perhaps in part because of it, markedly characterized by the preconceptions, the prejudices, and the uncritical sentiments of the social stratum from which in most part college students come—that somewhat indefinite but exceedingly important part of the population known as the middle class.

They had little or no conception of scientific method or of an objective approach to social problems. Their tendency was toward dogmatic assertion and judgment on the basis of the socially inherited sentiments of their class. Their criteria of criticism and valuation were their own likes and dislikes. In short they were, as was to be expected, deeply marked by what is referred to in this book as popular-mindedness.

In some slight measure to modify this psychological situation, I thereafter began the course with a few lectures on scientific method and attitude, democracy and class point of view, individualism and social cooperation, and conservatism, liberalism, and radicalism. The modification of attitude apparently resultant upon these cursory lectures was so marked that as time went on it seemed profitable to expand the preliminary discussion of social viewpoints and attitudes, until finally it covered a full term.

What had at first been undertaken to meet an immediate pedagogical situation came to enlist a closer attention on my own part, and I became interested in the psychology and the causation and effects of the sentiments which long observation had taught me were of major significance in the determination of attitudes and thence of judgments and action. The present book is the result.

The book is thus, in a sense, the product of a by-current of interest followed up in the intervals available from other lines of thought and work. But it is a by-current, which, I believe, leads into a highly important phase of social psychology and practical ethics.

An economist may be criticized for invading the fields of social psychology and social ethics, and especially for presuming to discuss attitudes, a subject now beginning to enlist the lively interest of sociologists. I shall offer no excuses, however. There is a real need, both for college students and for the general reader, for a book which attempts an objective analysis, not too technical and not, perhaps, hopelessly superficial, of the central social viewpoints and attitudes now crucially signicant in the perpetuation of sentimental conflict, of subjective approach, and of interest-bias in the formation of "public opinion" on fundamental social issues.

At a time when conservatism and radicalism are both regarded, by their respective adherents, almost as religions, and the conflict between reactionism and liberalism is sharper than at any time before within the memory of living man, no apology need be forthcoming for an attempt to arrive at a critical understanding of the psychology, and the probable ethical value, of these attitudes. There is much confusion of thought and sentiment, even among trained sociologists, over "democracy" and "individualism"; every one talks of democracy, but few have a definite idea as to its meaning or ultimate ethical implications. Our American tradition of self-help individualism is in conflict with the growing perception of the necesstity for an ideal and a process of social coöperation more in keeping with our present state of culture and technical development. Any serious attempt, therefore, to throw light upon the fundamental character of these sentiments and attitudes should be welcome. And when there is such a notable lack of understanding of the use of the scientific method and the ethical function of the scien-

tific attitude, when the psychoses resultant from a world war
have transmuted the little objectivity we had into sentimental
hysterias and praise-and-blame obsessions, a presentation of the
scientific attitude and the elements of scientific method in relation to the solution of social issues, especially of interest-conflicts, can hardly be said to be a work of supererogation. Nor
can a simple analysis of the contrasting subjective popular
attitudes.

Had I been able to discover that anyone else had attempted
this task this book would not have been written. But I have
been able to find but few, and no sustained, attempts to analyze
conservatism and radicalism as central social attitudes. And
so far as I know there is not available what I have attempted,
an exposition, simple without being superficial, of the social and
ethical function of scientific method and attitude in the solution, or at least the mitigation, of interest-conflicts, now so
commonly pursued and inflamed by the passionate, praise-and-
blame propagandas of sentimental, egotistical, and class, conscious reactionaries, conservatives, and radicals.

The main purpose of this book is to present a dispassionate
analysis, as objective as I could make it, of the sources, characteristics, and the socio-ethical bearing of the attitudes treated.
But in working out the probable social effects of the several
attitudes, and especially in the attempt to indicate the fundamental social and ethical function of scientific method and the
scientific attitude, it became necessary to touch upon the problem of fundamental ethical norms, both of ends and of means,
and attempt, as is done in Chapter X, on Individualism and
Democracy, to indicate the psychological basis for an objective
ethical norm. The critical reader may find in this chapter,
and perhaps in some of the discussion of scientific method, evidences of *a priori* assumption, contrary to the scientific spirit;
but the conclusions drawn rest upon only one outstanding fundamental postulate, namely, the assumption of a consistent
mechanistic, deterministic view of nature, man and his social
relations included. I have been driven to this postulate because
it seems to be the only one in accord with rational experience,
and the only one which affords a sure basis of understanding
of phenomena, both "natural" and "social."

Consistently with this deterministic position goes adherence to behavioristic psychology as the only psychology which gives promise of consistent scientific quality. But I have not deemed it necessary, with the extreme behaviorists, to reject the concept of consciousness; and in the analysis of the motivation of radicalism I have used the psycho-analytical terminology. I do not think it inconsistent with scientific behaviorism.

Philosophical subtleties have been avoided, and only in Chapter V and the closing pages of the Introduction is there more than incidental use of technical psychological terminology. It is important to note that where the term instinct is used it is used in a very general sense, hardly more definite than would be connoted by the phrase "inherited tendency."

Part of the chapter on the Motivation of Radicalism has appeared in the *Psychological Review*. The chapter on Individualism and Democracy, in abridged form, appeared in the *International Journal of Ethics*. An article on "Emotion, Blame, and the Scientific Attitude in Relation to Radical Leadership," published in the *International Journal of Ethics* for January, 1922, and one on "The Rôle of Sympathy and Ethical Motivation in Scientific Social Research," in the *Journal of Philosophy* for April 26, 1923, have been drawn heavily upon. A part of Chapter II has appeared in the *Scientific Monthly*. Cordial acknowledgment and thanks are due the respective publishers for permission to use these articles.

Parts of the manuscript have been read by Professors F. A. C. Perrin and A. P. Brogan, of the University of Texas, by Professor T. V. Smith, of the University of Chicago, and by Binnie D. Pearce of Austin, Texas. To all of these persons I am indebted for valuable criticism. To my former colleague, Professor Max S. Handman, of the University of Texas, the value of my six years' intimate association with whom I can hardly overstate, I owe special acknowledgment, for most stimulating criticism and suggestion. More than to anyone else I owe thanks to Clara Snell Wolfe, first for reading and correcting the page proofs entire, most of all for her penetrative appreciation and criticism of the subject matter, both in its final form and during the years of its development and organization. I wish also to take this opportunity to express my appreciation for the helpful suggestions, which have come from stimulative contacts with the students in my class on social problems during nine years teaching in the University of Texas.

A. B. W.

Austin, Texas, September 6, 1923.

CONTENTS

CHAPTER   PAGE

I. INTRODUCTION 1

II. CONSERVATISM AND RADICALISM—DEFINITIONS AND DISTINCTIONS 11

III. DISINTERESTED CONSERVATISM 21
    1. The Motivation of Disinterested Conservatism   21
    2. Characteristics of the Conservative Mind .   31
    3. The Making of the Conservative   42
    4. The Methods of Disinterested Conservatism   60

IV. THE MOTIVATION OF INTERESTED CONSERVATISM .   61
    1. The General Motivation of Interested Conservatism   61
    2. Interested Conservatism in the Different Social Classes   63
    3. Some Psychological and Social Characteristics of Interested Conservatism   76

V. THE METHODS OF INTERESTED CONSERVATISM . .   82

VI. THE MOTIVATION OF RADICALISM 119

VII. THE ORIGINS AND CHARACTERISTICS OF RADICALISM   139
    1. The Selection of Progressive and Radical Types   139
    2. Radicalism as an Impulse to Freedom . .   145
    3. Some Characteristics of the Radical Mind .   157

VIII. THE METHODS OF RADICALISM 168
    1. Psychological Phases of Radical Method; Emotion and Blame in Relation to Radical Leadership   168
    2. The Specific Methods of Radicalism . . .   181

IX. SCIENTIFIC METHOD AND SCIENTIFIC ATTITUDE .   200
    1. The Relation of Scientific Method to Interest Conflicts   200
    2. The General Features of Scientific Method .   203
    3. Characteristics of the Scientific Attitude .   215
    4. Difficulties and Obstacles   220

CONTENTS

CHAPTER

PAGE

X. INDIVIDUALISM AND DEMOCRACY 252
   1. Individualism of Ends 252
   2. Society as Means 261
   3. Democracy 263

XI. THE ETHICS OF CONSERVATISM AND RADICALISM . 276

XII. THE PRESENT SITUATION AND THE WAY OUT . . 294
   1. The Present Situation 294
   2. Is There a Way Out? 304

Conservatism, Radicalism, and Scientific Method

CHAPTER I

INTRODUCTION

A MAN'S point of view determines the perspective and the light in which he looks at things. The apparent shape of an object depends upon the direction from which it is viewed. Two individuals looking at a cylinder, the one broadside, the other endwise, would differ hopelessly as to its shape, if they could not shift their positions. One would hold it to be rectangular, the other circular. The configuration of a landscape appears very different in certain atmospheric conditions than it does in others; the only sure way of knowing what it actually is is to make an accurate topographical survey of the country. The surveyor, climbing from peak to peak, threading his way from valley to valley, comes to know the real lay of the land. But the tourist comfortably viewing the landscape from the hotel veranda knows only how it looks from that point and under the atmospheric conditions of the day he happens to be there.

It is much the same in human affairs. Appearance and reality seldom coincide. Our social viewpoint determines both the direction, the perspective, and the light in which we see the social landscape, so far as it comes within our vision at all.

Some people think about social relations and problems. More do not. Many who do think, think in personalistic terms and only on problems which affect them in some immediately personal way. Most persons, however, do not hesitate to entertain "views" and express "opinions" on social issues. In a minority of cases only are these views or conclusions real opinions, the result of logical thinking based on more or less informa-

1

tion, even though we include erroneous information and fragmentary knowledge beside the point. The vast majority of persons have opinons, properly speaking, on only a limited number of matters. It cannot be otherwise. All individuals, however, have sentiments and more or less emotionally tinctured beliefs, which have been either acquired uncritically from popularly accepted "authorities," or absorbed unconsciously through association and from what happens to be "in the air."

But whether an individual thinks or not, whether his thinking is connected and logical or fragmentary and full of fallacies, whether he has intellectually supported opinions or merely sentiments, whether he is credulous or critical, open-minded or narrowly prejudiced and intolerant, he has some viewpoint from which he looks out upon life. He cannot escape having attitudes toward the world of his experience and the issues which come to his attention, however transitorily. Judgments and pre-judgments (prejudices), sentiments, opinions, valuations, estimates of good and evil, of right and wrong, of expediency and inexpediency, are always the product of experience (taking the word in a broad sense), which has determined the individual's point of view and attitudes.

Attitudes and points of view are thus of immense importance in human affairs. In fact, attitudes, whether regarded as traits of personality or as types of reaction or "approach" to the social environment, now constitute a most significant subject-matter of psychological and sociological research. Difference in point of view or in "feeling" and sentiment may lead either to fruitful intellectual stimulus, discussion, and creative thinking, or to irrepressible class conflicts and world wars, with all their barbarous waste and brutalization. Reflection upon these different consequences puts us in a position to realize that a careful understanding of social attitudes has an intensely practical, as well as significant theoretical, bearing.

A thorough study of viewpoints and attitudes has not yet been made, either by the psychologists or the sociologists. Such a study must involve consideration of the nature and significance of attitudes in general, and especially of those which have played major roles in history and cultural development. It must also include inductive research for the purpose of discovering the causes of the various attitudes and analyzing critically and objectively their respective social effects. Particular attention must be given to oppositions and incompatabilities between attitudes, and to the social and ethical results of attitudinal conflicts.[1] The present book undertakes no such comprehensive purpose. We shall arrive at an objective and thorough understanding of attitudes only through much co-operative research on the part of all the social sciences. In the present book, the purpose is to analyze, as briefly and with as much freedom from technicalities as is consistent with clearness, certain great types of attitude of great practical significance at the present time.

Every period of history, however "static" it may appear to be, is characterized by some change or drift in social organization and cultural processes. But in some periods change is so slow that it can be detected only by careful historical comparisons, while in others it is so rapid and violent that it can properly be called revolutionary. Since the end of the eighteenth century an unchanging, static society has been hard to find in the Western World; since 1914, it is scarcely needful to say, there is scarcely a society of any importance anywhere in the whole world which is not experiencing something akin to revolutionary change. In both hemispheres there is a rapidity and a depth of transformation, accomplished and in process, paralleled in history only in such crises as the Reformation and the French Revolution. Such sweeping social and economic changes are taking place as those which marked the break-up of feudalism and the march of the Industrial Revolution. Change is slower and less vividly present to casual view in some countries than in others. Doubtless it is likely to be less pronounced and on the whole more tardy in countries, like the United States, the most prosperous and the least vitally and directly touched by the war. Few will question, however, that even here significant shiftings, if not transformations, of thought and attitude are in process, which must sooner or later eventuate in significant modification of the social topography. If one questions the presence of a momentum of social change in the Orient, he has only to remember the political and cultural

---

[1] See J. M. Williams, *Principles of Social Psychology, as Developed in a Study of Economic and Social Conflict*, 1922.

transformations going on in China, the widespread and persistent Nationalist Movement in India, and the seething of political thought and sentiment in the Moslem world.[2]

No period is free from attitudinal oppositions and interest conflicts which ruffle the peace of society and the comfort of individuals. But without falling into the fallacy of superlatives we may regard our own period as one in which chaos of attitudes, confusion of thought, and intensity of class and nationalistic conflicts have rarely been paralleled. A noteworthy characteristic of the present historical crisis is our lively awareness of our disorganization and uncertainty. We are conscious of the dangers, not only to special class, institutional, and national interests, but to civilization itself, involved in the emotionalism, passion, dogmatism, and intolerance of present conflicts.

If history may be conceived broadly to be characterized by comparatively quiescent epochs alternating with crises of change and revolution, unquestionably we are now at one of history's great critical points. All such crises are preceded and led up to by slow process of social drift and cumulative maladjustments in organization and sentiment. Conflicts of interest go through an unseen gestation, to burst into the world's consciousness as the throes of a social revolution. The present crisis is no exception. It is the inevitable result of great movements and slow attitudinal changes, the real significance of which escaped the notice of all but a few farseeing, analytical minds, and the outcome of which no one now living should have the temerity to predict. Among these movements may be catalogued: the growth of natural science and especially the application of scientific knowledge to industrial technique, the intensification of nationalism and the rise of modern imperialism under the stimulus of economic rivalry, the phenomenal spread of communication and education, the slow drift toward humanitarianism—when it did not interfere too much with economic interests,[3]—unprecedented expansion of population and development of intricate inter-racial contacts through migration, cul-

[2]On the latter see Lothrop Stoddard, *The New World of Islam*, 1922.
[3]If this seems to the reader an unduly cynical aside, let him recall the history of the struggle for the abolition of the English slave trade. See for example, A. W. Benn, *Modern England, a Record of Opinion and Action from the Time of the French Revolution to the Present Day*, 1908, Vol. I, pp. 25-27, 50, 51, 73.

tural and attitudinal modifications incident to urbanization of an ever-increasing percentage of the people, and last but not least that rather indefinite but momentous movement called democracy. Such a complexity of developments, taking place in one short century, and involving practically every aspect of human life, could not fail to create problems and induce conflicts beyond the capacity of the peoples caught in the swirl and impetuosity of their own cultural flood to solve peacefully, rationally, and objectively.

So we have staged today the drama, in which we are all, whether we like it or not, the actors, of a gigantic conflict of interests, with a plot of intricately confused and ill-understood attitudes, sentiments, inherited beliefs, attachments and loyalties; rebellious iconoclasms; thunderous clashes of economic institutions; apologetic murmurings of academic philosophies; by-play of ecclesiastical dogmatism; and cheap, melodramatic posings of self-appointed defenders of the faith and guardians of law and morality. Notwithstanding the seeming intricacy, however, fundamental issues are clear enough. The struggle is not only between interests, material and otherwise, but between certain outstanding types of attitude derived from or giving force to the interests.

It is a conflict first of all between attitudes having to do with change itself—a conflict which runs the whole scale from the most uncompromising reactionism to the highest pitch of radicalism. It is secondly a conflict of sentiments or valuations with regard to distributive justice or economy, of material wealth and income, and of the opportunities associated with them. It is in short a conflict of democracy with class interest. In the third place, it involves fundamental divergencies of sentiment or intellectual conviction with regard to means and ends in human life—a conflict between individualism and socialism. And this conflict doubles back upon itself when we remember that individualism and socialism can each be either a calculus of ends or an organization and a philosophy of means.[4] And

---

[4] The term "socialism" as used in this book, unless the context clearly indicates otherwise, means social co-operation in a broad sense, mutual aid, mutuality, concerted volition and action for what are commonly called social ends. It has no reference to any specific kind of economic or political organization.

finally, it involves what is perhaps most important of all, contrasting and mutually incompatible methods of conceiving and evaluating things—namely, the scientific attitude and the scientific method, in contrast to the attitudes and methods of the popular mind, with its sentimental traditionalism, its weddedness to authoritarianism, and its facile formation of snap judgments.

Conservatism and radicalism, scientific objectivity and popular sentimentalism, democracy and class interest, individualism and socialism, do not, of course, exhaust the list of social attitudes. We might add, for instance, optimism and pessimism, courage and cowardice, contentiousness and forbearance. Distinguishing between generalized attitudes and attitudes on special issues, we might in the latter category catalogue nationalism and internationalism, fundamentalism and modernism (as exemplified by current theological controversies), federalism and states' rights, feminism and anti-feminism—and "pro" and "anti" this and that to the end of the chapter. Such a list would be as long as the catalogue of issues, but it would serve no present practical purpose. The attitudes and the four-fold conflict which we have singled out above for analysis are all generalized attitudes, that is, attitudes which will characterize the individual in whatever situation he may be placed or with whatever issues he may be confronted. Moreover, a calm analysis and objective understanding of these particular attitudes seems most urgently needful at the present time.

We may close these introductory explanations with a brief statement of certain distinctions and definitions of psychological terms. Formal definitions of the terms "attitude" and "sentiment" are not absolutely essential to an understanding of the chapters which follow, and the reader may skip the rest of this chapter if he so desires. Nevertheless it is always some satisfaction to be clear as to what we are talking about. Before we proceed to a critical examination of conservatism and the other attitudes which we are to consider, it will be useful therefore to state as accurately as we can what we conceive to be the psychological nature of attitudes.

Popular usage of terms is almost always undiscriminating. Take the queries, "What is your feeling about this matter?" "What are your sentiments on this?" and "What is your attitude toward this?'' In popular phraseology they all mean about the same thing. It will be evident from what follows, however, that useful distinctions can be made between ''feeling,'' ''sentiment,'' and ''attitude.''

If we find a certain deficiency in accuracy and refinement in popular language, the layman who turns to the psychologists for his definition of terms finds accuracy and refinement enough, volumes in fact, but unfortunately no widespread and established agreement upon a consistent set of definitions or usage of terms. Moreover, comparatively few psychologists have attempted to analyze the nature of sentiment, although an increasing number are inquiring into attitudes as elements in temperament, character, and the complex thing called personality. To add to the confusion, sociologists are using the terms sentiment and attitude in a variety of loose and shifty senses and with connotations often different from those implied by the psychologists.

We shall therefore attempt to give a clear and concise statement of the meaning attached to these terms in this book, without asserting that our use will meet with the approval of the psychologists or please the sociologists. If the reader is thereby helped to a critical appreciation of the lines of thought in the succeeding chapters, it is of secondary import whether our definitions and our conception of the relation between emotion, sentiment, and attitude are acceptable to him in other connections.

Attitudes belong to the feeling side of mind, rather than to the intellective. If we start with feeling, we may accept Woodworth's statement that ''feeling is subjective and unanalyzed,'' or again that it is an ''undercurrent'' or ''background'' of consciousness.[5] Discarding figurative expressions, we may regard feeling as a quiescent organic state in which there is going on no special organic preparation for, or effort in, activity, and no consciousness either of well-being or illbeing. Feeling, in this sense, is the datum level from which ''the feelings'' and emotions rise and fall, like waves and tides on the sea. Between elementary feelings and emotions the distinction is one of degree and complexity, not of kind. Feelings

[5] *Psychology, a Study of Mental Life*, 1921, p. 172.

may be regarded as relatively slight departures from the mean level of feeling. They are produced by simple stimuli, not very strong and not very sudden. Emotions are conceived of by most psychologists as a "moved" or "stirred-up," an agitated, state of mind. By the large number of psychologists who accept the James-Lange theory of the emotions, an emotion is regarded as a "blend of organic sensations,"[6] a "sudden complex of bodily sensations arising from our instinctive reactions toward appropriate stimuli."[7] This distinction between feelings and emotions is doubtless of technical utility to the psychologists, but it is unnecessary for our purposes. We shall accordingly mean by emotion simply differential feeling, above or below the quiescent level, an affective state accompanying activity in response to stimuli which arouse the organism out of a quiescent condition.

In a broad sense we may regard an emotion as a vibration of the personality. It may exist without any outward and visible reaction toward the stimulus which produces it. Even so, with sufficiently delicate instruments its presence can probably always be detected in altered rate or intensity of organic functions. An emotion may thus be either a violent agitation —a veritable symphony of pleasurable experiences, or "sweet bells jangled out of tune, and harsh"—or a relatively mild and momentary differentiation of feeling, an evanescent rippling of the surface of consciousness. The "tone" of an emotion is probably always one either of pleasantness or unpleasantness, a fact which, if established, is of significance to an understanding of sentiments and attitudes.

A sentiment is an emotional complex definitely associated with some object—it may be an actual present situation with the involved stimuli, or a remembered, imagined, or represented experience—to which it is essentially a value-reaction made on the basis of the pleasantness or unpleasantness of the stimulus. "Our sentiments," as Warren says, "are generated within us; they are intimately personal, like pain, and yet they are excited by something in the external stimulus."[8] This "some-

---

[6] Woodworth, p. 173.

[7] Z. C. Dickinson, *Economic Motives, a Study in the Psychological Foundations of Economic Theory*, 1922, p. 132.

[8] H. C. Warren, *Elements of Human Psychology*, 1922, p. 219.

thing'' is the pleasantness or unpleasantness of the experience, and is what gives to a sentiment its character as a value-reaction. By value-reaction is meant simply that the person is placing a value on the situation as it affects his interests. Valuation is an estimate of importance, or utility, and there is consequently some ideational element in a sentiment.[9] There is always an element of attraction or aversion in a sentiment, a ''feeling for'' or a ''feeling against.'' There are, of course, mixed sentiments in which attraction and aversion mingle. If the attractive element dominates, a sentiment bears a certain analogy to a tropism.

One further, and important, feature of sentiment must be stated. A sentiment is produced by a *specific* object or situation. The stimuli of this situation, which constitute the occasion of the sentiment, may be very simple and momentary, but they arouse a complex of feelings and give rise to instant valuation (attraction or aversion, praise or blame) because they call into action memory, imagination, habit, perhaps in fact the major part of the whole personality, in reaction to a specific, immediately presented experience.[10]

We are now in position to define attitude. An attitude is the *type* of sentiment which the individual manifests upon the recurrence of a given situation. It is a behavior-pattern, with reference especially to the ''feeling'' side of response. It is, in Warren's definition, ''a permanent set of our mental and nervous system which modifies the effect of stimuli and determines how we respond.''[11] Instead of saying, however, that the attitude ''determines'' how we respond it would be more accurate to say it is how we respond. Since the valuation element is so strong in a sentiment, an attitude may be regarded also as a type of valuation-response. Knowing an individual's sentimental valuations in a sufficiently large number and variety of specific situations, we can predict the type of his valuations

---

[9] Cf. Warren: ''The prominent elements in the sentiment of beauty are a feeling and an idea of value'' (p. 219). ''The value idea is especially prominent in sentiments, a belief is partly an idea of the worth of some statement, partly a feeling'' (p. 219).

[10] This is in substantial accordance with A. F. Shand's conception of sentiments as complexes of emotions. See his *Foundations of Character*, 1914, Ch. 4.

[11] *Elements of Human Psychology*, 1922, p. 332.

—his attitudes—in any new situation. Attitudes are thus sentiment-patterns. When we say that an individual is characterized by a conservative attitude we mean that we expect him to manifest a certain type of sentiment, "for" or "against," in a large variety of specifically different situations. He is likely to be "for" familiar food, the Monroe Doctrine, strict and uniform divorce laws, a literally inspired Bible, and in general against the new and the unfamiliar. Similarly if a man has thoroughly accepted the scientific attitude we know that under no conditions will he jump to conclusions on hearsay, express dogmatic "opinions" without knowledge, or give way to the emotional reactions of the crowd. If we know a person's sentiment-patterns, that is, his attitudes, we can predict, at least roughly, his reaction in any particular situation.

Moreover, since the action of the group is that of its members, as influenced by its leaders, a knowledge of attitudes is essential to predicting the policy and action of the group. Understanding of attitudes is thus of great practical utility, both for the individual who wishes to "manage" others to his own purposes, and for him who desires to lead or persuade others to act for the best interests of society. A study of sentiments and attitudes is thus bound to be a very important part of all applied psychology.

Further, an understanding of attitudes is of incalculable value to the individual who has arrived at a stage of culture and courage where he wishes honestly to face and to know himself. Unremitting introspection and self-analysis is a morbid trait. A critical awareness, however, of the nature and causes of one's own impulses, sentiments, attitudes, and points of view may at times be a salutary asset.

CHAPTER II

CONSERVATISM AND RADICALISM—DEFINITIONS AND DISTINCTIONS

MANY years ago, Walter Bagehot [1] showed how necessary it is for every social group to acquire what he called a shell of custom—some form and organization of authority which shall hold the group together in physical and spiritual solidarity and curb the self-will of individuals who might endanger the co-operative cohesion and defensive powers of the group. But, as Bagehot goes on to suggest, once this shell of custom is set, it has sooner or later to be smashed, else it stifles growth and strangles the intellectual and moral evolution of the very society it was designed to serve. As a rule, when the provocation has become sufficiently great, men have risen who have not been lacking in the necessary courage and strength of character to undertake the task. Always, indeed, there have been would-be shell-smashers, men who rebelled inwardly or outwardly, and frequently with violence, against the particular controls and institutions imposed upon them by historical accretion, by the passive, non-resistant indifference of the phlegmatic or repressed masses, and by the special interests of powerful individuals or classes.

Thus sponsors of things-as-they-are and advocates of change, modification, and transformation are always set over against one another in an attitudinal and active conflict. The intensity of this conflict depends both upon the psychological temperament and character of the two groups, conservative and radical, and upon the degree of divergence or opposition of their respective interests.

The scale of attitudes which different men and women take toward social change may be compared to the solar spectrum. At the opposite ends stand extreme radicalism and uncompromising reaction. Between these extremes are conservatism and

---

[1] *Physics and Politics*, 1873, Ch. 1.

liberalism, or progressivism, each with its various degrees of intensity and its shading into the adjacent attitudes. Thus the attitudinal spectrum reads, from left to right, radicalism, liberalism or progressivism, conservatism, reactionism. Like the colors in the solar spectrum these attitudes grade each into the next so gradually that it is impossible to draw a sharp line between any contiguous two.

Conservatism, generally speaking, is simply that system of sentiments, that mental attitude, which causes the individual to accept with equanimity and approval things-as-they-are (or would be if liberals and radicals would only let them alone), which desires little if any change, and which opposes with vigor any proposal for radical transformation. The conservative does not so much oppose relatively innocuous temporizing and tinkering with unimportant social details. He does not so much resist the evolutionary drift which may mean in the long run very significant transformations, to which, indeed, he is ordinarily oblivious. In its purest form conservatism opposes thorough-going and consciously conceived and directed reform or revolution having to do with the more fundamental aspects of thought, economic organization, and social relations. Conservatism, if it could have its way, would thus stand still, maintaining social relations and processes, thought, belief, and culture practically as they happen to be at the time. It would resist on the one hand the innovations of progressive and radical, and on the other, with perhaps a little less enthusiasm, the reversionary ideals of the reactionary.

With reactionism the conservative is not in accord, because reactionism advocates a return to some previously current but now abandoned mode of thought and system of organization. The reversion advocated by the reactionary is distasteful to the conservative because it would mean a change in existing relations and activities which would interfere with his habituation and attachment to things-as-they-are. Nevertheless the thorough conservative is more nearly related to the reactionary than to the radical. Conservatism is opposed to radical thought and action, and is antipathetic to liberalism, because the conservative is not only averse to change of any significant kind but has a lively fear of the new and unfamiliar. Both the introduction of new and unfamiliar arrangements and a return to some previously existing order involve change and hence more or less disturbance of established habits and points of view. Both entail discomfort to the conservative, therefore, but the proposals of the reactionary are likely to seem less subversive than those of the radical, although as a matter of fact they may be quite as much so. The conservative does not want the existing shell of custom smashed or even appreciably bent, but if its form is to be modified at all he would rather go with the reactionary back to the once tried and once familiar than with the radical and his innovations.

Progressivism stands midway between conservatism and radicalism and partakes of the milder characteristics of both. The progressive welcomes and works for orderly and gradual changes which can be brought about by planned endeavor and the conscious direction of social evolution. He is not so deeply habituated to things-as-they-are as is the conservative nor characterized by the irrational fear of change which marks so many timid temperaments. But progressivism is not devoid of fear. It fears the disruptiveness and discontinuity of radicalism. Where the radical would smash the existing shell and substitute another, the progressive would rebuild it piecemeal, and in this process of gradual reconstruction remodel its form and content.

The progressive holds, in other words, that however rapidly human advance may be accelerated by innovative initiative and radical direction, it must nevertheless be evolutionary and continuous. The future must grow out of the present, as the present has come from the past, by a "natural," orderly process of development, not through those sudden jumps and changes of direction, those "discontinuous variations," to borrow a biological term, which constitute social revolutions.

Progressivism is, of course, vigorously if not bitterly opposed to reactionism, but it is almost as bitterly opposed to extreme radicalism; as, indeed, moderate radicalism is frequently also. While advanced progressivism can hardly be distinguished from mild or moderate radicalism, we may say that in general the progressive is averse to radicalism because he shares with the conservative a strong sense of order, a high valuation of past experience, and a firm conviction in the stability and unchangeableness of human nature. Moreover, where special interests,

economic or otherwise, are at stake the progressive, like the
conservative, may fear the results of radical change upon the
interests of himself and his class.

Liberalism in a general sense is practically synonymous with
progressivism, though the term may connote a slightly less
aggressive attitude than is commonly associated with progressivism.

More specifically, current usage applies the term liberal to
those who, though they break with conservatism and hold reactionism in contempt, still contend that the main contours of
our present political, economic, and social life are, if not ideal,
at least better than anything to be looked for through revolution or the quick transformations demanded by the radical.
The liberal may hold, speculatively, that in ultimate ideal our
present mode of life and social organization will be regarded
by the peoples of the distant future as just as crude, inefficient,
and inhuman as we now regard the life of our wholly barbarous forebears; and yet he will reject radical reform or
revolution on technological and especially on psychological
grounds. His attitude, and there is much to be said for it,
both from the standpoint of scientific psychology and from
any rationalist's observation of human nature in everyday life,
is summarized in the sentiment: ''Yes, all that would be very
good and attractive if human nature were different, but it
isn't.'' When it comes to the extreme speculative idealism of
a humanistic philosophical anarchist like Bertrand Russell, that
is the inevitable sentiment of all parties, from reactionary to
socialistic radical—and doubtless of Mr. Russell himself.

In a still narrower sense, the liberal of today, like the economic and political liberals of England and France of the
nineteenth century, is one who regards free competition, private initiative, and political government in the forms supposedly crystallized in the English or American system as approximately ideal. He is naturally averse to reforms leading
to government ownership or to socialism and to more governmental control than is essential to that somewhat traditional
and elusive thing, free competition.[2]

---

[2] Perhaps the best brief presentation of this type of liberalism is
Woodrow Wilson's *The New Freedom*, 1913. Contrast, for example,
M. P. Follett's *The New State*, 1920. Bryce's *Modern Democracies*, 2
vols., 1921, is also suggestive.

The more a term is on everybody's lips the harder it is to
define it. This is particularly true of the word "radicalism."
Etymology, as usual, gives us little help. The dictionary definitions are figurative and hazy. About all they tell us is that
"radical" and "radicalism" carry the double connotation of
change and thoroughness. But so may "reactionism." Radicalism and reactionism merely idealize and advocate change in
diametrically opposite directions, the one toward the old, the
other toward the new. Radicalism means innovation; reactionism suggests, literally, re-novation, a bringing back and renew-
ing of the old.

We may define radicalism as the attitude of those who desire
and advocate speedy, deep, and thoroughgoing innovative reform or revolution, either in regard to certain aspects of social
relations and processes or to the whole social order.

As both social evolution and social revolution have, on the
whole, during the modern period, led toward political and
social democracy and away from absolutism, authoritarianism,
and class privilege, radicalism has been, is at present, and for
a long time will continue to be directed to the project of securing rapid, accelerated democratization. If applied to a case
of extreme economic radicalism like the bolshevist régime in
Russia, this statement might be regarded as humorous, in view
of the autocratic methods of Lenine and Trotsky. The bolshevist reply is, of course, that these methods are merely a
necessary temporary expedient in the service of ultimate democracy. Final proof of the validity or falsity of this excuse
lies only in the future.

It should be noted that there may be two radicalisms, both
visioning thoroughgoing innovation, which point in different if
not opposed directions. Socialism and anarchism, for illustration, agree only in wishing the abolition of the present social
system; further than this they have little in common, for
anarchism, very credulous as to the innate goodness and rea-
sonableness of man, would abolish all coercive forms of social
control,[2] while socialism, with less childlike faith in human perfectibility and greater practical insight into the difficulties of
economic organization, looks forward, generally speaking, to a
very material increase in the amount and effectiveness of social

---

[2] Cf., for example, Bertrand Russell, *Proposed Roads to Freedom*, 1919.

control over the actions of the individual. Much the same kind of opposition exists between moderate socialism and communism. In England, in the first third of the nineteenth century, two radicalisms, Cobdenism (free trade, *laissez faire*) and socialism, were similarly opposed, though they were in agreement in demanding the abolition of the traditional, Tory mercantilist economic policies.[4]

In English politics the term "radical" was originally an opprobrious epithet applied by aristocratic Tory reactionists to a group of liberals who did not regard the Reform Bill of 1832 as the last word in the extension of the parliamentary franchise.

Since the world war there has been a noteworthy, and in some quarters, successful, attempt, to revive this opprobrious use of the term. The attempt has been especially general in the United States, where the tendency seems to many liberals to be less strong toward real democracy than it is in England.

The central social conflict of today is without doubt the conflict of economic interests. This struggle is waged along two intersecting planes, one of class, the other of nationalistic interests. In these respective planes the conservative and reactionary positions are held by the capitalistic employing class and the nationalists, while the extreme radical positions are held by those who aim at some form of comprehensive economic collectivism and in general are advocates of internationalism. This alignment is by no means mere accident, but is the historical and the logical result of the conflict of interests involved. Be that as it may, however, capitalistic, corporate reactionism stands in determined defense against the massed attacks of radical collectivist internationalism. Thus it becomes easy to associate "patriotism" and "loyalty" with capitalism and nationalism, while "radicalism" is made to carry the strong implication of crossing over into disloyalty (pro-Germanism during the war) and into socialism or "bolshevism." By this process of associative emotionalism, consciously aided and stimulated by a none too scrupulous system of well-financed propa-

---

[4] Leslie Stephen, *The English Utilitarians*, 1900, Vol. III, p. 38. As to the radical democrats in England from 1820 to 1870, see Bryce, *Modern Democracies*, 1921, Vol. II, p. 568.

ganda, "radicalism" and "bolshevism" have been made to mean practically the same thing to the average business man, and to many others, and that something a thing to be dreaded and fought against by every available means.

That this uncritical usage is unfortunate, entirely apart from the respective merits of capitalism and socialism or of nationalism and internationalism, a moment's reflection will show. In the first place such usage is the result of combative emotionalism and intolerance, and these sentiments rarely if ever advance the cause either of truth or of human welfare. In the second place such a narrowing of the connotation of the term radical deprives it of significance outside the field of the economic and political struggles. This leaves us without a term to denote the thoroughgoing innovative attitude in other phases of human life, for example in religion, ethics, and art.

A still weightier reason against this popular usage is that by no means all the individuals who advocate really radical measures or thoroughgoing innovation in some particular field of human activity, even in the economic, are socialists, or internationalists, much less communists or bolshevists. We should hardly withhold the term radical from the staunch single-taxer; from the advocates of the abolition of the United States Senate or the Supreme Court; or those who would initiate a wide-reaching system of governmental price regulation, divorce by mutual consent, or compulsory education of every normal boy and girl to the age of eighteen. Each of these is (or would be) but a limited radicalism, that is, radicalism applicable to only a single part or phase of our social organization. Nevertheless, within the scope of its interest, attention, and design, each is just as truly radical as is socialism or internationalism. It can hardly be said that the Eighteenth Amendment and the Volstead Act were not radical innovations. Curiously enough, however, popular usage has not taken to calling the prohibitionists socialists.

There is, then, in every field of human sentiment, thought, and action, a continuous gradation of attitude from reactionism to radicalism. The terms conservatism and radicalism, therefore, should always be regarded as relative, both to each other and to the standards of valuation or sentiment current at the time. What appears to one person, or at a given time, or in a given place, extreme radicalism may be to another person or in another time or place hidebound conservatism.. As there are degrees of conservatism, so there are gradations in radicalism. Comprehensive radicalism is revolutionary in thought and purpose. In method it may be either revolutionary or reformist. Less comprehensive or thoroughgoing radicalism may be reformist (as distinguished from revolutionary) in both aim and method. In general, history shows fairly well that the radicalism of today becomes the liberalism and progressivism of tomorrow and the conservatism of the day after. When the aims of the radicals of a particular epoch are accomplished they usually become conservatives. But however rapidly sentiments and standards of valuation may shift, the radicalism at any time existent is always an attitude which demands thoroughgoing change, through conscious innovation.

It may be suggested that a distinction should be made between radical desires and innovative impulses. In the absence of such distinction all innovators, like the inventors, Edison or Bell or Westinghouse, all creators of new architectural styles, all those who introduce new models in art or literature, would have to be classified as radicals. It might be convenient to think of thoroughgoing innovation as radical only when advocated or carried out against opposition. Radicalism would then be defined as desire for thoroughgoing innovation which is opposed by conservative objection and obstruction. While this distinction is logical enough, it has more academic than practical significance, as will be shown later.

Distinction between thought or theory and action should be kept in mind—a distinction somewhat more significant in radicalism than in conservatism. Conservative sentiment and conservative conduct may coincide without excessive expenditure of energy. On the other hand radical sentiment or theory may not produce radical action, because such action means not only doing something new, but doing it against the whole weight of conservative inertia and perhaps against the violent opposition of interested reactionism. Moreover, radicalism is in a sense a less "natural" attitude than conservatism, because the radical not only has to meet the pressure of conservative inertia and

---

* Pages 132, 133.

reactionary opposition of other persons, but also to overcome the conservative tendencies of his own nature.

Returning to the other end of the attitudinal spectrum, we find that some conservatism is the expression of sincere and relatively unselfish conviction, that most conservatism is the product of mere habit and uncritical fear, and that not a little of it is thoroughly selfish in its motivation and insincere in its expression and reasoning. So far as conservatism is the product of conscious motivation, two primary motives prompt it: the one is selfish, material interest, economic or otherwise, in the established order of things; the other is a temperamental attachment to things-as-they-are. This attachment may or may not be productive of good or logically justifiable. Nevertheless, the individual always finds, if forced to seek them, what seem to him good and sufficient reasons for such attachment, and hence for the essential propriety and rightness of the things—the ideas, beliefs, institutions, and relations—to which he is attached. Sometimes his reasoning possesses objective scientific validity, but it is quite as likely to be the type of reasoning for self-defense and self-justification which the psychoanalysts call "rationalization," that is, casuistry.

Because of this fundamental difference in motivation it is desirable, in an attempt to analyze the motives and characteristics of the conservative attitude, to distinguish what we may call, for want of better terms, *interested* conservatism and *disinterested* conservatism. Interested conservatism is motivated by narrowly selfish, egotistical, individual or class interests. The interested conservative invariably has an ax to grind, and it is distinctly his own. The motivation of disinterested conservatism, on the other hand, is due not to the calculating quality of the "narrower selfishness" or of conscious class interest, but rather to the pervasive influence of the instinct of fear, and of association, imitation, habit, and adaptation. It is thus both temperamental and characteristic.[6] Both interested and disinterested conservatism may be observed in the same

---

[6] Broadly speaking, psychology calls traits which the individual possesses by reason of organically inherited instincts or tendencies "temperamental," those which result from environmental influence, "characteristic."

individual, and they shade into each other in a manner which makes too sharp a distinction between them erroneous.

In a very fundamental psychological and ethical sense, it may be argued that there is no such thing as disinterested conservatism; or from the standpoint of conscious motivation only, a disinterested attitude of any kind, since we assume those attitudes which correspond to our strongest habits, desires, and interests. Any attitude may in this sense be regarded not only as the expression of the nature of the person, but as a servant to the functioning of his personality. Whether we have quick and sensitive sympathy, or are insensitive and unsympathetic; and whether we are broadly intelligent in finding our own happiness in conjunction with that of others, or are directly, narrowly, and unintelligently selfish, it may be maintained (again so far as conscious motivation is concerned) that we always do those things which, under the circumstances present to our appreciation, we deem will give us the most satisfaction.[7] We are not concerned at this point, however, with this broader, deterministic, and somewhat unconventional conception of self-interest. Whether all conduct be found in the last analysis to be self-centered or not, the practical fact remains that some people are temperamentally conservative and other conservatives are primarily so from conscious motives of material self-interest in the narrow sense. And this distinction proves significant and essential to an attempt fairly and objectively to analyze the psychology of conservatism and the influence of conservatism upon social ideals and social achievement.

---

[7] No crude hedonism is implied by this statement. It is not assumed that all human motivation, or even the major part of it, is conscious, or that all conscious motivation is intelligent.

CHAPTER III

1. *The Motivation of Disinterested Conservatism*

THE motivation of disinterested conservatism boils down to fear and habit. All conservatism, both interested and disinterested, is essentially a safety-first attitude. Its root is desire for security. This desire is in great part the result of cultural contacts and training in conformity to the demands of the social environment, but it undoubtedly has also a very deep-seated instinctive or temperamental root. In interested conservatism the desire for security is consciously centered upon specific ends or values—the maintenance of property rights, keeping one's job, and upholding by hook or crook the social controls by which these established rights and privileges are secured against the threats and dangers of social change. In disinterested conservatism, the desire for security is less consciously formed, although it is no less real. Here it is nearer the level of inherited temperament, broader and more varied in its content, and less definitely associated with specific interests.

The safety which the disinterested conservative desires—even though he may not consciously formulate his wish—is security in the wonted performance of his habitual routine of activity. Grant him to possess a certain range of inherited aptitudes, modified and developed by individual training, or compressed by social pressure into a more or less stereotyped character, such an individual finds this security when the social environment in which and to which he has been adapted is maintained without sudden or substantial change. For in such an environment and in no other, he functions freely and agreeably, through habit.

Disinterested conservatism is thus not entirely, or even mainly, a rational attitude. It is, the rather, a matter of sentiment, both in the popular, and in the technical sense of the term. It is characterized and motivated by sentiment in the popular sense of the word because it is essentially a "sentimental" attachment to things-as-they-are. Examples a plenty will occur to the reader, for the conservative frequently opposes change which he admits might be desirable on rational grounds, because sentiments dear to the heart attach to the old and familiar thing. No one, in fact, is free from this type of conservative sentiment. More significantly, however, conservatism is a matter of sentiment in the technical sense, namely pleasant feeling in the presence of a familiar environment plus some idea of its value.[1] Sentiment in this sense of a valuation is felt in the presence of the familiar object or situation; just because the individual feels at home in it, is oriented, and can respond to it with the ease of habituation, the situation is valued highly.

This sense of wontedness and smooth functioning of capacities may under certain conditions be regarded as the pleasant feeling which results from self-expression in work. It is probably unnecessary to single it out as an "instinct" of workmanship, to use Veblen's expression, but certainly every worker not too thoroughly mechanized by modern division of labor and scientific management has a pride in work well done; and he knows that he cannot do his accustomed work well and easily in a new and unfamiliar *milieu*. The worker not endowed with extraordinary originality and adaptability therefore clings conservatively to the standards and traditions of his craft. Man is not, of course, unique in this disposition to security. All animals, when not under the stimulus of some counteracting instinctive emotional complex, such as the mating instinct or the sentiments of maternity, exhibit this trait in their behavior. For the impulse to seek safety is a fundamental prerequisite to the preservation of the life of the individual. In man the desire for security is, on occasion, counterbalanced not only by the essential instinctive complexes involved in mating, food getting, and protecting the young, and in some cases by desire for adventure and the like, but by powerful group sentiments such as the glory of martyrdom or the discipline, the *élan*, the hypnosis, of group morale in combat. The

---

[1] Cf. H. C. Warren, *Elements of Human Psychology*, 1922, pp. 219, 298.

moment the occasion of combat or exposure to danger is past, however, man, like other animals, seeks safety.

Man thus comes by the conservative attitude naturally. He gets it from his ancestors who practiced it for countless generations, back to the time when the first bit of living protoplasm stretched out toward food and shrank back from foreign substances. It is bred in the bone. But its hold upon him goes beyond that. It is more than mechanical reflex in any simple sense. For with the development of the power of memory and ideation, of emotional association, and of reflective thought, the *idea* of security has been caught up and made the center and locus of the conservative sentiments. Security has become a *value*, a state to which a conscious significance and importance is attached. And through the agreement of individual valuations—an agreement based partly on the similarity of individual needs and inherited temperament, partly on social pressure of various kinds, it has become a *social* value—an idea or a state with a utility which is collectively recognized not only for the individual but for the group.

Not only is conservatism indicative that an adjustment, a working relation, has been established between the individual and his environment; it is also, as we shall see, the product of a prolonged and complex process of adaptation which has resulted in more or less complete habituation and attachment. In other words, conservatism is very largely the product of the habit-forming agencies, and conservatism and habit are roughly synonymous. But there is also an element of organic inheritance in this adjustment and attachment, namely the limits set by inherited temperament and aptitudes. Not only do we like to live in an environment which is familiar and wonted, and in which our activities are relatively easy, because habitual, but there are some environments more suited to our inherited nature than are others. If we are fortunate enough to be placed in such an environment the process of adjustment through training and education is much more rapid, easy, and effective than it can be if we are placed in a social situation which runs counter to our natural bent. Favorably placed, we are loath to change, not only because of orientation and habituation, but also because of the more deeply seated conformity between environmental opportunity and native aptitudes. Unfavorably placed, we either change our environment, or endure a hard process of discipline which not infrequently represses and wastes valuable natural talent. Through a prolonged process of repression and discipline we may become adjusted to an unsuitable environment and habituated, to a fair degree of thoroughness, to the attitudes and activities demanded by it.

Habitual adjustment, conventional attitudes and actions (whether we are placed in favorable or unfavorable environment), thus become a part of us—''second nature.'' We cannot entirely divest ourselves of our inherited aptitudes, though they can be repressed or greatly modified through training. We can change our habits, but we do not like to do so, chiefly because of the fact that they are the expression of what we have become, partly also because of the sentiments which attach to habitual attitudes and activities. The fact that we do not like to change our ways is indication that they have become characteristic of us. Where conservatism is the product of habituation, we may therefore properly call it ''characteristic'' conservatism.

In its higher forms the impulse to security becomes a rational, thought-out desire. Its primitive emotional content is disciplined and directed by knowledge and belief. Habit and wontedness are given the sanction of rational calculation. But below this higher level of disciplined minds, the desire for security exhibits, with greater clearness as we go down the mental scale, its instinctive emotional nature and its unthinking attachment to the merely wonted situation.

If what we here venture to call ''characteristic'' conservatism is the product of processes of adjustment and habituation of the individual to a specific situation, we may, on the other hand, without drawing a too sharp and consequently untenable distinction between instinct and habit, distinguish another type or phase of conservatism which we may call temperamental or protective. Remembering that all human instincts are very much overcast, modified, and complicated by imitation and training, the fact remains that beneath all the adjustment and habituation which we have suggested lies the primitive, fundamental fact of fear emotions and fear reactions.

The fear element in conservatism has both an inherited (instinctive) and a cultural basis. In its instinctive aspect fear must be regarded as a defense mechanism or "set"—a state of preparedness of the whole organism to meet danger, either by flight or by fight. It makes little difference whether, with McDougall, we regard fear as the emotion accompanying the "instinct" of flight (as he makes anger the emotion accompanying the "instinct" of pugnacity) or regard fear itself as the instinct. However much psychologists may differ as to the nature and number of instincts, and however cautious they may be in the use of the term instinct, they are in agreement that fear is in a fundamentally significant way a part of our organically inherited equipment, and that it serves a fundamental and universal function in the process of adjustment between organism and environment. The biologist sees constantly fear functioning as a protective agency. The sociologist sees in it not only one of the most powerful motives making for the effectiveness of social control, but also an agency in the social selection of types of character. And the moralist has always appealed to fear, doubtless entirely too much so, to secure "right" lines of conduct.

Throughout all the varied manifestations of fear on the part of the individual in a social complex, its fundamental nature remains the same. It is always essentially a defense mechanism or state. The essential difference is that the stimuli to fear have now come to be other than they were under "natural" conditions. While the wild animal shows instinctive fear in its most unmistakable form, and while in men some survivals of this form of fear may be observed, modern man exhibits fear emotion most frequently when the culturally acquired adjustment between himself and his environment is threatened. The animal fears for his life; man fears for his habits. In a broad sense, and to no small degree in a very specific sense, man fears what he has been taught—not always intelligently—to fear.

The fear which motivates individuals in a social complex is thus a very much complicated product of instinct and the stimuli of social environment and tradition. Instinctive fear, temperamental timidity, is only the groundwork upon which social relations have constructed a "pain economy."[2] There

---

[2] See Simon N. Patten, *The Theory of Social Forces*, 1895, pp. 75ff.

are of course other motives of conduct which in many situations are more effective than fear. One need mention only love, sympathy, good fellowship, curiosity, desire for the beautiful, and the impulse to workmanship. Yet the functioning of all of these positive and dynamic tendencies or motives is generally more or less guided, held in check, and repressed by protective fear. That fear may be groundless or hypertrophied, even to the point of paralyzing all power of action, does not alter the main fact. It is always, if not actually present, at least near at hand, to hold up a warning finger. "Thus conscience doth make cowards of us all!" The individual may wish, as Cooley suggests,[2] to write " 'whim' on the lintel of his doorpost;" but he is usually afraid to do so, knowing that if he "lets himself go" society (that is, his temperamentally conservative, habituated, and repressed neighbors) will make him suffer, physically, socially, or economically, as one who infringes upon the established conventions and controls. What he does may do neither himself nor any one else any harm, in fact he may perform some of the occasionally useful functions of the iconoclast, but society will not put up with too whimsical a person, unless he succeeds in getting himself known as a genius. For one thing, his more conventionalized and less individualized neighbors find it hard to interpret him in terms of the fixed formulae of sentiments or habits of thought which are their customary standards of judging people. They are consequently uncomfortable and uncertain in his presence. They fear him as they fear the unknown.

The essential facts with regard to the fear-habit motivation of conservatism may be summarized as follows: The individual once adjusted to a given environment, in such a way that most of his responses and activities are of a habitual, routine character, is normally in a psycho-physical state which we may call contentment. (This, of course, is on the assumption that his habitual physical needs are met, and that he is not subject to balked dispositions arising from unsatisfied desire to emulate persons financially and culturally adjusted to a different, "higher" environment than his own.) When this adjustment, this working relation, to the environment is broken in upon

---

[2] *Social Organization*, 1909, p. 46.

by change, or threatened change, the contentment-repose van-
ishes and the organism undergoes an active internal turmoil
of adjustment to meet the impending change, either by flight
or by combat. The emotion of fear (very likely accompanied
by emotions of anger or of sorrow) immediately appears because the habit-routine of the individual is endangered. It
makes little difference, in principle, whether this habit-routine
is one of physical activity, of sentiment, or of thought. In
any case, just because the behavior-pattern has become habitual,
we cling to it, and any threatened necessity for modifying it
arouses fear and resentment. In such a juncture we are conservative from active fear. We seek safety, that is, a condition
in which our habit-routine can continue unmodified, by resist-
ing the threatened environmental change. When no change
threatens and consequently habit-routine is not endangered, we
are conservative in a passive sense; that is, we simply go on in
the accustomed routine of sentiment, thought, and action.

In general, therefore, the function of the attitude of conservatism is to protect the working relation between aptitudes and
habit on the one side and the environment on the other. While
this attitude functions through some form of fear, it will add
to our understanding to note somewhat more specifically what
it is that we are afraid of, whether by instinct or by training.

We find in the first place that fear of the unknown or unfamiliar is one of the deep roots of conservatism. The unknown
offers unlimited play for imagination and superstition, with
the result that even the common-sense mind of civilized and
disciplined man is not free from the primitive propensity to
people it with terrifying intangible dangers. The merely unfamiliar is not so much feared as simply avoided, because it
will require too great effort of attention to understand or
become adjusted to it. Habitual, repetitive, imitative lines of
thought—the only kind of thought most individuals indulge in—
do not move easily in an unfamiliar medium. The attraction
of the novel (appeal to curiosity, or to desire for distinction)
to some extent counteracts this fear of the unknown and lazy
aversion to the unfamiliar, but only partially, and not at all in
the more set type of conservative mind. As the average traveler
or hiker keeps to the blazed trail, and fears to venture into out-
of-the-way places or to set off across hill and dale for himself, so

the average citizen feels safest in the circle of his familiar thoughts, customs, conventions, and habits, and feels an uncomfortable sense of insecurity and shrinking at the thought of essential change or experiment in new social, political, or economic arrangements. Considered as a positive guide to conduct, the known and familiar must always carry greater weight than the unknown and unfamiliar. One's own experience, one's own interpretation of facts, one's own illusions, one's own imaginary facts, one's own valuations, are more convincing, more comforting, than the reassurances of priest or medicine man or prophet —unless, and until, these personages attain a degree of prestige, authority, and power of quasi-hypnotic impression which stimulates in us the propensities of self-abasement and hero worship. Such impressive prestiges, however, are palpably diminishing in strength and prevalence under the influence of modern science and democratization. Science and democratization have still a very long way to go. Democracy is in the nature of surface phenomena, as yet, and as far as application of scientific thought to the guidance of human affairs goes, science is held in check by an almost impermeable mass of superstition, egotism, and illusion. Temperamental, protective conservatism still results from unreasoning fear of the unfamiliar and untried, as well as from the authoritatively imposed habits of thought and belief inculcated by conservative leaders. These leaders themselves are not free from old illusions and attachment to the archaic, and incidentally they may sometimes have personal materialistic reasons for not desiring essential change.

We may also fear the relatively familiar if it is deemed disadvantageous to our interests or does not conform to our sentiments. Clericalism fears science, law-abiding citizens fear the deteriorating influence of the Ku Klux, one hundred per cent Americans fear the foreign born, one of our noted automobile manufacturers fears the Jews, and so on. Obviously fear of the familiar may lead to conservatism and it may not. Fear of the possible results of woman suffrage—a familiar enough *idea*— caused many persons to take a conservative or reactionary attitude on that issue. Some of these same persons voted for the radical eighteenth amendment out of fear of the familiar saloon. In many cases it is clear that fear of the familiar thing is really fear of the unknown factors in it. Thus fear of the Ku Klux is due in part to the secret nature of that organization. The same can be said of fear of science (Darwinism! Evolution!), the foreign born, Catholicism, the Jews, and vaccination. While knowledge does not drive out fear in cases where fear is rational, ignorance nevertheless is the mother of a vast amount of unnecessary fear.

Quite as strong as, and somewhat more definite than, fear of the unfamiliar is fear of social disapprobation.[4] We have here an explanation of the hold which conventional notions of propriety and conformity have upon the average mind. To uphold the old, to abide by the established, to refrain from much criticism of things as they are, to think none but conventional thoughts,—these are the avenues to day-by-day respectability. Divergence from them lays one open to the charge of being "queer," eccentric, a "knocker," and of being deficient in good taste and respectability.

There is, however, more in the motivation of protective conservatism than this self-regarding, egocentric fear. People hesitate or refuse to make progressive or radical social changes, not only out of personal interest or irrational dread of change, but from honest, rational belief that a given reform may unleash more social evils than it will remedy. There are times when any relaxation of social control or any great or sudden change in its forms and agencies may spell disaster, at least temporarily, not only to those classes who have enjoyed special privileges but to the group as a whole. And while the vast majority of conservatives who oppose radical economic reform probably do so because they fear for particular economic interests and privileges, there are still many, among whom are some who enjoy no special privilege, who have honestly convinced themselves that any essential alteration in the mass and incidence of social control, say of business enterprise (*e.g.*, centralized federal regulation, or government ownership of public utilities) would inflict a permanent economic loss upon people generally, producers and consumers alike.

---

[4] For a brief discussion of the relation of this form of fear to pride and to the possible instinct of gregariousness, see Z. C. Dickinson, *Economic Motives*, 1922, pp. 118-121.

Take an illustration in the field of social contact and segregation. The great mass of the population of the United States is either oblivious to the existence of a race (*i.e.*, negro) problem, or is content to let race relations rest in *statu quo*, for fear that the more these relations are discussed, and the more reform is admitted to be desirable, the more dangerous the situation will become. This is probably the average characteristic attitude in both races. At least it was so before the war. But there are radical reformers in both races who insist upon the ideal of social, as well as economic, equality, and who insist that agitation must be carried on in season and out for the practical realization of this ideal. Now the white people of the South (and a very large proportion of those in the North) are not likely soon to take kindly to the remotest suggestion of social equality, although there are many forward-looking, thoughtful people in the South, as in the North, who hold that provision for equal economic opportunity for the negro is a just and necessary reform. But any agitation for social equality, even though there be very little of it, produces a retardation in the acceptance of the ideal of equal economic opportunity. There are undoubtedly a vast number of persons in the South—cotton and sugar planters, lumber companies, employers of negro domestic labor—who cannot bear the thought that the negro should ever be anything but a hewer of wood and a drawer of water, one set aside by Providence to do the heavy, dirty, and unremunerative work, just as there are many employers in the North who look upon the immigrant laborer as an impersonal cog in the industrial machine.

These persons will, from entirely selfish, materialistic motives, oppose any step or drift toward economic opportunity for the negro, such as might flow from adequate schools and industrial and commercial training. But, as is the wont of special interests, they will not ordinarily give their real reasons for opposition; they will, the rather, raise the cry that social equality is being aimed at, and must inevitably follow from educational and economic opportunity. Hence the only safe course is a tight-sitting conservatism which will continue to see to it that the negro is kept in his place. Once the alleged issue of social equality is raised, all but the critically-minded find themselves confronted by the spectre of race amalgamation. Barring those with selfish interests, who with malice afore-thought draw the red herring of social equality across the trail of the real issue, the people who are honestly impressed with the fear that social equality is the real aim and that it would follow upon the heels of increased economic opportunity must be given credit for a conservatism motivated by considerations of public welfare, and this credit must be given whether one "believes in" racial "equality" or not. In other words, the fear which motivates them to protective conservatism is not egoistic fear (at most it is based on race egotism) but a fear for the safety of the social group.

Other and more generalized motives to conservatism are suggested in the next section, on conservative characteristics.

2. Characteristics of the Conservative Mind

Our analysis of the fear-motivation of conservatism has distinguished fear of the unknown, of the unfamiliar (and, under certain circumstances, of the familiar), of the unconventional, and of social disapprobation. These fears must here be set down as specific and salient characteristics of the conserva-tive mind. Desire for recognition and for distinction, later mentioned above, and the resulting susceptibility to prestige-attraction are characteristic of all minds, and so cannot be called exclusively conservative traits, although they are perhaps some-what more characteristic of conservative than of radical tempera-ments. The conservative conformist is more likely to control his conduct in accordance with the standard "What will people say?" than is the non-conformist radical. The specific conserva-tive characteristics, other than these, are: a group of traits related directly to the fact of attachment or adjustment, pride, loyalty, sense of order, deficiency in constructive imagination, and a tendency to base subjective valuations upon an exagger-ated regard for safety and past experience.

By "attachment" is meant that accommodation which results from the habit-forming agencies and processes discussed above. The central significant product of these processes is, as we have seen, the ability and tendency to react to a familiar, wonted environment in semi-automatic manner, without the intervention of conscious attention or "willed" direction of action. There is a close relation between conservatism and certain aspects of physical laziness, which plays its part in the development of the lackadaisical, passive type of conservative attitude. The smaller the variety and range of stimuli to which an individual or class is subject, the more likely is this physiological conservatism to be present. As Veblen points out, any class sheltered from the action of environment in any essential respect "will adapt its views and its scheme of life more tardily to the general situation" and "will in so far tend to retard the process of social transformation." This is one reason why, even apart from special interests which it consciously wishes to preserve, the leisure class obstructs change. [5]

A sub-type of lackadaisical conservatism is that of the people who are willing to have progressive things done if some one else will do them. After the hard, unpopular pioneering work of a movement is done, there are always a sufficient number of such conservatives to come forward in time to share in the congratulations. Both fear and desire for recognition and approbation play their part in this change of front. Fear of unpopularity keeps many people who have possibly considerable potential originality from arousing themselves to the effort of independent thinking or of lending their energies and influence to any unpopular cause. The effectiveness of this fear is enhanced by our pecuniary standards of social position.

A sub-characteristic of habituation is the craving for "principles" (which can be used as a credit currency in place of work and accomplishment), and for settled systems of thought and feeling—centers about which sentiment can revolve in a closed orbit. This is one thing that gives certain religions their hold. Hard and fast religious creeds, authoritatively imposed, enable their nominal devotees to escape the labor of critical thought and furnish a safe haven for those who have not the courage to face the stubborn realities of life, and have therefore to appeal to some kind of mysticism. Every individual has, and in the nature of things must have, some working philosophy of life, at least some fragmentary justification of his way of

---

[5] Veblen, *The Theory of the Leisure Class*, 1899, p. 193.

living. The difference between the conservative and the progressive in this respect is that one dislikes intensely to change his philosophy in the slightest particular, while the other adjusts himself to the repeated necessity of modification. The extreme radical, in this respect, resembles the conservative more than he does the progressive.

Curiously enough, this desire for a settled philosophy is prominent in a certain type of college student, especially among those who have had rigorous authoritative training. College students, after the Sophomore year, are usually old enough to begin to grasp something of the methods of unrest and criticism, of "drift," changing ideals, and the development of new standards and points of view in economies, politics, morals and religion. But as soon as the defects, the insufficiency, the non-adaptability of the old, are dimly realized, there is a strong tendency among them to demand a new system, a new philosophy, ready made and cut to fit, neatly arranged and labeled, so that they may immediately put it in the place of the old. And if college students can be addicted to this sort of superficiality, in which a man knows not the reasons for the faith which is in him, but takes the way of least resistance, whether it lead back to a comfortable, flabby conservatism or off into a superficial radicalism, we certainly have no cause for surprise to find the populace at large characterized in great measure by a certain mental stolidity, quite as much as by actively protective conservative attitudes.

Active conservatism may be regarded as a phase or by-product of loyalty—loyalty to principles, to institutions, to ideals, and to persons. Unfortunately "loyalty" is one of those much used and of late grievously abused terms which among the unthinking passes for full-weight, sterling metal. Among the more critical it has come to be regarded as a somewhat depreciated currency. Most people use the term without any definite idea of its significance. Of late, regrettably, it has come into frequent use by special interests who wish to make it synonymous with reactionism. According to this usage, anyone who dares to criticize the existing economic and political order is "disloyal," just as formerly anyone who did not accept the doctrine of the virgin birth of Christ or the literal inspiration and infallibility of the Bible was an "infidel" or "atheist." This conception of loyalty as an attitude excluding independent thought and adverse criticism is probably very old, and it is the one most common to-day. The "loyal" undergraduate frowns upon any open adverse criticism of "the team," the local business man dislikes unfavorable publicity for his town, the rank and file of trade union members turn a deaf ear to anyone who tries to convince them of shortcomings in union leaders or policies, and so on. Now, from a rational point of view, this sensitiveness to criticism is foolish and costly, because the group ought to find in criticism a stimulus and means to improve its services to its members. But from the point of view of "practical politics," as well as from consideration of historical origins, it is easy to see why any great amount of open adverse criticism receives a cold welcome. Not only does it offend the pride of members of the group, but it may cause internal dissensions and produce a lack of unity which will be injurious to the group in its competition or conflict with other groups. No army leader wishes the enemy to know the weakness of his forces.[6]

Loyalty, in its historical development and its practical application is thus a *defensive attitude,* and it is not without significance that etymologically the word is closely related to "legal." Loyalty is a trait highly useful to protective conservatism. It gives confidence in group solidarity and in group support of the individual. It is not surprising, therefore, that in war-time it becomes the first of the cardinal virtues, or that always one of the easiest ways to ward off investigation and rob criticism of effect is to raise the hue and cry that the group is being traitorously attacked. The "herd instinct" will do the rest.

Moreover, "loyalty" serves a useful purpose to the group and to group leaders in that it removes or diminishes the necessity for giving *raisons d'être* or justifications. If my attitude is to be "my country, right or wrong," there is no pressing reason why my country should ever be right. Such an attitude, literally carried out in any institution or group, would stifle every vestige of internal criticism—which is usually the most effective kind—and peaceful progress would be impossible.

---

[6] Sinclair Lewis' much read novel, *Main Street,* is a suggestive study of mediocrity's sensitiveness to criticism, and at the same time imperviousness to it.

Protective conservatism is peculiarly loyal to institutions as such. Its reverence for established institutions, in their existing form—especially the family, the church, private property, and nationalism—would lift them above the reach of criticism and practically make them ends in themselves—a curious ethical inversion of ends and means.

Loyalty to persons is a trait of both conservative and radical. The Chinaman with his ancestor-worship, the precinct man with his unquestioning fealty to his boss, the revolutionary socialist with his reverence for the memory of Karl Marx, and the Mohammedan with his "There is no god but Allah and Mohammed is his prophet" are all, so far as personal loyalty is concerned, in the same class. They all flame out white hot at criticism or opposition.

Personal loyalty is akin to the so-called herd instinct, which can be observed in animals, and strong survivals of which persist in civilized man. The more closely knit a group, the less contact its members have with other groups, the more uniform and homogeneous their experience—in a word the greater their group isolation—the more completely is the personality of the individual shaped and "set" in conformity with group viewpoints and standards. Under such conditions the individual is likely to have an exaggerated idea of the authoritative quality of his group's beliefs and ideals.

Herein lies a partial explanation of the intense loyalties, institutional and personal, and the dogmatic conservatism of many young people during the adolescent period. While the loyalties of youth are doubtless more easily reshaped and rationalized than are those of age, provided one authority or prestige be set against another and the youth thus led to think for himself, the immature personality bears the impress of the group quite as plainly, though not so deeply, as does the settled character of older persons. It is only the plasticity and elastic rebound of youth that prevents a permanent "set" of these impresses into practically ineradicable prejudices. Everyone who has had to do with the mental processes of youth must have noted in how many instances any adverse criticism or even questioning of the ideals, beliefs, sentiments, and institutions to which the adolescent mind has been trained arouses instant defensive reaction. While it is less tenacious, it is often as intense and intolerant, for the time being, as that usually shown by men and women of more mature years. The more authoritative and the more preclusive of independent critical thought this training has been, the more do these tenaciously loyal minds fail to open up to rational processes. It is in the sphere of religion that this exclusive authoritarianism has been of longest standing and is most persistent in institutional folkways. As a result, hundreds of young men and women in some church schools and seminaries never catch even a glimpse of the constructive philosophical and ethical thought of the "higher criticism" and the modern tendency to give Christian ethics a social rather than a narrowly individualistic implication.

Loyalty, of course, is not a trait exclusively of conservatives. No one can be more loyal than are the dogmatic and uneducated members of some radical groups. There is a sort of conservatism, however, even in such loyalty, for it bespeaks a sentimental attachment which will not brook, and cannot understand, any criticism of the tenets and sentiments of the group. There is in popular loyalty very little intellective element. While rational criticism and true loyalty—that is, devotion to the best interests of the person, institution or group to which one is loyal—are by no means incompatible, what usually goes as loyalty is mere unthinking sentiment. For this reason loyalty is in another sense than the one noted above a defense attitude. The loyal person, by his unquestioning devotion, and resentment or combat-reactions to criticism, seeks to protect the object around which his sentiments gravitate.

Unconsciously the personality of the young mind has become identified with the traditions, mental habits, and viewpoints of its institutional relations. Consequently pride enters in. The individual feels criticism of his group or institutional habits and ideals to be an attack upon himself. His self-regard and his group loyalty become essentially synonymous. This egotistical loyalty results in part from the fact that no mind likes to be re-made. Dislike to mental refurnishing is a matter of laziness ("motor-set"), of pride in consistency, of loyal attachment, and perhaps also of fear. The social order in which a man lives and to which his responses are habitually adapted becomes a part of himself. Change in it necessitates alteration in his personality. Even a change of abode is distasteful to those who have lived long in one place. If, as Giddings says, "the persistent desire of consciousness is to be clear and painless,"[7] opposition of thought and of sentiment is likely, in all but critically-intellectual minds, to induce a "balked disposition."[8] Physiologically this may be explained as nervous strain, but morally it is to be regarded as thwarted assertion of the ego, resulting either in combativeness or in hurt feelings and an increase of shyness and reticence. In any but the critically-intellectual mind, which takes intellectual opposition as a purely impersonal matter and welcomes it as an aid to clear thinking, difference of opinion or of sentiment is too commonly regarded as a personal affront. Thus the untrained or the too narrowly trained person is thrown into a personally defensive attitude and the blindness of his devotion to his sentiments is intensified. The egotistical person has a distinct and conscious pride in his loyalties, which intensifies both his virtues and his faults, but in particular has a tendency to deprive him of objective critical capacity. Both individuals and groups may thus become conservators of beliefs and viewpoints which continue to claim loyalty only because they are by pride protected from effective criticism.

On the group's side—more specifically on the part of its most narrowly "loyal" and conservative leaders—care is taken to see that this egotistic and unquestioning faithfulness to group institutions and ideals is not allowed to diminish in intensity or exclusiveness. What may be called group-egotism is cultivated. One's group is the greatest, finest, most enlightened of its kind. Sufficient illustration of this sort of group-utilitarian sentiment will occur to the reader. Its favorite haunt is chauvinistic nationalism. One does not have to go to Germany to encounter it. Sectionalism and sectarianism are green pastures for it. Certain radical groups are strongly characterized by it.

The sincere conservative always has a strong sense of order. This may be merely an unthinking dislike of disturbance of any kind, coupled to the feeling that all radical change is

---

[7] *Readings in Descriptive and Historical Sociology*, 1906, p. 126.
[8] See Graham Wallas, *The Great Society*, 1914, pp. 64ff.

somehow connected with "lawlessness," or it may be intellectual conviction that social order as it is, in all its essential details, has been too hardly won and is too sacred to be subjected to the risks of reform. Usually, however, the cry that order is being disturbed comes from vested-interest conservatism.

Sense of order, and fear of change in social order, are to be associated, where some special interest is not at stake, with a lack of constructive imagination. The conservative is adept at conjuring up a list of imaginary evils sure to flow from a change in institutions, economic relations, or moral standards, but he lacks either the will or the capacity to form a mental image of benefits to flow from new arrangements. The more radical the proposed change, the more it stimulates his pessimistic forebodings, and the less able is he to see any possible good in it.

The conservative looks at his entire familiar environment through the eyes of habituation and at any different environment through the eyes of fear. All elements of life are evaluated primarily with reference to safety or security. Since the existing environment is usually the present product of the past, from which any change has been gradual enough to permit unconscious adjustment, the conservative generally sets an exaggerated valuation on the past. Whether from the influence of the schools, and specifically from the study of history as it is too frequently taught, or from other causes, such for example as family pride and the appeal of the antique and archaic to the imagination, our attachment to the tried and familiar is turned into a reverence for the past simply because it is the past. Thus the social organization and ideals of the past take on a sanctity and authority out of proportion to their real value.

The extent of the part which fear and habit, conjoined to an uncritical attachment to things as they are and the easy belief that the past contained all wisdom, play in life, depends largely upon the degree to which the individual's life is governed by objective knowledge and critical reason as compared with subjective sentiment and prejudice.

We shall later, when we come to consider the characteristics of the radical mind, have occasion to allude to the idea of mental types, and specifically, to refer to a rough classification, based on the degree to which the individual's mental processes are characterized by emotion and intellect respectively, and his actions governed by emotional or rational guidance.[9] We shall there point out that the nearer the mind comes to the objective, scientific ideal, the more it reaches conclusions on the basis of factual evidence, the more it is characterized by intellectual and rational processes, rather than by reflex and habitual motor reactions or by subjective emotionalism, the nearer it comes to the qualities necessary, not to the exigencies of field combat between conservative and radical interests, but to the constructive inventiveness and engineering capacity essential to social readjustment reasonably rapid, yet reasonably consonant with social stability and safety. Needless to say, comparatively few minds, whether conservative or radical in tendency, approximate this creatively intellective type. The majority of minds are with respect to most interests either ideo-emotional or dogmatic-emotional. A mind either highly emotional or markedly dogmatic is uncritical.

Certainly the mass of conservatives are characterized either by a conspicuous absence of critical capacity or by the determination not to allow criticism to be directed against the institutions, ideals, etc., to which they pride themselves on being "loyal." This leads to an avoidance of issues, refusal to face facts, and to a vast network of "rationalizations"[10] and casuistries by which the world is made to seem what it is not and worse reasons the better.[11]

From this "rationalizing" trait, as well as from loyalty, refusal to face facts and issues, and the tendency to deceptive idealization, springs the conservative's bland optimism, "God's in his heaven, all's right with the world"—why worry!

Few minds are wholly either conservative or radical. Fear, habituation, inertia, loyalty, and bovine contentment may produce in some cases a nearly absolute conservatism, but there are few persons who will not, upon occasion, manifest at least some *interest* in criticism, in change, and in the new; and interest may pave the way to accommodation to innovations,

---

[9] See pp. 174, 175, 181, 316-318.
[10] In the psychoanalytical sense.
[11] See the later passage on symbolical conservatism, pp. 127-129.

if not to actual approval of them. So also will a sense of the inevitable. It was some gain for political democracy, for instance, when hide-bound conservatives reached the point of saying of equal suffrage, "Oh, well, it's coming, I know that!" Conservatism of this stoic type, however, would be of comparatively little significance did it not always lie as an inert mass weighing the scales down heavily against the critic and the innovator. It forms a mass whose votes and implastic sentiment the progressive or radical always has to contend with in his attempts to turn public opinion and concerted action in the direction of reform.

Even the best of minds has its compartments. Some of them are duly lighted and aired, and swept out with exemplary frequency, and old junk and lumber are never allowed to accumulate. Others are tightly closed and have a musty odor like an old parlor. Sometimes, doubtless, fine sparkling wine of thought is drawn from some dark cellar-hole of the mind where it has lain long and matured in the calm of unruffled meditation. Mostly, however, these closed or half-closed areas are merely the catch-all places of ideas, loyalties, habits, and attitudes which we are too lazy or too preoccupied to dust out. We cannot always be changing and redisposing, it is true; some resting place for the really valuable we must have; but if some fine day we wake up to the fact that much that we have cherished is no longer precious, or if upon our demise our executors pitch the whole content into the discard, we cannot complain.

Your true conservative, however, does not use his mental compartments intelligently—as intelligently at any rate as a modern business office does its filing system. He allows no cross references, and his follow-ups are persistently along one line, even though it be unprofitable. Ideas are valuable only in pairs or multiples. Ingrown philosophies grow stale and lose their savor. Cultures are best when cross-fertilized.

But a mind constructed wholly on the compartment plan is practically idea-proof. Such a mind may exhibit the most startling contrasts and inconsistencies. Such a man's life is not a unit. The different phases of his experience, however broad the ground covered may be nominally, remain unco-ordinate. What he gets, or might get, from variety of group contacts, from acquaintance with different fields of thought, is kept tied up and put away in its own proper cubby hole. The cards are never shuffled. There is no cross fertilization between the various kinds of knowledge or culture which such an individual may have acquired. A resourceful and inventive engineer may be a dub when it comes to politics. Many a priest and many a professor says one thing to-day and thinks another to-night, because his real outlook upon the present spiritual and social needs of the world would play havoc with his religious or educational formulas, did he not keep the two prudently segregated. The compartmentized mind is thus both a result and a cause of conservatism—fundamentally of laziness and of fear.

Specialization thus has a bearing on the psychology of conservatism and radicalism. In the first place, a man's vocational and business interests make him conservative, in matters where they are concerned. Specialism, making a man an expert in a narrow field but leaving him essentially ignorant otherwise, probably exerts some tendency toward the continuance of that quasi-instinctive fear of the unfamiliar which we have seen to be an important factor in the conservative attitude. On the other hand, it must be confessed that not a few specialists who rightly deprecate the intrusion of untrained laymen into their fields, often themselves rush into the territory of others, where angels fear to tread, with consideration so crude that it reveals at once the egotism of their ignorance. Whether specialism tends to make a man conservative, progressive, or radical, in matters upon which he is not specially trained, will depend upon the nature of his work and upon his temperament. It is safe to guess that there are not many socialists among Catholic priests or many educational reformers among professors of Greek.

The cleavage between radicalism or progressivism and conservatism or reaction in the same mind often is on the line dividing aim from method, end from means. History affords striking illustration of the fact that conservative aims are often attained through radical innovation of method—witness the United States Constitution. Contrariwise the older leaders of radical movements generally show a noteworthy tendency to become conservative in the methods they sanction—witness the history of trade unionism, and the stagnation of the woman suffrage movement until in England the militant "suffragettes" and in America the National Woman's Party put life into it and by radical methods made it a national political issue. The tendency for aging leaders to harden into the shell of conservative sentiment and procedure, and the counteracting impulse of new blood to dissatisfaction with established policies that lack spirit and effectiveness, explain the schisms to which all lasting reform movements and organizations are sooner or later subject. Witness the development of sectarianism in the church, the break-up and realignment of political parties, and the continual rebudding of new schools of art and criticism.

Having attempted to suggest the sources in instinctive fear and social habituation of the disinterested conservative attitude, and to point out the more significant features of the conservative mind, we must now examine more in detail the processes by which the conservative attitude is developed and fixed in personality.

3. *The Making of the Conservative*

The ultimate sources of conservatism, especially in its temperamental or instinctive aspects, must be sought in the facts of biological evolution; specifically in the necessity for adaptation of the organism to its environment and the consequent development and fixation in heredity of the traits requisite to survival.

Ever since the work of Charles Darwin, sociologists and anthropologists have applied the doctrine of struggle for existence, natural selection, and survival of the fittest to the explanation of social evolution and the development of types of society. For a time, especially after the publication, in 1885, of August Weismann's theory of the non-inheritability (in organic heredity) of acquired characteristics, many writers on social evolution placed almost exclusive emphasis on elimination of the unfit and selection of the fit as the only permanent method of progress. Crude analogical application of the doctrine of natural selection to human affairs was the fashion of the time,[12] but riper and less one-sided scholarship has shown that selection is only one of many agencies of social evolution.

---

[12] Perhaps the most typical example of this type of social theory was that advanced in Benjamin Kidd's *Social Evolution*, 1894.

Nevertheless, certain important facts remain. Nature is the realm of an unceasing struggle for existence (*a*) between individuals of the same species (where mitigating influences do not enter in), and (*b*) between species. The success of the individual in this struggle depends primarily on his own characteristics (his "fitness") and secondly, upon the degree to which cohesion, mutual aid, and co-operation have been developed in the group to which he belongs. The characteristics of any individual are the combined product of his organic heredity—the potential characteristics he has at birth, if we disregard the ante-natal environmental factors—and of suggestion, training, education, and experience. Through organic heredity, variation, and selection, the species is adapted to its environment. This process we may call phylogenetic adaption. Those individuals survive which have the hereditary traits suitable to adjustment to the environment. Given this hereditary basis, adjustment to environment is further brought about by habituation and (when we reach man) by training and education. In general, the fitting of the individual to his environment through individual habituation and experience may be called ontogenetic adaptation. Ontogenetic adaptation is impossible or imperfect in the case of those individuals who lack the proper phylogenetic characteristics. Thus the hereditarily feeble-minded are phylogenetically unfit for successful individual adjustment to the demands of life in modern society.

The psychology of this ontogenetic adaptation or habituation is succinctly set forth by Veblen:

"What men can do easily is what they do habitually, and this decides what they can think and know easily. They feel at home in the range of ideas which is familiar through their everyday line of action. A habitual line of action constitutes a habitual line of thought, and gives the point of view from which facts and events are apprehended and reduced to a body of knowledge. What is consistent with the habitual course of action is consistent with the habitual line of thought, and gives the definitive ground of knowledge as well as the conventional standard of complacency or approval in any community. Conversely, a process or method of life, once understood, assimilated in thought, works into the general scheme of life and becomes a norm of conduct, simply because the thinking, knowing agent is also the acting agent. What is apprehended with facility and is consistent with the process of life and knowledge is thereby apprehended as right and good. All this applies with added force where the habituation is not simply individual and sporadic, but is enforced upon the group or the race by a selective elimination of those individuals and lines of descent that do not conform to the required canon of knowledge and conduct. Where this takes place, the acquired proclivity passes from the status of habit to that of aptitude or propensity. It becomes a transmissible trait, and action under its guidance becomes right and good, and the longer and more consistent the selective adaptation through which the aptitude arises, the more firmly is the resulting aptitude settled upon the race, and the more unquestioned becomes the sanction of the resulting canon of conduct.'' [13]

Within a given group, the struggle for existence is tempered and modified. The herds of wild horses on Asiatic steppes, and human beings, may compete in internal strife with one another with brutal intensity, but the individual horses which compose a given herd will join forces in repelling attacks by carnivorous beasts,[14] and the human inhabitants of a country will combine, in spite of bitter internal struggle for subsistence, to the best of their ability to repel a foreign invader. Mutual aid, as Kropotkin and others have pointed out, thus becomes an important factor in survival. Co-operation depends on the cohesion and organization of the group. The group which stands together survives; that which does not, perishes. In species below man, group cohesiveness is based mainly on instinct; in man partly on instinct, partly on habituation and adjustment.

Thus, through various selective processes in human society, a premium is put on conformity, loyalty, and obedience to authority. Intolerance of nonconformity, of individuality, and of independence of judgment becomes a social virtue. Public sentiment becomes an intimidating force, and fear hastens conformity to its behests.

It is impossible at present to say to what degree tendencies

[13] "The Instinct of Workmanship and the Irksomeness of Labor," *American Journal of Sociology,* Sept., 1893, p. 195.
[14] See P. Kropotkin, *Mutual Aid a Factor of Evolution,* 1902, Ch. 2.

to conservative conformity to the group's needs or supposed needs are due to organic heredity, and to what degree to onto-genetic adjustment. It is possible to argue that in the long evolutionary struggle of group with group the "brain patterns" proper to conservative conformity and group cohesiveness were developed through variation and selection and handed down by organic heredity. These inherited behavior-patterns would consist of certain sets of synapses, nerve-cell connections, such as would produce conservative, protective attitudes and reactions on the part of the individuals of each successive generation. In the light of advances now being made in our knowledge of the physiological bases of human behavior, the analysis would run not in terms of brain patterns but in terms of the inherited structure and nature of the "organism as a whole"—neural, glandular, and muscular. On some such lines would be laid down the argument for the hereditary nature of conservatism. It is quite within reason to suppose that long ages of fear-reactions and life in groups, both in the human species and its ape-like progenitors, may, through selective processes, have developed an organic type which would necessarily involve, even in the absence of ontogenetic adaptation and the compul-sory influence of authority and public sentiment, a temperamen-tal conservative tendency.

Even though organic inheritance of conservative behavior patterns may not enter into the problem, the selective influences brought to bear upon the individual in any society are sufficient as an anthropological explanation of the prevalence of the conservative attitude. As Lapouge[15] and others have shown, those who have not conformed to the economic, political, moral, and religious prescriptions of their time and society have fallen prey to factional conflict or been put under the ban of the law, and if not actually killed off, as in the Roman proscriptions and the Inquisition, have been put to such economic and social disadvantage that they have either left the country or failed to transmit their nonconformist tendencies to a numerous progeny.

Only in times of rapid social change are the conservatives as likely to be eliminated as are progressives and radicals. In

[15] *Les Sélections Sociales*, 1896.

times of revolution they may be in even more danger, and may
die in great numbers, as the French and Russian Revolutions
show, because revolutionary radicalism is not likely to be more
fastidious in method than is counter-revolutionary reactionism,
and because, also, habitual conservatives lack the power of
flexible adjustment to changing social norms and group
needs.[16]

While biological selection is undoubtedly at work in human
society, and while normally it probably tends to the survival
of conservative rather than radically inclined types, it is'
obscured by ontogenetic selective adaptation—the training of
individuals to habitual adjustment to a given social environment.
In the making of the conservative the learning process plays
a much more prominent part than does hereditary adaptation.
The hereditary foundation is present but the superstructure
is the product of adaptive education.

A baby comes into the world with no equipment save a few
simple reflexes, useful in the initiation of immediately necessary adjustment, and a few potential instincts. Some of these
will help to adapt it to the demands of the social environment,
and some will very likely prove to be impediments to that adaptation. The child is thus preponderantly a social product, as
Cooley means to say when he says that "Self and society are
twin-born," and as a long line of psychologists have pointed out.
Into the hereditary vessel, if we may speak figuratively, is put,
through the learning process and the pressure of social controls, such mental content—habit, knowledge, sentiment, in
short, behavior-patterns—as society deems expedient. The vessel itself is plastic, within limits, and as the growth process
goes on, the direction and extent of that growth is determined
by the nature of opportunity offered and the stringency of the
controls operative.

It is important, in arriving at an understanding of the development of conservative or radical sentiments, to remember that
the growth and adaptation of the child's mentality consist not
only in developing powers of perception, knowledge, intelligence,

---

[16] On selection in relation to conservatism, see Veblen, *The Theory of
the Leisure Class*, 1899, especially the two illuminating chapters on
"Industrial Exemption and Conservatism" and "The Conservation of
Archaic Traits."

and rational faculty, but also, as human life goes, much more significantly, in the development of sentiments and attitudes and in the special trend or training given the child's emotions. In fact, most of our popular educational institutions, home, school, church, athletics, and amusement, seem to be much more concerned with emotional reactions and sentiments than with the intellective side of personality. In other words, a very large part of the social disciplining of child and youth is inculcation, through association, imitation, emulative stimulus, and direct precept, of the *sentiments* assumed to be proper to the social environment in which the child is to live.

This sentimental adjustment is never, of course, quite completed in anyone's life. The individual himself changes; from the organic changes incident to increasing age, if from nothing else. Minor readjustments of habit-routine are constantly necessary, as there is no such thing as a completely static, changeless society. Thus both from within and without, the individual is forced to readjustment, which at times may approach a catastrophic character, as at adolescence, but which ordinarily may be made so gradually as not to awaken any great fear or seriously disturb the equilibrium of contentment. In periods, unlike our own, not marked by extraordinarily rapid social transformation, an adjustment, a working basis of habit-response, once established, may remain relatively unchanged during the individual's entire life. Barring periods of catastrophic revolution or exceptionally accelerated evolution, nine-tenths of the life of each one of us is lived out on the plane and within the fabric of this habituation to existing institutions, customs, and controls.

And that is almost equivalent to saying, that however "progressive" or "radical" our sentiments and desires may be with regard to important phases of life, we are at bottom nine-tenths conservative. Like Crusoe, we carry over into a new situation all the established habits which we can make work there, and, as every revolution shows, a distressingly large number which we cannot make work under the new conditions.

Full understanding of conservatism and other social attitudes, and especially of the way attitudes are produced by the operation of social influences, cannot be reached without detailed study of the various forms and agencies of social control. These agencies, as discussed by Ross,[17] are public opinion, law, belief, social suggestion, education, custom, religion, social types and personal ideals, ceremony, art, illusion, social valuation. These are not all co-ordinate in character or importance, and some of them overlap. Other agencies which will suggest themselves to the reader are family environment, economic processes and industrial organization, literature (including the daily newspaper), and political organization and ideals. All of these are important forms or avenues of control, but most of them perhaps might be included under one or more of Ross' heads. We shall not attempt to touch upon the influence of all these agencies, but will confine ourselves to a few observations, largely upon the educational process as related to the production and perpetuation of the conservative attitude.

An extremely important fact to be kept in mind is that the pressure of the whole social organism, intent with all its authority, controls, institutions, and processes, on the creation and perpetuation of proper sentiments and attitudes, is thrown upon the individual during the most formative years of childhood and youth when he has the least defense against it.

The family, with its parental solicitudes and disciplines, is some defense against external social pressure, but is itself usually a faithful reflection of the society round about it. Family training is authoritative, and from the first, in the very nature and purpose of its function, has to be highly and directly conservative in its influence. The child is trained to his parents' conceptions and standards of life, and so long as the parents can prevent it, is not ordinarily encouraged, or even permitted, to deviate from those valuations. As they see the world, they expect him to see it. In a measure, this authoritative imposition of habit, values, and viewpoints is necessary to the protection of the child; but practically it usually means that he has much to unlearn later on.

It is worthy of remark that the moral function of the family is very generally extolled as precisely this function of inculcating conservative, conformist attitudes. This means usually that in the family, as in the church, constant attempt is made to fix in the child's personality sentiments and standards at a

[17] See E. A. Ross, *Social Control*, 1904.

time when he has no critical capacity to judge their value. In fact, about the last thing the family or the church does is to encourage the development of the critical faculty. The child's own moral judgments, should he betray any incipient tendency to form any, are too frequently peremptorily cut off. There is good psychology in the declaration traditionally attributed to the Jesuits that if they can have the training of the child until he is seven they care not who has him thereafter. The moral right of parents to impose their sentiments and attitudes upon the child is seldom questioned,[18] although it must be confessed that the effectiveness of parental discipline seems to have waned greatly, under the strain of competition with other and somewhat commercialized formative influences.

The school subjects the child to a second set of habit-forming influences, in part similar to those of home, in part additional and different. As the school's chief function is to enable the child to live in the social group, it naturally teaches first of all, like the home, the things most prized by the group, the things considered most necessary to survival and success, both of the individual in the group and of the group itself. The central foundation of education is the established and the generally accepted—the conventions, beliefs, judgments, and valuations sanctioned by the authority of use, traditional continuity, public sentiment, and whatever prestiges and prejudices happen to be prevalent. Much effort as has been, and may be, spent on the "enrichment" and humanizing of the school curriculum, the fact remains that practically all that the child learns in the grades and most that he learns in the high school, if he is fortunate enough to get that far, is learned through a process of authoritative imposition, and in great measure mechanically. Not only that, but it also consists of subject matter designed to give him the simple mechanical, symbolical, and logical equipment necessary for every-day life and communication—reading, writing, composition, arithmetic, language, and the orientating subjects of geography and history. Some slight contact is occasionally afforded with the interesting fields of science, literature, and the fine arts, and some training in the healthful and efficient

---

[18] But see Havelock Ellis' Essay on "Religion and the Child," in *The Task of Social Hygiene*, 1912.

use of the human body. On the other hand, the average school commonly grants to the average boy or girl little scope for individuality, small outlet for the aptitudes of self-expression and workmanship. Least of all is any attempt made to awaken and develop the critical faculties. The child has to acquire so much necessary *information,* and is made to acquire so much that is useless if not *mis*information, the impedimenta of tradition, that he is not given time to think, even if he is so disposed. All this information is absorbed from authority of teacher and textbook, chiefly in a memorizing process—which may ultimately land the student into the ranks of Phi Beta Kappa, yet leave him devoid of wisdom and understanding, and almost certainly deficient in what Dewey calls creative intelligence.

The influence of the school, in short, is almost as productive of uncritical conservatism as that of the home. This is true even if we leave entirely out of account the patent fact that the schools consciously devote themselves to the inculcation of conservative attitudes and if we refuse to believe that special vested interests, under one pretext or another, use our educational institutions for their own propagandistic purposes.

The existing and accepted social order, which thus somewhat inevitably lays its whole pressure upon developing youth, is itself the product of socially planless accretion from a past which is dead in fact, but vicariously living in the present. The past stands in a relation of causal organic continuity to the present. It has an interest both in its own right, as any story or drama has, and also because it contains, if it can be located, the key to the explanation of the present. We turn to the past for poetic and dramatic material, because there is something there which makes a powerful appeal to sentiment. But we also, in a more intellective and rational way, appeal to the past to give up this key of explanation. Both barbarous and civilized men seek genetic explanations of phenomena. Since the present contains the accretions of the past, crystallized and encysted in custom, political organization, religious belief, philosophies, literature, economic processes, and inherited conventions of thought, it is natural that educational processes should give much attention to the past, and that history especially, and to a lesser extent literature and languages, should be studied primarily as records. This is now done, however, without any very intelligent attempt always to relate the experience of the past to the problems and tasks of the present.

The mind of child and youth in the schools is rarely turned to the future, except in so far as the schools recognize and utilize the "life career motive"—the future vocational interest—to secure attention and application to work. We are occupied with the formal and symbolical subjects of language and mathematics, with geography and science (which we may, or may not, realize to have some connection with the present), and with history, which is always written in the past tense. Sometimes our teachers draw historical parallels between the past and present for us, but we—and sometimes they—know so little about the real organization, the real movements, and the real issues of the present, that somehow the parallel fails to seem strikingly significant. Sometimes, too, they attempt to predict or moralize for the future, on grounds of historical experience. This sounds reasonable and of value at first, but we become mildly skeptical—if our youthful tendency to be critical is not too much repressed—when we discover that nearly everybody who has a pet aversion to a given present tendency or proposed reform manages to convince himself, and tries to convince us, that something very similar was the cause of the decline and fall of the Roman Empire. The net result of historical study in the schools is in favor of conservatism, although this need not necessarily be so.[19] Every observant teacher knows that examination papers are nearly always written in the past tense, as if all that the student is ever concerned with is the history of dead men's ideas.

The net result of school and home training, as well as of general social pressure, is to cause youth to accept the society into which he is born, and to which he is trained, as a static and final thing.[20] Much of our education, accordingly, tends to perpetuate

---

[19] See J. H. Robinson, *The New History*, 1912, Ch. 8, on "The Spirit of Conservatism in the Light of History." See also *The Mind in the Making*, 1922, pp. 18ff, by the same writer.

[20] It is true nowadays that many children are born into families that belong to social ranks in which radicalism is prevalent, and the present order is habitually held in disregard, in which there is a sort of blind, religious faith—an uncritical faith—that socialism or some other *ism* will soon usher in a glorious and flawless future. But if this uncritical radical spirit is all that surrounds the child, it can hardly

the class standards and interests which have been developing in this country as surely as they have developed and perpetuated themselves in older countries, however much our conventional "democracy" tradition and "equal-opportunity" cant may lead us to ignore or disguise the fact. Vocational education, necessary and progressive movement as it is, may still further increase this tendency to training that develops class distinctions and class ideals. It is quite likely that "training for citizenship" in unintelligent hands or under the semi-official auspices of vested interests, may contribute to the same result.[21] Conservative training, both secular and ecclesiastical, has generally aimed at contentment and subserviency on the part of the masses. Higher education, until the Germans made it a matter of *Kultur* technique, was mainly a matter of "culture" and the "gentleman" ideal. It largely remains so, where the individualistic vocational motive has not made inroads. The American high school, especially, imitating the curriculum and the spirit of the American college, fell victim to its appeal. Thousands of American parents at each June commencement season feel a glow of pride that their children have secured a high school "education." This is due not so much to a supposition that the high school has fitted Tom and Jennie for a useful occupation (for it usually has not) as to the fact that they have studied (?) solid geometry, Shakespeare, and French (which they will never use); aped the fraternities, the rushes, the yells, the dances, and the general "varsity" air of the colleges; and are felt to be a little superior to the ordinary common run of boys and girls. It is of course natural that Tom and Jennie should share in this family and class pride, and accept the superior (though in part somewhat shoddy) opportunities of their class as their natural due—as perhaps they are.

Should we turn from the day schools to the Sunday schools and to the general routine and ceremonial of the church we should find influences and agencies even more conservative of traditional values and attitudes. Comparatively little of the so-called religious training of the child and adolescent in Sun-

---

be said to give promise of a scientific attitude, or to be less dangerous to productive originality than is the prevalent authoritative conservative spirit.

[21] Cf. J. H. Robinson, *The Mind in the Making*, 1922, pp. 20-23.

day school is calculated to develop anything but unquestioning and unintelligent acceptance of a list of static moral maxims. The major portion of moral and religious education has been a training in acquiescence to authority, with little vision of any possible, other, or better system of moral, economic, or political ideals than those which are now nominally accepted if not put into practice. Sunday school literature has scarcely anywhere got beyond the conception that moral relations are all personal. It still dwells on personal sins and the personal conventional virtues, and does not realize the pressing need of a new code, or a restatement of Christian principles to fit the impersonal, corporate relations and processes of our modern industrial society.[22]

The general influence of the church, however, has noticeably declined, so that its importance as a conserving agency, except perhaps in the more rural regions of the South and West, may easily be overestimated.[23]

In so far as the church is an effective agency for education in social ethics and not merely a medium for the perpetuation of archaic ceremonial and ecclesiastical intolerance, its decline may be regretted. For while many thinking people believe that ethical training, which the Greeks made a central feature of their educational practice, should be largely taken over by the public schools, and divorced from mysticism and supernaturalism, the public school authorities have either been too timid or too preoccupied with other matters as yet to have made much headway in this direction. Ethics and other social ''sciences,'' except history and a formalistic civics, have been left to be studied by the small percentage of young men and women who go to college, and by only a fraction of them. So that the non-church-going youths of to-day—doubtless the vast majority— are left to absorb their general ethics, as they absorb their sex ideas, from the highways and byways of chance association.

---

[22] See Ross, *Sin and Society*, 1907. Reference may here be made to the "Children's Code of Morals" for elementary schools, by President William J. Hutchins, of Berea College. While this Code is mainly in terms of personal morality there is strong suggestion of the social element. The pamphlet may be had from the National Institution for Moral Instruction, Chevy Chase, Washington, D. C.

[23] See Bernard Iddings Bell, "The Church and the Civilian Young Man," *Atlantic Monthly*, September, 1919.

Not only is the shaping power of the existing social organization and social institutions thrown against developing youth
with all the weight of authority, and all the logic of the necessary adjustment of the individual to the ways of the group;
his susceptibilities are played upon with all the attractive force
of their respective prestiges. A social agency is influential,
other things being equal, in proportion to its power of impression. Everybody knows in a superficial and general way
what prestige is, no one entirely escapes its influence, and most
people consciously set a high valuation upon it. Those who do
not have it would like to attain it, and those who have it usually
guard it as a valuable asset. Yet it is hard to define; and the
ultimate motives behind its influence are complex and variable,
probably resting back upon instinctive characteristics.

Webster's Dictionary defines prestige as "the influence which
accompanies or follows successful accomplishment,"—a defective definition in that it does not apply to people who have not
themselves accomplished anything and who, judged by any
standard of social utility, amount to little or nothing yet still
have prestige. A definition more to the point is that given by
Ross: "Prestige is that which excites such wonder or admira-
tion as to paralyze the critical faculty." [24] It is this impairment
of the critical faculty (paralysis is perhaps too strong a term)
which gives imputed superiority its magnetic or impressive
power.

Prestige flows from the possession or the reputed possession
of characteristics which people value highly. It derives its influence from two sources: (1) the power, or supposed power,
which its possessor (whether individual, class, or institution)
has, and (2) the quasi-instinctive desires for recognition and
distinction, and the allied tendency to self-abasement. The
individual who possesses power—it may be either the financial
ability to purchase a better automobile than his neighbor, the
power of a pretty face to attach admirers, or the power to throw
the whole world into war—feels a sense of differential importance and therefore of distinction. Wherever there is power

---

[24] *Social Psychology*, 1908, p. 30. Even this definition leaves much to
be desired, but it would take us beyond our present needs to pursue the
subject here.

of any kind there are people to look up to it, envy it, aspire to it, and seek to ally themselves to it. Prestige is thus based on scales of valuation and sentiments centering about types of character and conduct.

Every person consciously or unconsciously sets some sort of valuation upon himself. Every individual desires to convince himself that he is somebody. Naturally and properly, no one desires this more than the developing young man or young woman. One's own opinion of one's self is not wholly satisfying, however, except with extraordinarily egotistical and self-confident temperaments, unless it has at least some slight evidence of corroboration in the opinion of others. Every individual therefore desires recognition. Even "cold-blooded" scientists sometimes contend acrimoniously for the credit of priority in discovery. If recognition comes from reputed superiors, it is that much more elevating to self-regard. Recognition is your great vanity-tickler. Generally speaking, the more self-regard the individual has the more he desires the recognition of superiors. This desire, manifesting itself in a thousand ways, many of them concealed and unacknowledged by the individual even to himself, gives the superior person or class great power. This fact is one of the sources of a whole stream of psycho-social processes in the nature of suggestion, imitation, emulation, and impression.

Ross finds that prestige may be due to a variety of factors or characteristics—namely, numbers (prestige of the crowd or of the majority), age (prestige of the elders), prowess (prestige of the military caste, especially the officers), sanctity (prestige of the priestly class), "place" (prestige of the official class), ideas and learning (prestige of "highbrows" and the mandarins), and wealth (prestige of the leisure class).[25] To this list should be added birth (prestige of family connection), and sex (prestige of the male), and also such agencies as tradition, ritual, and æsthetic mysticism.

The influence of prestige is not always necessarily toward conservatism, but it is commonly so. Prestige is so valuable an asset that people do not lightly jeopardize it by non-conformity.

---

[25] *Social Control*, p. 79. See also Lewis Leopold, *Prestige, A Psychological Study of Social Estimates*, 1913, Bk. II, Ch. 5.

Moreover those who enjoy prestige are able in a measure to set the standards of sentiment and behavior to be imitated by others. In matters which are not essential to the foundations of prestige the models set may be subject to innovation and even kaleidoscopic changes in fashion, but in matters which concern directly the social basis of the continuance of prestige those who hold the established positions will insist upon a prescriptive following of the old norms. This means conservatism.

It would take us too far beyond present purposes to try to discuss the influence of all the prestige-agencies in the production and perpetuation of the conservative attitude. We may, however, comment on those of wealth and age.[26]

Wealth is the strongest and most pervasive source of prestige. It has been so in all times and climes. Moreover, wealth is the basis of prestige not only directly and in its own right, but indirectly, in many ramifying channels. If it is not the basis, it is at least one of the buttresses of the prestige of the military caste; certain churches; family position; and much of the higher learning. Its power lies primarily in its influence upon subjective standards of living. We ape the rich because riches connote either "family" or, in our American morality, "success." It is well-recognized that wealth gives freedom, as well as opportunity for display and scope for the instinct of domination. The relation between wealth-prestige and conservatism is well described by Veblen:

"Since conservatism is a characteristic of the wealthier and therefore more reputable portion of the community, it has required a certain honorific or decorative value. . . . Conservatism being an upper class characteristic, is decorous; and conversely, innovation being a lower class phenomenon, is vulgar. . . . The fact that the usages, actions, and views of the well-to-do leisure class acquire the character of a prescriptive canon of conduct for the rest of society, gives added weight and reach to the conservative influence of that class."[27]

The prestige of age is less certain but is widespread and of great importance because of its strong tendency to impress

---

[26] The conservative influence of wealth is treated more fully in Chapter V.

[27] *Theory of the Leisure Class*, 1899, pp. 199, 200.

youth. Because of their superior experience and acquired wisdom (real or supposed), the elders have a preponderant voice in the fixing of social controls. It is a stock truism of popular psychology that as a man reaches middle age he grows more and more conservative. Most men and women undoubtedly do. They lose the rebound of youth, they become more and more the products of long-continued habit and routine, in sentiment, thought, and action; they acquired property and other interests dependent upon the continuance of the *status quo;* and very possibly experience has taught them to fear life and to wish to protect their children from the dangers (healthful and developmental as some of those dangers are) which attend one who gets off the beaten trail.

Speaking in general, parents desire two things with regard to their children; they want their companionship, and they want them to be "successful." But parental ambition, as the biography of many a famous man shows, is not always intelligent, or in line with youth's ideas of its own future. The parental desire for success engenders the demand that children shall conform to the accepted conventions, which set the standard of success. Parental ambition is thus an influence tending strongly to the inculcation of the conservative attitude. Moreover, in spite of some twenty centuries of Christian—or at least so-called Christian—discipline, of overmuch talk of "democracy" and "citizenship," the average parent sets greater store by individual, material success than even the children do.

The claim of the parent upon the child's time and companionship is most striking in the case of daughters. Modern movements, especially that complex of tendencies called the woman movement, cause a rapidly increasing number of girls to desire economic independence and freedom to captain their own careers. But any experienced teacher of live American college girls knows that in four cases out of five the girl has to assert her right to leave home to work, although there is hardly ever any objection to her leaving home to marry. There are some cases where this parental obstructive attitude cannot properly be called selfish; there are some which no other term will fit. But whether selfish or not, the parents' sentiments are ordinarily those of attachment to traditional statuses, and their influence is nearly always perpetuative of conservative attitudes.

Home and school influence, and parental control, are becoming, however, less surely effective agencies for the promulgation of conservatism than formerly. The youth of to-day is brought under a multitude of influences to which his (or her) parents were not in their youth subject, and enjoys what are, with all their shortcomings, incomparably better educational advantages than were available for the parents. In the field of manners and proprieties the younger generation seems to many of the elders to have taken matters into its own hands, to the injury not only of manners but morals.[28]

Age has a proverbial tendency to forget that "it was young once itself." For this there is sufficient psycho-physical cause. Middle age is characterized by different intensities of instinctive complexes than is youth; its "motor sets" have become more static and habitual; its character is more stable, less dynamically impulsive, less audacious, than that of youth. Its valuations of what experience can yield in the way of pleasure and happiness are different, partly because it knows more, partly because experiences which are to youth full of novelty, mystery, and perhaps strange beauty, unfortunately tend to become prosaic matter-of-fact, if not unwelcome, to age. It is not surprising, therefore, that youth and age rarely understand each other. Age is far less idealistic than youth, left to itself, would be; less hopeful and self-reliant, far less convinced of its ability to do things, less willing to try out new ways—to "take a chance." In a word, it is far more distinctly marked with the characteristics of conservatism than is youth.

---

[28] In this connection see a series of entertaining and informing articles in the *Atlantic Monthly*, 1920: A. N. Allen, "Boys and Girls," June, pp. 796-804; K. F. Gerould, "Reflections of a Grundy Cousin," August, pp. 157-163; J. F. Carter, Jr., "These Wild Young People, by One of Them," September, pp. 301-304; "Good-bye, Dear Mr. Grundy," by a "Last Year's Debutante," November, pp. 642-646. The literature of the conflict between youth and age is extensive, especially if fiction be included. Noteworthy here are: Bernard Shaw, *Parents and Children* (the Preface to *Misalliance*); Samuel Butler, *The Way of All Flesh;* Robert Louis Stevenson, *Virginibus Puerisque;* Edith Wharton, *The Age of Innocence.* Reference should also be made to the "Youth Movement" (*Jugendbewegung*) in Germany. On this remarkable revolt of youth against conservatism, see the article by Bruno Lasker in *The Survey*, Dec. 31, 1921, pp. 487-493, 537-540. For a thoughtful article by a parent with conservative fears see also Mary Briarly "The Man, the Woman, and the University," *Scribner's Magazine*, November, 1922, pp. 591-595.

All this would be of less significance to society, had age not acquired the intrenched position of a vested interest, from which it proceeds to demand deference and obedience from youth, as well as to exercise a variety of differential privileges over it.[29] Tribal society is governed chiefly by the elders. Modern communities reserve their most important offices to men advanced in years. That this prestige of the elders tends strongly to perpetuate conservative traditions can scarcely be open to doubt.

Touching this point in his discussion of "ossification," Ross says:

"Even the strong minds, the highly educated men, tend to abide by their earlier judgments, and to retain the emotional attitudes of their youth. If, then, the control of affairs is in the hands of the old, the effete thing will longer escape notice and be longer tolerated than if young men are at the helm. If education falls out of step with life, if knowledge grows beyond the creeds, if laws fail to keep up with the development of social relations, the unprejudiced young will realize it first and will demand changes which the old see no reason for."[30]

E. B. Gowin finds that in ten historical epochs of reform or revolution the average age of the dozen leading men in each period was from 32 to 46 years, while the average age of their chief opponents or of the leaders in quiet periods varied from 54 to 66 years.[31] Ross further notes that "a group of 55 persons averaging less than thirty years of age abolished the shogunate in Japan in 1867 and turned the face of Nippon toward the rising sun."[32] And who can well doubt that if four young men, instead of four old ones, had dictated the terms in Paris in 1919, the Peace Conference would have been far less likely to yield to the reactionary cynicism of old-time secret diplomacy and to the too-familiar demands of nationalistic greed and hatred?

---

[29] See Elsie Clews Parsons, *Social Rule, a Study of the Will to Power*, 1916; also *Social Freedom, a Study of the Conflicts Between Social Classifications and Personality*, 1915, pp. 9-23; Leopold, *Prestige*, 1913, pp. 163-165; W. G. Sumner, *Folkways*, 1906, pp. 321-324.

[30] *Principles of Sociology*, 1920, p. 502.

[31] Quoted by Ross, *op. cit.*, p. 503, from Gowin, *The Executive and His Control of Men*, 1915, pp. 264-270.

[32] Ross, p. 507.

4. *The Methods of Disinterested Conservatism*

Were the term "disinterested" to be taken in other than a relative sense, it would follow that the type of conservatism we are now considering could not be regarded as having conscious methods, since total disinterestedness would mean complete indifference. As a matter of fact, the methods of disinterested conservatism are less definite, less highly organized, and less consciously pursued than the methods of the vested interests, to be discussed later.

These "disinterested" methods are matters of psychological process and attitude quite as much as the result of conscious design. Only in part do they rise to the level of policy. They may be summarized under the following heads: inertia and indifference—sitting tight and doing nothing; appealing to tradition and "experience"; reliance on the prestige of the established and the momentum of things-as-they-are; avoidance of issues, minimizing the seriousness of maladjustments and other evils, throwing the burden of proof upon the progressive and radical; rationalizing [33] situations and keeping up a show of sentimental optimism; holding discussion to a personalistic praise-and-blame basis, with a parading of outraged sentiments at adverse criticism or non-conformity (taking it for granted that whoever else may be discommoded, the feelings of the conservative must not be hurt); discussion on an impersonal plane but within limitations beyond which discussion must not go, and with certain matters dogmatically exempted from criticism; control of educational institutions and processes (as by insisting on "safe" teachers) in the interest of conservative security; and finally political action, coupled with definitely supported propaganda and "education."

An extended discussion of these methods is needless at this point and would be tedious. Later, in our consideration of the methods of radicalism,[34] it is found necessary to recur to the methods of disinterested conservatism, and there the reader will find their significance in the opposition between conservatism and radicalism briefly analyzed.

[33] In the psychoanalytical sense.
[34] Pages 181-184.

CHAPTER IV.

1. *General Motivation of Interested Conservatism*

WE HAVE thus far sought to consider conservatism as uninfluenced by motives of selfish personal or class interest. We have treated this disinterested conservatism as the product of instinctive fear and of association, imitation, adjustment, and habit, and have so far as possible rigidly excluded consideration of the influence of special personal or class interest.

We now have the less agreeable task of analyzing the influence of these special interests in the motivation and perpetuation of what we have called interested conservatism.

The basis of this type of conservatism is desire for security in possession. Desire for security in enjoyment of rights and privileges, and fear of losing them, are the two sides of the same motive-complex. This desire is not ordinarily consciously formulated, but is rather the whole complex "motor set" of our organism in a familiar matter-of-course environment. It becomes conscious only when habitual functioning is impeded or threatened. At this juncture fear enters, and we may consequently regard fear as the proximate actuating motive to the interested, as it is of the disinterested, conservative attitude.

Conceiving himself as having a special stake in things-as-they-are, the interested conservative looks upon that stake as a kind of vested right. Interested conservatism is not confined, however, to the propertied and privileged classes with whom the idea of vested interest is ordinarily associated. Three broad types can be distinguished, corresponding roughly to as many graduations in the social scale.

(1) Some classes which have little or no stake in things-as-they-are are nevertheless conservative from selfish interest.

61

They exhibit the *conservatism of necessitous condition*. (2) Another class, composed mainly of white-collared salaried employees, has some economic interest in things-as-they-are, but is motivated mainly by imitation and emulation of the propertied and directive classes, and is consequently characterized by what may be called *emulative conservatism*. (3) What we shall designate *vested-interest conservatism* is confined to those "upper" classes of individuals who stand possessed of property, power, prestige, and privilege, to which the support of existing legal principles, political habits, and social sentiment are the guarantees, and which are felt to be immediately jeopardized by any serious or essential alteration in hitherto accepted precedents, established habits, and conventional sentiments. For an interest remains "vested" only so long as the sanctions which uphold it remain unimpaired.

For our purposes it is sufficient to regard a vested interest as a right which is recognized and enforced, in favor of its possessor and against all others, by some one or more effective agencies of social control. The chief and most reliable sanction, or agency, of enforcement of economic vested interest is the law; although lawyers are chary of defining the term "vested right." Law, however, is only the set and hardened expression of the real sanction which is general sentiment, or, under effective republican forms of government, the acquiescence of the majority, upon those matters which it has been deemed necessary or expedient to reduce to formal rule and procedure. There are other guarantees of vested interest, not inferior to formal law in their effectiveness—convention, custom, public sentiment; in a word, the established habits of thought, sentiment, and action to which the mass of individuals have been trained and accustomed, and which constitute the set of patterns to which education, both formal and informal, requires the young to conform.

Where the investiture of an interest has not attained the formality of law or the prescriptive inviolability of a hard shell of custom, its continuance depends largely upon the ability of its possessors to maintain prestige. In such cases the interest has not become "a complete and consummated right." It lies in the borderland of vested interests proper. And yet its possessors feel it to be something in the nature of a property right, something due them; they fear and resent any questioning of it, or any encroachment upon it, with as great intensity as those who stand possessed of consummated and established property rights resent intrusion.

2. *Interested Conservatism in the Different Social Classes*

The propensity to fear any alteration in the *status quo* is widely diffused. It is to be found even in those lowest classes who possess no property, who enter into no contractual relations which will do them appreciable harm if they are broken, and who are devoid of elements of prestige. These classes can hardly be said to have vested interests, yet they not infrequently act as if they cherished a vested right to their poverty and dependence.[1]

Any insecurity generates fear. In the lowest classes fear has its definite economic objectives—fear of ejection when the rent cannot be paid, fear of those who have control over one's livelihood through the autocratic processes of hiring and firing. This is the sort of fear which governs all animals subject to the law of survival in the struggle for existence; it necessarily generates conservatism of necessitous condition. Such conservatism rests directly on the instinct of self-preservation, which is brought brutally to the surface in the social ranks where life is summed up in an unremitting struggle for existence.

The extreme of the fear-complexes which produce conservatism of necessitous condition will be found in the most abjectly dependent classes. Formerly it characterized the psychology of the slave and the serf, as it does to-day that of the Mexican peon. In the modern period it is still, in spite of some mitigation of the brutal struggle for existence, a prominent feature in the psychology of the lower, unorganized ranks of wage earners, at least in countries which have not been deeply permeated by socialistic propaganda. It has also been characteristic of the vast majority of women throughout history. It is a well-known and significant fact that the lower the standard of living, the more depressed in physical health, and the more fatalistically

---

[1] At the still lower extreme the pauper feels that he has a right to public charity.

contented people are, the harder it is to secure their interest in their own betterment or to get them to put forth any effort or to take any risk to that end. The lowest dregs of humanity are not good material for even the wildest radical to work upon. The more temperate radical and social reformer makes practically no impression upon them.[2] In times of social upheaval this lowermost class, under stress of sufficient emotional stimulation and the chance to gather up such unconsidered trifles as camp followers usually lay claim to, may turn "radical"; but their radicalism is likely to be of the same stamp as their conservatism—the result and expression of opportunist characteristics molded in a sordid and none too scrupulous struggle for survival. It is a significant fact that not a few members of these lowest ranks do not hesitate to become the hirelings of reactionism.

It is not to be inferred that the great mass of non-propertied, unskilled day laborers are to be included in this lowest estate. The great mass of unskilled workers are propertyless, dependent, comparatively ignorant, and motivated in their day by day conduct by considerations of their necessitous condition. But events of the past few years have shown pretty conclusively that their sense of dependence, and the paralyzing fear flowing from it, can be overcome through organization and leadership, until a sufficiently strong sentiment of mutual aid and class solidarity may transform their erstwhile indifferentism and conservatism into a real and dynamic radicalism of no inferior social significance. Left to his own unaided resources, the propertyless unskilled worker is a helpless pawn on the chess board of corporate business and can hardly be otherwise than selfishly conservative. Organized with his fellows under competent leadership, his necessitous condition, coupled with an awakened consciousness of injustices, real or fancied, leads to radicalism, often of a revolutionary type. This is the psychology of the migratory "working stiff" of the western farms, ranches, and lumber camps, to whom the philosophy of syndicalism as

---

[2] It was perhaps an intuitive recognition of this fact which caused one employer of low class labor to oppose abolition of the liquor traffic because "the only way to keep them where they belong is to keep them half full all the time."

preached by I. W. W. agitators appeals as the only philosophy of hope.[3]

When we come to the working classes who have a little property, we encounter a different psychology. Unlike the "submerged tenth" these people have something to lose, and a lively realization of the fact. Change in the *status quo* may not only throw them into unemployment but may take from them what little property they have. The European peasant, for instance, with his small holding, is notoriously conservative, deficient in sense of social responsibility, and hard to move. Like those far above him in economic status, he possesses a vested interest, however small, and in his case it is proper to speak of vested-interest conservatism, albeit in a somewhat Pickwickian sense.

In the ranks represented by the semi-skilled machine tenders and the skilled workers, the forces tending toward conservatism diminish. Most of the members of these classes, under modern urban conditions, do not own their own homes and are not burdened with a great amount of property; but they have, generally speaking, an earning capacity which lifts them above the more sordid struggle for existence onto a plane where the struggle takes the form of endeavor to maintain the standard of living to which they are accustomed.

In this there is as yet no vested interest recognized by society, but the feeling in the worker's mind is suggestive of some such idea. He feels that in justice he is entitled to such a vested right; but realizes that it is his problem to force or persuade a reluctant society to recognize and guarantee it. It follows that once tolerably effective means have been found for protecting the standard of living, they will neither be lightly surrendered to the onslaughts of selfish reactionaries nor readily modified or exchanged for the possibly more promising, but less certain, plans of the radicals.

If, as has been the case, the skilled workers have been able to raise their standard of living through trade unions, and partly through such policies as restricted apprenticeship, limitation of output, and the closed shop, they are not likely soon to forego

---

[3] Much has been written about the western migratory worker and his social attitudes, but no one has written with greater insight and scientific sympathy than did Carleton H. Parker. See his *The Casual Laborer and Other Essays*, 1920.

the advantages derived from these policies. It may be pointed out by the employer and by the logical theorist that such practices take a leaf out of the book of monopoly and that the closed shop, for instance, when coupled to the "closed union," is a palpable case of restriction in favor of those already on the inside. The employer and the ruling propertied class, on the one hand, may cry out that the fundamental right of every man to work is being set at nought, and the I. W. W. and radical socialists, on the other, may charge that the unions of skilled workers are the selfish aristocracy of labor, bent only on advancing their own interests, with no care for the right or advancement of unskilled labor. These charges may or may not be true. It is not likely in any case that the skilled trades will soon recede from their policy of protecting what, by practically a century of struggle, they have won. Fear of losing what they already possess holds them back from the risks involved in attempting to get more through radical methods.

The interested conservatism of the skilled workers is a species in the genus "guild self-interest," as Ross calls it.[4] The restrictive regulations of the mediæval craft and merchant guilds, the social and economic barriers erected against the entrance of the common man into the professions, the enactment of sumptuary legislation to protect the prestige of the spending classes against the corroding imitation of the masses, the opposition of men to the entrance of women into remunerative pursuits or into the ancient and honorable society of scholars, the tacit and universal agreement, alluded to in Adam Smith's famous passage,[5] among employers not to raise wages, and the gentlemen's agreements and "inside management" of modern business men's associations, are all branches of the same trunk of collective self-interest. It is evident that this guild interest, with its conservative opposition to a larger public spirit, is not confined to any one class or rank. It is a prominent aspect of skilled laboring class conservatism largely because standardized wage scales and working conditions, collective bargaining, and a respectable standard of living constitute the only thing adumbrating a vested interest which this class has. Other classes also are

---

[4] *Principles of Sociology*, p. 504.
[5] *Wealth of Nations*, Book 1, Ch. 8.

motivated by the guild spirit; but they have other vested interests, definitely formulated and recognized in law and custom.

When we come to the propertied and active business classes we enter social ranks with which it is somewhat more customary to associate the thought of vested rights, if not of special privilege. Speaking in the by and large, the interests, sentiments, beliefs, and habits of these classes constitute the foundation of the greater and most effective part of interested conservatism. This is not saying that effective progressivism and even radicalism do not receive important support from certain elements in these ranks; the great mass of progressives and radicals, however, is to be looked for in the working classes, in spite of the individual worker's immediate motives to the conservative attitude. In the main, the classes possessed of vested property interests and special privileges associated with prestige based on inheritance, on social position, and on contractual and prescriptive advantage of one sort or another, are openly, consistently, and aggressively conservative—conservative because of desire to protect, retain, and augment these interests and advantages.

Vested interest conservatism, in these classes, as in the classes hitherto discussed, while not by any means entirely of an economic hue, is largely so.

Confining our attention, at present, to the influence of economic interest, we may for convenience divide these well-to-do conservatives into two main classes, (1) the *rentiers* or receivers of funded income from property and investments of various kinds, and (2) the active business men, professional men, farmers (in large part), and the great majority of the "white-collared" employees of active business.

The *rentiers* include those who are not engaged actively in any productive pursuit, who live off the receipts of real estate rentals, interest on bonds and mortgages, and stock dividends, royalties of mines, etc. In the second, or active, class are to be included: active business men, from the ultra-wealthy and powerful captain of industry and financial magnates to the ordinary small town merchant or real estate dealer; bankers, big and little; railroad executives of all the higher grades; the owners of newspapers and magazines (excepting the labor press, but not excepting the small town or country newspaper), etc.

Probably the vast majority of American farmers must usually be classed here also, although one must have in mind such movements as the Granger Movement of the 70's, Populism in the 90's, the farmers' adherence to greenbackism and free silver, and of late such manifestations of radicalism as the Non-Partisan League.[6]

To the active class also belong two other groups: the professional men—especially lawyers, physicians, clergymen, and teachers, to whom may be added most government employees of whatever rank—and finally, the great mass of clerical, office, and executive employees, whom we may call the white-collared class.

The motivation of the conservatism of the *rentier* class is clear. Their opposition to reform is due to conscious self-interest. Change is resented and opposed because of the fear that it will result in a reduction of rents, interest rates, and dividends. Social and political movements are judged primarily by their effect on the stock market or real estate values. Conceptions of public interest are not broadly developed; public interest is usually interpreted to mean the interest of the propertied and employing classes—especially the *rentiers* themselves. Any proposal for social betterment requiring increased taxation, or any legislative or administrative change not on its face promising advantage to the funded income receivers, is examined first of all with reference to its financial bearing. Any change, however demonstrably it may be to the public interest, is regarded as an invasion of established rights if it adversely affects the financial interests in question.

This *rentier* conservatism is widespread and of insidious influence. We can hardly expect a person whose main income is derived from land values to give open minded consideration to proposals for progressive land taxation, or one who expects to

---

[6] The American farmer, owning his own farm, has always been recalcitrant to social classification. Usually temperamentally conservative he may, when sufficiently aroused, become markedly radical, but his radicalism rarely takes the direction of co-operation with that of the industrial workers. On this point see E. G. Nourse, "Harmonizing the Interests of the Farm Producer and the Town Consumer," *Journal of Political Economy*, October, 1920, pp. 626-657. For an acute inquiry into the reality of the farmer's vested interest, see Veblen, *The Vested Interests*, 1919, pp. 165-174. See also, below, pp. 135, 187.

come into a large inheritance to look with favor upon increased inheritance taxes.

The conservatism of active business men, like that of all other conservatives, is motivated by fear and desire for security. But the operation of these motives is slightly different in different ranks of the business classes. The small business man is ordinarily very dependent—dependent on the good will of his customers, and hence afraid to take an unpopular stand on any public question; dependent on his creditors, especially on the banks, which have power to refuse him much needed loans; and dependent upon the good will of his business associates. He must not too far transgress the business standards and ethics of the community (for instance with regard to price competition), he must not offend any large group of people, he must be, if not without pronounced convictions, at least very tactful and circumspect in their expression. He thus comes to shun anything very far removed from the commonplace.

Indeed, it is possible that his sense of dependence is exaggerated and that he is a more abject victim of fear than he need be. More especially in the smaller towns and cities, is he careful to conform to the accepted standards of respectability. Moving in a small circle of associates, meeting the same sort of routine problems daily, dictating the same letters with the same vocabulary, and not accustomed to broad vision ahead, he usually is the victim of incapacity and habitual disinclination to face new conditions or to meet new problems. This is one reason why he fears change. The more essential reason, however, is that, like the *rentier*, he dreads the financial loss which might result from a social or economic reform involving him in conditions on which he has not calculated. Moreover, his economic philosophy is of the old American self-made-man type. The older he is, the more his experience has been derived from the earlier, quasi-frontier business life of a new country, the less able he is to understand the need of new standards, of co-operation to social ends, and of more effective social control of business and industry.[7]

---

[7] On the business man's control of the average American town, see Veblen, *Imperial Germany and the Industrial Revolution*, 1918, pp. 315-322.

"Big business" may be either conservative or radical, as its special interests dictate. Big business itself is the result of daring, and frequently unscrupulously radical, changes in business methods and industrial organization. These changes have involved great costs, not only to business men themselves, especially those unsuccessful in the competitive struggle and "squeezed out" in an era of combination and monopoly, but to the working classes, through unemployment and other maladjustments attendant on rapid change, and to the general public, in the upbuilding of huge vested interests and irresponsible power which at times have been practically uncontrolable.

Once established, big business is conservative, but its conservatism is far more intelligent (judged from the point of view of special interest) and far more aggressive than that of the common run of business men. As its vested interests are huge, and its privileges valuable and peculiarly liable to attack, it organizes economic and political conservatism into a system and a creed.

But for the fact that both conservatism and radicalism are the products of association and temperament as well as of special interest, and that an individual or class conservative in one matter is likely to be conservative all the way through, many business men would be radicals, as many actually are progressives, in matters which have no material bearing upon their financial interests.

Wherever these self- or class-interests are threatened, however, fear, habit, and training all conspire to present a solid front of conservatism. In periods of actual social and economic unrest, aggressive radical criticism and attack produce accentuated self-interest reaction. Radicalism to-day expresses itself in three main ways, (1) in the labor movement (including socialism, etc.), (2) in the movement for internationalism, involving disarmament, and (3) in the general trend and urge toward a real and effective democracy. These movements and tendencies mean that the great working masses, taken as a whole, are pushing, with organized weight and intelligence, against the social institutions, the economic organization, and the standards of distribution of wealth, income, and political power which the ruling propertied and big business classes have come to regard as fixed, just, and sacred. When revolutionary radicalism makes the disastrous and successful attacks it has made during the past few years on the very foundations of the business order and the business man's control, it follows that the conservatism of the business and propertied classes will be heightened and that it will develop an aggressive defense of these foundations. When the issue is one, or is described as one, between the vested privileges of capitalism on the one hand and the demands of the workers for democratic control and the abolition of special privilege on the other, conservatism and radicalism are not only attitudes, but come to be regarded respectively as duties to one's class in the class struggle. In this conflict of interests—whether we call it class conflict or not—in which the working masses are making demands unheard of hitherto in the world's history, or unheeded as merely visionary and academic, it is not surprising that the propertied and business classes should labor under a rebellious sense that justice and the fitness of things have been outraged.

For from the beginnings of history the privileged and fortunate or energetic and more intelligent few have resisted the struggle of the masses for freedom and higher standards of living. The masses have been in the position of servants to the classes, and the employing class, with property, power, and prestige, early developed a master-class conception of the proprieties of social and economic relations which it has never entirely lost, and which indeed underwent considerable development with the transition from the old hand and domestic system to the modern factory system and big business.

That the business man's reaction to economic and social radicalism in almost any of its forms and degrees, is usually so bitter and so extreme may be explained partly on the ground that he has developed something of an *übermensch* psychological complex, and that one of the foundations of his belief in order—his unconscious adherence to the master-and-servant type of ethics —has been endangered by the constant pressure of liberal progressivism and aggressive radicalism. In other words, beside the main fact that the danger of revolutionary economic radicalism has filled the propertied employing classes with a very real and lively fear for the safety of the whole system of hitherto recognized and accepted conventions upon which their vested interests and privileges are based, there is the additional significant fact that the superiority complex which can be found in every typical member of the upper and middle classes— his pride of position and association, and in freedom from rough-handed work—has been outraged by the attitude and demands of labor. It is mainly endangered material interests which have developed the class struggle, but this pride of mastership, hitherto the possession of the ruling classes only, now gives rise to more subtle and less consciously expressed or formulated fear and disgust, which are not without profound influence in the causation of conservative and reactionary attitudes.

Pride of position is contagious, and is the chief ground for class distinction between the skilled manual workers and the white-collared workers. In intelligence, breadth of information, and moral character, it may be doubted whether the general run of white-collared workers behind shop counters and in business offices are much, if at all, superior to the skilled and semi-skilled manual workers, upon whom they look down, and with whom they refuse to associate. Excluding the upper ranks of office help, buyers and department superintendents in stores, and the like, it is doubtful if the white-collared positions yield a larger income than do the manual jobs, though they perhaps afford greater continuity and security of employment. But the office workers are nearer the executives; they live in the same atmosphere of "business," they are actuated by and are expected to cultivate the same acquisitive spirit, and by a praiseworthy desire to rise to positions of responsibility and trust. They know that advancement is conditioned not only by ability but by unquestioning loyalty to the employer and to his projects and methods. When they think of the firm or the company they pretend to think "we"; they regard themselves as a part of it; whereas the manual workers in the shops or yards are much less likely to have this feeling, and are regarded by the office and sales force not as a part of the concern, but as "employees" or "hands." Office employees and sales people have little of the independent feeling of class cohesion or solidarity which tends to develop in the manual working classes. The white-collared employees do not in their own minds constitute a distinct class with special interests of its own. Nowhere are they organized. They regard themselves, if not as members of the capitalist-employing class, at least as closely allied to it. They are led to this attitude both by the subtle motives which underlie most emulation, and by material self-interest.

For these reasons, most men in white-collared positions hold the attitudes and look at things from the viewpoint of the propertied, employing class, and are consequently conservative. Their conservatism is at once that of ignorance, of dependence, of material self-interest, and of a sort of vicarious snobbishness.

The conservatism of the professional classes, the last of the vested-interest groups to be considered, is due to special interest, to temperament, and to the influence of occupational specialization and environment. It would be a mistake to suppose that all professional men and women tend strongly to conservatism, or that when they do, all their conservatism is attributable to motives of vested interest. Yet such interests are present and are doubtless influential.

Lawyers as a class are notoriously conservative, if not reactionary. Their life and work is wrapped up in the institutions of property and contract, in the settlement of disputes by appeal to precedent, and in technical knowledge of the extreme and to a certain extent unnecessary intricacies of legal procedure. The legal profession has certainly not been vigorous in pushing forward the reform of legal procedure and the codification of law, in spite of some talk in the American Bar Association and the crying need, admitted among thoughtful lawyers, of such reform. It has been charged that these reforms have made no headway because the lawyers fear that simplification and codification would reduce litigation, but the main cause of the inaction is probably to be found in mere habituation, specialization, and engrossment in the business affairs of the moment.

In economic interest and affiliation lawyers are obviously most closely associated with the propertied *rentiers* and active business classes. Legal work for corporations is the chief source of the large fees of the best lawyers. It is not to be supposed that the average corporation lawyer will be other than conservative, or that he will usually have a point of view which will put public welfare above the pecuniary interests of his corporate employer and himself.

In professional callings other than the law, conservatism is perhaps not so characteristic. Still there are not lacking special material interests productive of the conservative attitude. The rank and file of the medical profession have not been overly zealous in advocacy of efficient public health departments, nor, in the non-urban districts, have they been active for the establishment of community clinics and other means by which competent medical and surgical aid can be afforded to the poor as well as to the well-to-do. On the other hand, physicians, unlike the lawyers, have always provided a large amount of free service; and medicine, both in its scientific aspects and as a social art devoted to social ends, has advanced much more rapidly than the law.

Conflicting special interests hold back progress in both fields. The business men who "run" the average American town are very likely to oppose any exposé of conditions calling for more effective public health administration, involving closer inspection of markets, restaurants, dairies, etc. Druggists are commonly found to be hostile toward any movement for limiting the manufacture and sale of fake patent medicines. In so far as the business-ethics ideals of *caveat emptor* and charging what the traffic will bear, and the convenient fiction that public interest is sufficiently served by a balance of power between private interests each looking out primarily for itself, continue to be permitted a strong influence in law and medicine and pharmacy, no large progressive social spirit is to be looked for in the rank and file of the members of these professions.

The teaching and clerical professions are probably no better and no worse. In spite of high-sounding addresses before the National Educational Association, state teachers' meetings, and county institutes, it is common knowledge that public school administration is too frequently carried on in an atmosphere of political wire-pulling, favor-currying, and personal interests, more suggestive of petty ward politics than of a whole-hearted and honest devotion to the effective education of the nation's children. This is due partly to the personnel and spirit of school boards and partly to the competitive ambitions and egotisms of school superintendents and principals. It is due also to the well-known fact that salaries in the teaching profession are so low in proportion to the cost of living that comparatively few men of high calibre remain in public school work and that those who remain are often forced into conservative, time-serving attitudes by the struggle for existence. It is further due to the fact that four-fifths of American public school teachers are women, usually overworked, existing on salaries that have been a disgrace to the nation, and in such financially necessitous status that they perforce accept whatever conditions school boards and superintendents see fit to impose. It has long been charged, furthermore, that public school administration is so undemocratic in character that initiative and progressiveness in the rank and file are discouraged.[6]

Clergymen stand in much the same position as lawyers, in that their training has been based largely on the conservative foundation of precedent and authority, and in the same position as teachers because they are even nearer the poverty line and under the necessity, if they are to keep their jobs, not to offend the conventional attitudes or the special economic interests of their congregations.

The professor in a denominational college is in a scarcely more favorable situation. If he be intellectually original and if he tell his honest thought to his students he is liable to be charged with heresy by some ultra-conservative church official.

The preacher and the professor, both in privately endowed colleges and in universities supported from public funds, are liable to find their ideas in conflict with the economic special interests; and themselves subject to attack, if they tell what they know or say what they think. The result both in church and university is that to a certain extent, which of course differs with time, place, and circumstances, freedom of speech and of thought are limited by the intimidative power of special interests, here ecclesiastical, there economic. These interests attempt to take advantage not only of their preponderant influence upon governing boards but of the conservative and conventional sentiment of a public which is not sufficiently tutored

---

[6] See what is said below, pp. 87, 88, on economic intimidation in the teaching profession.

and sophisticated to understand the issues involved, a public not sensible enough of its own interests to know the great danger to liberty and progress involved in restriction, or censorship, of thought, speech, and publication.[9]

3. Some Psychological and Social Characteristics of Interested Conservatism

Wherever there is conflict or lack of agreement between a person's subjective moral ideals and his actual conduct, or between his actual and his expressed thought, a situation exists which cannot be said to be characterized by complete honesty. There are, indeed, few human situations or relations in which complete honesty and fearless frankness are possible. It would be too harsh to say that this lack of correspondence between ideal and action, or between thought and expression, is commonly the result of conscious, designed hypocrisy. In many cases, the individual frankly recognizes the conflict and admits, to himself at least, that not being a hero or martyr, he will, when confronted with the practical necessity of compromise, choose the line of action which best subserves his immediate interests. In other cases, perhaps most, to save his self-respect, he resorts to self-deceit, which he accomplishes through casuistry. In other words, he devises specious arguments—excuses and justifications for doing things which he knows are contrary to public welfare and to his own moral principles, but the doing of which protects his material and domestic interests. "Wives and children," says a recent writer, "are both rewards and hostages. Every householder thinks more radically than he acts, because he is fearful of losing what he has gained under the established rules."[10] He is conservative from personal interest, but the conservatism goes against the grain.

A survey of the different classes would reveal least of this casuistic conservatism among the workers, and most among the white-collared commercial workers and professional men, especially teachers and preachers. It is at a minimum in the

---

[9] Restrictions on thought can, of course, be indirect only, through limitation of speech and publication, but they are none the less effective for that reason.

[10] Maxwell Anderson, "Modern Casuists," *The Freeman*, August 25, 1920, p. 565.

lower ranks of the laboring population because they either frankly accept the philosophy of "looking out for number one" or, turning radical, regard dissimulation as one of the weapons in the class struggle. It is also at a minimum among the higher propertied and employing classes, because in these classes one has, relatively, power and freedom to do as one pleases.

Nowhere, however, is there absolute freedom from external pressure. Expediency—sometimes, indeed, exigencies of life and death—require a certain degree of conformity. "When one is among wolves one must growl a little." A known capitalistic or royalist reactionary gets short shrift amongst bolshevists in revolution. An "infidel" did not fare well at the hands of the Inquisition. Even Roger Williams was *persona non grata* to the Massachusetts Puritans; and the life of a labor organizer is in some jeopardy in West Virginia today. But the real rebels, dying bravely on Lexington Green, or calmly and alone suffering ecclesiastical persecution, or holding aloft before White House gates in the presence of hostile crowds the banner "How long must women wait for liberty!" or slowly starving to death in prison for the cause of Irish freedom—are few. After all, most people, when not affected by the hypnotic hysteria of crowd contagion, or under iron discipline, prefer to save their skins. And they are the more impelled to such expedient conduct by certain unavoidable conflicts of obligation.

There are but two classes who might consciously be wholly honest and frank, with themselves and with others, in thought, feeling, and action—those who desire nothing, and those who have everything they desire, or who are independent, at least economically, because of ownership of great wealth.

Few, however, are in fact even economically independent. The wealthiest family may be at the mercy of its servants; the bond-holder is ultimately dependent upon the employees of the corporation or upon the voters of the country whose bonds he holds; and no business man, amid the complex organization of modern industry and finance, can for a moment be independent of the business system and all that it may entail for his success or failure. Accordingly, we must expect to observe, even in the upper economic ranks, a certain compromise of de-

sire and conduct, a casuistry of expediency, a tendency to adaptation to conditions which one might wish to ignore.

It must not be supposed that all such tendencies are entirely
to be regretted or condemned. On the contrary, were there no
such characteristics of conduct, social life and co-operation
would be impossible. The fact of expedient adaptation, the
habits of tact, reserve, moderation in speech and action, con-
siderateness, and "good breeding" are but the component parts
of that discipline which makes human association possible; and
they may be at times far removed, in their motivation, from
narrow selfishness.

Pursuit of such considerations, however, would take us off
the main line of our present inquiry. The consideration in
point here is that the well-to-do, propertied, and employing
classes are under no such necessity of conflict between inner
conviction and external conduct as are the other ranks of
society.

It cannot well be doubted, however, that there are many
members of the vested interest classes who by temperament and
character are broadly social-minded and who in a different class
environment, would be liberal, progressive, or radical. This is
especially true among the younger members of such classes.
Not a few of these younger men and women do, in fact, in spite
of all the strong environmental stimuli to the contrary, become
more or less permanently influenced by modern liberalisms and
radicalisms. A still larger number, without taking on any of
the specific doctrines of radicalism, get in one way and another
a larger, more effective, and less sentimental conception of
public interest and public service than the general run of their
contemporary elders have had. But there is always a strong
tendency to slip back into the habits and thought and point of
view of class-interest conservatism. Everywhere, among friends
and acquaintances, the young man is thrown into the atmosphere of "business" and of self-interest. If, then, his inner
or temperamental tendency toward progressivism or radicalism
is not very strong, it will be overborne by the whole attitude of
those with whom he associates, through sheer unconscious imitation if in no other way, and his own material self-interest will
gradually get the better of his more social-minded self. This

is what happens in greater or less degree to nine out of ten college men and women who may at some time in their educational course catch glimpses of less materialistically selfish planes of thought and feeling, but whom the business of getting a living, combined with social emulation—keeping up with the Joneses—sooner or later pulls back to the plane of narrow self-interest and interested conservatism.

In these younger men and women the ethical conflict may be very real, either in economic matters, or as was formerly more common, in matters of religious belief. To the extent that the individual is drawn back into the interested sentiment of his class, the ethical conflict will be solved by a sublimation of temperamental radical tendencies through work, through a dilettante pursuit or art and literature, or through the soothing satisfaction of philanthropy and honorific public service. Compensation for temperamental repressions will be found in the satisfaction of special interests and privileges well guarded by conservative sentiments. There are of course some temperaments in which such compensation never takes place. They become the leaven of their class.

Somewhat allied to the casuistry of certain types of interested conservatives, but of far more fundamental significance, is what we may call the sense of social contract—the feeling that society owes to individuals, and possibly to classes, protection and guaranty of possession of what it has allowed them to acquire and to which it has both permitted and encouraged them to become habituated. Something of this feeling is doubtless inherent in all conservatism, especially when it is subject to criticism or attack. Where vested interests are threatened, this contractual sentiment is elaborated into a logical defense of the conservative position.

All conservatism, as we have seen, is at once both cause and result of a continuous process of adjustment of the individual to a social environment into which he is born. This adjustment is by way of habituation to a system of institutions, itself the product of historical evolution and prescriptive accretion. To the degree that the individual is habituated or adjusted to a position of superior rights, perquisites, and privileges in this system of established and conventionalized relations and institutions, he will have strong interest in the preservation of the *status quo,* and be ready with plausible, if not valid, argument against progressive or radical movements which would interfere with his vested interest in things-as-they-are.

Security in the possession and enjoyment of valued rights and privileges is essentially a matter of convention or agreement (tacit or overt) on the part of society (that is, other individuals) not to interfere or permit interference with them, at least so long as they are not abused in a way too conspicuously traversing the accepted canons of public interest. To the extent that other individuals or classes refuse to admit the social utility of these conventions, the rights and privileges sanctioned by them are impaired. To the degree that they are recognized as valid, the resulting protection and guarantee may be regarded as a quasi-contractual sanction of their use and enjoyment.

Were there no established habit of regarding conventions as binding, at least to a certain degree—in other words were there no conventions—a state of chronic anarchy would exist. The fact that a multitude of conventions do exist and make association possible, whatever the sanctions of those conventions may be, is indicative of a certain contractual character to all social relations. The theory tacitly held to by interested conservatism is that there is an implied contract that no convention will be altered or abrogated without due notice and that all members of the social group will abide by it.

This contractual concept may be embodied in law (common or statute), where its chief manifestations are the law of property and the law of contract; or it may be only in custom or other forms of social control, such as conventions in the narrow sense of the term. But however embodied, it connotes reciprocal duties between the individual and society. It implies especially, the reasoning runs, the obligation of society to protect the individual in what he has or does under existing law and custom. And this implies, if not a guarantee against any change of law or custom adversely affecting his interests, at least a promise that he will be reimbursed for any injuring or diminution of the rights and privileges hitherto enjoyed. Every vested interest, whether acquired by legal process or by mere prescription (unquestioned exercise of possession and use), is entitled to guarantee against change of the *status quo*. Society can make no alteration, however beneficial, without obtaining the consent of the individuals or classes whose special interests are affected.

It is not to be supposed that the vested-interest conservative always reasons consciously in this manner, but this, if not the argument which he advances in so many words, is the logic clearly implied.

Nor is it to be supposed that vested-interest conservatism is an attitude to which the individual arrives by his own unsupported feelings. To re-emphasize what was said above, the interested conservative is the product of the system into which he is born, and all the powerful stimuli of family and social environment conspire to produce an early and fixed adjustment to it. This is a principle well understood and consciously applied in those authoritatively directed processes of habituation commonly called religious training and education for citizenship, as well as in the general adaptation of young persons to the existing economic system. As vested interests are themselves the product of historical processes of acquisition through acts ranging from robbery, conquest, and restriction of output, to gift, bargain and sale, thrift, and actual production, so the attitude engendered by these interests, and functioning for their defense and perpetuation, is also but to-day's aspect of a psychological complex handed down from generation to generation in an unbroken continuum of concepts of differential privilege and vested right.

CHAPTER V

THE METHODS OF INTERESTED CONSERVATISM

HAVING completed our attempt to suggest in outline the more significant aspects of the nature and motivation of interested conservatism, to estimate the degree and causes of its prevalence in different social classes, and to suggest its relation to the social processes of historical accretion, habituation, and adjustment, we might assume our task of analysis to be finished. Any study of interested conservatism as a social viewpoint would be lacking in practical bearing, however, if it stopped short of some consideration of the methods adopted for the protection and enhancement of established rights and interests.

The great clash between conservatism and radicalism to-day is staged in the field of economic interests. Viewed broadly, it is the battle of the "haves" with the "have-nots"; of the privileged with the non-privileged; of the powerful with those whom they have, to various degrees, in their power; of those with prestige with those, without it, who challenge it. There is what Adam Smith would have called a "natural propensity" in men, once they get a good thing, to hang on to it. This, in fact, is the plain essential of vested interest conservatism—to have and to hold. Classes possessed of special privileges, of prestige, and of power have rarely been known to give them up or to abate their use and abuse unless under pressure or compulsion. And few individuals, whatever their claims to Christian disinterestedness, and however great their consciousness of self-rectitude, voluntarily renounce or even question the rights and privileges of which they stand possessed.

More than that, those many individuals who possess little except a propensity for acquisition, or a strong desire for that distinction and prestige which, according to popular standards of respectability, flow from the possession of considerable wealth, will never countenance overmuch questioning of the reality or worth of pecuniary prestige or of the methods open, to those not too sensitively scrupulous to use them, to obtain it. When the central motif in a class or community is individual material "success," all the tenets and methods of economic vested-interest conservatism will be accepted as right—rules in the game of acquisition—by those who hope to secure, as well as by those who have secured, power, position, and prestige. It follows that they will not be backward in devising and putting into practice methods of protecting and augmenting their interests, actual or hoped-for.

All methods of protecting vested interests are methods of control—control of knowledge and information, of public sentiment and public opinion, of economic relations and ideals, of governmental functions, of the organization and processes of social institutions in general. These methods include force, intimidation (especially economic pressure of various kinds), manipulation of political machinery, espionage and censorship (including control of the press and limitations on freedom of teaching and preaching), prestige, the absorption into vested interest classes of erstwhile progressive and radical leaders, and finally propaganda, both honest and dishonest, the latter including various devices and processes classifiable as shibboleths, claptrap, and chicane.

The ultimate basis of control, the final resort when other methods fail, is force. Between nations this means war. Between classes in the same nation it means revolution and counter-revolution. Between corporation and worker it means violence in labor disputes. At the least, the appeal to force on the part of the defenders of the *status quo* always means the exercise of the police power, backed by police force and militia.[1]

The police power may be used for the introduction of radical change—as when it is appealed to, successfully, in the courts to validate labor legislation. Force, it is true, is a sanction to which both conservative and radical can and do appeal. But the conservative has usually been in better position to use it. Those in control of governmental machinery and of the wealth

---

[1] An exception must be made of lynching, and of the extra-legal and illegal violence to which in many places supposedly disloyal persons were subjected during and after the war.

of a country have always sought either by actual force or the threat of its use to dampen the ardor and confidence of individuals or classes desiring radical change. That is one tacitly recognized value of standing armies, universal military service, and state constabularies.

Intimidation may be applied through show of military or police power, or through a system of espionage, or through various types of economic and social pressure.

Force, show of force, and espionage are relatively crude and expensive forms of control. Far more economical, more pervasive, and more flexible are the various types of economic pressure which the vested interests are commonly able to bring to bear upon critics and opponents. Economic pressure may be directed either against the workers and other classes dependent upon the vested interests, or against wayward members of the vested-interest classes themselves.

The power of discharge is the fulcrum of the most common type of economic pressure. When it is a question of behaving as your employer wants you to behave, or of losing your job and facing, if not starvation, at least a temporary and possibly permanent lowering of your standard of living, you are going to think twice before committing any act or taking any overt attitude which he may disapprove.

It is in the employer's unlimited power of hiring and firing that workmen have found one of the strongest motives to the formation of trade unions and to their struggle to establish the practice of collective bargaining. For where the individual workman is helpless, especially if the employer be a large corporation, the whole body of employees, welded into organization for concerted action, may be able to bring to bear enough economic pressure to offset that of the employer—in which case the employment contract will be made between parties who bargain on somewhat more equal terms. This is why conservative employers fight the unions, see no rule of reason or justice in collective bargaining, and, latterly, welcome a reactionary [2]

---

[2] Reactionary in the sense that it would abolish collective bargaining even where it has been established and proved satisfactory and go back to conditions which have long since been regarded as undesirable not only by workers but by many thoughtful employers. The "open shop" as currently advocated is a closed non-union shop.

"open shop" movement. If successful this movement could have but one of two results—namely, either to throw all workers into individual economic dependence upon the corporations who control productive resources and can grant or withhold employment at will; or to drive the whole organized labor movement underground into secret societies, such as the Knights of Labor were in their earlier years, with all the attendant evils of secrecy, suspicion, and irresponsibility. Where the economic pressure involved in the privilege of hiring and firing at will is not present, employers will have recourse to the blacklist, the shutdown, and lockout (corresponding to organized labor's unfair list, boycott, strikes, and "vacations").[3]

Here again actual resort to these measures may not be necessary. Threat or hint may be sufficient to intimidate the workers. Without threatening a general shutdown the employer may cause the impression to go abroad that action which workers may contemplate taking would produce conditions in which reduced wages and unemployment would be inevitable. It has been alleged, for instance, that some concerns which in the past have profited handsomely from high protective tariffs have forestalled any propensity employees might evince to think favorably of free trade or tariff for revenue only, by letting it be known that a Democratic victory would be followed by a shutdown or a reduction of wages. Whether such claims had any foundation in truth is not here the question. The threat might be effective even if the reasons alleged for it were entirely false, provided the workers had reason to suppose that the employer would carry out the threat regardless of the truth or falsity of his allegations. Threats of like nature have of late been frequent as an intimidation device to obstruct the further organization of labor or increase in its collective bargaining strength. It is perhaps open to question now, however, whether labor has not

---

[3] It is worth while to note here the perfectly known fact that where the vested business interests are in virtual control of legislation, if not the courts, labor's freedom to use these, and other weapons, like picketing, is very greatly curtailed by legal enactment and judicial decision—especially in the form of injunctions. The very great—and from the standpoint of labor, and perhaps that also of the rest of the public—exceedingly dangerous extensions of the sphere of injunctions as upheld in recent Supreme Court decisions, offers additional testimony to the power of vested-interest attitudes.

attained to such sophistication and has not now such able advisers and leaders that such threats rather stimulate than retard what they are aimed against.

The more powerful a person or class and the greater the ability to make use of intimidation, the less scrupulousness there is likely to be in its use. Power tends to become irresponsible —in the sense that it does not have to answer for its acts before any bar which can effectively convict it—and intimidation is often an easier method than rational persuasion.

It is to be expected that powerful business concerns will intimidate the smaller ones whenever the latter threaten to become troublesome. The history of the trust movement is full of instances in which firms have been compelled, under threat of being driven out of business, to sell out to the "combine," on the latter's own terms. The trust movement may be regarded as an excellent example of the unscrupulous radicalism of method to which conservative but powerful vested interests will resort when it is profitable to do so.

Touching more people, and somewhat more within the intimate knowledge of the average man, are forms of economic intimidation involving the withholding of patronage and credit, or threats to do so. A large, if not the greater, part of the diplomacies and amenities of business relations are based upon fears arising from the presence of this power.[4] Interesting and informing illustrations could be drawn from the inside chronicles of big business, of railroad finance, of combinations of buyers to depress the price of raw material, like crude petroleum, live stock, etc., but these are matters of hearsay to the average citizen. Everyone can understand, however, that the average merchant or manufacturer does not go out of his way to offend his banker. Neither do the small banks, except under extraordinary provocation, attempt to declare their independence from the large ones. A small town bank has the power to withhold loans from a business concern whose methods do not please it or the wife of whose manager is *persona non grata* to the wife of the bank's leading director. This is not necessarily saying that such power is frequently used, but every business

---

[4] Sinclair Lewis has made it one of the motifs in *Babbitt.*

man knows that it is there. And under present-day business organization power over credit is practically power of life and death over all but the largest business concerns.[5]

In farming communities, where social and economic conditions make for the presence of a large number of dependent tenants—a situation met with everywhere in the South—economic intimidation is widely prevalent. The tenant is not infrequently so poor in earthly possessions that he can live until the next crop is harvested and sold, only if the landowner or banker or store-keeper (sometimes one and the same individual) "carry" him by loans, either of cash or of food and feed. In such situation he may be for the time being little removed from the position of peonage.

The following incident is of not infrequent occurrence in certain more backward agricultural communities of the South. A local school district has an election to decide whether more money shall be raised for the schools the coming year. If the school is held for six months instead of five, or if the teacher's salary is raised, taxes will be increased. In some districts the greater portion of the land is owned by a few large land hold-ers, who live in a neighboring town where their own children have comparatively good schools, but where they do not pay taxes on their land. Not wishing to be taxed for even the ele-mentary education of negroes, Mexicans, and poor white trash these landowners give notice to their tenants that they will be dispossessed at the expiration of their annual lease if they vote the increased school tax.[6] In many cases such threats are successful, and in part serve to explain the pitiful inadequacy of the rural schools in some of the richest and wealthiest agri-cultural regions of the South.

Economic intimidation is very effective when applied to the members of certain professions. Even lawyers and physicians

---

[5] Interesting material on the power of the great banking interests can be found in the Report of the Committee Appointed Pursuant to House Resolutions 429 and 504 to Investigate the Concentration of the Control of Money and Credit (The Pujo Committee Report), 1913, and in John Moody, *Masters of Capital*, 1919.

[6] See, for example, A. C. Burkholder, "The Rural Schools of Hays County, Texas," *Southwest Texas State Normal School Bulletin*, Feb., 1918, p. 10.

are somewhat exposed to it, but salaried people, like teachers, are not uncommonly in abject subjection to it—another case of the hiring and firing prerogative of those in power. In many localities the private conduct of public school teachers is subjected to regulations galling and degrading to self-respect. In many small towns they are given definitely to understand that they must not play cards or attend dances. It is said to be not uncommon for the school board to rule that teachers shall not receive callers or attend social functions or public entertainments on evenings preceding a school day. Court decisions have held that a school board has no power to impose contractual conditions governing teachers' time outside of school hours, but the teacher who fails to conform to whatever regulations the board sees fit to lay down, or who does not conform somewhat carefully to the conventions and ecclesiastical predilections of the community, knows that she will be dropped at the end of the year and find it difficult to secure another position. Economic intimidation compels her to swallow her self-respect.

It may be noted, further, that from time immemorial women, have been economically dependent, and to a very great extent still are so. This dependence has been an important factor in the apparently "natural" conservatism and timidity of women. And it certainly has been one of the main factors in the development of those feminine characteristics—reserve, deference, conventionality, "indirect influence," etc., which, in the past at least, seem so to have appealed to men as constituting the essentially womanly character. Men have exercised the right of economic pressure without always understanding how far-reaching its results are sure to be. Many women reared from childhood in an atmosphere of the subtle chicane of "charm" and tactful "management" of fathers and husbands have themselves lost power to evaluate frankly at their true moral worth the attitudes and methods suitable to economic dependence.

Economic pressure is an effective device, but in and by itself is not sufficient. Law may be made a powerful ally of the vested interests. Hence they have always, so far as possible, retained control of the law-making function and fought vigorously and bitterly every attempt of the non-possessing masses to gain a voice in government. Many illustrations will occur to anyone even superficially familiar with political history. The various franchise reforms in England, the successful resistance of the Prussian junkers to abolition of the three-class voting system, the fight everywhere waged against woman suffrage, the resistance to abolition of the property qualification in the American Colonies, the opposition of conservative interests to the direct primary, the initiative and referendum, the direct election of senators, etc., are examples in point.[1]

And where the people, including the industrial and agricultural workers, have gained the formal right to a voice in the election of representatives, the special interests have been effectively ingenious in devising means by which the right should be deprived of a too real content. It is not a matter of chance or accident that in the past, at least, the United States Senate has had so many members who notoriously represented the big business interests instead of the people; that lawyers predominate in the personnel of the House of Representatives; that commissions and boards do not always place public interest above corporate and private privilege; or that the courts are so meticulous in their protection, and so broad in their interpretation, of intangible assets and matters of like financial importance to the investing and speculating classes.

The solid business interests have in large measure retained control of political machinery, especially of the nominating machinery (in spite of direct primaries), and have thereby been able not only to prevent, or retard, reform legislation, but partially to nullify through executive and administrative channels the legislation that is passed. If the courts at times represent the special interests rather than the people at large, that may be due to the fact that the judges are elderly lawyers who acquired their economic and legal training a generation ago, and who have been little influenced by the modern social point of view. That this may not be the sole reason, however, is suggested by the storm of criticism which enveloped President Wilson when he appointed to the Supreme Court a prominent

---

[1] See any good history of England; W. H. Dawson, *Evolution of Modern Germany*, 1914, pp. 434ff. A. S. McKinley, *The Suffrage Franchise in the Thirteen English Colonies of America*, 1905; A. B. Wolfe, "Manhood Suffrage in the United States," in the *Woman Citizens' Library*, Vol. 7, 1913.

lawyer known to be sympathetic toward labor and critical of the wasteful financing of American railroads.

That the vested interest conservatives have gone perhaps a bit too far in their control of governmental functions is indicated by the growing favorable attitudes toward "direct action," guild socialism, sovietism (representation by trade or industry instead of by geographical districts) and like current ultra-radical doctrines, on the part of significantly large numbers of the citizens of nearly every industrial country of the Western World.

To combat these movements, justly recognized to be dangerous to vested rights and subversive of traditional standards of law and equity, the war, fortunately or unfortunately, according to the point of view, has brought to the assistance of the vested interests a device of which, while not hitherto overlooked custom, law, tradition, and public opinion had permitted only a limited use.

Freedom of speech, press, and assemblage were definitely guaranteed in America by the framers of the United States Constitution.[8] But under pressure of the war, of fear of German spies, of the foreign language press, of Bolshevism and other agencies menacing to established vested interests, this constitutional guarantee was set aside by the Espionage Acts of 1917 and interpreted away by court decisions.

Into the question, however deep its significance for the liberties and safety of American people and American institutions may be, of the justifiability or unjustifiability of the Espionage Acts, the criminal syndicalism statutes and their interpretation by the courts, or the Postoffice Department's irresponsible censorship of the press, we will not here enter.[9] But there can be no gainsaying that espionage and censorship systems are

---

[8] The first Amendment to the Constitution reads: Congress *shall make no law* respecting an establishment of religion, or prohibiting the free exercise thereof; or *abridging the freedom of speech or of the press; or the right of the people peaceably to assemble and to petition the government for a redress of grievances.*

[9] An admirable treatment of the subject in its legal aspects is Zechariah Chafee's *Freedom of Speech*, 1920. It is worthy of note that certain organized interests sought to have Professor Chafee discharged from his position in the Harvard Law School for the writing of this book. For bibliography see Chafee, and Theodore Schroeder, *Free Speech Bibliography*, 1922.

most powerful weapons of repression in the hand of those in possession of governmental machinery, whether they be flag-waving representatives of vested economic interests in American State legislatures or autocratic Bolshevist officials in revolutionary Russia.

When espionage and censorship are engaged in by private organizations, the invasion of civil liberties is almost as dangerous and irresponsible as governmental invasion. When the two systems are co-ordinated, the situation is dangerous in the extreme. Among the weapons of the industrial vested interests is the spy system employed by many large corporations to keep tab on radicals and union organizers in the ranks of their employees and weed them out as fast as they come in.[10] Such spy systems, especially where *agents provocateurs* are employed, are effective in impairing the morale of the groups spied upon. In the long run, however, they react unfavorably on the interests which make use of them. Another device is control of the police force and the local government officials, who then are the creatures of the interests and regard the repression of radical free speech and free assemblage—and especially the hampering, arrest, or deportation of union organizers and agitators—as one of their chief functions.

Allusion was made above to the economic pressure which vested interests, large and small, are able to bring to bear upon teachers and preachers. Such pressure amounts practically to censorship.[11] There are not lacking cases in which it approaches the character of private and irresponsible espionage. Freedom of thought and freedom of teaching are recognized everywhere by liberal-minded people as a condition necessary to real education. But there is a very large number of people who do not see this, and who want "safe" teachers—that is, teachers who

---

[10] See Interchurch World Movement, *Report of the Steel Strike of 1919*, pp. 221ff; Interchurch World Movement, *Public Opinion and the Steel Strike*, 1921, Chapter I, on "Under-cover Men." See also "The Labor Spy"; (Digest of a Report Made under the Auspices of the Cabot Fund for Industrial Research), a series of articles in the *New Republic*, 1921.

[11] A case has recently come to the writer's notice in which a normal school president forbade teachers in the English Department to use the *New Republic* in their classes—presumably not on the ground that the *New Republic* disseminates models of poor syntax.

will not seriously investigate the untoward side of the established order and who will not venture seriously to criticize the point of view, the standards, ethics, or methods of the current vested interests.

But the matter does not stop there. The economic vested interests, or individuals who are associated with them and have their point of view, are largely in control of educational administration. It is of course a notorious fact that before the war no professor could long retain his place in certain of the larger German universities unless he took at least a complacent attitude toward the militarism and imperialism of the ruling classes. In this country the history of interference with academic freedom is a long one, beginning back in the days when the churches were fighting the theory of evolution and the denominational colleges were attempting to hamper the development and besmirch the reputation of the state universities.[12] Teachers of biology were thus the first group, in recent decades, to have to meet the attacks, not always intelligent or scrupulously fair and honest, of the vested interests. In this case, however, the attacking interests were not economic, but ecclesiastical. Later, during the free silver agitation of the 1890's, several professors of economics and political science lost their situations because their expressed views on the monetary issue did not agree with those of trustees and financial supporters. This period marked, in most parts of the country, the gradual cessation of attacks on the biologists,[13] and the beginning of the attacks and pressure which the reactionary economic vested interests have from time to time put forth against the teachers of the social sciences. These attacks have increased in number since 1914, and especially since it became apparent that non-orthodox economic theories had something more than an academic or foreign interest, and that the economists and sociologists were developing a disagreeable habit of probing beneath the surface of corporate affairs and vested-interest business methods.

There is probably not a direct representative of the indus-

---

[12] See Andrew D. White, *Autobiography*, 1905, Vol. I, Ch. 24.

[13] The present recrudescence of the ignorant hue and cry against "the teaching of evolution" in schools and colleges may be regarded as an adventitious piece of sentimental crusading expressive of the demoralization of rational balance incident to wartime nervous strain.

trial working classes on the board of trustees of any important American university. The members of governing boards are not unnaturally drawn mainly from the business classes (especially financial men) ; and the great majority of members will be found to belong if not to the higher income classes at least to those well-to-do ranks in which the middle class, vested-interest attitude is pretty sure to be prevalent.

This being the case, it should be noted to the credit of human nature that interference with academic freedom is not more frequent. But the mere knowledge of the presence of individuals who are allied to powerful and conservative vested interests, and who may at any moment make trouble, is a deterrent upon freedom and honesty of teaching. That there are many hypocritical teachers is as certain as that there are many soft-stepping preachers. Both fear the loss of their jobs, and thereby their livelihood.[14]

Of all forms of censorship, however, that of the press is most effective and far-reaching. The press, as the leading disseminator both of information and misinformation, is an influence transcending all others in the formation of public sentiment and opinion. There was a time when almost anything in print would be believed, provided it did not appear in a newspaper whose political affiliation was opposed to that of the reader. That time is past, however, as is also the day when metropolitan dailies and country weeklies were all staunch and unwavering party organs. Today many newspaper readers—all sophisticated ones—have become skeptical as to the trustworthiness of the news they read, and still more critical and cynical toward editorials, when the latter are read at all. Nevertheless, much of the old uncritical, credulous spirit remains, and even where it does not, the daily newspaper, together with the weekly journals read by a large part of the more intelligent public, constitute the sole avenue through which the world's current events are made known to the people.

Opportunities for censoring and "doctoring" the news by the news gathering agencies, editors, and proprietors are thus of great significance. Certain developments of the past ten

---

[14] Records of cases of dismissal on grounds of economic heresy can be found in the *Bulletins* of the American Association of University Professors.

years or so have made it probable that news doctoring and censorship are now much more common than formerly. The establishment and operation of a city daily require large capital. In the past decade many formerly well-known papers have suspended publication, and there is a continued strong tendency toward the concentration of the ownership and management of metropolitan dailies into the hands of a few wealthy capitalists who have extensive commercial and industrial interests. In the second place, the modern newspaper subsists much more on income from advertisements than on its sale of the news. This is even more true of the popular magazines. And in the third place, the newspapers are largely dependent for their news upon the great incorporated news gathering and distributing agencies. If the news agency is inaccurate or unfair in its news dispatches, the newspaper will almost inevitably reflect the same defects.

Vested-interest control is exercised directly by the owners, who have the power of hiring and firing the staff, from newsboy to managing editor. Naturally the owner has a "policy," and naturally that policy is not likely to be one which will injure his other business interests or run counter to the principles and prejudices of his class. He hires editors and managers who will carry out his policy, and they in turn hire reporters who will report the news with the sort of bias demanded by the owner. Most people know that when they read an editorial they are not necessarily getting the editor's honest opinion but opinions which he is paid to write. News goes through three editings, with three opportunities for suppression and "doctoring" before it reaches the public—first by the news gathering agency, second by the editors, and finally by the headline writers.

Vested-interest control and censorship of news and editorial opinion is further exerted by the big advertisers. Nothing unfavorable to the great department stores ever gets into the metropolitan dailies; these advertisers hold a club over the papers whose chief financial support they are. There are a few outstanding exceptions to this general statement, but only a handful.

Furthermore most owners and editors belong to the capitalistic employing class, hold its views, take its attitudes, and defend its interests. They have greater interest in the affairs of this class than in those of the working classes, and they see industrial unrest, labor difficulties, and the progressivism and radicalism of the non-capitalistic classes from the point of view of the employing class. Even were there not definite and direct financial control, the conservative attitude would be widely reflected in the press.

The result of these influences is that the so-called "capitalist press," which includes practically all but a handful of metropolitan dailies, three or four weekly reviews, and the labor and socialist press, even where it gives true news as to laboring class interests and movements, too frequently gives it in such one-sided and incomplete form that it is equivalent to false news. There is reliable evidence as to downright, conscious, and malicious misrepresentation, also.

It must in fairness be said, however, that labor is perhaps partly to blame for this state of affairs. Ordinarily, perhaps, when local issues are not too passionate or stale, newspapers will publish labor news without conscious bias. One reason why they do not publish more of it is that they think the "public" is not interested in it; another is that whereas the capitalistic interests are adept at publicity when they want publicity, labor has until very recently taken no steps to furnish the newspapers with news stories.

All this censoring, repressing, "doctoring," "faking" and misrepresentation has had profound effect in keeping general public sentiment true to the conservative mold. But it is a game at which radicalism can play also. One who wishes full information on labor's activities and news of the radical movements abroad must turn to certain labor and socialist papers. But here also he must remember that there are "policies" and controls. Much of the labor press is as inaccurate and vituperative with regard to capital and employers as the capitalist press is of organized labor and socialism. If the radicals had control of the press, as in Russia they have, it can scarcely be open to doubt that they would pursue much the same tactics of misrepresentation, distortion, propaganda, censorship, and repression with which the "kept press" of the vested interests is charged, not without good evidence, with pursuing.[15]   This does not alter the fact, however, that control and censorship of information constitute one of the most effective weapons and methods of vested-interest conservatism.

Control of the press is a method of purchasing influence.   The vested interests, on occasion, also resort to the more direct methods of bribery and distribution of patronage.   The annals of the relation between business and government yield copious illustration of known graft and bribery, suggestive of an immense additional mass which never comes to the light of common knowledge.

An effective indirect method of purchase, also, is to draw the able leaders away from progressive and radical camps, or out of poorly paid governmental positions in which they are devoting their energies to the public welfare, by offering them higher salaries and the prestige of rising above their class.   The lure of social prestige and a comfortable income is hard for some temperaments to resist.

The forms of interested conservative control thus far outlined involve compulsion or pressure.   Those which follow, namely (a) prestige, and (b) propaganda, shibboleths, slogans, and chicane, involve not so much compulsion, or pressure, as persuasion and suggestion.   Political control, however, partakes of both compulsion and suggestion.   Political control is realized through the legal processes—legislative, administrative, and judicial—which collectively involve the compulsion connoted by law.   But the control of political machinery and of legal processes, is not, except through comparatively rare *coups d'état* or revolutions, attained by force.   Ordinarily it is obtained, and retained, either by honest discussion and threshing out of the issues of the day, or by the more common processes of appeal to

---

[15] A copious literature on the subject of the press and its control has grown up in the past few years.   An excellent book, because it gives both sides, is *The Profession of Journalism*, edited by W. G. Bleyer, 1918. It contains a useful bibliography.   Another book of different type, but quite as significant, is Upton Sinclair's *The Brass Check*, 1920.   It is a savage attack on the capitalistic press by a socialist who has had abundant journalistic experience.   Mr. Sinclair backs up his accusations with definite evidence, giving names, dates, and detailed circumstances.   See also Walter Lippman, *Liberty and the News*, 1920, and *Public Opinion*, 1922 (especially pp. 334-337, and Ch. 24).

prejudice and sentiment, of persuasive trickery. It employs the usual devices of self- or class-interest which are embodied in disingenuous, if not dishonest, propaganda, and in the chicanery which notoriously characterized "politics" in the bad, and unfortunately, popular sense of the term.

The first of the suggestive or persuasive agencies of control is prestige. Because of their wealth and the social position which goes with wealth, the vested-interest classes enjoy a prestige to which other classes cannot lay claim. They are thus able to supplement the compulsory forms of control with this attractive influence, which, so far as it can be made effective, leaves far less sting than economic pressure. We saw above [16] that the prestige of wealth is the strongest, the most wide-spread, and the most persuasive of all prestige, because it attaches not only to wealth *per se* but to many other characteristics which are based upon wealth. We saw also that prestige is usually in inverse ratio to the development of the critical faculty. Now whether from the development and the freer functioning of critical capacity or from a more open and fiercer hostility of class interests, the prestige of wealth, financial interest, and social position has of late suffered some diminution. Doubtless this helps to some extent to account for the present bitterness of class animosities. Encroachment upon the exclusive prestige of vested interests is resented, much as a man resents injury to his vanity. Moreover, any successful attack upon the vested interests, or limitation of their powers and privileges, reduces their prestige. Hence such attacks would be resisted, even apart from materialistic considerations.

But while prestige—and especially the prestige of wealth and social position, in a somewhat militantly democratic age—has to be guarded by all the known devices, it continues to have a certain very great power of self-protection and self-perpetuation. Herein lies its utility to the vested-interest classes.

It is the privilege of economic and social prestige to set the standards of respectability upon which hinge the processes of social approbation and recognition. Prestige perpetuates the tradition that the guardianship of civilization lies in the middle and upper propertied classes, and in the continuance of economic

---

[16] Page 56.

and social institutions in the form in which they have come down to us from the past. "The dominant class," says Ross, "through the thousand channels it controls, always propagates the idea that social distinctions have originated in differences in personal capacity and virtue and that they owe nothing to crime, fraud, corruption, favoritism, or privilege."[17]

It is interesting to remember in this connection that the word "prestige" formerly meant "delusion," and was originally derived from the Latin *praestigiae*, jugglers' tricks.

The effectiveness of the prestige of the privileged and vested-interest classes varies inversely with the informedness and enlightenment of the other classes. The more ignorant and superstitious a class, the more it is impressed with the outward show and trappings of putative greatness, the more credulous it will be of jugglers' tricks, and the less able to recognize the real merit of individuals and institutions.

This latter fact is what makes revolutions so costly. Ignorance and credulity, dangerous as they are to civilization, are the products of poverty and lack of opportunity. "The abjectly poor," as Veblen says, "and all those persons whose energies are absorbed by the struggle for daily sustenance are conservative because they cannot afford the effort of taking thought for the day after to-morrow."[18] Upon the poor, plays from one side the glamorous light of fine living, which they neither understand nor hope to attain, but which impresses them with a sort of transcendental prestige, and from the other side play the hopes and hatreds engendered by emotional radicalism. This glamour of wealth and leisure, these fierce invectives against capitalism, exploitation, and the leisure class, and the beatific pictures of the future social state drawn by imaginative utopians have a greater appeal to the working classes than they would have, had prestige, on one side, not elevated wealth into an end in itself, and history, on the other, not infected manual labor with the taint of servile status.

From one reason and another, probably because it was during long periods of history performed only by women and chattel slaves, and hence came to be regarded not only as tiresome and

---

[17] *Principles of Sociology*, 1920, p. 237. See also pp. 340, 341 of the same work.

[18] *The Theory of the Leisure Class*, 1899, p. 204.

dirty, but as an indication, if not of servitude, at least of a subservient position, manual labor is still regarded as a badge of inferior social status if not of inferior native worth. The phrase "self-respecting workman" is a subtle though unconscious suggestion of this valuation. People consequently avoid manual work if they can do so, prize leisure, which is an indication of freedom from the necessity of working, and seek those occupations which suggest leisure, and in which at least the evidences of toil and subordination can be effectively washed away or disguised in non-working hours. To the horny-handed son of toil this is not possible. The fairly well-paid sales girl may be indistinguishable, in the subway or on the street, from the well-to-do mistress of the suburban home. But the industrial worker or the bronzed farmer of the plains knows no disguise. Hence the shop girl looks down on the factory girl, and Zenith draws an ever-swelling tide of young men and women from Gopher Prairie and the rural districts. Leisure, freedom from dirty and irksome work, rests largely upon the possession of income-yielding wealth. Here then is another reason why vested-interest conservatism seeks to perpetuate the eighteenth century ideal of self-help and the devil take the hindmost. The task, on the one hand, of extolling the dignity of manual toil and the duty of the self-respecting workman to be content with his lot, and on the other hand, of applauding the individual who, drawn by the prestige of wealth and the comfort of leisure, "rises above his class" and thereby demonstrates that he "has good stuff in him," is a delicate one, but one not beyond the casuistic capacity of many vested-interest conservatives. In part, the maintenance of leisure-class prestige rests upon this welcoming of the exceptional emergent individual, and upon the concomitant perpetuation of the tradition—whether true or fictional does not here matter—that those who do not rise in the world are lacking in sense, thrift, industry, and loyalty.

Unfortunately, few people are impersonal enough in their attitudes or disinterested enough in material ways, to accept the idea of full, free, and informed discussion of social and economic problems. Usually, someone wants to bar the discussion of certain topics, and frequently animosities and recriminations arise in what should be impersonal and objective exchange of evidentially supported opinions. Even the "open forums" established here and there in the larger cities and dedicated to such an objective, have not been entirely free from difficulties of this kind.

There are two sorts of personal or subjective influence upon discussion and argument. The first is in the nature of unconscious bias and predilection. Every individual believes, to some extent, what he wants to believe. While it is one of the principles of good debating to understand the case of the opposition as well as you understand your own, the accepted morals of public discussion leave it to the opposition to state its own case, even though it be done in what you know to be a poor and inadequate manner. (More than that, as we have seen, instances are frequent in which the "public" at the time in control will not allow the opposition to state its case in any manner.) The second kind of personal influence is more positive, still more vicious, and can be classed only as a form of dishonesty. It consists of skilled special pleading, claptrap, chicanery, drawing red herrings across the trail of inquiry, purposely confusing issues, maliciously and mendaciously misrepresenting the other side, calling names, and appealing to unreasoning sentiment by adroitly conceived shibboleths, slogans, and "principles."

Whenever the issue between conservatism and radicalism is sharply joined in a real conflict of basic economic or political interests, we must expect, unfortunately, to see the uglier traits of human nature come to the surface on both sides. Both parties or groups will make use, not only of all the evidence and arguments, specious, *ad hominem*, and otherwise, at their disposal, but of all the known devices for intensifying passion, developing prejudice, manipulating sentiment, consolidating loyalty, and preventing objective criticism. Propaganda, honest and dishonest, a storm of slogans and misapplied platitudes, fervent appeals to home, country, and almighty God, the passionate shrieking out of half-truths, the solemn assertion of things which every intelligent person knows to be untrue—in a word, maudlin sentiment, claptrap, and chicane—become common weapons on both sides. Their manner of use may be crude, or it may be so clever and subtle (especially in the case of chicane) as to deceive all but the exceptionally well-informed and critical.

It is well to remember that argument or propaganda put out by any special interest, however plausible it may sound, or however scientific and objective it may appear to be, should be regarded with skepticism. It is to be noted, too, that vested-interest propaganda and chicane may find their way even into the reports of Congressional committees and governmental administrative departments. It would be interesting to know, but probably never will be known, to just what extent war and navy department demands for huge armaments, in England, France, Germany, Japan, and the United States, have been due to the influence of armament manufacturers.[19]

It is difficult to discuss the claptrap and chicane of sinister special-interest reactionism without falling into unintentional unfairness to the honest conservatism of honest vested interests and the sincere conservatism of temperament, because all three use much the same vocabulary and make their appeals to much the same sentiments and principles.

Where, however, the appeal of the sincere and honest conservative is to real principles, that of the unscrupulously self-seeking special interests is to the *names* of popular principles or ideals, under which they can hide the selfish purposes really at stake—the most effective trick of dressing up the wolf of special interest in the sheep's clothing of whatever "principles," shibboleths, or catchwords may be popular at the time. The name of every ideal or set of principles tends to go through some such degradation. Originally advanced sincerely and thoughtfully, it tends, in proportion to the degree to which it gains superficial acceptance, to be repeated in more and more parrot-like fashion, and finally falls prey to any sinister use which designing selfish interest may see fit to make of it.

Patriotism, loyalty, Christianity, the will of God, law and order, democracy, Americanism, Americanization, "the principles laid down by the fathers in the constitution," the majesty of the law, equality of all before the law, free competition, freedom of contract, the right to work, education for citizenship,

---

[19] Much interesting light is thrown upon this question by J. A. Hobson's *Democracy After the War*, 1917, and by H. N. Brailsford's *The War of Steel and Gold*, 1914.

public interest,—these and many other names for ideals or principles have been prostituted to base uses by unscrupulous private and group special privilege.[20]

The insincere use of shibboleths and of sentiments dear to the popular mind is much too extensive to permit more than cursory analysis. The types of sentiment and of shibboleths may be roughly classified, however. They relate to, or are drawn from, (1) legalistic tradition and sentiment, (2) business, (3) labor relations, (4) politics, (5) religion and ecclesiasticism. Doubtless those sufficiently familiar with art, literature, and educational doctrine can find ample illustration of claptrap in those fields also.

The interested conservative makes much use of legalistic ideals—when it suits his purpose to "have the law" on his progressive or radical antagonist. Industrial corporations, at the very time that they may be employing astute lawyers to show them how to evade some inconvenient law, or inciting employees to violence, indulge in much virtuous talk about "law and order," "respect for the constituted authorities," "the sanctity of the law," and the like. Law and order, it goes without saying, are the necessary condition of any organized form of social relations. Without order neither safety nor achievement is possible. The philosophical anarchist thinks that human nature under complete freedom would be so good that peace, justice, and co-operation would flow smoothly and automatically from natural, spontaneous impulses. But there are few, even among idealistic radicals, who share this view. Evolutionary psychology lends as little countenance to it as to the opposite doctrine of the innate depravity of man. But the phrase "law and order" is so frequently and so vociferously in the mouth of special interests which do not hesitate to evade the law or to set order at defiance, when it is to their material profit to do so, that this fine and necessary sentiment, like so many other ideals, is made a cloak to chicane and exploitation. It becomes a shibboleth to be repeated in parrot fashion, and

---

[20] It is to be clearly understood that in pointing out this fact no criticism, either constructive or destructive, of the principles or ideals themselves is involved. Justly understood and sincerely applied, they may, or may not, each and all be valid and necessary, but that is not here the question. It is the claptrap use of them to defend or enhance special interests that is under consideration.

applied by a confiding public in the formation of judgment on situations, of the real facts concerning which it is in ignorance. The facts are particularly hard to ascertain at those times when the passions run high in bitter disputes between employers and employees. That violence may be instigated and committed by either side is well known. It is known also that the side which cries out most loudly for "law and order" is not always the one least guilty of violating both. The dispassionate student of violence in labor disputes will be slow to condone or to condemn. He will get the facts as to motives and actions on both sides, as nearly as he can, and form his judgments accordingly, and where he cannot get the facts he will refrain from forming any judgment at all.

Much could be said of the disingenuous sentiment over such legalistic shibboleths and slogans as "equality before the law," "due process of law," "class legislation," "states' right," etc., but further comment is unnecessary. It is but too evident, to any observant person who follows current industrial and political issues and who occasionally reads the decisions of the higher courts on matters involving labor legislation and the legal regulation of industry, that these slogans are amenable to skillful use in special pleading for vested interests.

The great antithesis to law and order is war. And most modern wars are held on good evidence to be due usually to a conflict of special commercial concession-hunting, profit-seeking interests. War may be brought on by international commercial rivalry without direct design. International violence may also be instigated by special interests. "Trade follows the flag." It may be the "manifest destiny" of one nation to invade the sovereignty of another, and the public may adroitly be led to support a war of commercial exploitation under the sincere belief that it is fighting for that as yet unsatisfactorily defined thing, "national honor." There have not been lacking, for instance, business interests and powerful metropolitan newspapers to preach law and order at home and at the same time argue that the United States army should go in and "clean up" Mexico. How much indignation at the killing of American citizens who took the risk of remaining in Mexico during a period of successive revolutions, and how much the existence in Mexico of vast exploitable oil, mining, lumber, and ranching resources have to do with this ethics, we need not here attempt to say. The life of an American in Mexico, however, seems to be worth more than the life of a Mexican in the United States.

This sort of dualistic ethics is not limited to commercial and labor interests or to sentiments with regard to international relations. "Lynch law" and mob violence constitute another striking illustration. In the South fervent appeals to reverence for the law and eulogies of the law-abiding citizen are not less frequent than in the North, though they probably display a higher average of flowery rhetoric. Yet both North and South are theaters of mob violence, of lynching bees, of orgies of revengeful bestiality which too few of the "leading citizens" ever condemn—or even refer to—and which indeed are sometimes led by some of the men who in their saner and more human moods are full of much oratory about the majesty of the law. The pinnacle of this sort of regard for "law and order" is reached in the Ku Klux Klan. It would be an enlightening study in psychology could we really determine the ratio of honest conviction to simple mendacity and gullibility in the membership of the Klan, which has repeatedly, with an air of outraged virtue, tried to make the public believe that it stands for the upholding of the law.

Touching on issues involving proposals for a less archaic and legalistic interpretation of the United States Constitution or for the revision of the fundamental law embodied therein, we have much sentimental appeal to the eternal verities, especially for "reverence for that incomparable document, the United States Constitution, which in their God-given wisdom the fathers drafted and bequeathed to posterity." There is of course no hint that the Constitution itself was the result of a compromise between contending material interests or that the men who framed it had personal prejudices and interests, class viewpoints, and sectional biases. Nor is there any recognition of the fact that no generation possesses all wisdom or that there may be a few men to-day comparable in insight, public spirit, and statesmanship with the fathers, nor again of the fact that the Constitution has come through a century and a quarter of Supreme Court interpretation (besides various popular emendations) which has so changed its meaning that the fathers might have difficulty in recognizing it. This appeal to the Constitution as if it were a changeless set of first principles, where sincere, is indication of a curious pessimism, for it betrays a belief that constructive political and legal wisdom reached a glorious apotheosis in the period of Alexander Hamilton and James Madison, and then declined, until to-day we do not know enough to fit fundamental law to our own generation's needs.

Whether appeal to reverence for the Constitution is sincere or insincere, it is an appeal which relies for effectiveness not on critical judgment but on the well-recognized popular sentimental proclivity to revere the archaic. It is another phase of the ancient habit of appealing to the elders. Too frequently such appeals betray either a futile desire to stay the moving hand of time or an inability to see that the men of one age cannot possibly foresee the problems and needs which will be encountered by the generations to come. That men of the period in which Adam Smith's Wealth of Nations and Rousseau's Social Contract were the last word in economics and political philosophy could lay down a body of fundamental law which would continue to meet the requirements of a world so full of rapid change, of industrial development, and of dynamic energy as the Western World has been since the eighteenth century is an amazing proposition. Yet reactionaries and vested-interest conservatives are able to propound it with straight faces.

Cant and humbug and pose are to be found in all professions and all classes. But they are perhaps most characteristic of the business world. This is due primarily to the fact that under law and sentiment, developed through long periods of materialistic individualism, business has become a field staked out with a multitude of ramifying, interlacing special privileges and legalized vested rights, many of them detrimental to social welfare, but defended by their possessors and beneficiaries with every means in their power.

The slogan "Don't injure business!" can be heard throughout the land, in wartime and peacetime, in prosperity and in depression, but most clamorously when business interests are threatened, or seem to business men to be threatened (there is a real distinction), by legislative or administrative reform.

This is natural enough. The business men and their retainers, the lawyers, regard themselves as "the public." In the industrial States of the Northeast and even in the agricultural regions of the South and West, the real control of government is commonly in the hands of these two allied groups. Under such conditions it is entirely natural that the primary function of government should be considered not only as the time-honored "protection of private property" but the protection of particular vested interests, business organization, and business ideals as they are. Under the external form of geographical representation, there is really a significant element of business sovietism, for the business men take care that individuals friendly to their interests are elected to office, and in addition spare no expense for the maintenance of skilled lobbies. Were labor in substantial control of government, as business now is, it is likely that the point of view prevalent in town councils, legislatures, and Congress would be that of labor almost exclusively, and that the chief purpose of government would be conceived to be the protection of the worker and the advancement of wages. "Labor" would be made an end in itself; the slogan would be "Don't injure labor!" The general public welfare—inclusive of all classes—would be made secondary, although there would be as much talk about it as there is now.

Actually, the facts are very much the reverse. "Business," being in control, though not indeed without powerful opposition on the part of the agricultural and labor interests, more or less consciously regards labor—including the farmer—as a means to business "prosperity." And prosperity is generally conceived as rising prices and high profits. Profits are the business man's standard of measuring "public welfare." Any change which may conceivably involve a reduction of dividends, or subject to criticism the current ideals and practices of business, is pilloried as dangerously perversive of law and order and the cherished foundations of our free government.

Business men during the nineteenth century—at slightly different periods in different countries—had to fight the landed aristocracy for control of the legislative function in government. In this country they have had control ever since the framing of the Constitution.[21] But with the spread of education, the development of strong groups of organized labor, and in this

---

[21] Cf. Charles A. Beard, *An Economic Interpretation of the Constitution of the United States*, 1913, and J. H. Smith, *The Spirit of American Government*, 1907.

country the growth of a very numerous class of farm owners and farm renters who on the whole are more and more adding their force to that of labor, the business control of government is seriously disputed. Business men in politics, with the narrow business tradition ingrained in their nature, and too frequently with economic axes of their own to grind, find themselves confronted not only with a new level of general public sentiment but with the unpleasant pressure of a none too polite and not too modest democracy of work people and progressive farmers. When these interests become strong enough to threaten control, or actually for a time secure control, the business world invariably sends out its S. O. S. call—"Don't injure business."

It cannot be denied that the appeal is telling, and at times necessary. For as long as the process of producing wealth is organized on the basis of private, or corporate, responsibility no one but an extreme radical who feels that anything, even a general crash of the social structure, is better than the present waste and injustice, will be blind enough not to see that when business men find production unprofitable and have to run their plants at a loss, everybody suffers—and the laborer most of all. Consequently the business world is in a strategic position, able to call itself the goose that lays the golden egg.

But business has a habit of crying before it is hurt, and those business organizations most inimical to real public welfare are normally the first and the loudest in their condemnatory protests. Not the least evil flowing from this habit is that the uninitiated public, and even business itself, cannot always clearly distinguish between a real danger to legitimate business, and an imaginary one.

A common form of the "injury to business" bugaboo is the cry that reform legislation will drive business to another State. This argument has probably been more instrumental in the defeat of salutary labor legislation than any other one plea. Time and again child labor bills, workingmen's compensation bills, bills regulating hours and conditions of work, providing for safety devices, etc., have gone down to defeat when some employers' association or some corporation lobbyist started the cry "Do you want to drive industry out of this State!" The average uninformed legislator, having himself the narrow business point of view, and deficient in a sense of social ethics, regarded this as convincing argument against the bill.

The legislator, and doubtless to a certain extent his constituents back of him, thus stand under the charge of motivation by local selfishness. They would rather have the industry, with all its evils, in their State than by cleaning it up run the risk of driving it elsewhere. There is a certain blindness in this attitude; for the people rarely stop to examine critically the claim that industry would migrate, or to consider what existing conditions—supply of raw material and labor, transportation facilities, and markets—may make it practically impossible for a whole industry, or even a given concern, to move. In other words, vested interests have long since learned the secret of stampeding public sentiment by appeal to the selfish material interests of individuals, and to inherited sentimental prejudices, while the intelligent public at large is only just beginning to develop defenses against this sinister use of crowd psychology.

Another cry of vested business interests is that industry cannot stand the added cost of reform. Opposition to minimum wage legislation, to prohibition of child labor, etc., not infrequently features this plea. That the added cost, if any, can usually be shifted to the consumer is overlooked; that profits may be high enough to allow the business prosperous continuance without raising prices to the consumer is never for a moment admitted; to read the manufacturer' pleas one would suppose that all business is carried on under a régime of cutthroat competition, with every concern on the verge of collapse. There are beyond doubt cases and perhaps whole industries in which additional costs cannot with justice be forced upon employers without permitting and expecting them to shift the extra charge to the consumers. But in many cases the cry that business cannot stand the increased cost is both false and insincere. Moreover, as the advocates of minimum wage legislation consistently reiterate, if an industry is so precarious in its hold upon the public demand that it cannot run without hiring child labor and without paying starvation wages, that industry should go out of business. The people who buy its products, yet who would be unwilling to pay a price sufficient to give the workers a living wage and the employer a fair profit, are not paying their way: they are in a sense objects of charity, for the laborers are donating work to them for which there is no adequate payment. But this is a point of view beyond the powers of comprehension of the average business man or corporation lawyer.

Captains of industry are no doubt often sincere in their premature warnings of impending injury. Business is proverbially timid, and it would be unjust to think that the hue and cry against reform legislation is always raised merely to protect unsocial and uneconomical privilege; but society at large cannot afford to overlook the fact that the interests of any class are likely to be exaggerated by the members of that class, and that the more prestige and power a class has in governmental affairs, the better is its position to impress unthinking people at large with the sanctity and inviolability of its "rights."

Another business slogan, in prominent use of late, is the sentiment with regard to every man's right to run his business as he sees fit. Probably few, if any, progressive laws limiting the power of business men to run business as they please, from the first English child labor act in 1802 to the Interstate Commerce Commission Act of 1887, and the minimum wage legislation of recent years, could be found to which a large number, if not the majority, of business men, individually and by collective organization, have not made more or less bitter opposition.

Those who have power which can be used for private ends nearly always oppose any diminution of that power, ostensibly because they hold such diminution to be derogatory to public interest, but really because they do not want to give up, whether in the public interest or not, any power or privilege. This is the real secret of the sentiment about "the right to run your own business in your own way" without "interference" from "meddlesome" governmental agencies, or associations of workingmen. Society, however, is coming to see that no such unrestricted right can be permitted, and progressive business men are willingly recognizing that fact.

The same motivation by self interest is seen in the favorite business slang "Don't knock, boost!" and in the aversion to criticism of business practices or to the calling of attention to shortcomings of local government or local public utilities which it reveals. This "don't-knock-boost," ostrich-like habit of hiding your head in the sand in an attempt to ignore facts uncomplimentary to your town or city, which if published, are likely to reduce trade and "scare people away," was formerly very prevalent among chambers of commerce and like organizations, but is said to be becoming less so. Still, very few real estate dealers—who are a class commonly influential in the average American town—like it to become known that the local water supply is infected with colon bacilli, or that the school system is backward.

Of course, the greater part of the insincerity of business-interest conservatism is not reducible to catch phrases. There is, for instance, a fixed and constant pressure of propaganda to discredit progressive movements of any kind, if they seem likely to have any adverse effect on profits or funded incomes, to limit monopoly power, to strengthen labor, or to give greater regulative power to the people through governmental ownership and operation of public utilities. Some of this propaganda is fair and sincere. Much of it is insincere and unscrupulously and willfully misrepresentative.[22] Partly because "business" has inherited the individualistic *laissez faire* sentiment from English classical political philosophy and from frontier conditions in America, but more because of conscious self- and class-interest, "the commercial class has long played upon a popular suspicion and jealousy of government inherited from the eighteenth century when government was an alien arbitrary agency over which the commonalty had no effective control."[23] One of the most common devices to this end is to exaggerate the incompetence and wastefulness of governmental operations and to maintain a judicious silence as to incompetence and waste in the private corporate conduct of business.

To-day the greatest chicane, the loudest claptrap, the most passionately unscrupulous vituperative propaganda are associated with the labor conflict. Ample illustration can be found on

---

[22] To analyze this unscrupulous propaganda would require volumes. Instances can, however, be found everywhere. See, for example, the publicity work of the steel companies during the strike of 1919 (see Interchurch World Movement, *Report on the Steel Strike*), the propaganda of the railway and business interests against the Federal Railway Administration in 1918 and 1919, and the literature of banking journals against the postal savings system.

[23] Ross, *Principles of Sociology*, 1920, p. 505.

both sides, but there is not lacking evidence that labor, as it has gained coherence and a reserve of income usable for its collective ends, is turning, at least in Great Britain and the United States, more and more to inductive statistical research to prove its case, while the business interests are tempted to passionate denunciation and reliance upon their ability thereby to hold public sentiment to the side of the employing class.

In this third group or field of social relations, shibboleths and slogans play an important role. "The right of every man to work" is a sentiment more frequently in the mouth of the employer than in that of the worker. Curiously, the employer is more likely to express this sentiment at times when profits are low, demand for product slack, and unemployment rife. At such times it would seem that it is regarded as the right of every man to close down his plant without notice and that this right is paramount to any vested interest which in other junctures the workingman may theoretically be implied to have in a job.[24] As a matter of fact, it is well recognized that "the right to work," under a system in which capital is organized into huge corporations, and employers into manufacturers' associations, but the workers left unorganized and with no recourse except to individual bargaining, is illusory. It is merely another name for the necessity of accepting whatever wage and working conditions the employer may see fit to grant. Those who oppose collective bargaining on the pious ground that it interferes with the individual laborer's right to work are less honest than those who oppose it frankly on the real ground that it may reduce profits and always means limitation on the employer's practise of running the business to suit his own love of unrestrained autocracy.[25]

[24] Here again fairness demands that cognizance be taken of the fact that some more enlightened and far-seeing employers are beginning to think constructively of methods by which the heavy burden of commercial depression, slack demand, and unemployment may be removed from the worker, or at least greatly reduced. See, for example, Henry S. Dennison, "Depression Insurance; A Suggestion to Corporations for Reducing Unemployment." *American Labor Legislation Review*, March, 1922, pp. 31-36.

[25] The reader may analyze for himself the phraseology and meaning of the following open shop advertisement which appeared in the Dallas News, January 23, 1922.

In the courts this right to work is commonly referred to under the rubric ''freedom of contract''—but freedom of contract in labor cases means in the mouths of judges trained in the *laissez faire,* individualistic business tradition, in point of fact essen-

---

THE OPEN SHOP WORKINGMAN'S
DECLARATION OF INDEPENDENCE

I claim the right to dispose of my time and skill in a manner that will be most advantageous to myself and on terms satisfactory to my employer.

I protest against any attempts to abridge my right to work uninterruptedly or to deter me from sustaining myself and family in honor and respectability.

I hold that outside of my employer no one has the right to demand that I discontinue my employment without my distinct sanction and approval.

I claim protection against any act of annoyance, coercion or intimidation aimed at me because I refuse to subject myself to those whose authority I do not recognize.

I insist that in keeping with the American spirit I have the right to choose my own affiliations whether in church, lodge, labor or society.

I refuse to associate myself with any organizations that demand rights, privileges, concessions or exemptions not granted to all citizens.

I stand unqualifiedly against any attempt to make of me a tool in the hands of agitators for accomplishment of their selfish ends.

I shall not engage in any activities aimed at my fellow-toilers which will deprive them of the right to work upon terms and conditions with which they are satisfied.

I resent the suggestion that I should limit my daily output or reduce my efficiency or in any way fail to give an honest day's work for a full day's pay.

I maintain that to create misunderstanding or friction between my employer and myself is to destroy all wholesome ends; that it benefits neither him nor myself and is against all public interest.

I stand for absolute freedom in thought and action, consistent with laws of our land and resent the unsolicited intervention of any man or combination of men, who, as a minority, arrogate to themselves the authority to speak and act in the name of the workingmen of America.

I declare for loyalty of the average workingman, the man who actually toils.

If you need skilled mechanics or help of any kind
Y 3985   CALL   X 5425

(SEAL)   DALLAS OPEN SHOP (SQUARE DEAL)
ASSOCIATION OF THE
CHAMBER OF COMMERCE
"It's in Dallas"—Open Shop

tially just what "the right to work" means in the master-and-servant ethics of the capitalist employer—the "freedom" to sign whatever sort of labor contract the employer may see fit to present as a condition to employment.

It is not meant to imply, of course, that all advocacy of freedom of contract and the right to work partakes of the nature of disingenuous claptrap or chicane. Some of it is mere doctrinaire tradition unthinkingly learned in the law schools and elementary courses in economics, and perpetuated by habit in the general population. It is possible to hold, of course, as many radicals do hold and many thinking liberals are coming to hold, that once society permits an individual to come into existence the duty should devolve upon it of finding him place and means of earning a living, but this fundamental, social-obligation aspect of the matter does not appear in the current business attitude. That attitude is that the worker is entitled to a job, under free, individual contract, *if he can get one.* The obligation to supply jobs is but imperfectly felt.

There is also much disingenuousness in the charges against labor for "restricting output," "limiting production," "soldiering on the job," and in general for profiteering and failure to deliver "a day's work for day's pay." In all this there is the implication that only the employer is to be the judge of what a day's work for a day's pay is. There is also the flagrant misimplication that business concerns never limit output and restrict supply by shutting down plants, suppressing progressive inventions, and by other methods, when it will enhance profits to do so.

During periods of "industrial unrest," that is, periods in which labor feels powerful enough collectively to push claims for better wages, better working conditions, collective bargaining, and perhaps, as at present, some share in industrial management, "unrest" itself becomes a term of opprobrium in the mouth of the average conservative business man. There is always unrest among those who do the manual toil of the world, but it is only when it becomes articulate, organized, and collective, and hence begins to have power, that interested conservatism condemns it. When it appears only in relatively sporadic and isolated cases it is praised, as evidence of thrift, ambition, and desire to improve one's condition or to rise above one's class.

When unrest becomes effective in stimulating demands for general improvement in the position of the working classes, the vested interests can find no condemnatory word too strong. It becomes socialism, bolshevism, communism, anarchism, disloyalty; it is aimed at overthrowing all law and order, at undermining the foundations of Americanism, and destroying civilization. It is chiefly the result of the diabolical machinations of irresponsible and self-seeking "agitators," who are nearly all anarchists or "reds" in the employ of the Russian government, men without scruple or education, "ignorant foreigners" who have come to this country to enjoy our free institutions, and now set about to destroy them.[26]

Even in normal times the able and courageous people who have revealed, not infrequently with all the paraphernalia of weighty if not indisputable evidence, gross evils, dishonesty, and efficiency in our governmental and economic processes, have been attacked and held up to scorn as "hare-brained reformers," and "theorists." Witness the hue and cry against the "muck rakers" of the late 1890's and early 1900's, the denunciations and misrepresentations of such organizations as the American Association for Labor Legislation, the American Public Health Association, the leaders in graft prosecutions in San Francisco and elsewhere, and the campaign of vituperation against the Interchurch World Movement Committee's steel strike investigators and the distinguished clergymen who constituted the Committee and issued its Report.

This device of trying to kill a movement by attacking individuals or calling names is of course not confined to vested-interest conservatism, much less to purely economic vested interests. Wherever met with, it is an evidence of vulgarity, sometimes clever (as in the case of cartoons), and nearly always designed as an appeal to prejudice, although it may pose as an

---

[26]That this characterization of the vested-interest conservative description or conception of the labor organizer and all but the most conservative national labor leaders is not overdrawn will, it is believed, be the conclusion of any open-minded person who will take the trouble to glance through the files, say of the *National Civic Federation Review*, or almost any financial journal for recent years.

appeal to reason. With the uncritical mind, habitually nursing and feeding its own prejudices, it is as efficacious in preventing open-mindedness toward the opposition's ideas as is the adroit use of shibboleths and rallying cries in creating and maintaining an unquestioning loyalty to the ideas and interests of one's own camp or clique. We are here touching upon one of the costly shortcomings of the popular, as contrasted with the critical or scientific attitude, but it is just this lack of critical capacity—one might almost say of critical will—which gives conservative vested interests their hold, and which, once that hold is broken, tends to produce an almost equally uncritical and credulous rush to the extreme of interested radicalism.

In the field of politics it is evident that slogans, shibboleths, claptrap, and chicane still play, as they always have played, important rôles. This is true, whether we have in mind those larger but somewhat purposely obscured special interests which it has been the function of the chicanery, deceit and skillful lying of secret diplomacy to further, or merely the coining of popular election slogans like the vulgar "full dinner pail" or the more dignified but in the light of swiftly following events ironical "He kept us out of war," and "back to normalcy."

When nationalistic sentiment runs high, as in spite of high-flown idealism, it has run, even in "disinterested" America of late years, when popular feeling has been stirred to the depths, and popular indignation at international injustices fanned into furious heat and unreasoning hysteria, certain words—names of ideals—become invincible slogans. To this class belong "patriotic," "loyal," "American," and their antonyms, "unpatriotic," "disloyal," and "un-American."

In the fervor of nationalistic sentiment a new sort of patriotism, a sort of super-patriotism, is conceived of, and christened "one hundred per cent Americanism." Now the point here is not that patriotism, nationalism, loyalty, and Americanism (even of the "one hundred per cent" variety) are, or are not, praiseworthy and desirable. The point is that these terms are seized upon by every sort of special designing interest, person, or group, and prostituted to the furthering of selfish materialistic ends. If prohibition interferes with brewing profits it is "un-American"; if effective labor organization raises wages, it is "unpatriotic"; if critical scholarship questions the motivation of conduct of the war it is "disloyal." In general anything that does not involve putting social institutions and economic conditions back where they were in July, 1914, falls short of the magic standard, "one hundred per cent American."

Unfortunately the good term "democracy" has not escaped similar prostitution. The vested interests which have been financially discommoded by the income tax, the excess profits tax, the Clayton Anti-trust Act, the Federal Trade Commission Act, and by the public utility commissions, etc., see much merit in the "democracy of our fathers," which, being of a *laissez faire* type, was not effective in preventing the development of powerful special privilege, and which, if it could be restored, would remove even the feeble restrictions which we now have. The simple truth is that no special interest has any use for a real and effective democracy, and vested-interest talk about democracy is largely chicane and claptrap.

It would take us too far afield to attempt to discuss even in outline the methods of vested-interest conservatism in religion and ecclesiasticism. That there are ecclesiastical interests which consciously and designedly oppose progress in religious thought and ethics is patent. What is called cant may be either the result of designing selfishness (economic interest) masquerading under the forms, ceremonies, and vocabulary of religious observance, or it may be merely the reflection of the uncritical popular habit of accepting words at par value without impulse or capacity to inquire closely into their significance.

There are other conditions which contribute to the success of even transparent dishonesty and chicane on the part of selfish interests. These are to be found in the apathy of the general public and the constant alertness and activity of the interests themselves.

It is an old cynical saying that "what is the public's business is nobody's business." In so far as this is true, it may be explained as the natural outcome of the selfish, *laissez faire*, "self-help" theory upon which popular organization and economic processes have been conducted, with important modification it is true, since the Industrial Revolution. Especially in a new country and in the geographical zone known as the frontier,[27]

[27] See **F. J. Turner,** *The Frontier in American History*, 1920.

where great natural resources await private appropriation and exploitation, and where the uppermost thought of every individual and every family is to "get on," it will be true that few will be willing to take time or thought away from private affairs to devote to public interests. Where public and private interests seem in conflict, private interests make the first claim to attention. The same holds true in those great commercial and industrial centers in which the central controlling motive is "business." Not only, then, does public apathy—that is, absorption in private material interests—furnish a fruitful culture medium for the political corruption and gross inefficiency of government, especially municipal administration, which has been the disgrace of America, but in a broader and not less significant way it has supplied just the requisite condition under which vested-interest conservatism could manipulate governmental agencies and public sentiment to its own designs.

At those times when public sentiment has been aroused to a wave of zealous political house-cleaning, the special economic and corrupt political interests have momentarily bowed to the storm, in the faith, based on sufficient experience, that it would soon blow over and the virtuous citizens settle back to the calm pursuit of their own personal affairs. At other times the interests find it most expedient and effective simply to sit tight, say nothing, and ignore the attacks of progressives and radicals. This of course points to the advantage which all conservatism enjoys, namely, that it is in an entrenched position, which progressivism or radicalism can carry only by a frontal attack or a prolonged and costly siege.

To assert untruths or half-truths, to play upon prejudice and passion through the use of rallying cries, shibboleths, and slogans, to create prejudice through calling names, through cynical ridicule and caricature, to appeal to local enthusiasms, arouse local fears, and fan sectional loyalties, to discourage objectivity, open-mindedness, and fair criticism—these are the too common and conspicuous methods of vested-interest conservatism. They overshadow in volume and out-balance in weight the justifiable methods of objective presentation of evidence, honest propaganda, and fair consideration of the other side, methods open to all parties, and all shades of opinion, which may be practiced by honest conservatives and sincere radicals alike.

It would be difficult to determine how much of the defensive

propaganda of interested conservatism is honest and sincere—
based on a sincere conviction as to the social value of the interests and *status quo* defended—and how much of it is consciously
and designedly "bunk" and claptrap. Where the motive is
assuredly individual- or class-selfishness, how fully conscious of
this fact are the conservatives? How much human sympathy
have they? How much knowledge of social conditions do they
have? How much knowledge of "how the other half" lives do
they *care* to have? However much sympathy and public sentiment interested conservatives may have in concrete cases—as
for instance the care of conspicuous destitution or the institution of "good fellow" Christmas dinners for the poor—there is
room for some question as to the reality and breadth of their
"public" and "progressive" spirit.

CHAPTER VI

THE MOTIVATION OF RADICALISM

GENERALLY speaking, radicalism is the product of unrest. Unrest is the expression of personal discomfort. Thoroughly comfortable individuals never become radicals. The main reason why people desire innovation is that they are uncomfortable under the existing *status quo* and see no prospect of relief in change in the direction of reactionism. This is not saying, of course, that all discomfort, even when extreme, leads to radicalism. It may lead to hysteria, to a contented disbelief in the efficacy of human effort, to sullen stoicism, to mob violence, or to patient, painstaking effort, often successful, to adjust the personality to the existing environment, rather than to any serious attempt to change the environment itself even in superficial ways.

Discomfort may not lead even to mild progressivism. The individual's life may be so dominated by fixed habits that failure of certain aspects of his personality to obtain adjustment and healthful functioning may not be sufficient stimulus to break down the inertia of his established routines and attitudes. Similarly, his social or economic position may be such that no ordinary amount of discomfort or maladjustment serves to overcome his fear. This is notably the case in certain types of what we have called the "conservatism of necessitous condition."

When the uncomfortable person contemplates no other method of removing his discomfort than those at the time recognized and practiced as conventionally right and proper—for example, the business principles of self-help, *caveat emptor,* charging what the traffic will bear, individual energy, initiative, and thrift, and the "go get it" spirit, or the Christian virtues of modesty, humility, self-criticism, conscientious soul-searchings, and conviction of sin and unworthiness—the radical attitude does not develop.

119

Only when discomfort or dissatisfaction creates a desire for significant changes or transformations in social organization, relations, or standards, does it lead to other than habitual conservative attitudes. When the desire for thorough-going, fundamental, and rapid change of the environment in essential respects is present, the sources of this desire will always be found to be some maladjustment between the individual and his surroundings such that he is consciously uncomfortable and restless. It is not essential that he know the causes of his discomfort or that the objective changes he desires be such as would remove the real causes.

Desire is always a disposition to change—to do something that one is not doing, or to be something other than one is or thinks one is at the particular moment. Desire is the result of stimulus, and stimulus always leads to some sort of bodily or psycho-physical activity. The stimulus, whether from some part of the organism itself or from the external environment (physical or social) produces a disequilibrium, which is normally balanced by the appropriate reaction or response. The normal, healthy conservative lives a life of short-cycle routine (largely habitual) in which organic disequilibria, physical or mental, are balanced, and the energy of desire or unrest released in a fairly regular rhythm. In individuals who become radicals, this short-cycle ebb and flow of disequilibrium and equilibrium, of desire and satisfaction, of stimulus and releasing reaction, is broken into by desires or interests which do not find release or expression in normal rhythmic response. A state of more or less chronic unrest ensues, and may become the basis for definitely formulated desire for fundamental change in the environment.

Any impulse to action, any "motor set," desire, or disposition, the carrying out of which is impeded, prevented, or balked, gives rise to organic unrest, which may be merely physical, or "spiritual."[1]

---

[1] All unrest has its physical basis. Even "spiritual" disequilibrium may—when physiological psychology attains more adequate analytical power than it now has—be explained in physical terms, if any gain in clearness of understanding is to be had thereby. The terms physical and spiritual are here used in a somewhat popular or conventional sense. A man may be restless because, unconsciously to himself, his thyroid

Now what happens when a desire or a complex of desires (interest) is balked? Normally an unbalked desire or interest is fulfilled and terminated by the appropriate motor activity.[2] Fulfillment of desire or interest is accompanied by the appropriate emotions, mostly of a "pleasurable" or satisfying character. When the interest is impeded or balked, however—that is, when the normal motor response which would release the energy of the desire cannot take place—the emotional accompaniment is different. The energy held back is likely to go into a ferment, at least until it can find some other outlet than the one to which the desire or interest was at first directed. The central emotion of the balked disposition is "hurt feeling," resentment, or anger. Accompanying emotions may also be fear, discouragement, or simply a generalized and diffused sense of uneasiness. Which emotions or emotional complexes are most in evidence will depend on the type of temperament and character.

It should be understood that the initial anger is not due to loss of the object of the desire or failure to achieve the aims of the interest, but follows immediately in a purely reflexive manner upon the balking of the wish, or the damming up of the motor activity appropriate to the realization of the wish. The organism is "set" for a given line of action, and when action cannot be carried out along that line the universal first impulse is toward those motor reflexes which are the manifestations of anger, in some one of its many forms, and which are classified under the general term pugnacity.

One of these initial reflexes, and perhaps fundamentally the one most important in its social consequences, is the tendency to blame somebody—some person—as an object upon whom the angered organism, now set for combat, may make its attack.

---

glands are overactive; because he is conscious of hunger, or because he wishes to solve a mathematical problem, rescue a fellow-man from suffering, is himself suffering under a "conviction of sin," or is irritated by a consciousness of the waste, disorder, and ugliness of a social system.

[2] This statement will hold whether the desire is a simple physical "appetite," an urge to intellectual activity, or an impulse to "get in tune with the infinite." On thinking, for instance, as motor activity, see Watson, *Psychology from the Standpoint of a Behaviorist*," 1919, p. 15 and Ch. 9.

Reflexive anger, blame, and set-for-combat are the initial effort of the organism to prepare itself for action in a new situation involving a break in the regular routine of habit or obstruction of the carrying out of desire and interest. But anger and fear are closely associated; are perhaps but the two sides of one shield. Whether the combative impulse associated with anger, or the avoidance impulse attendant on fear, shall guide and motivate subsequent activity can be foretold only if we know both the general situation and the character and temperament of the individual. In any case the individual is confronted with the necessity of making some sort of readjustment between himself and his environment. He may attempt to accomplish this by attack upon the environment, or may elect, under the influence of fear (timidity, lack of self-confidence, etc.), to modify his desires and docilely accept whatever the situation may hold in store for the meek and non-resistant personality. If attack rather than self-repression is the chosen mode of readjustment, the resulting attitude may very well be radical, although it might be reactionary. In the higher mental types the combative impulse may give way to curiosity and contrivance impulses, and the attack be carried out not so much in a militant as in a workmanlike manner.

Speaking in the by and large, readjustment will take place through one of three processes—(1) repression, (2) substitution and transference, and (3) reinforcement. In the first, the obstructed desire or interest is repressed or totally suppressed. In the second, it is "sublimated" through the substitution of other desires or interests and transfer of attention to them. In the third, attention is concentrated upon the obstructed desire and it is reinforced by the determination to remove the obstructing agency. The method of readjustment obviously has important causal bearing on the psychology, and especially the motivation, of conservative and radical attitudes.

(1) *Repression or total suppression.* Where the readjustment is accomplished by a recession of the obstructed desire, the desire (a) either drops automatically out of the individual's life (that is, is completely forgotten) and retains no influence even in the unconscious, or (b) is suppressed—driven out of the

individual's life by conscious act of will (desire to be rid of it),[2] or (c) apparently totally suppressed, it may be in reality only held in durance vile in the subconscious or unconscious by the "censor," which may be for the occasion either conscience, or fear, or rational control.

In case the desire is relatively superficial and unimportant, it is simply dropped and forgotten, without struggle or effort, and without appreciable disturbance to the personality. Where it is of greater amplitude and intensity, involves a significant disequilibrium of energy, and is regarded as important, the individual can dismiss it from his life only by conscious specific attention and act of will accomplishing complete suppression. In this case, the individual gives the desire concentrated attention for the time being, not with the idea of its realization in spite of all impediments, but with the conscious purpose of getting rid of it once for all. It is highly important to him, but, from whatever reason, he prefers not to push for its fulfillment. His will to forgetting or suppression is really the stronger desire to avoid the disagreeable results probably involved in effort to overcome the obstacles to the realization of the original desire.

With the balked disposition totally suppressed, the individual can proceed to other interests, untroubled and unhampered by the disturbing emotions experienced at the time of the balking. The *idea* or the purpose of the desire is dismissed, and with it the desire. The energy which would have gone to its realization, had the individual been left free to carry out his purpose, is now free to be applied, without ulterior motive, and without regrets or hesitancy, to other interests which can be pursued without impediment from the existing social *status quo*.

Where complete suppression takes place in this manner, and the individual turns his attention and energies to conventional interests, it is obvious that the reflexive anger and resentment attendant upon balked desire do not afford any effective impulse toward progressive or radical attitudes. In suppression of desire and acquiescence in the continued existence of the obstruction we have further light on the psychology of the easy-going, flabby conservative. If, in such an individual, an incipient

---

[2] The stickler for strict psychoanalytical procedure may object that this is only a type of sublimation.

radical impulse does arise, it is immediately suppressed, and by reason of repetition of this suppression process the acquiescent do-nothing habit is firmly established.

The term suppression, or total suppression, is meant to signify that the desire is gone out of the personality completely— that it does not hang around in the subconscious or unconscious, seeking egress into consciousness again at some favorable opportunity. Some psychologists hold that there is no such thing as total suppression of a wish while others hold that there is.[4] The psychoanalytical view is that once a desire is experienced, even though it never reach formulation in words (ideas), it is never so entirely destroyed, suppressed, or repressed that it may not return, though perhaps in disguised and symbolical form, to plague the individual. According to this view the desire is either held down in the unconscious by the main force and watchful police functioning of the conscientious "censor," or through sublimation (the second of our above-mentioned methods of readjustment) is allowed to drain off its energies in collateral, and perhaps diluted, streams of interest. If by the "unconscious" is meant instinctive impulses which are not usually defined in idea form and which are habitually inhibited or unconsciously sublimated, or, from the behavioristic standpoint, obscure physiological processes (reflex arcs and arc-complexes) of which the individual is entirely unaware, it is reasonable enough to suppose that no desire ever occurs without leaving some trace of characterization upon the personality, some latent tendency for the obstructed reflex-complex to be carried out should opportunity and stimulus to it ever recur.

Indeed, from a scientific, deterministic standpoint some such trace of characterization must always remain. The individual is the product of all his past reactions, both releases and repressions. This is succinctly put by Watson when he concludes, in italics, that "youthful, outgrown and partially discarded habit and instinctive systems of reaction can and possibly always do influence the functioning of our adult systems of reaction and influence to a certain extent even the possibility of our forming the new habit systems which we must reasonably be expected

---

[4] The latter view is supported by Dunlap's somewhat caustic criticism of the psychoanalytic position, in his *Mysticism, Freudianism, and Scientific Psychology*, 1920. See especially, pp. 46-50, 95, 105-108.

to form"; [5] and again, where, by implication accepting the psychoanalytic view, he says:

"Unquestionably the completeness with which old habits and the emotional factor connected with them which do not work are put away when the new situation is faced, tremendously modifies the type of personality each individual develops into. . . . Possibly no one of us escapes unscathed through the childhood and adolescence stages. The early situation when again faced by the adult may not call out the overt infant reactions but they do not wholly lose their power to stir up the old implicit emotional activity. . . . A great many individuals have water-tight compartments filled with old reaction systems which resist the storm and stress of adult life." [6]

While the reference here is to childhood desires and tendencies, the thought applies equally well to any balking of desire or interest which necessitates readjustment of reaction systems.

It should be remembered, however, that the psychoanalysts' conclusions have thus far been derived almost entirely from observation of mentally pathological individuals, in whom old and obstructed desires or "complexes" have not been discarded or even effectively repressed. Had they given more attention to normal individuals, it is quite possible that they would accept the idea of total suppression. In the case of normal personality, it makes little difference whether we call the process of getting rid of a desire which one does not care or dare to push against social obstruction, total suppression, or repression into the unconscious. The fact remains that so far as the individual's conscious life is concerned he does get rid of the desire and of the emotions experienced at the time of its obstruction, and that he has accomplished this riddance by a conscious exercise of will, by "direct action," without the conscious aid of sublimation devices. The bearing of these facts on the formation of social attitudes is that suppression, or repression, is not at all likely to produce radical attitudes.

(2) *Transference and substitution.* The second method of readjustment is by way of what the psychoanalysts have named sublimation—the substitution of other desires or interests and

---

[5] *Psychology from the Standpoint of a Behaviorist*, 1919, p. 408. See also Frink, *Morbid Fears and Compulsions*, 1918, p. 520.

[6] Watson, *op. cit.*, p. 416.

the transference to them of the attention and energy which would have gone to the realization of the old desire.[']

Substitution and transference may be consciously and purposefully undertaken and directed, or may be largely an unconscious process. New interests may be created, or old interests given greater attention, with the direct and conscious purpose of "taking the mind off" the disappointment and unrest occasioned by obstructed desire. The existence of this original desire is frankly recognized, but there is no attempt to suppress or repress it. It is simply deprived of support and is atrophied by disuse, since attention is withdrawn from it, and interest in it diminished, in proportion to the degree that they are transferred to the interest in process of substitution. The energy which would have gone into the realization of the original desire, had it not been balked, or which might have been used in attempts (perhaps successful) at suppression or total repression, or into the conflicts of a disorganized personality in the event that repression proved a failure, is now switched to other tracks which gradually develop capacity to handle the whole traffic. When this stage is reached and the old desire reduced to innocuous desuetude, the process of substitution and transference is complete. The abnormal disequilibrium produced by the balking of the original desire is corrected; the personality is compensated by the new interest. The individual's energies now continue to function with unabated vigor, though in new directions and to altered objectives.

This whole process may be carried out unconsciously, and perhaps is so in the vast majority of cases. Attempts at repression may be made and fail, or prove only partially successful. The repressed desire escapes the watchfulness of the "censor," but in disguised or symbolic form, in which form it may in weak temperaments play pranks enough to bring on a neurosis,

---

[']The term "transference" is used by the psychoanalysts in a highly technical sense, practically synonymous with the "conditioned reflex" of the behaviorists. (See Frink, *Morbid Fears and Compulsions*, 1918, pp. 192-197.) That is no good reason, however, why it should not be used in the way suggested in the text. There is no other term which suggests so accurately and definitely just what takes place in this second method of readjustment. Frink's term "displacement" and Dunlap's "drainage" mean the same thing, but do not seem to be as suggestively descriptive as "transference."

or may unconsciously be directed to new objectives which in conscious activity symbolize it and give release to it.

The final results of such unconscious transference and substitution may not be essentially different from those of conscious transference, except that where the process is consciously directed, intelligence has a chance to prevent or minimize the tendency to dispersion of interests and to the dilettantism likely to attend unconscious transference.

We are now in a position to note the influence of transference and substitution upon social attitudes. Whether the new interests to which the attention and the energy of the old desire are directed are of a conservative or radical nature will depend primarily upon the temperament and previous habituation of the individual. If he is of a non-resistant type, strongly motivated by fear complexes, or if he is deeply habituated to the existing general order of things—in brief, if he is a temperamental conservative—his transference will be to substituted interests not in conflict with the existing conventional order or the main trend of sentiment in his class and locality. If in such a temperament transference to radical interests does take place it is probably a case of "compensation," in the technical psychoanalytical sense. The non-resistant worm does sometimes turn, and when he turns, it is likely to be with tiger-like ferocity.

If on the other hand the individual be of a more assertive and pugnacious temperament, transference is much more likely to be of radical interests. In either case the new interests, especially where the transference is unconscious, are in a measure symbolical of the balked desire, and we may accordingly, for convenience, speak of symbolical conservatism and symbolical radicalism.

This kind of conservatism is very common. A vast amount of interest in and devotion to conventional social and religious activities has this background and motivation. No small amount of "social service," in charity work, social settlements, mission work, both home and foreign, "crusade," and "uplift" movements, is indulged in by individuals who are unconsciously compensating for balked dispositions. This is particularly true of volunteer work, and is probably truer of women than of men. Women are by no means alone, however, in this symbolical conservatism. Checkmated in the struggle for "success" on the commercial battleground, our male friend joins the army of back-to-the-land sentimentalists. Failing in his ambition for distinction in his field, the mediocre professional man settles down to routine work and creature comforts, and finds soothing release in an arm chair, popular magazines, an automobile and golf, and vicarious interest in the ambitions and activities of his children.[8]

It is now well recognized that much of the restlessness of modern women comes from the fact that the domestic duties of the home, under the modern small family system and since the factory and other non-domestic agencies have taken over so much of the work which formerly had to be done in the individual household, are not sufficiently engrossing to occupy the attention or to give outlet for instincts of workmanship and self-expression. This is especially the case with the woman whose children are "married and gone." She needs new interests to which to transfer her activities, now balked for lack of objective. Bridge and the movies are but imperfect substitutes, as any psychopathic clinic, or observation of the average highly domesticated "postgraduate mother," will bear evidence. Consequently certain aspects of the woman movement are not so wildly radical as some short-sighted opponents suppose. It can scarcely be considered irrational radicalism to ask, for instance, for such change in social conventions as will allow the postgraduate mother to transfer her now balked attention and energy to substitute interests of more social utility than the organized futility of social functions and "literary" clubs, without feeling that she is violating the accepted canons of taste and respectability.[9]

In temperaments strongly actuated by fear-complexes, desire-obstruction and transference of attention may lead to a different type of symbolical conservatism. The anger and resentment which in one form or another always accompany the balking of a wish and which usually produce the impulse to blame

---

[8] It is commonly said that children help to keep parents young (via this vicarious interest), but there is perhaps quite as strong an influence toward hastening the oncoming of attributes of age.

[9] Cf. Anna Garlin Spencer. *Woman's Share in Social Culture*, 1913, Ch. 8.

somebody are turned inward upon the self. The painful emotions of the obstructed desire are reinforced by self-castigation, the conviction of having made an ass of oneself, or a sense of sin. Under the impression that the desire was improper or sinful, the individual may resort to philosophical or mystical doctrines of resignation and renunciation, and in order to realize these ideals in his living he reinforces the consciousness of wrong-doing or of sin, and then proceeds to the task of self-reform through repression and sublimation. The resentment which in some cases might have been directed against other persons, against the social organization, or "fate," is turned upon the self, and the energies of the balked interest transferred to the task of reshaping the personality. Personal "salvation" becomes a leading interest, symbolical of the obstructed desires.

It needs no erudite analysis to suggest that here has been the opportunity of the church, managed by conservative interests, to utilize the processes of sublimation and transference to keep restless individuals suffering from the social and economic obstruction of legitimate desires and ambitions, from turning their baffled energies to the reform of social relations. As long as religion could be kept a matter of sense of sin and personal salvation, producing, through various types of mystical sublimation, acquiescent attitudes of resignation and contentment, it remained a powerful agent for conservative control. It is of very great significance when the church, as in America at the present time, begins to turn its attention, in part at least, to the removal of social and economic obstructions to the development of strong and symmetrical personalities. It indicates that the old processes of repression and introspective transference are recognized to be inadequate to the development of the type of character demanded by the conditions of modern life. Where the church until recently encouraged the dissipation of personal energy in repression or mystical idealism and self-reform, practically to the ignoring of social and economic causation of "sin" and misery, the more intelligent and progressive part of it now seeks to direct the transfer of balked-interest energy to channels and objectives which may prove quite the reverse of conservative.

Symbolical radicalism results from unrest and disequilibrium when the attention is transferred from impeded interests to radical movements or "causes." It is not essential that the movements to which the energy is transferred should be such as would, if carried through to success, remove the specific obstructions to the balked desire. The repressed energy may be placed at the service of the first radical movement which claims attention. All radical social movements aim at thorough-going change of social organization or relations in some one particular or more, and the motive to the desired change is the removal of obstruction of some kind. Hence any radical movement may take on, for the individual in question, a symbolical character. Since one cannot satisfy the original desire, although it is felt to be entirely normal and legitimate, and realizes that the seat of the obstruction is somewhere in the existing social *status quo,* and also perhaps believes that the specific obstacle cannot be removed, attention and energy are turned to another type of obstruction or to generalized revolt against all and any of the elements of control in the present social system. In extreme cases this leads to the anarchistic attitude, and it summarizes some of the psychic processes of the "working stiff" and I. W. W.-ism, to whose abnormal but natural and perhaps justifiable complexes Carleton Parker and others have so strikingly called our attention.

Symbolical radicalism, due to more or less unconscious transference of the energy of balked or repressed interests, may be found in the intellectual type of mind, but is more prevalent in emotional types. Such radicalism is likely to be superficial, emotional, lacking in settled principle, and unstable in its aim or object of attack. There may be a sort of serial transference. When one line of attack or radical project encounters difficulties and does not move rapidly toward consummation, it is given up (a wish easily balked) and the attention turned to some other project which for a time elicits equally emotional enthusiasm and serves as another temporary outlet for the energy of the balked or repressed desire. There may thus develop radical fashions and fads and a sort of lo here! lo there! radicalism, which never "stays put" long enough on one thing to accomplish any thoroughgoing objective change in social organization. Such radicalism is merely a sort of spiritual *Wanderlust.*

(3) *Reinforcement.* The third method of readjustment con-

sists in conscious reinforcement of obstructed desire. Instead of suppressing the balked disposition, attempting to repress it, or "sublimating" it by transference and substitution, we make the desire a conscious, dynamic, motivating force to its own realization in spite of obstacles. This involves bringing to its support the determination to remove the obstructions and "see the thing through," perhaps against all odds. We put on our fighting clothes, and instead of wasting energy in repression, self-pity, split personality, or symbolical and diffused sublimation, we proceed in militant or workmanlike manner to clear the ground for the realization of the obstructed interest.

This is the central line of radical motivation and action, so far as the radical attitude is the result of balked dispositions. Where obstruction and reinforcement reaction lead to absorption in the radical movement or program designed to remove the specific obstructions, the final result may amount to a practically complete transference, for the time being, of the interest of the original desire to interest in winning the victory over the agencies which have occasioned the obstruction. But the results of such transference are different and more pointed than those likely to flow from the transference hitherto noted. People who know what they want in the way of radical change, and why they want it, and who go out vigorously to accomplish the change, are far more likely to accomplish definite results (whether for good or ill) than those whose radicalism is of a symbolical and dilettante variety. In general, one of the mainsprings of progress is the aggressive reinforcement of impeded interest—the active, dynamic, and *directed* discontent which drives people to attack the obstructions to wish-fulfillment.

In Chapter VIII it is shown that the method and the effectiveness of desire-reinforcement vary with the degree to which the individual or group is dominated by emotion or by intellectual control. The practical, socially significant results of balked-interest motivation and reinforcement depend quite as much upon the method of reinforcement as upon the strength or amplitude of the unrest and discontent caused by the balking of desire and interest.

In the preceding discussion the motivation of radicalism has been found in the incompleteness of habituation and of acquiescence to the existing *status quo* and in the unrest and desire-obstruction which result from conflict of social interests and standards—the conflict between the tried and familiar and the novel and ideal.

We have now to raise the question whether all radical motivation is properly to be explained in terms of desire-obstruction and reinforcement, or whether there are instincts and proclivities which would produce the radical attitude even in the absence of obstruction and restrictive external controls.

That there are positive instinctive tendencies which give rise to desire for innovation cannot well be questioned. These include curiosity (the tap-root of all science), workmanship and contrivance (the root of the practical arts), and æsthetic self-expression (the root of the fine arts). There are also, in any differentiated social organization, proclivities such as imitation and emulation, sympathy and antipathy, desire for distinction, and the like, which certainly constitute impulses to innovation.

But whether these positive instinctive urges and socially aroused interests would in themselves produce the radical attitude depends, as was above suggested,[10] somewhat on the meaning which we are to give the term radicalism. If "radical" is a term to be applied to all desire for thoroughgoing innovation, it will apply to those who have such desire whether they encounter any social opposition or not. The great inventors and artists—all innovators—would then be classed as radicals. But if radicalism connotes innovative desire *opposed*, not by the difficulties involved in control of physical nature, but by social obstacles, socially unrestricted instincts of workmanship, contrivance, curiosity, etc., would not be regarded as motives to radicalism. This view of the matter would amount to drawing a distinction between innovative and radical desires. Innovative desire would then be called radical only when opposed. Such a distinction, while logically proper, is in fact somewhat academic, because in actual life there is scarcely any innovative desire, especially desire for thoroughgoing and fundamental innovation, which does not all along encounter more or less social opposition in the form of conservative and reactionary obstruction. In a society without serious conflicts of narrow selfish interests, and with freedom for the functioning of the

---

[10] Page 18.

instincts of curiosity, contrivance, and æsthetic self-expression, the inventor, the artist, and the engineer would be producing enormous changes in our mode of living. The motivation to their work would be the creative impulses and we could leave socially balked desires and obstructed interests out of the discussion. But we have no such society, and are not likely soon to have it. The very existence of self-expression instincts, seeking outlet in innovation, arouses opposition and institutes that balking of disposition and that unrest which we have described as the main source and cause of the radical attitude.

Conservatism (or reaction) and radicalism, as we have noted, are the opposite ends of the attitudinal spectrum. Innovation always has to contend against habit; social sympathy and co-operation against intrenched special interest; rational construction against sentimental dogmatic conventionalism, and courageous curiosity against fear. To all practical intent there is hardly a human interest or impulse which, if it involve any very serious innovative desire, will not encounter social opposition and become to that extent an obstructed interest.

From whatever reason, some individuals are temperamentally more inclined to innovative desires than are others. There are degrees of domination by fear and freedom from it, of originality and independence as contrasted with imitativeness and easy acceptance of authority, of habituation and refusal to become habituated. These differences of temperament appear in connection with all the great interests of life—curiosity and intellectual interests in general; workmanship, contrivance, and æsthetic expression; religious, ethical, and political interests; and acquisitive interests involving subjective standards of living, ambition, economic emulation, competition, and co-operation. Equally important temperamental differences exist with regard to motivation by egotism and sympathy, by hope, faith, loyalty, suspicion, distrust, desire for distinction, and desire for obscurity.

Now while desire-obstruction is probably the source of all radicalism, partly, as we have just seen, because any desire, or proposition, for innovation is sure to be opposed, it does not follow that the obstructed desire is always of a nature which popular ethical parlance would call "self-seeking." If there

.is a disinterested conservatism, it is quite as clear that there is also a disinterested radicalism.

Indeed, it is pertinent to ask whether there is a type of radicalism corresponding to the conservatism of direct, self interest, and whether "interested radicalism" should be set apart for separate treatment such as we have given interested conservatism.

It does not seem necessary or even feasible, to draw so sharp a distinction between interest and disinterest in the motivation of radicalism as we drew in the analysis of conservatism. This conclusion may seem illogical and even biased; but there are compulsive reasons to it.

In a sense, as was suggested in the discussion of conservatism, all human conduct—both "selfish" and "unselfish"—is interested, for we always follow the strongest urge, whatever it is, and it is the strongest urge which practically constitutes the self of the moment. In this deepest sense, radicalism as well as conservatism is, of course, "interested." But in a less recondite sense, most radicalism may be regarded as "interested." Radicalism is a product of discomfort; and most of the personal discomfort which drives people into radical movements is material, financial, maladjustment—a conflict between their subjective standard and their actual level of living.

It should not be held against radicalism that this is so, or written too fully to the credit of conservatism that there are so many disinterested conservatives. For it is difficult not to be self-centered when you are suffering from balked dispositions, and relatively easy to be tolerantly urbane, and appreciative of the beauty and balance of things-as-they-are when things-as-they-are make you pretty comfortable.

In a narrower sense still, there is some grossly, directly self-seeking radicalism, and some dishonest radicalism. A few members of the lowest classes, and possibly here and there representatives of other classes, are radical when it pays to be so. In times and places where militant radicalism is in control there are doubtless many individuals, conservative at heart, who simulate an insincere radicalism in order to save their own interests, perhaps their lives. Revolutions always draw in their train the criminal riffraff who love to fish in troubled waters.[11]

---

[11] G. Le Bon, *The Psychology of Revolution*, 1913, p. 99.

The same crowd will follow any counter revolution. Their existence should not be charged against either radicalism or conservatism.

A more legitimate illustration of self-interest in radicalism is to be found in those partial radicalisms—radicalisms *ad hoc* —which become defined whenever conflicts of special interests are sufficiently acute. Here may be mentioned as illustrations, the radical tendencies of the cattlemen, who, in their fight against the meat packers, have proposed measures radically at variance with the "American" idea of non-interference on the part of the government with business. The American farmer, in his hitherto futile attempts to protect himself from the organized commercial interests, has time and again manifested this *ad hoc* radicalism: granger legislation, greenbackism, populism, free silverism, co-operative marketing, "un-American" agricultural blocs in Congress, non-partisan leagues, and proposals for governmental fixation of farm-product prices, are all illustrative. Incidentally he has never failed to be roundly lectured for his foolishness. He has never been a real radical-from-principle, however. There would never have been a Non-Partisan League had the grain dealers not pressed the wheat growers a trifle beyond the limit of endurance.

It may be, however, that an interest-group, like the wheat-growers or the cattlemen, once pushed into an *ad hoc* radical channel and kept there for some time by the obstinate selfishness of other vested interests, will become used to the idea of radicalism and remain at least "progressive" even after the special evils they fought against are removed.

Certain types of radicalism are the result of desperation, of legitimate desires and interests so chronically balked, of such personal insecurity and exploitation, that the individual, normally of a conservative temperament, may be goaded into a violently radical (usually blame-anger reflex) attitude. Such misery, whether it arise from poverty or from exploitation and persecution, may lead to sympathetic grouping and assimilation of sentiment among large numbers of people. The solidarity of laboring class radicalism, with its collective sympathy within the working classes, may be regarded as a sort of pooling of individuals' balked desires. The lack of a more dependable solidarity may be due to a deficiency in sympathy and to the hard struggle which the workers are constantly compelled to make to retain living standards already won. Laboring class radicalism partakes somewhat of the characteristics of "gentlemen's agreements," and as is always likely to be the case with such loosely organized interests, there are always some who will violate the agreement as soon as personal advantage is to be gained by so doing. The average radical is perhaps no better, and no worse, than the average conservative in this regard.

By no means all radicalism, however, even in the lowly rank and file, has this type of life-history or this materialistic motivation. Direct personal and material discomfort may be the most effective motive to radical desire-reinforcement, but it is by no means the only important source of radicalism.

There is a spiritual maladjustment, a vicarious desire-obstruction, as well. The obstructed desire which produces radicalism may be, and often is, one arising from sympathy, rather than any form of narrow selfishness. Radicalism is then due to sympathetic understanding of the maladjustments, the untoward lot, of other individuals.[12]

A social radicalism may result also from an outraged sense of order, of economy and efficiency, or of beauty, not in regard to matters touching the immediate, much less the material,

---

[12] Mr. Victor F. Yarros ("Induction and Radical Psychology," *Psychological Review*, May, 1922) criticizes the analysis of the motivation of radicalism as it has been presented in this chapter and as it first appeared in practically the same form in the *Psychological Review*, July, 1921. His criticism is based on two counts: first, that analysis of radical motivation should be inductive, based on a study of the lives of great radicals, whereas the present analysis follows psychoanalytical lines; and second, that such an inductive study would reveal the fact that many men have been radical, not from balked disposition, but from sympathy and intellectual conviction as to the waste and inefficiency of the existing order. There can be no question that the suggested inductive study should be made, but it may confidently be anticipated that it will reveal in every radical some obstructed desire, though he may not be conscious, as Mr. Yarros apparently is not, of obstruction. That many men and women are radicals from sympathy, and from intellectual conviction as to waste and maladjustment in a society which has given them materialistically and personally little to complain of, was noted by the present writer in an article on "Emotion, Blame, and the Scientific Attitude in Relation to Radical Leadership and Method" in the *International Journal of Ethics*, January, 1922. There is thus little difference between Mr. Yarros's views and those of the present writer, who is as far from charging all radicals of *materialistic* balked desires as from holding that all conservatives are calculatingly selfish.

interests of the individual, but in regard to social maladjustments which offend the (otherwise comfortable) individual's
sense of justice, fitness, and balance. This is cogently put by
Achille Loria.[13]

"It is unquestionably one of the strangest of anomalies exhibited by the polychrome flora of human thought that revolutionary blossoms should so frequently spring from aristocratic seeds,
and that the most incendiary and rebellious spirits should
emerge from a domestic and social environment compounded
of conservatism and reaction. Yet when we look closely into
the matter, we find it less strange than it may have appeared
at first sight. It is, in fact, not difficult to understand that
those only who live in a certain *milieu* can fully apprehend its
vices and its constitutional defects, which are hidden as by a
cloud from those who live elsewhere. It is true enough that
many dwellers in the perverted environment lack the intelligence which would enable them to understand its defects.
Others, again, are induced by considerations of personal advantage to close their eyes to the evils they discern, or cynically
to ignore them. But if a man who grows to maturity in such
an environment be at once intelligent and free from base elements, the sight of the evil medium from which he himself has
sprung will arouse in his mind a righteous wrath, and a spirit
of indomitable rebellion will transform the easy-going and
cheerful patrician into the prophet and the revolutionary. Such
has been the lot of the great rebels of the world, of men like
Dante, Voltaire, Byron, Kropotkin, and Tolstoi, who all sprang
from the gentle class, and whose birthright placed them among
the owners of property."

Most radical leaders, from whatever rank of society drawn,
are men and women of broad sympathies and much capacity
for self-sacrifice, in the accepted sense of the term. The life
of the radical leader is not usually the type of life that an
inherently selfish individual would choose.[14]

There is current much conservative allusion to "self-seeking
agitators," sponging off the rank and file, which should be
taken for what it is—propaganda,—but it cannot be gainsaid,
on the other hand, that some radical leaders do not rise above

---

[13] Karl Marx, 1920, pp. 37, 38.
[14] Cf., for illustration, Ernest Poole, *The Harbor*, Ch. 8.

narrowly selfish motivation.[15] It is to be recognized also, that some persons join radicalism from such superficial motives as desire for momentary distinction, straining after originality through difference from the common run of their class, or simply because radicalism may be fashionable. Doubtless some intellectuals have been drawn into radical associations and movements not so much from spontaneous sympathy for the working masses as by a chance to escape the boredom of their class and to experience the interest of the novel and perhaps not quite "respectable."[16]

In spite of exceptions, however, it remains true that the average social radical is a man of wider, or at least of more intensive, sympathies than is the average well-to-do, contented conservative. Many a radical leader knows from personal experience what the repressed and obstructed desires and interests of the working classes are. He is also in position to have a keener realization of the divergence which exists between social activities and the principles which are supposed to underlie them and to give them ethical support.

In the socio-economic field, narrowly egoistic interests are not likely to lead to a sincere radicalism, the real radicalism of principle; at most they may lead to the symbolical radicalism resulting from random transference, mentioned above. Social radicalism, while it quite naturally has an admixture of motive resulting from balked personal ambition, is mainly the result of balked social sympathy and of reflective impatience with existing social wastes and injustices. No one can say truthfully that the world's great radicals, in whatever field, have not been sincere, or that they have opposed the established order out of selfish personal motives. The way of the non-conformist leader is never so easy that men and women would seek it from other than motives of high idealism.

---

[15] See, for instance, Ferrer, *The Origin and Ideals of the Modern School*, 1913, Ch. 1.

[16] Cf. J. S. Shapiro, "The Revolutionary Intellectual," *Atlantic Monthly*, June, 1920, pp. 820-830.

CHAPTER VII

THE ORIGINS AND CHARACTERISTICS OF RADICALISM

THUS far we have analyzed only the more individual or personal aspects of radical motivation. It is now necessary to inquire into the social conditions and processes which tend to create the situation in which interests are seriously obstructed and desire for innovation stimulated. Examination of the social sources of radicalism will throw additional light on its motivation.

1. *The Selection of Progressive and Radical Types*

We saw in Chapter III that in organic evolution and social selection are to be found certain influences tending to the development and perpetuation of the conservative temperament. Once a species has become adjusted to a tolerably stable environment, natural selection continually eliminates the individuals that depart far from the structural and functional norm appropriate to survival and success in that environment. In the great sweep of biological and anthropological development man has been no exception to this rule. The biologically unfit perished. And when the stage of social organization, however crude and simple, was reached, social selection—the elimination of non-conformists—began. It is well to keep in mind that social selection—especially in its milder types currently active in civilized societies—ordinarily functions not so much by killing out the undesired individuals and types as by placing them under such handicap that they are deprived of success, prestige, and influence.[1]

---

[1] For illustration, take the situation in England about the time of the Reform Bill of 1832, "The Whigs formed an aristocracy of great families exclusive in their habits and associations, and representing the tastes of the old *regime*. The new men (the so-called 'Radicals') . . . were no congenial associates for the high-bred politicians who sought their votes, but not their company. . . . The Whigs held all the offices, and engrossed every distinction which public service and aristocratic connections confer." May, *Contitutional History of England*, 1863, Vol. II, pp. 72, 73.

Not always, however, is the selection, survival, and success of conservatives favored by the social situation. There are other aspects of the selective process.

In the first place the exceeding multiplicity of nearly related biological species and genera shows that many different types of organism can be adapted to the same environment. The whole process of organic evolution, especially to the extent that it has been due to wide mutations, is evidence that nature's analogy to the radical—the biological mutant—sometimes is far better adjusted to environmental exigencies than was the previously existing type. When the environment changes, readjustment in the structure and functioning of the species is necessary, with the result that what would have been in the old environment aberrant individuals now may be the fittest to survive. Capacity for readjustment becomes a prime requisite for survival. If the demands of the environment change (for instance through physiographic and climatic changes, or the incoming of new organic forms through immigration or successful mutation), the requisites for survival change, and survival then takes place either through the selection of new types or through the ontogenetic re-adaptation of individuals to the new conditions.

It is not desired to push this biological analogy very far, nor is there need to do so. Nevertheless it helps to an understanding of the fact that there are occasions on which the radical stands in closer relation to the natural order of things than does the conservative.

Many persons discount the historically plain fact that human society, in its structure, institutions, and processes, is by no means a static, changeless thing, but on the contrary highly changeable and dynamic.[2] They do not perceive that social institutions and relations, in their present form the result of the exceedingly rapid social evolution which has been going on in the century and a half since the political and industrial revolutions at the end of the eighteenth century, can hardly be, expected to retain their present outlines indefinitely. It has

[2] For what purports to be a scientific view of the psychology of radicalism, but which grossly exaggerates the static quality of human society and of the adjustment of human psychological reactions to a fixed social environment, see Stewart Paton, "The Psychology of the Radical," *Yale Review*, Oct., 1921, pp. 89-101.

always been the characteristic of shallow, dogmatic thought to take it for granted that the social organization and ideals existent at the time are final, and that sc .al change and evolution, except for minor and relatively insignificant details, have come to an end.[3]

Changes have been due to a variety of causes. Alterations in the physical environment have been widely influential.[4] Transformations in productive or predatory technique, sometimes traceable in their origin to climatic changes, more often to the dynamic influence of instincts of curiosity and contrivance, constitute a second group of causes. Altered relation between the size of the population and natural resources has in the past been a very powerful stimulus to social change,[5] both to technical progress and to the development of militaristic proclivities. Many other factors, some doubtless of a non-economic character, such as the growth of science and scientific method, the progressive rationalizing of the higher mental types, the rise of social stratification, and the development of social and humanistic ideals, have played their part.

It is but judicial, therefore, to realize and admit that the requisites for social survival and success have in the past been subject to change, and at times to revolutionary transformation. What Elizabethan courtier, for instance, would feel at home in the present court of St. James? What mediæval seigneur in contemporary rural France? What seventeenth century guildsman at the council table of the American Federation of Labor? Or what East Prussian junker in the Berlin of to-day? There is no reason to think that the requisites for adaptation are not changing to-day as rapidly as at any time in history.

Generally speaking, those societies and those individuals lacking in power of flexible adjustment are at a disadvantage.[6]

---

[3] Even radicals are not free from this "finality" sentiment, as concerns the state of society, once their particular reforms or revolutions are accomplished. See William Clarke, "Political Defects of the Old Radicalism," *Political Science Quarterly*, March, 1899.

[4] See Elsworth Huntington, *Civilization and Climate*, 1915.

[5] Cf. Spencer, *Principles of Biology*, 1866, Vol. II, Ch. 13, Sec. 373, 374.

[6] A classic exposition, one of the clearest ever penned, of the need of flexibility is that by Walter Bagehot, a conservative, in Ch. 2 of his *Physics and Politics*. Although written in 1869, it may still be read with profit.

Static conservatism in a dynamic environment is always fighting a losing battle. The progressive and radical attitudes thus have an important function to perform in the social evolutionary process—the function of furthering necessary readjustments.

Given an individual with certain potential capacities, given an environment with a certain wealth or poverty of resources, of opportunity, and of stimulus, free and effective functioning, and the happiness which comes from it, are conditioned by the degree of adjustment between the individual and the environment. Were the environment changeless, the problem could be solved once for all by the genetic selection of adaptable stocks and by the ontogenetic habituation of their individual representatives to the static society into which they were born. The problem would be simply that of maintaining a *status quo* from generation to generation. But no such changeless environment exists. Even those would-be hermit groups or nations which might prefer, like China, to be let alone, to pursue undisturbed the ways of their fathers, are not permitted the peace, the somnolence, of isolation. The rest of the world compels them to break their shell. The world has reached such a stage of technological interdependence that they cannot maintain their isolation. The Western World cannot, if it would, prevent its dynamic unrest from filtering out to the ends of the earth.

In a static society, restless radical temperaments, if they appeared at all, would be repressed into submissive conformity. In a dynamic state no such policy of suppression can succeed. In the long run it will produce catastrophic revolution in the place of evolutionary readaptation.

In fact, a policy of repression can succeed only for a time even in a relatively static society. The great mass of men may perhaps be habituated for a time to any kind of social organization, even one, of slavery and tyranny. Always, however, obscure currents of malcontent, restlessness, and aspiration work their way through portions of the population. If they do not break through to the surface in some spontaneous movement of reform, sooner or later some temperamental radical appears on the scene, with vision, with daring, with dynamic stimulative energy, to focus and make articulate the undertones of unrest; and a revolt movement, long in unseen gestation, is born with a sud-

denness stunning to the contented, unambitious, and unimagina-
tive conservatives.

The "great man," however, is not the cause; he is but the
expression of radicalism, of the hitherto inarticulate and unorganized desire for readjustment. The real cause lies in a progressive maladjustment in institutional organization and process, and in a shifting of internal, spiritual needs. Both the
individual and the social environment undergo change, but not
always at the same rate, or in the same direction. The balking
of desire and interest, to which we have traced the main motivation of radicalism, is in large degree the result of social
changes altering the demands made upon the individual.

These demands change more for some classes than for others.
Some sections of the population are relatively exempt from
institutional changes which cause a profound transformation in
the position of other sections.[7] The Industrial Revolution, for
example, produced a much more sweeping change in the lot of
the working class than it did in that of the landed aristocracy.
The introduction of labor-saving devices not infrequently throws
a whole craft into unemployment, but causes hardly a ripple of
adversity on the life of those modern absentee owners, the hold-
ers of corporation securities. This difference in the directness
and intensity with which outward changes impinge upon different classes goes far, as Veblen points out, to account for the persistence of conservatism in the "industrially exempt" classes
and the growth of unrest and radicalism in those classes upon
whom falls the major force of change in industrial organization
or technological process.

Those not exposed to the new conditions are exempt from the
necessity for readjustment; they are not made immediately
uncomfortable by the change; hence they see no need of social
or ethical readjustment, and remain conservative. Those exposed to the full force of the altered environment have to
readjust their habits and point of view.

"Anyone who is required to change his habits of life and his
habitual relations to his fellow men will feel the discrepancy
between the method of life required of him by the newly arisen
exigencies, and the traditional scheme of life to which he is

---

· See Veblen, *The Theory of the Leisure Class*, 1899, Ch. 8.

accustomed. It is the individuals placed in this position who have the liveliest incentive to reconstruct the received scheme of life and are most readily persuaded to accept new standards; and it is through the need of the means of livelihood that men are placed in such a position." [8]

But this explanation of the difference in the attitudes of different individuals and classes, while it undoubtedly hits upon the main line of causation, does not tell the whole story. External pressure, chiefly of an economic sort, is the same as the "obstruction" to wish-fulfillment which we have treated as the central psychological cause of radicalism. But we have not closed the door to the recognition of temperamental radicalism and conservatism—born radicals and born conservatives. [9] Periods of rapid change in economic technique, in shifting of influence and power from one section of the people to another, and in material standards and manner of living, will inevitably give freer scope to these nervous, restless temperaments, which in more static conditions have little opportunity to express their restlessness in an articulate or organized manner.

That there is a valid distinction between the phlegmatic temperament, not easily rendered prey to discontent, and the alert, nervous temperament, quick to irritation by stimuli or conditions which have little effect upon the easy-going, few will be disposed to question. There is good ground in the facts of physiological psychology, imperfect as our knowledge in this field is as yet, for such a distinction. It is popularly known that a dyspeptic or a man suffering from over-fatigue is very likely to be "touchy," irascible, and difficult to please. It is known, too, that variations in the secretions of the various ductless glands, especially the thyroid and adrenal, produce profound changes in metabolism, in physical health, and in emotional tone. Attitudes, including conservatism and radicalism, are the result of complexes of instinct, emotion, and habit. All of these have their physical basis in body structure and process. It would not be strange, therefore, were it ultimately demonstrated that

---

[8] Veblen, *The Theory of the Leisure Class*, 1899, p. 195.

[9] It should be noted that Veblen also keeps in mind the fact that there may be in a changing society a selection of conservative or radical types, as well as ontogenetic adaptation of individuals to changing conditions.

the glands, and the autonomic nervous system, developed to different degrees of functional activity in different individuals, were in large part responsible for difference in emotional type and temperamental attitude. The more sensitive, keyed-up, and active the individual is made by excessive secretion of his thyroid or adrenal glands, for instance, the more likely he is to be critical of his surroundings and irritated by them. He is not inclined, indeed, oftentimes not able, to take desire-obstruction with the same philosophical or cynical equanimity with which more phlegmatic persons meet it.[10]

Frink, an able psychoanalyst, sees a direct connection between high nervous tension and radicalism:

"It is nothing to the discredit of any movement to say that perhaps many of its conspicuous supporters are neurotics, for as a matter of fact it is the neurotics that are pioneers in most reforms. The very normal people who have no trouble in adjusting themselves to their environment, are as a rule too sleek in their own contentment to fight hard for any radical changes, or even to take much interest in seeing such changes made. To lead and carry through successfully some new movement or reform, a person requires the constant stimulus of a chronic discontent (at least it often seems so) and this in a certain number of instances is surely of neurotic origin and signifies an imperfect adaptation of that individual to his environment. Genius and neurosis are perhaps never very far apart, and in many instances are expressions of the same tendency."[11]

We need not go so far as Frink does in this suggestion, yet that there is a casual relation between nervousness and radicalism cannot well be doubted.

2. *Radicalism as an Impulse to Freedom.*

To great extent, especially at junctures necessitating choice, human beings act as if they were driven by two fundamentally

---

[10] On the relation of the ductless glands to emotional tone, see Watson, *Psychology from the Standpoint of a Behaviorist*, 1919, pp. 181-193, 219-226. For fuller exposition see: S. W. Bandler, *The Endocrines*, 1921; L. Berman, *The Glands Regulating Personality*, 1922; W. B. Cannon, *Bodily Changes in Pain, Hunger and Rage*, 1920; Benjamin Harrow, *Glands in Health and Disease*, 1922; E. J. Kempf, *Psychopathology*, 1920.

[11] *Morbid Fears and Compulsions*, 1918, p. 136.

opposed motives—fear and courage. Fear means the impulse to seek safety; courage implies impulses to self-expression and the desire for freedom. These fundamental tendencies and some of their derivatives may be contrasted in some such tabular form as the following:

Fear	*Courage*
timidity	aggressiveness
self-abasement	self-assertion
acquiescence	resistance
indifference	interest
avoidance	curiosity
imitation	contrivance, workmanship, innovation
seeking safety	seeking freedom

With the radical, whether he be so from external circumstance or from temperament, the desire for freedom is stronger and more active than in the conservative, because the conservative either sets a lower valuation on freedom or represses his desire for it.

There are many reasons for thinking that desire for freedom is the ultimate, though not always conscious or expressed, motive to most radicalisms. There is every reason to suppose, also, that as life becomes more rationalized, the demand for freedom will undergo growth in amplitude and intensity. The demands that individuals, especially the working classes, make on life are constantly increasing. The objective standard of living has been rising, at least if we take long enough periods for comparison, but subjective standards—the way people think they ought to live—have been rising much more rapidly and persistently.[12]

It is impossible to put a definite limit on aspiration, to say

---

[12] If we take only the period since 1890 in the United States the rise in the objective standard of living is problematical. The most painstaking statistical analyses, while they leave much to be desired with regard to the sufficiency of their data, reveal no increase. See especially, I. M. Rubinow, "The Recent Trend of Real Wages," *American Economic Review*, Dec., 1914, pp. 798-817; H. P. Fairchild, "The Standard of Living—Up or Down," *American Economic Review*, Mar., 1916, pp. 9-25; F. W. Jones, "Real Wages in Recent Years," *American Economic Review*, June, 1917, pp. 318-330; P. H. Douglas and Frances Lamberson, "The Movement of Wages, 1890-1918," *American Economic Review*, Sept., 1921, pp. 409-426.

that the actual living standard can rise so high and no higher; and there is no inherent reason why the working classes should be satisfied with any particular standard, *e.g.*, with a "living" wage.

The more control we acquire over nature, the greater the development of our technological productive power, the more education, culture, and opportunity we have, the more we demand. Those who get a real taste of the cup of life wish to drink ever deeper. With the one great exception of war—and perhaps even there—the world appears to become less tolerant of waste and maladjustments which impair the value of living. Even in complacent, tolerant America, long so sentimental about "our exhaustless natural resources," and still of all the leading western nations the most careless of human life, such diverse movements as prohibition, conservation of forests, child welfare, reduction of infant mortality, the Sheppard-Towner Maternity Act, and the Federated Engineering Societies' Report on "Waste in Industry," [13] show a strong and healthy tendency to increased demand on life and on the efficiency of social organization and control.

The growth of population and the revolutionary rapidity of change in economic technique and organization since the Industrial Revolution have brought a host of new evils, but we no longer regard them with fatalistic resignation as unavoidable visitations of a disciplinary Providence. This growing intolerance of evil, and these increasing demands on life, are but illustration, in both material and spiritual realms, of what the political economists long ago discovered as the "expansibility of human wants." The truth of this concept was much larger, however, than the economists imagined. Wants have not only indefinitely expanded, but have deepened in intensity, and, in spite of some indications to the contrary, probably in refinement. The expansion of wants is by no means confined to the realm of material commodities and services.

A little reflection on the trend of social history for the past hundred, and especially the past twenty, years will suggest some of the main causes of this modern expansion and intensification of desire and interest, and the attendant persistent demand for

[13] New York, 1921.

greater individual freedom. The labor movement, the woman movement, the movement for constitutional democracy, the demand for the rationalization and democratization of family relations, the revolt against the narrower Puritanism in art, morals, and literature, the fight now being waged again against those who would shackle freedom of speech, press, and assembly —all these are among the expressions of this demand for freedom, itself in large part the result of expansion, refinement, and rationalizing of desire and capacity to live.

We live in a larger world to-day and know more about it. Communication, cheap printing, almost universal literacy, have made the masses immensely more alert and more aware of their relative situation than they ever were before. Public education has formed the basis not only of industrial efficiency, but of industrial unrest. The growth of democracy and the doctrinaire emphasis, in America at least, on individual worth have made the working masses resentful of class distinctions.[14] This resentment, positively formulated as demand for equality of opportunity and the elimination of waste and exploitation, has been furthered by a host of organizations and propagandas, each in its way an educative influence. Authoritarianism has broken down. Except where the expediencies of social conflict bring it back in the form of party discipline—especially in the socialist parties—its place is taken by a developing rationalizing of life. The decay of religious and moral authoritarianism gives the emotional capacities of man freer scope, and this leads to a keenly felt conflict between established norms and the demands of the personality.

---

[14] Karl Kautsky, in a recent work, expresses some doubt as to the influence of democracy: "Democracy develops mass organizations involving immense administrative work; it calls on the citizen to discuss and solve numerous questions of the day, often of the most trivial kind. The whole of the free time of the proletariat is more and more taken up with petty details, and its attention occupied by passing events. The mind is contracted within a narrow circle. Ignorance and even contempt for theory, opportunism, in place of broad principles, tend to get the upper hand. . . . On the other hand the degenerating influence of democracy on the proletariat need not be exaggerated. Often it is the consequence of lack of leisure from which the proletariat suffers, not of democracy itself. . . . On the contrary, the antagonisms in capitalist society become more acute and tend to provoke bigger conflicts, in this way forcing great problems on the attention of the proletariat, and taking its mind off routine and daily work." The Dictatorship of the Proletariat, pp. 38-40.

It is to be remembered, moreover, that the personality, and the desires and interests which characterize it, are in great measure the result of imitation and emulation. In a definite class or caste system the range of emulation is strictly limited by class lines. The amplitude of desires and interests for any given class, especially the lower classes, is circumscribed. Habituation to status precludes the rise of wants which are normal to classes above. There may, in consequence, be but slight development of a consciousness of unfreedom and little apparent discontent or restlessness. As soon, however, as even vague intimations of democracy dawn upon a people, and class lines become less keen-cutting, class itself becomes a powerful stimulus to unrest. For now imitation can cross class boundaries; it becomes emulation in one of its most virulent forms. The high regard in which prestige models, consciously or unconsciously supplied by, and embodied in, the upper classes, are held, fans the emulative desires to an intensity beyond all opportunity for their realization. However much the upper classes may prize exclusiveness and isolation, they nevertheless, from commercial motives, encourage this emulation, through types of advertising that make insistent appeal to the emulative ambitions of the classes lower down in the social and economic scale.

Thus useless and conspicuous expenditure is encouraged, subjective standards of living rendered more elaborate and pretentious, and great masses of people are brought to sharpened discontent with their financial limitations. Here is a social significance of the doctrine of comparative poverty that is sometimes overlooked. The individual compares his lot not with that of his grandfather but with that of living contemporaries. Democracy, therefore, in conjunction with our so-called ''open'' classes, is itself bound to contribute to unrest, at least as long as it is not deeply enough founded to lift self-respect above the superficial level of emulative waste.[15]

Formal education also plays its part in the expansion of interest and the creation of desire for greater scope and freedom, and this in spite of the superficiality and pose of much of

---

[15] Cf. Cooley, *Social Organization*, 1909, Ch. 20, 21; Sidney and Beatrice Webb, *A Constitution for the Socialist Commonwealth of Great Britain*, 1920, pp. 59, 60.

our life and the shoddy character of much of our educational
fabric.

In spite of many indications to the contrary, it is safe to say,
generally speaking, that people to-day—perhaps even in Gopher
Prairie—are characterized by more alert sensitiveness, broader
and more rational appreciation, and greater disinclination to
submit to unnecessary repression or sublimation of legitimate
desires than ever before. In every social rank and field of
human interest, there is more sophistication, more *savoir faire,*
more tendency toward critical rationalism, more questioning of
the credentials of inherited authority. If we live in a period
of revolt, we are also the beneficiaries of an age of enlightenment. We are thus the heirs to a more alert and stereoscopic
awareness and a less easily opiated or discouraged idealism than
was the immediately preceding generation.

It is clear that these liberalizing processes and attitudes,
which are so prominent a feature of our life to-day, cannot but
greatly increase the probability and the prevalence of desire-
obstruction. The greater the range of an individual's contacts
and experience, the more likely, at least within a certain limit
of culture, he is to encounter objective obstruction, and hence
balking of his now multiplied and developed interests. And
the more he is removed from domination by irrational or super-
rational controls and authorities, the more the natural sponta-
neity of his temperament will be in evidence, and the more he
will demand freedom. This may go to lengths destructive of
all discipline or sense of social responsibility, or on the other
hand, may lead toward a clearer conception of the necessity for
cordial and effective social co-operation. But that is beside the
present point. Whether expansion of interests and of desire
for freedom leads to anarchy or to social processes better adapted
to serve human needs, the great probability remains that desire-
obstruction, and thence radical sentiments, will multiply.

On the other hand, we must not overlook the fact that there
are some temperaments which seem instinctively to dread experience. In individuals who approximate this type, experience
may engender both a poignant fear of living and a desire for
more freedom, a craving to escape their own timidity in the
presence of life. In times of rapid social evolution, when conventions and moral emphasis are changing with confusing quick-

ness, such individuals are the victims of an intense inner conflict. Whether experience will give them courage and impulse to desire-reinforcement, or intensify their timidity and their tendency to repression and conservative sublimation, cannot be told beforehand.

The chief barrier to the multiplication and refinement of interests is fear. Other things being equal, the more an individual is governed by instinctive, primitive fears and traditional superstitions, the more closely he will keep within a limited range and familiar routine of sentiment and action, and the more he will withdraw from the supposedly dangerous influence of ideas and associations.

Specialization and isolation have this narrowing and deadening influence, as can be observed in backward agricultural communities, in groups kept closely within the discipline of economic or ecclesiastical sects, and even in business and academic circles where narrow specialization is the price paid for "success." To fear and specialization, as well as to visionless selfishness, can be attributed the dead-level monotony and philistinism characteristic of much of our middle-class life, of the "domestic virtues," of "Gopher Prairie-ism" wherever found, and even of certain academic communities.

To the extent, however, that a really liberalizing education, observant travel, diversity of social contact, and broad-minded, courageous journalism multiply the stimuli to which the individual is subjected, and force him to *select* ideas, attitudes, and responses—in brief, to the extent that narrow routine habituation is broken in upon—fear becomes rationalized, and with rationalization diminishes.

The obstacles to freedom are thus both subjective and objective, but the subjective are not likely to diminish unless there is some diminution of, or escape from, the objective obstructions to the free unfolding of the human personality.

Only the exceptionally privileged are in position to escape in large measure these quite often irrational and wasteful external obstructions. Wealth confers the opportunity—too often left unutilized—to develop capacity for spontaneous expression of the positive creative impulses of workmanship, curiosity, and æsthetic appreciation. It is no strange fact, then, that the demand for economic opportunity has always been at the center of radical programs, or that temperamental radicals set a very high value on freedom, and are always skeptical of the necessity or value of making "the social compromise."

The main sources of desire-obstruction under modern circumstances may now be passed briefly in review.

The first limitation on the fulfillment of desires and interests is the limitation of material opportunity, or wealth, which arises from restricted supply of natural agents and the finite character of man's control over nature. The orthodox economists of the past never tired of pointing out the significance of these limitations. On the "niggardliness" of nature they built up the "dismal science" against which Carlyle and later the socialists thundered, not always without telling effect. To-day, without accepting the excessive optimism of the utopian socialists as to the possibilities of indefinitely lightening the toil and expanding the income of the masses, we are not so pessimistic as were the classical economists as to the kind of living the world can reasonably be expected to yield to the general population—so long as population is kept, by means of birth control, within reasonable limits as to size and quality. We realize our tremendous productive powers, given only an efficient organization and proper motivation, and we think less of the conflict with nature than the race has ever thought before. Before the development of modern industry, toil was more generally long and exhausting than it is now. A much larger percentage of the population than now had to work hard for a living, and practically their whole time was taken up with the demands of physical existence. Interests were narrow and simple; neither the intellectual nor the emotional life was as complex as it is to-day, nor had it need to be so. On the part of the men, at least, there was far less occasion for balked interests than there is to-day, largely because attention had to be concentrated upon the business of subsistence.

Under such circumstances the typical blame-and-anger reaction of balked desire could not ordinarily take place. If the crops were poor, or if a storm at sea wiped out a fishing fleet, there was no one to blame but the gods—or God—and blaming the gods is dangerous business. Hence resignation to the inevitable.

Technical progress has lightened toil, greatly reduced man's

bondage to nature, and given him comparative leisure and a
wider range of wants and interests. His dependence on nature
is of course admitted once for all, but is regarded rather as a
truism than as a problem. His attention is freed for other
than physical subsistence needs and is more spontaneously
directed to social affairs. His interests now develop faster than
his opportunities; conflicts of wants now appear in greater force
and variety between social strata and classes, and the obstructions to wish-fulfillment consequently multiply.

The second, social, and infinitely more effective, source of
balked interests is thus opened up. Combative impulses, anger,
and blame now assert themselves against the obstructions placed
in one's way by other individuals and other classes. Limitations
on individual liberty all seem to be due to the unfair aggression
or obstructionist attitudes of other people.

This seeming is in part truth, but only in part. For much
of the restriction of freedom and opportunity is, and will
always remain, due to limitations on our utmost power to
utilize material nature.   Where the dividing line between
natural limitations and restrictions due to social maladjustments lies no one can state with accuracy.   To realize what
latitude of opinion there is on the question one need only compare the views of the orthodox socialist with the orthodox
Malthusian's, or those of the biological eugenist with the environ-
mentalists.' The fact, however, that some individuals may discount our dependence on nature and wrongly attribute most
opportunity-obstruction to the machinations of exploiting classes
does not alter the force of the resentments felt or of their
tendency to create dogmatic-emotional radical attitudes.

In the third place, conflicts of interest between individuals
produce interminable conflicts within the same person.   Every
normal human being has illimitable possibilities of experience.
No one, at least no one who has not reached the neutral spiritual
state of an Indian yogi, escapes having mutually incompatible
desires. Logical limitations of time, place, and circumstance
give us only one actual life to lead as against the infinite number of possible lives we might lead. It results that even the
most staid and practical-minded person occasionally indulges
in ideals and day dreams, consciously or subconsciously. Day-
dreaming and the like may be only harmless ways of momen-

tarily escaping actualities, a sort of vicarious escape from specialization and discipline. Every individual has some time imagined himself to possess capacities and talents which he did not possess, and never would. But on the other hand there can be no doubt that in many if not most persons, there are, or have been, capacities, talents, proclivities, which have had no opportunity for development or expression, by reason of the necessity for specialization. In the processes of suppressing these possibilities and sublimating these interests, we are always in a sense killing ourselves—some one or more of our many potential selves. In general, the radical temperament, with its strong desire for freedom and self-expression, objects to more of this spiritual suicide than is necessary.

This desire for freedom gives additional weight to the conclusion that obstructed interests are the main source of radicalism. Constantly, in history and in social relations, we encounter this desire and the conflict it engenders between those in authority and their dependents—ruler and subject, husband and wife, parent and child, owner and slave, employer and employee. The struggles for political liberty, for religious toleration, for economic opportunity, and for intellectual freedom are all branches of the same tree of desire to escape bonds which tie down, formalize, or atrophy human personality.

Many individuals who do not overtly enter any of these struggles are at heart rebels and radicals, but are restrained from expressing their resentments and aspirations by various types of fear and considerations of expediency. That is one reason why radical movements, once well started, often grow with extreme rapidity. Many individuals who have been suffering from legitimate interests, balked by obstacles which the movement gives promise of removing, and who see that there is a growing and respectable company in the same situation, now take courage to recognize their desires and to join others for their collective reinforcement.

It is well to note, moreover, that thwarted instincts, repression, and the resulting sense of injustice and perhaps persecution, may produce in certain temperaments a fixed and ingrained attitude of irreconcilability. Thus may develop a chronically dissatisfied and thoroughly unreconstructible element in the population. How many such temperaments there are in the ranks of the various radical parties and movements no one knows. The number is probably grossly overestimated by conservative critics.

The radical's high valuation of freedom does not necessarily mean that he is in revolt against social control as such, but only that he objects to the way in which certain institutional limitations on freedom now operate. A certain type of radical, indeed,—the philosophical anarchist—does object to all forms of social control not the result of spontaneous and unforced concert and co-operation of individuals. But this attitude is so obviously based upon a thoroughly unscientific ignoring of human nature as it actually is (whatever it ideally should be) that it may be left out of consideration. Many radicals, not classifiable as anarchists, not to speak of many individuals and groups who would resent being regarded as radical, advocate diminution of this or that institutional limitation of personal liberty. This attitude may result from the suppression, by law or other forms of control, of habits and activities previously countenanced but now regarded as injurious to social welfare. Those most inconvenienced by the new dispensation may violate it simply because of the power of habit, or they may oppose it, sometimes sincerely, sometimes otherwise, on the ground that it is a dangerous step toward undue centralization of authority, and hence toward tyranny. Some of the opponents of prohibition, for example, are undoubtedly actuated by purely personal self-assertiveness—the product of pathological thirst or the human desire to do something forbidden—while others act under a sincere conviction that the Eighteenth Amendment sets a dangerous precedent with regard to the powers of the Federal and State governments.

On the other hand, far from insisting upon a direct and unmediated personal liberty, the radical may hold that individual freedom can be attained only through great increase in the effectiveness of social control. Nearly all socialists, whether of the state collectivist or the guild socialist school, hold this view. In this the radical is at one with the moralists of all ages, who have never wearied of sermonizing on the fact that liberty can be had only under law and order.

The radical differs very essentially from the conservative just here—in that he is thoroughly dissatisfied with an ''order,'' a system of organization and control, which seems to him to give little promise of furthering the solution of the difficult, but basic, problem of combining efficient social co-operation with individual liberty. The average advanced, thoroughgoing radical wants a social structure which will insure and promote genuine personal liberty. He regards the liberty so often extolled as the product of present organization as a somewhat Pickwickian matter.

It is not to be overlooked that insecurity is a very important cause of radicalism. Paradoxically, it may be said that many men are radical because they are naturally conservative. They wish, that is, assurance of a living at some customary standard, with which they would be, or at least think they would be, content for the rest of their lives. But they find that the existing social organization fails to assure them even reasonably continuous employment—in spite of the reiterated ''right to work.'' Consequently they maintain a deep-seated distrust of the existing order and come easily to believe that only revolution and transformation can give them security of employment and of life.

Industrial insecurity is regarded by Professor Commons as the central cause of economic radicalism. ''The greatest self-cure that it [capitalism] needs today is security of the job, for it is insecurity of jobs that is the breeder of socialism, of anarchism, of the restrictions of trade unionism, and a menace to capitalism, the nation, and even civilization.'' [16] Commons certainly over-estimates, however, the results which would flow from mere security of industrial employment. There are other and equally important sources of insecurity and obstructed liberty. As a perspicacious reviewer of Commons' book says:

''These chapters do not show us how capitalists can employ labor when they cannot sell their goods, how they can or will stop the pitiless drive for world markets in which to sell their goods, how they can or will prevent devastating imperialist wars such as the recent unpleasantness, or how they can or will stop the endless quest of human nature for something that it

---

[16] John R. Commons and Associates, *Industrial Government*, 1921, p. 272.

does not have, even after warm beds and full dinner pails have been provided." [17]

3. *Some Characteristics of the Radical Mind*

The radical lacks the conservative's attachment and conformity to things-as-they-are. His habituation and adjustment have been broken by social changes and intellectual stimuli from which the conservative is relatively exempt, or to which he is temperamentally impervious.

Feeling his maladjustment, the radical tends to become increasingly sensitive and critical. He persistently questions, or dogmatically denies, the rationality of his lot and that of others of his class and station. His spirit not infrequently becomes hypercritical.

With this, especially in the rank and file, goes a tendency to make impossible demands—sometimes impossible simply because the radical does not sufficiently understand the necessity, or know effective methods, of persuading enough people to see things as he does, sometimes physically as well as psychologically impossible. In other words the extreme radical may be, though he is not necessarily so, a visionary utopian. As the proof of the pudding is in the eating thereof, so the present value of an ideal depends, in great part at least, upon its chances of acceptance and application—a truism which the radical frequently overlooks.

On the whole the radical is more imaginative than the conservative. Either from personal experience or from a greater sensitiveness to maladjustment and a quicker sympathy with its victims, he draws a vivid picture of the untoward lot of the masses. The easy-going, comfortable conservative draws no pictures at all, or else a fancifully roseate comparison of the lot of the masses today with that of his grandfather, because his personal interests are not touched and he is not fired by the impulse of socially creative workmanship. A certain type of radical has constructive imagination. Not only does he see and feel present evil and ugliness, but he conceives a structure in which the major injustices and maladjustments would be avoided. If he be one of the increasing number, but still too few, practical

---

[17] Charles A. Beard, in the *Nation*, Nov. 9, 1921, p. 543.

radical idealists, his imagination is fertile in devising working programs by which the ideal may be approximated. At this point it is difficult to draw a line between the rational, hard-headed, moderate radical, and the advanced idealistic progressive or liberal.

It must be said that the mass of economic radicals, however, are almost as deficient in constructive imagination and practical innovative capacity as is the average conservative. They are quick to follow the lead of an intellectually powerful or sufficiently vituperative critic of the present social order, but they contribute little or nothing to constructive programs.

Nearly all men and women are victims of what the psychologists call "language habits." Words and phrases are reiterated and passed back and forth, until, if they ever had any definite meaning, they lose it. Formalistic verbiage takes the place of constructive, analytical discussion. A very heavy percentage of socialistic literature, as well as of criticism of socialism, is practically nothing more than empty verbiage revolving around the academic phraseology of Marxian economics. Just as liberal and conservative talk *ad nauseam* of "democracy," often without knowing what they mean by it, so the average rank-and-file socialist has contented himself with repeating, parrot-like, "class struggle," "increasing misery," "surplus value," and "exploitation."

Nevertheless, in spite of the prevalence of empty language habits, there is probably more real thinking done in radical than in conservative circles. If one were not brought to this conclusion on the *à priori* ground that discomfort, unrest, and a quick sympathy give radicals more to think about, and more stimulus to think, than the comfortable conservative has, observant association with both groups would force one to it. The intellectual radicals, at least, try to get down to basic principles; the conservatives regard basic principles as settled. To them these matters have become fixed habit, established matter-of-course—and as a result conservative talk, where not forced into pugnacious defense sentiment by the attacks of critical propaganda, too often degenerates into personal pleasantries or matters of repair and depreciation account.

While the mind of the rank-and-file radical may become just as set and inflexible as that of the uncritical conservative, the very stimuli which create radicalism tend to produce and perpetuate a certain mental alertness and flexibility lacking in the mind that habitually takes things-as-they-are as matter of course. The mind of the more intellectual and the more constructive radical of today is especially characterized by this flexibility, although the dyed-in-the-wool followers are strikingly lacking in it. He is constitutionally averse to accepting his ideals on traditional authority, not bound down to the intellectual and moral conventions of a self-complacent class or community, unfettered by any worshipful attitude toward the superior wisdom of the past, not afraid of social experiment, and as yet not a slave to the dictates of some radical party organization. So the intelligent, progressive radical is temperamentally never satisfied with the transformation or progress which, even with unbroken peace, society can accomplish in one individual's span of life. No sooner is one job done, than his active mind has conceived and planned another.

For this reason, if for no other, when society once begins consciously and effectively to rationalize its relations and to direct its own evolution toward ends of real justice, economy, and efficiency, we must expect to see progress accelerated to a degree now scarcely thought of. That we were already, at the outbreak of the war, entering upon such a period in this country can scarcely be doubted by one who will take the pains to study the history of social legislation and of change in social viewpoint during the past fifteen or twenty years. And no one doubts that the war proved a tremendous impetus to radicalism the world over.[18]

But the alertness and elasticity of the radical mind has another side. The instinct-like conservatism of youth has been alluded to. Every college teacher knows, however, another, though rarer, type of youthful mind: the enthusiastic, volatile temperament which seizes with avidity every new "ism," every new ideal or proposal for reform, and rushes, with a pressure so high that it is soon exhausted, into this and that movement, without pausing to understand or criticize its practicability or real desirability. This is the emotional radicalism of youth,

---

[18] See the *Nation*, Dec. 27, 1917, "The Proper Attitude Toward Socialism."

which, if not tempered and curbed by intellectual and critical discipline, leads either to early moral exhaustion, with its logical result—a sinking back into a humdrum acceptance of things-as-they-are—or to early crystallization into the dogmatism and irreconcilability of orthodox radical parties and sects.

If we find that radicalism perhaps tends to less equanimity, poise, and balance than does conservatism, we should undertand this as a natural consequence of the different relation in which radicals and conservatives respectively stand to the existing order of things. In normal times, the conservative is not subject to abnormal strain; he does not feel that society is not granting to him what is due him and his class; he moves among people who think and act and live as he does. Such stress as his nervous system endures comes from the ordinary cycles of life and from those competitions and conflicts of interest and ability which he accepts as a part of the order of nature. The radical, however, is usually in the minority. He is swimming against the current of established habit and sentiment. The burden of proof, and of being understood, is laid upon him; and the conservative takes care that it is not light.

Moreover, the radical is an idealist; the conservative is, in a sense, a realist. The conservative lives in what he calls a real world, and he is in the habit of parading the sentiment that it is a world of cold, hard facts. The radical lives in the world of facts, but also in that of his ideals. In a sense he is the victim of a divided personality; the gulf between his actual and his ideal world, or self, is such that he cannot help being in a state of more or less continuous mental unrest. The conservative is an idealist in a different sense, in that he idealizes the actual world by shutting his eyes to its maladjustments and deformities.

The alertness, flexibility, and idealism of the radical give a different texture and trend to his loyalty attitudes than have those which characterize the conservative. Like the hide-bound conservative, the doctrinaire radical is loyal to his principles, with a loyalty so intense, so dogmatic, and so uncritical that it blinds him to objective truth. But the radical is not attached to institutions as they are, and consequently not "loyal" to them —at least in that popular conception which regards loyalty and adverse criticism as mutually incompatible. He regards institutions as means, not ends; and as means they are not only open to scientific analysis and criticism, but to rational adaptation or transformation. The radical has usually found too many institutions standing in the way of his ideals to have much institutional reverence. It is precisely a certain institutionalizing of thought, belief, and sentiment, which constitutes the shell of custom and habit, which the radical has always to contend with. If the radical is marked by institutional loyalty at all, it is of a deeper and more philosophical sort, because his loyalty is to institutions idealized through his critical faculty and constructive imagination—to institutions as he hopes they will become in the future.

With regard to loyalty to persons, submission to the prestige of leaders, and hero worship, it is hazardous to draw comparisons. The "take-a-lead" instinct, and the human propensity to idealization for the sake of hero worship, are strong in all but the most highly trained and intellectual individuals. That radicalism is not free from these sentimental proclivities, that the average radical is almost as quick as the conservative in his respect for dogmatic authority, is evidenced by the conduct of the early Christians—certainly an extremely radical group in their time—and by the various socialist groups, each with its own prophet.

Nevertheless, the radical leader, unless he possess very unusual personal magnetism, like Lassalle and Marx, usually has a much more difficult position than does the conservative leader. He cannot appeal to such a complex of highly organized special interests—financial and otherwise. Nor can he escape the basic fact that all radicalism, in its very nature, is a criticism of, and in a measure a revolt from, existing controls and authorities. Something of this revolt from authority is bound to last over, to produce a separatist tendency within the radical groups themselves.

Evidences of this fact, apart from whatever personal acquaintance one may have with radicals and liberals, is to be found in the intense partisan quarrels which seem sooner or later to break out in all radical movements. Witness the bitter controversies between Marxians and Revisionists in the socialist congresses, the friction between "militants" and conservatives within woman suffrage organizations, and the great difficulty liberals in religion have in getting together in effective organization. The history of Protestantism is thickly sprinkled with the droppings away of sect after sect, in striking contrast to the remarkable and in itself magnificent solidarity of the conservative Catholic Church. And a certain suspicion of authority and discipline, together with an over-developed individualism of self-expression and narrow self-interest, must be a part of the explanation of the seeming incapacity of labor to obtain solidarity of organization and action.

This individualistic tendency, and the effort to curb it, explain the iron-bound rules of official radical parties—discipline which defeats its own end by limiting party membership and association to the relative few who can subscribe to doctrinaire creeds and submit to autocratic control. The discipline of some of the socialist parties has been quite as zealous as that of the Victorian church in the pursuit and expulsion of heterodoxy. The radical's aversion to authority is overcome, in his own organizations, only by constant reminders of the tactical necessity of solidarity and by provision for drastic discipline of the recalcitrant member.

Outside of his own organization, if he belong to one, the radical is a less obedient slave to the instinct of the herd than is the typical conservative. Not infrequently, he scorns, or affects to scorn, the public sentiment of a society which he believes to be crushed under a shell of thoughtless formalism. He comes to move as one apart, and the further he drifts from the main current of popular sentiment and prejudice, the less influence he has, unless he be possessed of unusual tact and a striking personality. To be a radical, or in some sections and classes even a liberal, means a certain degree of isolation, unless the individual can find enough others of his kind to form a supporting group. To be a radical is to be different; it is to be a non-conformist with the established standards of thought and belief; and the nonconformist is always drifting out of the current or swimming against it. Moreover he is always the object of a certain clannish suspicion and enmity. The herd does not take kindly to the stranger, whether in deed or in thought. Fear of this herd instinct, whether it be expressed quietly in simply letting the radical alone and thus making him feel that he is one apart, or in active opposition, prevents many persons from having non-conservative convictions, or when they do have them, from exhibiting the courage which is supposed morally to go with them.

As progressivism and radicalism gain ground, however, they gain adherents and numbers, and the erstwhile isolation of the nonconformist is broken. He finds himself one of many like-minded persons, and discovers that he has a part to play in an organized movement for a common end. When this stage is reached, radical discussion turns from criticism of the existing order to tilting as to the best means of reform or tranformation, and the way is opened for those internal dissensions which may retard the whole movement.

It is clear that the radical's whole scale and system of valuation differ in important respects from those of the conservative or even of the progressive. Values, whether economic, æsthetic, moral, or religious, are highly institutionalized and conventionalized. They are in a broad sense social. We prize what others prize. In any of the great fields of human interest values are largely the result of imitation.[19] But the radical, as he breaks with existing institutions or finds fundamental defects in them, logically and perforce first questions, then rejects, many of the values derived from their influence and conventionally accepted by the uncritical. Every institution tends, for the most part unconsciously and unpremeditatedly, to make itself an end rather than a means. The radical, on the other hand, with his institutionally balked interests, and his fundamental desire for scope and freedom, is an individualist in the truest sense of the term. Unconciously, radical parties and movements may forget for the time being their essential function as means, and come to be served practically as ends in themselves, but the insistent individualism of their members, and of other radicals not members, tends to keep alive and alert the recognition of the fact that the party is means and individuals the end. Hence it is generally true that the radical's standards of valuation are in one sense more directly individualistic and less conventional and traditional than those of the average run of the populace.

---

[19] For an illuminating discussion of the institutional nature of valuation, see C. H. Cooley, *Social Process*, 1918, Part VI.

We have noted the conservative's high valuation of "order" —by which he means the existing institutional controls and conventional relations. The radical, on the contrary, does not set a high valuation upon this order, because he is convinced that it is essentially not order, but confusion and disorder. He is impressed by the working at cross purposes, the lack of co-ordination of plan and effort, the waste and inefficiency, of our present society, especially in its industrial aspects.

The liberal has rather a sense of progress than either an exaggerated appreciation of the beauty and fitness of things-as-they-are, or a too violent reaction to the ugliness and injustice about him. The radical differs from the liberal in that his theory of progress is apt to be mutative. He assumes that progress takes place by jumps and crises—while the liberal's theory is rather that progress takes place opportunely, by small steps and continuous readjustment and improvement.[20]

What the conservative regards as his high valuation of order is often nothing more or less than a craven fear of the new and simple dislike of the inconveniences of readjustment. Moved by conviction of the insufficiency and hollowness of an order which he thinks does not promote progress in justice and freedom, with his critical eye on the defects of the present system rather than on its beneficent aspects, with a keen desire for accelerated and directed progress, and living as much in a world of ideals as of actualities, the radical welcomes every change which he thinks will bring society nearer to the standards which his constructive imagination has more or less definitely formulated as the next step in social evolution.

Placing a low regard upon the justice, efficiency, and progressiveness of the present order, in whole or in certain of its aspects, the radical naturally has little of that reverence for the past which is so striking a characteristic of conservative and reactionary. The radical sees the past as a period in which the passions of men retarded the development and use of constructive reason. He sees the whole social organization and point of view of the past so different from the present that he

---

[20] Herbert Hoover, for example, is quoted as saying that "the opportunity for advance in living standards lies more surely in the steady elimination of these [industrial] wastes than in great inventions," but he was speaking of mechanical, not social, progress.

concludes that past experience—recorded with more or less subjective bias by the historians—has little value as a guide to future constructive effort, unless it be to show us what to avoid. He sees the past so bound by superstition, dogmatism, and authority, of both political and ecclesiastical absolutism, not to mention scholastic metaphysics and mystical obscurantism, and so deficient in scientific knowledge and spirit, that to him it appears incapable of giving us much of value in the development of a rational organization and control for the democratic ends of health, opportunity, and happiness for all.

He has the less faith in the value of traditional viewpoints and standards because he finds, in the political field, that individuals have been regarded as existing for the state, and the state for the interests of a limited group or ring of privileged people, and in the economic field, that most of the economic thought— or language-habits—of the conservative and reactionary interests who oppose organization and regulation of economic relations for democratic ends are drawn from the doctrinaire individualism of the 18th century—a *laissez faire* policy which is incapable of just and effective application today. He sees the conservatives themselves apparently learning no lessons from the past, but continuing in one breath to cry for an impossible cessation of governmental regulations and restrictions and in the next for protective tariffs, state aid to private banking corporations in forcing loans upon reluctant, but weak, foreign nations, and government subsidies to shipping and transportation companies—policies which in principle are but a twentieth century application of the mercantilist policies of the sixteenth and seventeenth centuries.

It is not surprising, therefore, that the radical is far less actuated by fear than is the conservative. His intellectual attention, his quasi-religious attachment to the idea of change, his faith in the perfectibility of human relations, his critical capacity, and his constructive imagination greatly reduce, for him, the area of the unfamiliar; his mind is accustomed to functioning in realms of prophecy and speculation which the matter-of-fact conservative dreads to enter. Moreover, radicals very commonly have little to lose and much to gain from social change, even of a highly questionable and experimental nature. This last, however, is true only of those men and women, chiefly self-sacrificing leaders, who have freed themselves from bondage to material things.

The fear which influences the radical is suspicion—distrust of the motives of the classes that have power and prestige. Every movement and organization which preaches or acts upon the doctrine of class antagonism increases the depth and scope of this suspicious attitude.   The socialist class struggle theory has done so, the syndicalists and I. W. W. make it the basis of their creed and policy, while on the other side employers' organizations, open-shop associations, and, abroad, the erstwhile domination of church and clerical parties by the political authorities [21] have done their part to increase the gulf between the masses and the classes, and to make it increasingly difficult for either to understand the other's point of view or see any good in it.

But if the radical is characterized by an over-measure of distrust, and exhibits too frequently and without due respect for the feelings and sentiments of others, its derivative, a somewhat egotistic pugnacity, he is also the vessel of undaunted hope and abiding faith—hope in future realized ideals, faith in the ultimate rationality and perfectibility of human nature. It is this larger faith in man, in what life may be, and specifically in our ultimate power to organize collective life for the ends of individual freedom and personality which, perhaps more deeply and

---

[21] See, for example, Adele N. Phillips and Russell Phillips, "The Decline of the Berliner," *Atlantic Monthly*, January, 1918, pp. 19-20.

"In the episcopal oath of fidelity to the Crown, which all must take who seek to preach the divine word, the solemn oath is administered. 'I will be submissive, faithful, and obedient to his Royal Majesty,—and his lawful successors in the government, as my most gracious King and sovereign; promote his welfare according to my ability; prevent injury and detriment to him; and particularly endeavor carefully to cultivate in the minds of the people under my care a sense of reverence and fidelity toward the King, love of the Fatherland, obedience to the laws, and all those virtues which in a Christian denote a good citizen; and will not suffer any man to teach or act in a contrary spirit.   In particular, I vow that I will not support any society or association, either at home, or abroad, which might endanger public security, and will inform His Majesty of any proposals made, either in my diocese or elsewhere, which might prove injurious to the state.   I will preach the word as His Gracious Majesty dictates,'—and so forth. . . . In consequence of the strange words uttered in the pulpit, the people, being aroused, distrust the church.   They fear that it has been subordinated to the political system."

fundamentally than any other trait, characterizes the radical mind.

The active radical simply cannot be a cynic, though he may tire us with his refrain, "Eventually, why not now."

CHAPTER VIII

THE METHODS OF RADICALISM

1. *Psychological Phases of Radical Method; Emotion and Blame in Relation to Radical Leadership*

IT IS not our intention to discuss in detail the specific methods practiced by radicals. There is a copious literature, condemnatory and otherwise dealing with this subject; no small part of the internal discussions and dissensions of radical groups and parties revolve around questions of policy. Our discussion of specific methods will be confined in the main to bringing out certain comparisons and contrasts with the methods of conservatism. The main purpose at this point is to attempt further analysis of the psychology of radicalism in the hope that light may be thrown upon some of the less evident aspects of method. An attempt at something more than the usual superficial survey is essential to later evaluation in relation to social achievement.

The conflict between conservatism and radicalism, wherever and however it may be staged, is, in all its protean forms, a struggle for possession of the means and agencies of social control. That extreme radicalism contemplates and strives for the abolition of some (in the case of anarchism, all) of the existing institutional controls does not alter this fundamental fact. The extreme radical may desire to abolish many specific institutions, but for the most part he expects other institutional controls to be put in their place. (Here, again, the nihilists and philosophical anarchists must be excepted.) The syndicalist, for example, is strictly speaking not an anarchist; his "dictatorship of the proletariat" does not mean unrestrained individualism. It merely means that he expects the workers to substitute their own control of industry—in whatever form it may work out— for the present control by the capitalistic bourgeoisie.

Similarly, in whatever field other than the economic, *e.g.*, in art, or literature, or ecclesiastical policy, conflict between conservative and radical tendencies may arise, the struggle is for control, now of the authoritative offices, now of the positions of prestige, and always of the attention, sentiment, and allegiance of the rank-and-file public concerned.

Any radical method involves three tasks. First, the nature and causes of the conditions which the radical wishes changed must be determined, and the human responsibility, if any, for their continued existence fixed. Secondly, this done, people must be brought to see the nature of the objectionable conditions, their causes, and the agencies responsible for their existence. And third, action must be instituted and carried through for their removal. The first is the stage of investigation; the second is that of propaganda and organization—in brief the formation and unification of opinion and sentiment; the third is that of attack, which may be either a combat of social groups, or the carrying out of a technological, social-engineering project.

The first task is that of diagnosis. Let us for a moment resort to a trite analogy. The cure of disease obviously is conditioned upon a correct diagnosis of the trouble, a true determination of its cause. It follows that diagnostics is a most important, as it is a most difficult, medical art. First-class diagnosticians have been comparatively rare; today diagnosis is becoming more and more a co-operative process carried on with the indispensable aid of clinical laboratories. As nearly as may be, it is a strictly scientific procedure.

The case of social maladjustment is not essentially different. The effectiveness of whatever measures may be taken to remedy or to cure it clearly must depend upon the accuracy and truth of the analysis of its causes. Inasmuch as the radical is bent on curing certain social maladjustments through thoroughgoing treatment of some kind, it is important to analyze his mind with regard to its fitness to diagnose the disease, and to estimate the probabilities of his choosing the right remedy.

Returning to our concept, desire-reinforcement—the determination to remove the obstacles to the fulfillment of specific desire or interest—it is obvious that the effectiveness of this reinforcement in action depends upon the character of the individuals concerned, especially the leaders—upon their ability to single out the real causes of obstruction, in order that the plan for their removal may be intelligently conceived and directed.

We have seen that the emotional accompaniment of balked desire is very likely to be resentment, hurt feeling, and anger. We detected also the presence of a strong impulse to blame some person or persons and to make an attack upon them. There is always the impulse to kick, or at least to damn, the chair against which you have just barked your shin. The next impulse is to blame the person who left the chair in that place. It is not essentially different in a social situation involving obstruction of interest and activity. Here, also, the normal, naïve, "natural" impulse is to blame some *personal* agency for the obstruction. And the natural, undisciplined method of attempting the removal of the obstruction is to make an attack upon these personal agencies. The success of the attempt will depend upon the character and force of the attack—the strength and the organization of the attacking forces—and also on whether the right object of attack has been chosen.

It is therefore important, and especially so in the case of proposed radical action, to ascertain under what mental strains and stresses, and through what apprehensional biases, the obstructions are perceived, and whether attention and attack are directed to causes or to symptoms. A sick person, no matter how skilled a diagnostician he may be, may not be able to diagnose his own ailment correctly. Similarly, an angry person can scarcely be expected to make a dispassionate evaluation of the causes of his anger.

Not all obstructions or maladjustments, by any means, are due to the malevolence and maliciousness, or even the incompetency, of personal agencies, whether individuals or classes. Obstacles to wish-fulfillment, *e.g.*, to desire for greater personal freedom, for higher standards of living, for real democracy in social control, for new standards in art and literature—in fact the obstacles to progressive ambitions and ideals in general—are embodied partly in the conscious personal opposition of people or classes who can best profit by things-as-they-are, but partly also, in impersonal historico-genetic causes, and in physical limitations. To the extent, therefore, that the radical's diagnosis is based upon personalistic reactions, it may be far from the mark.

Mass-poverty, for instance, in a country like the United States with "boundless" natural resources, may be due, as the socialists and many liberals claim, to the unjust distribution of income and gross restriction of output attributable to capitalistic "business enterprise." Here the fixation of responsibility in personal or class terms may be in part valid. But mass-poverty in China, every once in a while involving starvation of some millions of people, cannot be attributed to class conflict or to corporate greed and inefficiency. It is patent that the causes there lie almost wholly in actual pressure of population on the land's utmost capacity to provide food. Further analysis shows that the cause of this redundancy of population lies in the historico-genetic tradition of ancestor worship, for which, certainly, no "blame" can attach to individuals as such.

Granting for the moment that the socialist explanation of poverty in America is substantially correct, it would follow that the capitalist-class, business-enterprise, production-for-profits obstacle to a higher standard of living for the masses might be removed through the agency of blame-fixation and militant attack, accomplishing the removal of capitalism from power. But no militant class conflict in China could by any stretch of the imagination remove the causes of starvation, which could be avoided only by a successful campaign of education for abolition of ancestor worship and the adoption of an intelligent policy of birth control.

Personalistic "blame" explanations of poverty are advanced both by individualists and by socialists. The latter fix the blame on the members of the capitalist-employing class and say that poverty is due to exploitation. The individualists place the blame on the poor themselves and assert that their poverty is due to individual shiftlessness. Both explanations contain some degree of superficial truth, but both are emotional explanations, and fail to satisfy or convince the critically analytical mind, which demands explanation not in terms of blame-fixation but in terms of mechanistic causation. The scientific, behavioristic student of poverty will want to reveal, on the one hand the social or historical causes of "shiftlessness," and on the other the historical and institutional causes or antecedents of "exploitation" and exploitative attitudes; and further he will insist on extending the search for causes to the possible limitations of the physical environment and of man's technological control over nature.

In the clash of interests between individuals and between classes, within and across national boundaries, so much desire-obstruction is involved that a chronic conflict psychology has been acquired. Perhaps the human race has been afflicted with the conflict complex from the start; it doubtless has instinctive and biological origins. Human institutions and moral codes have had as the major part of their purpose the diminution and control of conflict and conflict attitudes within the group, but it is patent also that some of these institutions and some parts of these moral codes have also operated, often designedly, to inflame and perpetuate suspicion, hate, and conflict between groups. Whether one's thought turns to the head-hunters of the Philippines or to the propaganda of hatred waged in Europe and no less in "Christian" America during the world war and after, evidences of the presence of the conflict complex, and the quickness and ease with which the hatred impulse comes to the surface, are everywhere at hand.

In one aspect, human progress is measured by the increasing size of the social unit, whether local neighborhoods or nations, within which hate and conflict are suppressed and good will and co-operation rendered possible. Many who hold that the world war and its aftermath have almost undermined civilization, and that another war would complete its destruction, have in mind, not so much the physical destruction of wealth and life, as a reversion to universal suspicion and hatred—the "Balkanizing" not only of Europe, but of the whole world. The effect of anger, hatred, and their whole tribe of related emotions is to intensify the conflict psychology, to render co-operation impossible, to atrophy the rational and judicial faculties.

To the extent, therefore, that the anger-and-blame reaction is allowed free scope, in the radical or in anybody else, we cannot look either for just diagnoses of the causes of obstruction, maladjustment, and conflict, or for rational and peaceful policies for removing these causes. Anger in itself never develops a reasoned plan of action, and without plan and program neither reactionism, liberalism, or radicalism ever accomplishes anything but discord and conflict.

Even where scientific analysis shows the obstructions to be due to the presence of personal and class interests or unbending bigotry—*e.g.*, the conservative vested interests discussed in

Chapters IV and V,—the radical cannot hope to remove them or appreciably diminish their power by objurgation and emotional indictment. Militant attack—propaganda, and perhaps in some cases, as a last resort, force, carefully planned and directed—will be the most effective and necessary method of liberal or radical reform, unless the obstructing forces can be outwitted in their own strongholds, diplomacy and professional politics. But the results of such attack may be no better than a conflict of special interests, and the radical group may be reduced to the moral level of the obstructionists, unless, after all, the personal obstructions are regarded in an *impersonal* light. This amounts to saying, as will be explained later,[1] that the reforming party must take a behavioristic and deterministic view of social relations. Such a view rules out of court anger and blame except as the initial accompaniments of the motivating balked interest.

Where, on the other hand, the obstructive causes are physical, impersonally institutional, or technological, the effective method of reform can be militant, militantly propagandistic, diplomatic, or political (in the narrow sense) only in so far as personal and class interest obstructs the carrying out of constructive technological reforms and advances. Unfortunately, one of the radicals' most telling arguments in favor of militant revolution is the fact that personal and corporate interests do stand in the way of technologically constructive reforms, both in organization and in processes, which could be carried out in workmanlike manner were the properly qualified experts free to apply themselves, unhampered, to the task.

There are, then, but two fundamental methods of removing the obstacles to the attainment of the ends desired by progressives and radicals—conflict, and constructive co-operation. By the conflict method, personal and class-interest obstructions are removed either by force, by political superiority (more votes and more political solidarity, greater skill in the political game), or by massed strength of organization in non-political lines. By the construction method, the problems and difficulties of organization and technical processes are critically and scientifically analyzed, and the technologists, whether engineers,

---

[1] See pp. 215-219.

medical men, economists or what not, set to work to solve them. Under the constructive method must be placed education of the people with regard to the actual nature of the obstructions, whether personal, institutional, or technological.

It should be noted that the blame attitude and the conflict method are always subject to the disadvantage that they tend to inflame and intensify personalistic opposition—the very opposition or obstructive agency against which they are directed, and that consequently they make harder their own task.

In any case dispassionate leadership is necessary. The outcome of the balking of interests and of desire-reinforcement will vary, in the absence of leadership and discipline, with different temperaments; and the methods of attempted reform will be as diverse as are the types of will and intellect. In some cases the net result will be mere reflex and unreflecting violence. At the opposite extreme will be cool-headed, scientific achievement. The more obscure and complex, the more powerful and subtle, and the more intrenched in human habituation the obstructions are, the greater is the need for inductive, objective analysis and the more imperative is rational and informed leadership.

We are thus brought to the necessity of comparing the psychology of radical leaders with that of their followers. It follows, too, that in temperament, in training, and in discipline are to be sought the characteristics which differentiate the leaders from the followers in radical movements; and the specific kind of contribution which different temperaments are likely to make to progressivism or radicalism.

Contemporary psychologists are wary of types and classifications. To speak of mental "type" seems to them to smack of an à priori, unscientific attitude, especially if a classification suggests a division into emotional and intellectual types. This caution is perhaps due to the observed fact that the same individual may exhibit a hair-trigger motor responsiveness and a thoroughly undisciplined emotional attitude in one sphere of interests, and a calculating, rational intellectualism in another. The fact that the average mind is compartmentized, and addicted to glaring inconsistencies of attitude and method, makes classification seem futile, or at least dubious.

All this may be admitted; and yet, not unscientifically, we may recognize different attitudes, different modes of response, different methods of attack, *when some particular type of interest*—say the economic—is balked. With regard to a particular situation, or a specific issue, it is difficult to see how it is possible to escape the conviction that some individuals react in a primarily emotional (praise and blame) way, while others react in a disciplined, rational manner.

Individuals may therefore be classified on the basis of the degree to which, with reference to a particular interest, they habitually subject their instincts and emotions to the control and direction of their intellects and reasoning powers, or in other words, upon the relative extent to which their conduct is determined by unreflective motor and emotional complexes and by judicial or scientific rational analysis.

For the purpose in hand, Professor Giddings' classification comes nearest to meeting our needs.[2] He distinguishes four mental types, ideo-motor, ideo-emotional, dogmatic-emotional and critically intellectual. These types correspond roughly to motivation and control by sensibility, emotion, sentiment or belief, and impersonal rational intelligence, respectively.[3] The first three types react more to convictions involving personal praise and blame; the last to perception of impersonal causes. The first three, whether they happen to hold any definite, conscious convictions as to "free will" or not, tend to reinforce their balked desires as if all obstructions were attributable to responsible personal agencies. The last type recognizes personal as well as impersonal agencies of obstruction, but regards the personal from the behavioristic, as it does the impersonal from the deterministic, standpoint.

The bearing of these typical distinctions on methods of desire-reinforcement, and on the psychology of rational leadership will be evident.

In the two lower types, the ideo-motor and the ideo-emotional, the fear-anger emotions attendant upon the obstruction of desire are most likely to find expression in blame. The obstruction is apprehended in terms of personal causation.

---

[2] "A Provisional Distribution of the Population of the United States into Psychological Classes," *Psychological Review*, Vol. VIII, July, 1901, pp. 337-349. Also *Readings in Descriptive and Historical Sociology*, 1906, pp. 236-239.

[3] Cf. Jastrow, *The Psychology of Conviction*, 1918, Ch. 1.

When natural persons are at hand to whom blame may be attached, the emotional temperament, undisciplined to scientific method and attitude, makes them the scape-goats. Anthropology furnishes boundless illustration of this personalistic fear-anger reaction, from the blame and punishment of mothers of twins [4] to the burning of witches and the deportation of bolsheviks. These blame-reactions are naïve methods of removing the obstacles to wish-fulfillment, especially to the desire for security.

When natural persons cannot be blamed for an evil, supernatural personal agencies are created for the purpose, and the world is populated with evil spirits, devils, demons, and ill-dispositioned gods. Belief in spirits and gods then re-directs fear, anger, and blame to natural persons, who are held reponsible for displeasing the gods and bringing down their wrath upon the social group.

Uncritical, naïve personification, or personalistic symbolization, is by no means limited to naturefolk, or to the realm of religion. The naïve socialist, however well-read in his Marx and Engels he may be, nevertheless welcomes the hog-jowled capitalist of Art Young's cartoons [5] as a personal object, not wholly of a merely symbolical significance, upon whom his hatred may find momentary release. In the same way the conservative, his equanimity and comfort disturbed by labor unrest, vents his blame on the "agitator." It was noticeable that the armistice day parades in 1918 carried many black coffins labeled "the Kaiser," or "Wilhelm"—a striking example of symbolization and blame-fixation through personification.

Such personal scape-goats, found or created as objects for blame and hate, serve in emotional minds as definite stimuli of reinforcement and motor-attack. They give definite objective for the aggressive disposition aroused by the balking of desire. In temperaments not so aggressively emotional, they are less likely to stimulate motor attack. Such minds find release in objurgation or verbal attack, which serves in part as momentary release of anger complexes and in part as a defense mech-

---

[4] Kingsley, *Travels in West Africa*, 2nd edition, abridged, 1897, pp. 323-328.

[5] See the files of the *Masses*, the *Liberator*, and the *Federated Press Bulletin*.

anism against consciousness of fear and disinclination to fight—
that is, against self-reproach.

Effective leadership and organization, holding the volatile-
minded rank and file to a steady program, is supplied by the
more persistent temperament of the dogmatic-emotional minds,
whose motor and emotional releases are of a less hair-trigger
type. Such minds are also given to intense resentments, but
their resentment is steadier and often amounts to sustained
moral indignation. They are given to personalistic fixation of
blame, but they may also have very considerable perception of
the non-personal causes of existing evils and obstructions, and
may consequently make use of the objective scientific analyses
furnished by the relatively disinterested critical intellectuals
not engaged in the actual "movement."

In the characteristics of the dogmatic-emotional attitude we
have the key to the explanation, as to the requirements, of the
actual, effective leadership of radical movements. Most active
radical leaders, so far as concerns the movement that claims
their major interest and attention, are of this type of mind.
It is therefore desirable to review its salient characteristics with
some care.

The dogmatic-emotional mind holds to its beliefs, valuations,
and "principles" with intense conviction and unswerving loyalty. Its principles may or may not have been arrived at
through objective processes of investigation and inductive logic.
Its observational and reasoning processes are more or less
strongly influenced by its emotional interests, and, while usually
biased by them, may be at times aided by them, *e.g.*, by sympathetic insight, where the colder critical intellectual would
fail to sense essential realities. In any case, its convictions,
once formed, are held to with dogmatic persistency. Argument
will not dislodge them. They become the premises of its reasoning, and by emotional attachment are placed beyond the reach
of criticism. In the more intense dogmatic-emotional types,
convictions are held to with religious devotion. We all know
single taxers, socialists, "open shop" propagandists, defenders
of the classics, advocates of vocational education, feminists and
anti-feminists, high protectionists, eugenists, devoted Christians,
and sincere atheists of this type.

The dogmatic-emotional mind is rarely cynical, as what passes for the critically intellectual sometimes appears to be, for cynicism is an attitudinal complex serving as a defense attitude, and the dogmatic-emotional individual is usually something of a fighter. If the dogmatic-emotional mind is ever pessimistic its pessimism is not the kind that paralyzes the will to action. It may be vindictive and domineering and it generally has an inward austerity and capacity for self-denial, which, however, may be disguised under a genial exterior. It may or may not be capable of deep and active sympathies. Where it is, they help to intensify its perception of social wrongs, and furnish part of the explanation as to why it is more persistently and intensely motivated by moral indignation than are the other, either lower or higher, mental types. It tends, more than the intellectual, to attach blame to persons or to classes of persons, and is likely to conceive reform and revolution in terms of militant combat (*e.g.*, class struggle), or of diplomacy and political intrigue.

When such a mind gets set in a conservative channel it supplies the stalwart, sincere conservatives, who are so, not so much from personal interest, as from strong moral and intellectual conviction.

When, however, the dogmatic-emotional mind happens to get directed into the radical channel, either because of balked personal interests, or because its keen sympathy makes the wrongs and obstructed interests of others its own, it attacks institutions with vigor equal to that with which the dogmatic conservative defends them, and conceives an equally strong antipathy, expressed in terms of personal blame, toward those who represent and defend the offensive institutions.

Since the dogmatic-emotional radical holds to his principles, be they economic, political, or moral, with religious devotion, it follows that he will not easily be drawn off from the attempt to put them into practice. That is, he reinforces his balked desires with vigor and determination. Obstruction and opposition merely increase his reinforcement and intensify his resentment, until finally his "cause" is made a matter of truly religious significance, of religious hope, and may even come to have some of the mystical and militant accompaniments of religion in the narrower sense.

Not all dogmatic-emotional radicals become leaders, of course. But the emotional and intellectual qualities of this type of mind

fit it for the development of the specific characteristics necessary in the successful active leadership of an unpopular radical
movement.   Such leadership calls for unremitting hard work,
sacrifice of all narrow and immediate personal interests, indifference to rebuffs and to the misunderstanding, contempt, and
insults of respectability, patience to withstand the strain of
waiting, without pessimism or cynicism, during the long, slow
period of growth of an unpopular movement, ability to visualize
distant ends, capacity for organization and inspiration, and
above all, such reinforcement of desire or interest as will create
that quality of dogged persistence and determination which
finally accomplishes the aim of the movement, if such accomplishment is humanly possible.[6]

In this effective reinforcement of desire the combative instinct plays an important part.   The active militant leaders
of progressive or radical movements opposed by powerful, entrenched personal and corporate interests, must not only be motivated by deep desires strongly obstructed, but also somewhat
amply endowed with the fighting spirit.   Such a temperament
has its advantages and disadvantages.   It will avoid the refinement of analysis, the meticulousness of judgment, which sometimes put the intellectual in the position of Buridan's ass,
starving between two hay stacks for want of decision.   It
will proceed to push a plan of reform through to success
against the determined obstructionist tactics of conservatives
and reactionaries, where the more philosophical, critically-
intellectual temperament would fail, because of indecision,
lack of personalistic aggression, or inadequate desire-reinforcement.

The combative temperament is likely, in its vigorous attack
upon the personal agents of obstructive institutions, to conceive
the problem of reform or revolution wholly in terms of conflict or of politics, whereas the fundamental obstructions, as
we have seen, may be of an impersonal nature and may require
for their removal not merely the combating or political outwitting of personal opposition, but painstaking scientific analysis of the whole situation.

The less decisive and combative intellectual will in the long
run delve deeper in critical evaluation of the obstructions to

---

[6] Cf. Buchanan, *The Story of a Labor Agitator*, 1903.

progress, find the impersonal forces back of personal attitudes, and by attention to these more fundamental causes, lay the foundations to thoroughgoing social transformation, while the more combative and emotional mind is planning a campaign to crush its enemies. The nature and function of the critically intellectual mind in relation to liberalism and radicalism must, however, be left to later discussion. It is evident that both types of leadership are necessary, as long as men are ruled by emotion so much more than they are by reason and scientific knowledge.

In the field of action, to summarize, radicalism has for its immediate purpose the wresting of control from the conservatives and reactionaries. Its object in acquiring control is to remove the obstacles to desire-fulfillment—fundamentally, to the desire for freedom. Radical method, to be effective, must therefore involve three tasks or processes: (1) social diagnosis, to determine the true causes of obstruction; (2) propaganda and education, in order that an effectively large number of people may be dynamically conscious of these causes; and organization, in order that their conscious knowledge may be effective in action; and (3) planned attack upon the obstructions.[7]

Obstructions to desire and interest are embodied in both personal agencies and in impersonal conditions, institutional and physical. This very important fact tends to be overlooked by the rank-and-file radicals, and by not a few leaders, because of the instinctive anger-and-blame reaction. There has thus developed, in both conservative and radical, a chronic psychology of conflict, a pugnacity complex, a tendency to give way to suspicion and hatred. The social conflict thus tends to be staged, not upon the plane of rational analysis of causes and workmanlike plan for dealing with them, but upon the plane of militant force, or political and diplomatic outwitting of human adversaries. In the clash of class and other conflicts, the deep-seated impersonal lines of causation are lost sight of or ignored. The initial anger-and-blame emotion incident to the original balked interest is augmented and intensified by the conflict itself; and the bitterness of the conflict is further intensified, until it becomes a headlong clash of special interests without probability,

---

[7] The second phase, propaganda, education, and organization, we have touched upon only incidentally.

of constructive results. Even for effective militant attack on personal obstructions, intelligent leadership is necessary, if radical action is to be effectively and constructively directed to the removal of both personal and impersonal obstacles.

In relation to qualifications for leadership, the question of mental types is of great importance. Accepting, as adequate to present purposes, Giddings' classification, we have seen that the rank-and-file radicals (like the general population at large) fall preponderantly under the two lowest and most volatile types, the ideo-motor and the ideo-emotional; while the radical leaders are mostly derived from the more stable and determined dogmatic-emotional type. The two lower types easily resort to violence, which may or may not be "radical." In any case, however, effective radical action is not to be looked for from these types, except where they are organized and disciplined by the more intelligent and steadfast dogmatic-emotional leaders. "Solidarity" and organization for attack are insisted upon as the prime essential of radical method by the leaders of extreme economic radicalism, who are mainly of the dogmatic-emotional type and who see obstructions as mainly embodied in class interest and selfishness. Further analysis of the characteristics of the higher dogmatic-emotional types shows that while they hold to and advance their convictions with a religious devotion, they may also approach the critically intellectual level, while at the same time they avoid the indecision likely to characterize the latter type.

2. *The Specific Methods of Radicalism.*

Generally speaking, the tone of specific radical methods is set by the type of opposition offered by conservatism. The interested conservative offers much more positive and pointed opposition than does the disinterested. We have considered the methods of the former type of conservatism with comparative fullness, but did not find it necessary to attempt an extended discussion of disinterested conservative methods, largely because they do not, so definitely as those of the vested interests, rise to the level of conscious policies. Nevertheless the radical has to deal with the attitudes of the disinterested, as well as with the consciously designed oppositions of the interested, conservative, and we will first consider briefly the radical methods bearing on these disinterested conservative attitudes.

It is easy to see, in general, how disinterested conservative methods, ranging from purely unconscious habitual inertia to definite and purposeful sustaining of educational programs, affect the radical's problem of policy.

One of the liberal's or radical's primary tasks is to overcome the indifference and inertia of the contented conservative. In most ordinary situations, the conservative has only to sit still and do nothing, holding "theorists" and "reformers" in good-natured contempt.[8] So far as he has to deal with the general disinterested conservative element the radical has to break the conservative's habit circuit and to the best of his ability destroy the (psychologically) impressive power of the established and conventional loci of prestige and sentimental, uncritical loyalty.

The conservative holds the defensive positions. The burden, not only of proof, but of persuasion—the breaking down of sentiment and prejudice—is upon the radical. If the conservative could always be brought out to fight in the open, these tasks would not be so difficult. But the conservative is an adept—often unconsciously so—at shifting his position and refusing to join issue. This trait results from his characteristic blinking of facts which he does not like, throwing into the spotlight those he does like, and his resultant skepticism with regard to social maladjustments and evils. Here the rose-colored optimism of comfort plays its obstructive and distortive part, and it is a task of no mean proportions for liberal or radical to counteract it by showing up the facts in the true—or what they at least think to be the true—light.

How dangerous to truth and objectivity this situation is, is of course clear. No brief can be held for the superior objectivity of radical as compared with conservative. Objectivity is at a discount in all but the highest critical minds in each case. The worst aspect of the situation is that avoidance and distortion (either conscious or unconscious) on one side occasion and necessitate a counterbalancing intensifying and centralizing of emphasis on the other.

When mere inertia fails, or when the optimistic bias no longer suffices, and the conservative is compelled to make some

---

[8] "Mere theorist . . . is a common taunt of men who cannot render a reason against men who can." Bonar, *Letters of Ricardo to Malthus*, 1887, Preface, p. xii.

kind of active defense, his loud appeal is first to precedent—to the experience and judgments of the past. When this appeal is frankly made on rational grounds, when it is based on actual analysis of the factual experience of the past, the radical's task of reformation may not be easy. That depends on the circumstances of the case—at least so far as concerns intellectual conviction. But when the appeal is made, as it usually is, on the sentimental ground of attachment and loyalty, the radical's task is much harder. Sentiment is less easily changed than opinion, and in attacking sentimental attachment to the past, the radical is likely to encounter a network of hidden prejudices inrooted in pride, in dislike of mental and moral effort, and in honest idealization, which are extremely difficult to loosen. Just here also, he will often fail to distinguish with sufficient care between the sentiment-mongering of vested-interest chicane and the honest, sincere sentiment, attachments, and loyalties of the disinterested conservative. Here, too, is where the radical, having cast off his own sentimental moorings, has need of a tact and diplomacy which he frequently does not evince. For in meeting sentimental objections, persuasion—the tactful meeting of sentiment by sentiment—is more effective than cold logic. With youth, scientific, objective reasoning may break up undesirable sentimental attachments, because they are not yet rooted deeply in long-standing habits of thought and attitude; but not so with middle age. Whatever be the diplomacy, or the lack of it, with which liberal or radical handles this appeal to the past, his method essentially amounts to opposing to it an appeal to the future, and in gradually causing the conservative to be a little ashamed of contentment with past mediocrities, deficiency in moral courage, and lack of constructive imagination. Liberalism and radicalism will naturally have an easier task of diplomatic persuasion in those times and places where "progressivism" is held in high repute. No one likes to be thought, even if he is not called, a fossil or mossback.

The conservative's next move is to seek limitation of discussion and criticism. Beyond question, many conservatives do sincerely feel that some principles, beliefs, and institutions should be held above criticism, and that it is disloyal and sacrilegious, or at the least an exhibition of impropriety, to discuss them in any other spirit than that of unquestioning reverence.

We are not here speaking of the interested conservative's device of censorship. The disinterested conservative's sense of propriety, his sensitive propensity to be "shocked," his avoidance of discussions which may bring out differences of personal opinion and sentiment on fundamental questions of politics and economics, and especially of religion, tend, however, to amount to the same thing as censorship. It took courageous radicals like Havelock Ellis, Prince Morrow, and Jane Addams, for instance, to lead the way in breaking down the conspiracy of silence which so long held up all intelligent attempt to solve the problems of sex hygiene and sex ethics.

There are important border line cases in which it would be difficult or erroneous to draw a dividing line between vested-interest censorship and the limitations desired by disinterested conservatives. This is notably true of restrictions on academic freedom—whether in cases involving economic issues or in those strangely anachronic cases in which attacks are made on the "teaching of evolution," or, more generally, where denominational institutions rigidly exclude the teaching of any scientific theories which by casuistic logic cannot, if occasion arise, be made to square with the Biblical account of creation. An illuminating collection of similar anachronical limitations could probably be made from the deliberations of school boards and text book commissions. But when this region is approached, the liberal and radical have to deal not only with sentimental avoidance, but with something that has the earmarks of sheer stupidity, the most difficult human trait to deal with.

Finally, it is to be remembered that the conservatives—usually a combination of disinterested and interested—commonly have control of most of our educational resources, including not only the public schools but boards and faculties of the institutions of higher learning, and the press and publishing business. Against these controls, liberal and radical bring to bear (a) the general propaganda resources—oral and printed—at their disposal, (b) the radical press, including some few publishing houses which accept, if they do not specialize in, radical matter which other companies avoid, and (c) the project now gaining headway, of workers' education through "trade union colleges" and "workers' universities."

Coming now to the center of the conflict between conservatism and radicalism, we have to pass in review the methods of radicalism against the great variety of policies practiced by the interested conservatives.

First of these, in point of the perspective of public attention, is violence. When the social history of the years 1914 to 1921 is objectively studied, men will marvel at the scope and abandon of the popular, and the inspired, literature devoted to anathematizing the violence of the radicals, at the very time when the whole respectable, conservative, "Christian" world was indulging in orgies of violence beyond the wildest fancy of a philosophical Sorel or a literary Sienkiewicz. But when the passions are stirred to the depths, and men think they are fighting for the preservation of institutions and principles which they are led to hold dearer than life and reason, consistency must not be expected. The only practical point is that while much that has been written about radical violence is sincere and some of it objectively truthful, much of it must be taken for what it is—at best, passionate rant, expressive of rage due to the balking of the desire for security; at worst, a clamor raised to draw attention away from the real issue of privilege versus democracy.

Let us pass by this rant and clamor—of both sides. It is unnecessary for us to attempt to say how much of an enemy of law and order the radical is, or just how dishonest and unscrupulously exploitative and self-seeking the vested-interest conservative. The primary function of the fair-minded student is neither to defend nor to condemn violence, but to find the fundamental causes, which explain why it is resorted to.[9]

---

[9] Here is a field singularly neglected by the psychologists and sociologists. There is no outstanding scientific literature on the subject. The literature of the "sociology of conflict" is concerned with general results, and with social and economic causes, rather than with psychological motivation. Aside from such historical studies as Robert Hunter's *Violence and the Labor Movement*, the various government reports on violence against the I. W. W., etc., during war time (see *e.g.*, the *Report of the President's Mediation Commission*) and such studies as the Interchurch World Movement *Report on the Steel Strike*, and the *New Republic's* series of articles on "The Labor Spy," 1921, about the only serious attempt in English to delve down to fundamental questions of motivation of radical violence is to be found in the various papers of Carleton Parker, and these leave something to be desired from the standpoint of an acceptable scientific psychology.

One salient fact is clear: violence is not confined to radicals. Impulses to violence are common to all. Into its probable primitive instinctive motivation we need not inquire. Generally speaking, violence, where not institutional (as in legal punishment), is always found in close connection with anger, and anger in connection with balked desires and activities. Much apparently spontaneous conduct is merely a method of desire-reinforcement on the part of hair-trigger ideo-motor temperaments which can brook no opposition, unless repressed by discipline and fear into a quasi-servile obedience to superior power and authority. In the somewhat higher, dogmatic-emotional temperaments, violence may eventuate only after a period of personalistic blame-reactions, often verbal—so verbal in fact that the whole anger-complex may be dissolved in words. Still, sufficient brooding upon wrongs and oppositions, sufficiently sustained, and voluble and dogmatic assertion of the rightness of one's own cause and the devilish depravity of the opposition may fire even peaceful temperaments to violent reactions.

Herd instincts, especially the immediate impulse to attack the stranger—an impulse partly due to fear, partly, perhaps, to innate sadistic tendencies—are also operative.

These herd impulses to the use of force become conventionalized and legalized. Violence, properly ritualized, becomes one of the recognized legitimate methods of conservatism. Were this not true, there never would have been a war between civilized peoples.

The motivation of these legalized violences may cover a wide range. Group safety is an ever-present motive; but acquisitive desire is a motive not merely sporadic in occurrence. From the exercise of the police power in the protection of property to wars of economic aggression, it plays its part.

Finally, a whole community or a whole people may get into a state of nervous irritation and fly into a rageful violence at the slightest provocation. Thus violence ranges all the way from neuropathology to law and statecraft.

We are now in position to understand that mere disorderly, violent attack upon institutions or persons who happen momentarily to be the termini of anger and resentment releases does not constitute radicalism. Discomfort, release of repressed energy, transference, and reinforcement may lead merely to hysteria and emotional slashing about, mob violence, and purposeless feudism. A lynching mob is usually composed of conservative citizens. The machine smashers in the English textile industries during the Industrial Revolution were not radicals; usually machine smashing was the result of reflexive anger expressing itself in organized rioting. Whatever else it may betoken, the breaking up of Non-Partisan League meetings by members of the American Legion does not represent radicalism, nor do the outrages attributable to the Ku Klux.

Violent methods may be used in the interest of either radicalism or reactionism, but radicalism as a social attitude involves the persistent desire for thoroughgoing and fundamental innovation, usually against opposition. Explosive release of repressed desire or impulsive anger-and-blame attack will occasionally take place in the rank-and-file representatives of conservative and reactionary, as well as of the radical, attitudes. Nevertheless violent action, not taking into consideration war and other legalized violence, is to be expected somewhat more frequently in those social classes in which there is the greater amount and intensity of desire-repression and obstruction of interest and ambition. For these classes have, in consequence of repression and obstruction, the strongest emotional impulses to resentment and blame, and the broadest rational ground for desiring thoroughgoing change.

Nevertheless, the difference between conservative and radical, with regard to tendencies to violence, is not so great as may at first appear. In the nature of things, the conservatives usually control social institutions and are consequently in position to legalize whatever violent methods and policies may be to their interest. The social agencies—notably the police power—may or may not be justly used, according as disinterested and dispassionate conservatives, or self-seeking and unscrupulous vested interests (whether economic, ecclesiastical, or racial), are in control.

Where vested interests are in control they can finance violence on a grand scale. And often it does not make much difference whether this is done in accordance with legal conventions or not. Examples enough will occur to any informed reader—the questionable use of armed forces in labor disputes, the hiring of professional "detectives" and strike-breakers (usually a

euphemism for thugs and gunmen), the forcible jailing or deportation of labor organizers in defiance of constitutional rights,
and the fomenting of disturbance and rebellion in foreign countries, usually the weak and backward ones. All these things are
respectable, right, and proper when done by those with sufficient
economic power, but when the same, or nearly the same, things
are done by radicals, no terms of condemnation are too strong.

We saw above [10] that the vested interests, standing for law
and order, do not always have to resort to actual violence. They
may use threat of force as a method of intimidation. But as
the world should have learned by now, this is a game two can
play at. Extreme radicals have not been slow to learn it.
Against the power and threats of reactionism they have matched
terrorism, through "propaganda of the deed." [11] Introduced
into theory first by the crazy anarchist Bakounin, and into
practice by the Russian nihilists, especially by that "incarna-
tion of hatred, malice, and revenge" the young revolutionist,
Nechayeff,[12] it was spread by the anarchists through Europe and
into America, and eventually became, under such names as
"direct action" and "sabotage," the official doctrine, as to
method, of the syndicalists and their American prototype, the
I. W. W. As is well known, the argument advanced for direct
action, propaganda of the deed—in short, terrorism—was and
still is that trade unionists and political socialists not only have
failed, but must continue to fail, to accomplish anything by
parliamentary, political, methods.

To attempt to trace the historico-psychologic causes for the
development of this doctrine would take us far beyond the
proper confines of this book.[13] But the general motivation to

---

[10] Pages 84, 85.

[11] See Hunter, *Violence and the Labor Movement*, 1914, Index, under
"propaganda of the deed" and "terrorism."

[12] Hunter, Chapter 1.

[13] The reader who wishes to pursue this subject will consult Hunter,
Violence and the Labor Movement, and Parker, *The Casual Laborer and
Other Essays*; and then the whole literature of syndicalism. The fol-
lowing works may be specifically mentioned: Laidler, *Socialism in
Thought and Action*, 1920, ch. 6; Levine, *Syndicalism in France*, 1913;
Brissenden, *The I. W. W.—a Study of American Syndicalism*, 1919;
Macdonald, *Syndicalism*, 1912; Tridon, *The New Unionism*, 1913; Rus-
sell, *Proposed Roads to Freedom*, 1919, ch. 3; *Revolutionary Radicalism,
Its History, Purpose and Tactics* (Report of the Lusk Committee to the

direct action is clear. It lay in ideo-motor impatience and anger at aspirations and programs seemingly checkmated everywhere, and in the resultant conviction (mingled with combat instincts and revenge motives) that the proletariat had but one effective method left. Appeal and argument had failed; nothing was left but action—force without stint.

A powerful contributive cause lay in the fact, also, that the leaders were more impatient, more revolutionary, and more ready—in theory at least, in spite of their bitter personal quarrels—to insist upon the necessity for discipline and organization, than were the masses of their followers.

A candid survey of history will show a very long series of popular uprisings against oppression and exploitation. But these revolts have been spasmodic; they do not occur until oppression becomes unbearable. As a matter of fact, the masses of humanity have always been conservative—at least until the exceedingly unsettling influence of the Industrial Revolution ushered in the dynamic nineteenth century. Uprisings and revolutions, from slave insurrections in Rome and revolts of German peasants to the Paris Commune and the Bolshevist revolution in Russia, have in the main been indubitable evidence of tyranny and exploitation so gross that it moved to concerted action even the thick intellects and the slow wills of the naturally conservative people.

The untutored masses may know only that they are miserable; they may be unable to single out the causes of their misery; they may not know exactly what they want or how to get it if they did. For these reasons, and also because of a certain inborn or acquired individualism, they are by no means always reliable and persistent in their attachment and loyalty to particular programs of reform or revolution.

If the balked aspirations of the masses could be co-ordinated, and their obstructed energy released under skillful organization and leadership, they would obviously constitute a force not lightly to be held in contempt or trifled with. Whether it be

New York State. Senate, 1920), Vols. I and II. This Report, whatever may be thought of the animus and ethics of the men behind it, is an invaluable mine of documents relating to revolutionary theories and programs. See, for illustration, the "Left Wing Manifesto" (Vol. I, pp. 716-738, especially pp. 730-736).

a fact fraught with danger or with hope, it remains a fact that the working masses constitute the great majority of the population in any country, and accordingly could legally and constitutionally carry through any program of change, however drastic, and however disastrous or beneficial, provided only that the minorities would abide by constitutional law and order. The industrial workers of America, if joined by the farmers, could, if they so desired and were solidly organized, amend the Constitution or abolish it and adopt another and very different one. But there is not the slightest immediate likelihood of anything of the kind. For there is far less class consciousness and class solidarity among the workers than there is among the ruling propertied classes. The workers are for that reason less amenable to discipline in a common cause than are the capitalistic vested interests. By the very reason of their many repressions and obstructions, as well as of their age-long training in subserviency to the power and prestige of superior classes, they are in fact hard to organize and still harder to keep organized.

In the absence of the essential organization and discipline, their desire-reinforcement is likely to be relatively futile. In spite, however, of the survival of a subservient spirit and of a safety-first attitude lasting over from earlier periods less touched than the present by democratic aspiration, few will deny that there is a vast reserve of energy dammed up in the obstructed and repressed desires of the masses. It is equally plain that this energy is kept from effectiveness largely by the futile propensity to personification, personal blame, and pointless objurgation, which serve as partial, momentary, and somewhat rhythmic releases of anger, and scatter, rather than focus, the energies of the obstructed interests.

Now it is precisely to concentrate these energies and to secure solidarity of organization that direct action, propaganda of the deed, and the less violent but no less effective measure of the general strike are advocated. The conservative interests have been altogether too successful, from the standpoint of the economic radical, in their policy of dividing and thereby holding in check the forces of radicalism. Hence the direct action policy is the result both of the inability and failure to organize the masses for unified political co-operation—failure perhaps due in part to the superior political capacity of the conservatives,—and of the violent and sometimes ruthless methods resorted to by the vested interests. It is safe to say that had the ruling powers not resorted to violence and had they not played their political cards so adroitly as to convince many radicals that the masses had no chance in *that* game, "propaganda of the deed" would have got a scanty number of adherents.

Before we leave this subject it should be noted that propaganda of the deed was a policy not invented by Bakounin. It has been the method of militarism from time immemorable, of imperialism and class rule from the beginnings of civilization. Not to go back to Egytian dynasties, or the tender policies of Hebrew Kings and Judges, to the glories of Rome, or even to the ministrations of feudal overlords and gentlemen of the manor, it has been a part of the conventional methods of the Germans in East Africa, the Dutch in Java, the French in Morocco, the English in divers places, and the Japanese in China and Siberia; and the Americans have not entirely escaped some taint of its use. We have had it with us very recently— not always in radical circles—in West Virginia, in Seattle, in Arizona, in Pittsburgh, in Haiti, and in Ku Kluxism everywhere. It is the primal eldest curse of man, the mark of Cain set upon us.

There is no sharp dividing line between violence and intimidation, or between intimidation and peaceful economic pressure. Nor is there a distinction of kind between the use of these devices by conservative labor groups and by radicals. The effectiveness of a strike or any other device to compel favorable action, depends, though by no means wholly, upon the amount of pressure it brings to bear upon the employer. On the pressure agencies—strikes, picketing, boycotts, unfair lists, etc.— we need not dwell, further than to note that they may be peaceful or violent. They do not directly concern the present inquiry, because they are not exclusively or essentially radical methods.

Even so, however, the conservative labor movement itself is continually confronted with new limitations upon the use of methods upon which it has relied ever since the modern organization of labor began. This is indication that trade unionism— the conservative wing of labor—is in many respects not much better a match, politically, for the capitalistic employing interests than are the radicals. Since the war, certainly, there has been a series of court decisions of no little significance, not only to labor itself, but to the student of methods of economic pressure; for there can be no gainsaying of the fact that the present judicial tendency in this country is greatly to limit, if not destroy, labor's power of action through organization and collective bargaining.

It is well to realize that the narrower the legal limits within which labor (whether such relatively conservative organizations as the American Federation of Labor, or in groups of more radical tendency) can bring to bear economic pressure to resist that of the capitalistic vested interests, the more likely it is to go over bodily to the advocates of the doctrine of direct action. Herein lies an important, though somewhat remote, limitation on the power of the vested interests to add legal intimidation to economic. Short of this danger of driving conservative unionism into the arms of syndicalism, the reactionary and conservative interests, as long as they remain in control of institutions and office, are in possession of a thousand and one intimidation devices not available to radicals.

Theoretically a general strike could take place without violence, although should the workers ever see fit to institute one, and be organized with sufficient solidarity to make it effective, it would be the most powerful weapon of economic intimidation ever put into their hands. Practically, as things stand in the Western World, a proposal to inaugurate a general strike is a proposal to meet violence with violence if necessary. Assuming that the striking workers could hold in check their own impulse to combat, and at the start refrained from all violent acts, it is very likely that ways would be found of forcing them into violence. The whole familiar round of charge and countercharge, display of police power, calling out of the military forces, serving of blanket injunctions, and raising of clamor would probably be repeated, and perhaps would result in emergency statutes making it a crime for two or more employees to agree to stop work together. Cognizance of what took place in the coal strike of 1919, what was threatened in the impending railroad strike of 1921, and did take place in that of 1922, suggests the question whether the vested interests and the government would permit a peaceful general strike. The motive back of such governmental policies is not in question; no one could for a moment doubt that it is for the protection of the public.

A peaceful general strike, were it possible, would be a type of passive resistance. Of this method of attaining ends the Western World offers few if any illustrations. But the Orient offers a magnificent example of what passive resistance (meaning by the term, absence of violence) can do—the Chinese students' strike of 1919, and the ensuing Chinese boycott of Japanese goods.[14]

Closely related to legal intimidation is political manipulation. In politics of the "practical" kind, it is possible that European radicals have attained a degree of technique rivaling that of the various conservative parties, though the post-bellum history of the British Labor Party (in point of policy and accomplishment) may throw some doubt upon this opinion. In America, however, radicals have not exhibited distinction in this interesting game. This is due, perhaps, to the fact that America is, in general, more conservative than Europe. Radicals constitute a small minority—minorities rather—and these minorities have shown a conspicuous lack of ability to get together.[15] This in turn is due to the traditional and ingrained individualism of the American people, plus the disinclination of any radical group to accept compromise.

On the whole it is probable that radicals are too conscientious idealists to make good use of the methods commonly employed, and regarded as matter-of-fact, by the conservatives, respectable and otherwise. Or at least a new type of practical radicalism, foreshadowed perhaps in Wisconsin and North Dakota, will have to develop. As matters stand, radicals are no match for the conservatives in political wisdom or experience.

The outstanding, traditional policy of radical parties in this country and the Continent, in contrast to England, has been the attempt to maintain the most stringent party discipline. No

---

[14] Another movement of the same kind and one which may eventually result in still more revolutionary consequences is the non-resistance, non-intercourse Indian nationalist movement led by Ghandi. There is ample evidence, however, that an intellectual idealist like Ghandi cannot hold the masses to non-violent methods. See, for instance, Sir Verner Lovett, *A History of the Indian Nationalist Movement*, 1920, chs. 6, 7.

[15] Witness the dismal failure of the attempt, headed by the Committee of Forty-eight, in the presidential campaign of 1920.

one has been considered a party member or allowed to have a voice in party policy who would not formally subscribe to a hard and fast Credo. So far as the socialists are concerned this has been the expression, in the main, of the heritage of an uncompromising Marxism imported from Germany during the trying years of the early struggles of German Social Democracy to obtain a consistent party organization.

This lack of elasticity and adaptability was thought to be essential to secure and maintain solidarity of spirit and team-work in action. But with the increase in the number of people socialistically inclined, and the demand for practical as well as academic programs, it helped to produce the thing it was designed to prevent—split and re-split in the radical wing. The socialists were agreed only in their opposition to capitalism, and in a general way, in their ultimate ideals (an agreement now shattered by the upstarting of syndicalism and guild socialism). With the appearance of revisionism and reformism in France and Germany, all probability of early agreement on methods of practical political procedure was at an end.

In espionage the radicals are at a hopeless disadvantage. The vested interests can place their spies in the inmost councils of every radical movement and every labor organization. They have the money, and can get the men of moral calibre suited to the office. The radicals, however, can scarcely hope soon to place any considerable number of hirelings on the directing boards of the steel corporations or the great banking houses. Whether the vested interests employ espionage widely is another question. They can, if they want to, and the results they momentarily reap are not confined to the inside information obtained; they include a not inconsiderable injury to radical morale. The long run results are not so certain.

Again, in the adroit use of seductive prestige the radicals can hardly hope to compete. Superior inducements of money income and social position are continually causing defection from radical ranks or preventing promising individuals from following the bent of their less materialistic impulses and join-ing the radical movement. The only seduction proper to radi-calism is its appeal to idealistic morals, and its promise of distinction through difference—an attraction not without influence upon certain types of young intellectuals and people of wealth grown tired of monotonous respectability.[16]

Propaganda and "education of public opinion" must, with few exceptions, be either oral or written. It goes without saying that radicalism generally makes all the use it can of agitation, oral propaganda, and published material, from penny pamphlets to ponderous books. In this it is not essentially different from conservatism. The only reason we do not realize that conservative propaganda or "education" is influencing us all the time is because conservatism is the medium in which we live. It is because the propaganda of radicalism is new and different, as well as dangerous, that it attracts so much attention—largely at second hand. As the arena of oral propaganda, the radicals have the soap box; their own indoor meetings—where allowed—the right to speak in a few open forums; the class rooms of the socialist schools and certain types of "workers' colleges"; possibly some social settlement clubs and classes, here and there; evanescently, a propagandistic teacher in the public schools and universities; and opportunity provided for scattering representatives in elective office to speak in legislative halls.

In printed propaganda they are somewhat more favorably situated, though still at a disadvantage. There is a large radical press, if judged by the number of radical periodicals. Their total circulation, while large in absolute figures, is small if compared to the aggregate circulation of non-radical periodicals. Half a dozen great dailies like the Chicago Tribune, the New York Times, the Los Angeles Times and the San Francisco Chronicle, probably have a circulation comparable to that of all the radical papers put together. As the chief center of economic radicalism in this country is New York City, which is also the great publishing center of the country, it is natural to find a large number of radical publications printed there.[17]

---

[16] See Professor Shapiro's article, "The Revolutionary Intellectual," *Atlantic Monthly*, June, 1920, pp. 820-830.

[17] The Lusk Committee Report gives a table of radical papers published in New York City or circulated there, the total circulation of which is put at 1,072,700. This includes everything from dailies to monthlies, publications in foreign languages as well as in English; and a group of liberal periodicals like the *Nation*, *New Republic*, *Freeman*, and *Survey*, with a total circulation put at 168,100. By adding the total circulation

There are, as noted above, a few radical publishing houses. Some of these, co-operative or otherwise, specialize in cheap reprints of radical classics and in pamphlet material; others, which have recognized standing in the publishing world, put out an increasing number of scholarly books not to be classed as propaganda.

Finally, with regard to news, the labor movement has founded the Federated Press, with its daily service to labor papers, and its weekly *Bulletin*.

Radicalism makes more use of certain forms of publicity, like parades and "demonstrations," than does conservatism. The "militant" suffragists made extremely effective use of parades and later of spectacular picketing at the White House and the Capitol. Their effectiveness, however, was greatly enhanced by the stupid way in which the situation was handled by the police and the authorities higher up. The rough handling of the pickets by the mobs, the arrests on trumped-up charges, often on none at all, and the ensuing illegal jail sentences imposed upon the women, not a few of whom were socially prominent, only served to give suffrage a publicity it would not otherwise have had, and undoubtedly forced the hand first of the President and then of Congress.[18]

The National Woman's Party, however, had one advantage which laboring class radicalism lacks. While the National Woman's Party succeeded in raising an astonishingly large amount of money in small contributions from all over the country, it was greatly aided, and tided over tight places, by the large gifts of a few wealthy and influential individuals.

---

of the periodicals published in New York City and the "circulation in New York City" of those published elsewhere, the Report leaves the reader to infer an enormous number of readers of radical periodicals in the Metropolis. See Vol. II, pp. 2004-2006.

[18] See Doris Stevens, *Jailed for Freedom*, 1920; Inez Haynes Irwin, *The Story of the Woman's Party*, 1921. Probably no finer exhibition of leadership and of political insight could be found than that of Alice Paul's management of the suffrage campaign. The history of the passage of the Nineteenth Amendment is a brilliant exemplification of what the leadership of a determined and able minority can do, especially when, as in this case, there develops a growing general sentiment that it has right on its side, and it can therefore rely not only on political pressure but on the shifting of public opinion in its favor, which eventually brings the political pressure to bear.

Only when solidly organized, with very large numbers of paying members, can labor organizations and radical movements escape in a measure the drawbacks of financial limitations. The expenses of propaganda and publicity are heavy. While there is a large amount of masked vested-interest propaganda in the newspapers and magazines, very little from the radical groups appears. They are often not even able to secure a presentation of their case in paid advertisements. Hence they must rely for publicity mainly upon their own periodicals and the cheap pamphlet literature so characteristic of radical movements. Even in this they are at a disadvantage, for they cannot stand the expense at the rate which the great industrial interests can and do incur.

The conservative interests—packers, banking houses, railway executives, employers' associations, public utility companies, etc.—are lavish in their use of publicity through letters and pamphlets, often very attractively got up. Most of this literature is free—to be had for the asking, and often without it. It gets into the public libraries and into the loan, or "package," libraries sent out by the extension departments of universities; it is used in class rooms without offsetting material, and its existence is a matter of bibliographical record and distribution in the Bulletins of the Public Affairs Information Service, for which most libraries of any size subscribe, and in which all "free" items are marked with a star. These Bulletins cite comparatively little radical literature, because it does not come so generally to their attention, and star still less, because the radical organizations cannot financially afford to scatter it broadcast freely.

While it cannot be called a "method" of radicalism, doubtless some of the most effective publicity radicalism gets, and often with surprisingly favorable results, comes from its opponents. Persecution is an effective mode not only of advertising your opponent's cause, but advertising it at your own expense. Allusion was made above to the publicity thus given the suffrage campaign. The expulsion of the socialist members from the New York State Legislature, and the breaking up of the mass meeting of the National Birth Control Conference, by the New York City police, led by the secretary of the Catholic bishop

(November, 1921) are striking recent examples. Through such forceful opposition the attention of thousands of people is drawn to an issue or movement, of which they would otherwise be but dimly aware, and sympathy is aroused where there would otherwise be indifference or antipathy.

Here, too, should be mentioned the frequent case in which radical, or even merely liberal, speakers, are refused the opportunity to speak in schools, colleges, and churches.[19] Professor John Dewey tells us that upon his arrival in Japan to give a series of university lectures he was tactfully requested not to talk about political or social questions, but to confine himself to abstract philosophy. When he adds that a year before it was dangerous to utter the word "democracy" in Japan, we know that the Japanese are still a backward people. We can understand that in the case of the Japanese.

More recently, the Y. M. C. A. of the University of Oklahoma summarily refused to allow the European representatives of the Youth Movement to speak in its hall. Permission had been granted but was withdrawn when the rumor arrived that the young men were "reds."

Finally we have to record the well-recognized fact that popular radicalism, in its propaganda and agitation, has never hesitated to meet the claptrap sentiment, the chicane, the shibboleths, and slogans of vested-interest conservatism with its own appeal to passion and prejudice, and a numerous species of radical cant and catch phrases. Most of the popular, and much of the academic and so-called scientific, literature of socialism, for instance, is liberally besprinkled with these stock terms, phrases, and sentiments. Their meaning or foundations the average radical reader no more stops to analyze or criticize than the average conservative questions the meaning and finality of the "eternal verities" and "fundamental principles" handed out to him in his favorite kind of literature.

But most of all it is the appeal to passion; the spirit of

---

[19] University authorities, for instance, are sometimes placed in a very trying situation between the demands of reactionaries and radicals. When the President, and on appeal of students against his decision, the Regents of the University of Wisconsin recently refused the opportunity for the students' open forum to hear Oswald Garrison Villard, Kate O'Hare, and Scott Nearing, the fact was published throughout the country.

personal blame and its attendant name-calling and revilings; the inability to see anything good in conservative and especially in propertied persons; and the one-sided absence of any statement of the case of conservatism, and especially of capitalism, which characterize radical talk and the popular radical papers. The headlines of some of the labor papers (not, however, the general run of trade union magazines) are as inflammatory as the worst of the capitalistic press. And certain radical papers do not hesitate to distort facts, and grossly misrepresent conditions. Most propagandistic cartoons are vicious in their appeal to prejudice, and those in radical publications are no exception. The radical press, like yellow journalism, has a decided penchant for sensationalism. It is said that the Federated Press cannot place its news items and write-ups with many labor papers unless they are written in a somewhat lurid style. Finally, that there is some—the amount, though, is exaggerated—truth in the conservative belief that many labor leaders and agitators are corrupt, given to double-dealing and a self-aggrandizement, and that their liberalism or radicalism is mere pose and chicane is only too well attested by known facts—as revealed, for instance, in the Lockwood investigation where collusion was shown between building contractors and the officials of certain building trades in New York City.[20]

When these lower strata of human character and conduct are tapped, it is evident that there is little to choose between the baser methods of vested-interest conservatism and dishonest radicalism.

Escape from the slough of passion, prejudice, and angry combat does not lie in any method likely to be proposed or adopted by ideo-motor temperaments. For that reason it is high time we turned our attention to the nature and social significance of scientific method and the scientific attitude.

[20] See the *Intermediate Report of the Joint Legislative Committee on Housing*, New York State Legislative document No. 60, 1922. It would be unfair, however, to charge the conditions revealed by this report to radicalism.

CHAPTER IX

1. *The Relation of Scientific Method to Interest Conflicts*

FUNDAMENTALLY, conservatives and radicals are in opposition because their interests conflict. In the absence of interest conflict there might remain some slight difference in intellectual attitudes and convictions, as two groups might differ as to the reality of certain alleged facts or as to the significance of facts unanimously recognized. Difference in intellectual emphasis, divergence of foci of attention, and variations in logical method might still occasion some misunderstanding and friction, but in the absence of conflicts of interests and sentiments these differences would be relatively insignificant.

Conservative and radical are unable to agree on facts, not only because of the great difficulty of ascertaining and putting in orderly array all the facts pertinent to a complex issue, but to very great extent because they do not want to agree. Neither will admit that he sees the facts as the other sees them, because his interests are the glass through which he looks. Each sees the facts distorted by the refractive peculiarities of his own glass. And if he views the facts myopically or astigmatically through subjective distortions, still more is he likely to draw twisted interpretations and inferences. It is but a short step from emotional astigmatism to intellectual chicane and shifty logic. Even with complete honesty in their conscious rational processes, however, the two may never come to a common meeting ground of agreement, or even of profitable discussion, because of intense sentimental opposition.

Here we must recall that the difference in the general motivation of conservatism and of radicalism is derived from the different relation in which conservative and radical respectively stand to the existing *status quo*. Generally speaking, those relations are such that the conservative is fairly comfortable and

200

satisfied, while the radical is uncomfortable, dissatisfied, and driven to more or less consistent reinforcement of balked desires and obstructed interests. The conservative thinks that his interests are fairly well subserved by things-pretty-much-as-they-are; the radical knows that his are not. This conflict exists not only in the economic interests, where it is at present, if not always, most widespread and bitterly fought, but in all the fields of human interest. It is a conflict not only of specific desires and interests, but of sentiments, and of general attitudes.[1] In the economic field the conservative-radical conflict is, as we have seen, largely one between vested interests and the exploited and excluded. Where we are able to speak of "disinterested" conservatism the conflict is one in which unbroken habit and attachment are on their defense against the innovative projects of elements whose sentiments and loyalties are in one way or another detached from the conventional norms and institutions. To a certain extent the conflict may rise above the level of mere sentimental attachment and detachment and be carried out on a semi-rational plane. To this extent it becomes a conflict of rational estimates as to the human values or social utilities derivable from existing institutions and processes, in relation to human ends—on which there may be agreement, but usually is not.

It is well at this point to recall from our introductory chapter certain concepts and distinctions. An attitude (like conservatism or radicalism, or the scientific attitude) is a type of sentiment, or sentiment-complex, reaction—a generalized behavior-pattern. The individual characterized by a given attitude will meet and evaluate a given situation in a way typical to the attitude and predictable from it. Sentiments are emotional complexes or states in the presence of specific objects or situations, to which a valuation (an estimate of significance or importance) is attached, instinctively, habitually, intuitively, or even through rational processes. This value or significance is always relative, not only to the situation, but to the situation

---

[1] This conflict or "rivalry" is discussed at length and in detail, and with great wealth of illustration, in J. M. Williams, *Principles of Social Psychology, as Developed in a Study of Economic and Social Conflict*, 1922, a book which did not come to hand until after the present chapter was written.

regarded (not necessarily consciously) as a means to an end—that is, with reference to its bearing on interests. The process of valuation may be entirely sentimental—a matter of immediate feeling—or it may be rational, intellectively mediated. In the later case it may or may not be scientific.

Omitting those relatively rare cases in which the situation is scientifically, objectively, and disinterestedly evaluated, the conflicts of valuation, being in the main reducible to conflicts of sentiment, are nearly always accompanied by the impulse to personal praise and blame. These in turn intensify the conflict. Sentimental valuations thus tend to produce groupings and group conflicts. For conflicts of this type there are three levels of solution. In the absence of tolerance the outcome will be determined by superior force. Where sufficient tolerance is present to give opportunity for negotiation, and where each group has a healthy fear of the other, the outcome may be an opportunistic compromise—each group giving in just as much as it has to and no more. Thus far sentiments are the basis of the solution. The third level is that of objective analysis of the facts and issues involved. This method may not be able to eliminate the fundamental interest conflict, but, if sufficient opportunity is given, it can eliminate, or at least surmount, the personalistic blame reactions resultant upon sentimental approaches to a problem. Finally, objective scientific analysis of the issue may prepare the way for constructive effort—"creative intelligence."

Given only open-mindedness and sound methods of observation and logic, any purely intellectual conflict, other than speculations based on mutually incompatible metaphysical postulates, can be solved by the accumulation of factual evidence. A conflict of interests, on the other hand, can be solved, if at all, only by the opponents coming to agreement on some common ethical ground, that is, by such re-definition of their interests and modification of their attitudes as will lead them to judge the facts of the situation by reference to some higher standard of ethical valuation.

Briefly, and excluding from consideration at this point the problem of deciding between ends, social issues, if they are to be settled fairly and as presumably rational beings should settle them, are not to be settled by brute force, dogmatic appeal to authority and precedent; or trickery, emotional frumpery, and chicane; but by the arbitrament of fact. They can be solved only through the objective, scientific method of investigation and decision. The leading social function of scientific method is thus to delimit emotional or interest conflict to the sphere of ends or purposes, and to diminish, so far as humanly possible, the rôle played by subjective illusion and emotional astigmatism in the ordering of human affairs. In a word, the moral function of the scientific method is to rationalize interest conflicts.

That is why it is necessary to give consideration to the scientific method and attitude in these chapters. Employment of the scientific method is necessary for the discovery of the essential factual data upon which the orderly solution of social issues must be based. The scientific attitude or spirit is necessary as a check, both upon over-sentimental, conservative attachment and upon too headlong radical reinforcement.

2. *The General Features of Scientific Method*

While there are analogies to scientific method in the mental activity of every normal individual, no one can use this method consistently, who has not acquired a consistent scientific attitude. Given the attitude the corresponding method will follow. In practice it requires a long educational discipline, with emphasis upon the sciences, to secure the scientific attitude in an individual—long not because of any inherent difficulty or complexity in the scientific method itself, since in its fundamentals it is comparatively simple, but because it takes time to dislodge the sentimental, subjective, and prejudicial attitudes fixed in boys and girls by the social controls which are constantly bearing upon them.[2] Few persons ever acquire even a passably consistent objectivity, especially with regard to social problems.

Our main concern in this chapter is therefore to explain, as clearly as we can in limited space, the scientific attitude, and to point out the obstacles and contrasts to it in the popular mind. Some of the most significant elements in the scientific attitude cannot well be understood apart from reference to scientific method. We shall not need, however, to give, even

---

[2] See above, pp. 48-53.

from an elementary standpoint, a full statement of the steps and characteristics of the scientific method. We will limit our discussion to such a statement as will bring out the salient characteristics of the scientific attitude, and give us a glimpse into the processes and problems of scientific method, as related to the investigation of social phenomena and the solution of social problems, especially that of conflict of interests.

Let us begin with that older type of science known as classificatory or taxonomic science. Its chief task was to classify phenomena. It was the delight and the great work of the old-time naturalists, men like Cuvier in zoölogy and paleontology, and Linnæus and Asa Gray in botany, to study the structure of animals and plants, and on the basis of their structure to classify them into families, genera, and species. Although the task of naming the animals had scripturally been laid upon Adam, Adam had not completed it, as there remained some millions of unnamed species. A family, in "natural history," is a wide group of organisms, animal or plant, having certain structural characteristics in common. A genus is a narrower group, composed of individuals which all have not only the structure peculiar to the family, but additional common structural characteristics. A species is a still smaller group, in which the individuals have the same family and generic characteristics and in addition certain common "specific" ones. All the members of a species are very much alike, those of a genus less so; those of a family still less.

Now it is clear that plants and animals, or for that matter any other objects, can be assorted into species, etc., only by observing likenesses and differences. The steps in the method of classificatory science have traditionally been stated as (1) observation, (2) analysis and comparison (observing likenesses and differences), (3) generalization or induction. While this statement will do provisionally, it will be evident later on that it gives only the skeleton of scientific method.

The first step in any scientific investigation or analysis is like the beginning of the traditional recipe for cooking a rabbit— "first catch your rabbit." Scientific method starts with observation of facts. The second step, or rather one which should be taken jointly with observation, is the recording of the observed facts, preparatory to their later analysis. Record is both an adjunct to memory (itself a kind of record, but an exceedingly unreliable one) and an aid to orderly and purposeful observation. The observing, collecting, and recording of facts is by no means as simple as it may at first thought appear. Later in this chapter some of the chief difficulties in the way of accurate and adequate observation, especially in fields intimately touching human interests and relations, are noted.[3]

When all the facts which essentially appertain to the particular phenomena under investigation, or as many of the facts as can be made available, are observed and recorded, the next step is analysis. Analysis is a complex process, involving (1) the splitting up of apparently simple facts into their elements, (2) observing the qualities or attributes of these elements, (3) comparison of these attributes, to discover likenesses and differences in the nature of the facts. Briefly, analysis is the process of finding out the nature of the facts and their relation to one another. These relations may be either relations of co-existence or of sequence, and in either case may or may not be "causal."

Analysis and comparison put us in position to classify, and to build up abstract or generalized concepts of classes. This process is generalization or induction. Induction is the process of reasoning from particulars to the general. Every concept is originally built up by a process of induction. Our idea of pine trees is the inductive result of observation and comparison of many individual trees, all more or less alike, yet more or less different. But the likenesses exceed the differences, or at least there are always certain common characteristics which we come to think of, apart from trees in particular, as the characteristics of a *type* which we call the genus *Pinus*. When we have observed and analyzed the facts of a sufficient number of similar events or phenomena, we are in position to observe in the various "cases" similarities of correlation and sequence. Not until we have made such comparison and classification are we ready to draw our induction—that is, to formulate a general statement of the relationships common to this kind of phenomena.

Inductive investigation comprises, broadly speaking, all the

---

[3] See pp. 234, 235, 242, 243, 248, 249.

processes of observation and analysis of specific cases to discover similarities of sequence and correlation. When these
similarities are found to constitute an invariable repetition of
similarity, sequence, or correlation, that fact is stated as briefly
and accurately as possible in a generalization or "law"—which
is merely a "brief, shorthand statement" of the observed relations and sequences. Briefly, induction is the derivation of a
generalization or "law" from experience.

In practice, every new scientific generalization is arrived at
not only upon the basis of observed facts, but also by a process
which includes not only inductive reasoning, but deductive application of scientific generalizations previously established.
Moreover, in the tentative formulation of a law much use may
be made of hypothesis as to the presence of significant facts not
yet made out. Such a tentatively formulated law must be
recognized as provisional, however, until the hypothetical elements are verified. Practically, therefore, no scientific generalization is made without a much more complex process of observation, analysis, comparison, and inductive inference than that
above suggested. Since every new scientific generalization is
based upon generalizations previously made and accepted,
every change or correction in these previous generalizations
requires modification in the laws or generalizations based upon
them.

It is evident that deduction—reasoning from the general to
the particular—is quite as necessary in scientific investigation
as is induction. The great difference in logical method between
modern science and the old time philosophy is that science checks
its deductive processes by continual reference to experience.
But scientific progress would be impossible, did not every scientist use, of course with critical care, the generalizations of
others, present and past, as part of the data for his own observational and logical processes. In thus using them he is not only
furthering his own inquiries, but is constantly putting these
prior generalizations to the acid test of truth—that is, whether
or not they will "work."

It is clear, of course, that every scientific investigator must
exercise care, not only to see that his observations and experi-
ments are free from subjective bias (that what he records as
fact *is* fact) and his logical processes free from fallacy (*e.g.,*

that his mathematical calculations are free from error), but that the generalizations he employs as guide to his observations or as premises in his reasoning are themselves scientifically well founded.

Evidently, then, certain things are essential to scientific method. These indispensables are: (1) a body of observed facts, (2) established generalizations, principles, or laws, the result of previous scientific work, (3) the fundamental laws of thought or logic. (Anyone who thinks that two and two make five, or who calls black white, will not make a successful scientist.)

To these fundamental essentials must be added certain other equipments or processes, namely, (4) scientific imagination, which aids in directing observation, analysis, and inference, and which enables the investigator to form (5) hypotheses.

An hypothesis is a more or less shrewd guess, formulated in reference to incomplete or incompletely analyzed data, as to conclusions or generalizations which may on further investigation validly be drawn from them. Or it may be an assumption with regard to the existence of certain factual data not actually observed. It was thus, for instance, that the planet Neptune was discovered, in 1846. The then outermost planet known, Uranus, was not behaving in its orbital revolution around the sun exactly as the computations of astronomers showed it should behave, on the basis of the gravitational influence of the then known bodies of the solar system. So the hypothesis was formed that there must be another planet outside the orbit of Uranus, causing the otherwise inexplainable perturbation in the movement of Uranus. This hypothesis was verified by the discovery of Neptune, after magnificent and independent mathematical calculations by Adams and Leverrier, which enabled them to tell observers approximately where they would, at a given time, find the new planet.

To hypothesis must be added (6) experiment; but as experiment is not usually possible, in the strict scientific sense, in the realm of phenomena with which the social scientist has to deal, we may pass it by without explanatory comment.

And finally, (7) analogy plays an important, but dangerous rôle, in scientific inquiry. At best, it is but a kind of hypothesis, or hypothetical reasoning, which one interested in unravelling the nature of social phenomena and social causation had best avoid. The main trouble with analogy is that it leads us to see likenesses and overlook differences.[4]

The foregoing attempt briefly to state the elements of scientific method has made no reference to "cause" or "causation." Properly amplified and illustrated it would constitute a fairly adequate statement of the method of the older taxonomic science, science in the stage of definition and classification. But science to-day has gone far beyond the taxonomic stage, though classification is still as necessary as ever; scientific investigation is now engaged primarily in problems of sequence or causation. We want to know not only what things are, and what their generic and specific relationships are, but why they act as they do. The emphasis of scientific investigation has swung from structure to function. In biology, for instance, we study the comparative anatomy of ascidians, not to classify ascidians into exact genera and species (for that in the main has already been done), but for the light comparative anatomy may throw upon physiological processes, a matter of causal relationships. And in economics, after a century of taxonomic discussion, which has not yet, however, produced a consistent and generally accepted set of definitions and concepts, we are to-day less interested in the classificatory relation of capital to other forms of wealth

---

[4] The reader who desires a more adequate undertsanding of the processes of scientific method than can be gained from the above sketch may consult the little book on the *Principles of Science*, by W. F. Cooley, 1912. It is perhaps the best available brief presentation of what scientific method involves. See also J. E. Creighton, *An Introductory Logic*, 4th edition, 1920, Part II. Readers interested in pursuing the general subject further should consult Karl Pearson, *Grammar of Science*, 2nd edition, 1900. (In the 3rd edition of this work, 1911, it was planned in two volumes, but only the first volume has thus far been published. The 2nd edition is thus the best for the general student.) John Stuart Mill, *System of Logic*, 5th edition, 1872; W. Stanley Jevons, *The Principles of Science, a Treatise on Logic and Scientific Method*, 1874; John Dewey and others, *Creative Intelligence, Essays in the Pragmatic Attitude* (especially the chapter of "Scientific Method and the Individual Thinker," by George H. Mead), 1917; Bertrand Russell, *Mysticism and Logic*, 1918, Chs. 2, 6, and 9; *The Problems of Philosophy* (Home University Library), Chs. 5-7, 12-14; *Scientific Method in Philosophy*, 1913. Suggestive matter may also be found in John Fiske, *Outlines of Cosmic Philosophy*, 1874, Vol. I, Part I, Chs. 1, 3, 5, and 6, and, in V. Pareto, *Traité de Sociologie Général*, 2 vols., 1917, especially Vol. I, Ch. 1.

than we are in the function of capital—what it does that interest should be paid to its owner.[5]

If we mean by scientific method merely freedom from subjective bias in observing and recording facts, mere observation, orderly arrangement, cataloguing, and description may be called "scientific." In this sense an accurate, objective description of the state of a city's streets, or of the physiognomy of thieves may be "scientific." A monograph describing the distribution of population by age, sex, conjugal condition, etc., is scientific in this descriptive sense. So is a table, based on objectively obtained data, showing the ups and downs of the bank discount rate, or the number of suicides or infant deaths by months and years.

But in a more accurate sense, such descriptive productions are but the raw material—the factual data—necessary to analysis and solution of problems of cause and effect—the problems which are now of primary interest to us.

We want to know *why* the streets are in the condition described, *why* the demographic distribution of the population is what it is, why discount, and suicide, and death rates fluctuate as they do. And, to the extent that we are objective and scientific, we desire solution of these "whys," these causation problems, not in the personalistic praise-and-blame terms of the popular-minded and usually more or less propagandistic conservative or radical, and not in terms of "final causes," which explain nothing, but in terms of impersonal, phenomenal correlation and sequence.

Generally speaking, naturalists before the time of Darwin were interested in species as species. The traditional authoritarian doctrine that each species was the result of a direct and special Divine act of creation, unintermediated by any evolutionary or developmental process, precluded much inquiry into the causation or developmental origin of species. Since the publication of Darwin's great work in 1859,[6] the interest has centered

---

[5] Nevertheless, as we shall see (pp. 245-247), one thing which still makes the application of scientific method to the investigation of social problems very difficult is the lack of a sufficient body of accurate and generally accepted definitions.

[6] *The Origin of Species.*

almost wholly in developmental or casual processes. The old geography which our parents and grandparents studied, to take another illustration, was a dry catalogue of rivers, cities, boundaries, and commercial statistics. The study of geography today, in good schools at least, has to do with causal relations between man, or human culture, and the physical environment—a much more interesting, as well as an infinitely more important study. Or take our chapters on conservatism and radicalism. There has been some analysis, defining, and classification, but not for their own sake, and only in so far as seemed essential to discover and elucidate the causes and effects of these attitudes.

Now what do we mean by "cause" and "causation"?

In the scientific sense, a "cause" is merely a fact, phenomenon, or event, which invariably precedes another. If the first event is the cause of the second, the second does not occur unless the other has taken place. More accurately, the cause of an event comprises all the preceding and co-existent events without which the event in question does not occur. Causation is invariable sequence. If we find that a particular type of event, B, never takes place until another event, A, has taken place, we say that event A is the cause of event B. Where we are observing and analyzing a particular event or phenomenon—one, let us suppose, unique to our experience—we cannot be certain that the phenomenon or event preceding it is its cause, in the sense that the same sequence would be observed in a second case. To conclude forthwith that event A preceding event B in this particular case is the cause of B, would commit us to the *post hoc, propter hoc* fallacy. We are conscious of the danger of falling into this fallacy, this false inference, because long observation has taught us that one event may precede another in a given case without doing so in another case. It is only after observation of *repeated* sequences that we are entitled to draw generalizations as to "causal" relations, or invariable sequences.

Readers of Mark Twain will remember that his Connecticut Yankee in King Arthur's Court got into a tight place at a tournament and was compelled to shoot a couple of knights, who were charging down upon him. There was a loud report and a dead knight—and a court thrown into consternation, because it had no experience of firearms and consequently was in no position to render the sort of verdict as to causation that a modern jury would render without hesitation. Subsequently, the world, through much repetition of experience, has come to know all about firearms and their causal sequences.

So, if we wish to state *causal* relations observed as parts of a given event, we have to collect the facts pertaining to a large number of similar events. Accepting as true the tradition about Newton and the apple, the one apple's fall was only a suggestive event to Newton, possibly productive in his mind of an hypothesis as to a possible "causal" law of gravitation. But his formulation of the law of gravitation came only after prolonged mathematical analysis and the use of observations and calculations by earlier investigators. More than that, the "law" was not accepted as true until it had been subjected, not only to rigid verification of the mathematical analysis by which it was arrived at, but to the test of experience, when it turned out that all observed bodies do "attract each other" substantially as the law describes.[7]

The reason we are continually cross-questioning nature with inquiries into What? How? Where? and Why? lies partly in the desire to know truth for its own sake, and partly to know truth which may have practical application in solving problems or meeting practical needs. Many scientists hold to the ideal "science for science's sake," but in practice an immense amount of scientific research is carried through with utilitarian ends in view.

It is argued with some cogency that there may be a tendency in the utilitarian aim to impair the scientific objectivity of an investigation. This danger, greater in social science than anywhere else, must be freely recognized. We must constantly be on our guard against it, but whatever the abstract ideal as to the proper motivation of scientific inquiry may be, it is clear that we are constantly confronted with social problems and issues on which objective data are needed and for which scientific solutions must be sought.

One reason why we seek a cause-and-effect analysis of phenomena is because we wish to predict and control. We not only

---

[7] "Substantially," not absolutely, if Einstein's revision of the law be proved, on further observation, to be necessary. It appears also that intra-atomic particles—ions—do not move in accordance with Newton's law.

want to know the facts about infant mortality in the present and the past, but we want to be able to predict the future effect of certain conditions, and, through our ability to predict, to modify these conditions and control the future infant mortality rate. In the case of such a social phenomenon or problem, the urge to research is a practical, moral motive rather than an expression of pure scientific curiosity.

It should be clear that rational control of phenomena (either physical or social) can rest only upon the basis of scientific investigation and knowledge of causes and effects. Control is impossible without prevision; prevision is impossible in the absence of knowledge of causal correlation and sequence. The ability accurately to predict is the test of the validity of scientific conclusions or generalizations.

Between scientific prevision (foreseeing) and popular prediction (foretelling) there is a world of difference. The latter is generally based upon inaccurate and ill-balanced observation and confused analysis, and not infrequently upon positive illusion and intellectual dishonesty. We saw, for instance, that conservatives are given to predicting that dire results will flow from innovation. Some predictions of that kind may be realized because they are founded on adequate experience; some are the result of sincere conviction, but are based upon inadequate experience and consequently would not necessarily be true; while some are the product of sinister interests which do not hesitate to distort the facts, to lie, and to arouse groundless fears, if only by so doing these interests can prevent undesired changes. Scientific prevision, on the other hand, is firmly founded on experimental, observational knowledge of facts and objective analysis of their causal connections.

Both conservative and radical are given to long-range prediction on slender data or experience. The enthusiastic radical is sure that his particular plan of reform or revolution will usher in the millennium. The dyed-in-the-wool conservative meets every proposal for innovative improvement with the objection "It can never be done!" Science realizes that "never" is a long word. That is one reason, perhaps, why scientific men are chary of making long-range predictions, especially in fields involving so many unknown data and such a variety of ill-understood forces as do social phenomena.

Prediction can be accurate, and the control dependent upon our power to predict efficient, just to the extent that the scientific knowledge upon which it is founded is adequate and exact. Put briefly and somewhat technically, reliability of prediction and efficiency of control depend upon positivity of knowledge. No scientific law or generalization is absolute. It is relative to the data from which it is derived and of which it is a "brief resumé" or shorthand statement.[8] A scientific generalization must always be read with the proviso "so far as we know," or "as far as observation shows." In general, the positivity or accuracy of scientific generalizations, and of the deductions and predictions drawn from them, are in direct proportion to the degree to which observation and inductive inference have taken account of all the facts pertinent to the phenomena involved. We can predict that the sun will rise to-morrow morning with greater certainty than we can say whether it will rise clear or cloudy.

Generally speaking, those sciences where the data is capable of accurate observation and measurement, which are accordingly called the "exact" sciences, are characterized by a high degree of positivity, while in those where the data are so numerous and so intricately inter-related that they are not easily reducible to accurate observation and measurement the degree of positivity is low.

The physical sciences, astronomy, physics, chemistry, and to a less degree biology, with its border sciences bio-chemistry and genetics, belong to the class of exact sciences—sciences in which accurate observation and record are possible, and in which analysis, both inductive and deductive, is carried on with the indispensable aid of mathematics and statistics. The social sciences, including psychology (which, however, in its fundamental aspects, may be classified with the natural sciences), economics, political science, anthropology, sociology, and ethics belong to the group of inexact or "synoptic"[9] sciences, although in all of them there is an increasing use of statistical methods.

Generalizations in social science are highly relative. To say, for instance, that population tends to press on food supply is

---

[8] Pearson, *Grammar of Science*, 2d edition, 1900, Ch. 3.
[9] See Pearson, *op. cit.*, pp. 513, 514.

true only for given conditions. It is generally not true in new countries, or among peoples who have learned to control their fecundity. That social inferiors tend to emulate their superiors may be true in general, but there are cases in which the opposite is true. We got ragtime, jazz, and the turkey trot from the savages of the South Seas or some equally heathen part of the earth, and fashions in women's clothes are said to be set by the fast women of Paris. That men consciously calculate pains and pleasures is true, but it does not follow that all economic acts' are the result of conscious calculation. That women are inferior to men in intellectual output is true, but that is not to say that they are so because of hereditary factors or that they must continue to be so. Illustrations of relativity could be multiplied practically without limit.

It must be admitted that writers and investigators in the social science fields have been slow to recognize this principle. The social sciences were offshoots of philosophy and metaphysics, and that, among other reasons, retarded them in acquiring really scientific methods of investigation. Psychology suffered from close association with deductive and absolutistic metaphysics. Economics was an offshoot of political and moral philosophy. Sociology built out "cantilever fashion," as Ross puts it,[10] from biology, and fell a prey to superficial analogical methods from which it has not yet fully recovered. Nearly all the social sciences were greatly retarded by the early desire they manifested to reduce everything to terms of some one or two or three "fundamental postulates." Orthodox economics had its "economic man" with his "economic motive," and its god "free competition." Socialistic economics followed with its "class struggle" and "surplus value." Modern political philosophy, the precursor of political science, started either with Hegelian absolutes or with "social contract" and "natural liberty." Anthropology had its "parallels," and sociologists vied in proposing "fundamental social facts" in terms of which sociological generalizations were to be formulated. All this, especially when coupled to a very prevalent tendency of social "scientists" to draw sweeping "laws" from very slender factual data, not unnaturally led the natural scientists to distrust and then to

---

[10] *Foundations of Sociology*, 1905, p. 50.

ridicule the pretensions of the social subjects to a scientific status. A part of this distrust, however, was due to a too narrow conception of science and scientific method—to limitation of the term scientific to investigations which could be carried on with mathematical or quasi-mathematical exactitude. This conception is fallacious, for reasons which it would take too long to explain here.[11] Science, indeed, may be regarded as measurement, and in this sense, it is always quantitative, but measurement, or valuation, to be a valid basis of generalization, prediction, and control, need not be reducible to exact mathematical units. Much pseudo-scientific work, indeed, has resulted, in the field of the social sciences, from premature attempts at mathematical method and statement—for instance, in much of the economics of diminishing utility and marginal productivity.

On the other hand, great promise for development of scientific knowledge in the social science fields now lies in the introduction, and in the rapid development and refinement of the use, of statistical methods of observation, record, and analysis. By reason of such comparatively recent developments, as well as the present widespread interest in scientific methodology in the social sciences, one need not hesitate to believe that scientific method will gradually supplant emotional conflict and personalistic discussion in large measure, at least among liberally educated people.

3. *Characteristics of the Scientific Attitude*

Before scientific method can be widely and confidently utilized to guide social policy, and before the general populace will be willing to adopt such guidance, certain difficulties will have to be overcome or greatly diminished, and certain very prevalent attitudinal obstacles, some of which have been suggested with perhaps sufficient fullness in the preceding chapters, will have to be removed. In a word, the application of scientific *method* to the investigation of social problems, and to the solution of social issues and conflicts, is conditioned upon the acquirement of the scientific *attitude.*

It must be firmly borne in upon us that the scientific attitude rests upon one, and only one, fundamental article of faith

---

[11] See Pearson, *op. cit.*, Ch. 12.

—faith in the universality of cause and effect. Without this faith, a steady, undaunted pursuit of scientific knowledge as a guide to action may be incontinently flouted whenever it interferes with special interest or prejudice.

Scientific generalizations are constantly undergoing revision, but that is true only because further observation and analysis correct shortcomings and defects in previous investigation. There is, as we have attempted to point out, nothing absolute about any scientific "law" or generalization; but that is so only because of our finite powers of observation and logical inference. What we ought to know is infinite, what we can know is finite, what we do know infinitesimal. A mind of sufficient power could formulate absolute generalizations or formulæ,[12] and they would never stand in need of revision, because they would take full account of every force in the universe.

If, however, the universe—that is, nature—were a realm of whim instead of a dependable mechanism, observation, classification, and analysis would obviously be futile. We might just as well look for the sun to rise in the west any day, a Bermuda onion plant to yield oranges one day and potatoes the next, or an angry man to be reasonable.

Science, in other words, is deterministic—must be so. No one who does not become a thoroughgoing determinist can ever completely acquire the scientific attitude. One who is able to take the scientific point of view, and to lay aside the idea that there is such a thing as whim or chance, sees the universe as a mechanism. A mechanism is an inter-relation of causes and

---

[12] "Taking all such functions for all the particles in the universe, there will be theoretically some one formula embracing them all, and this formula may be regarded as the single and supreme law of the spatio-temporal world."—Bertrand Russell, *Scientific Method of Philosophy*, 1913, p. 8.

"This notion of 'chance' is a misleading figment inherited of the modern world from the days of blank ignorance. The 'Nature-searchers' of to-day admit no such possibility as of chance. . . . A leading writer and investigator of the Mid-Victorian Era, the physicist John Tyndall, pointed out, in a celebrated address delivered at Belfast that according to the conceptions of the mechanism of nature arrived at by modern science, the structure of that mechanism is such that it would have been possible for a being of adequate intelligence inspecting the gaseous nebula from which our planetary system has evolved to have foreseen in that luminous vapor the Belfast audience and the professor addressing it!"—E. Ray Lankester, *The Kingdom of Man*, 1907, p. 8.

effects. It is something we can analyze. We can understand its processes, and in a measure control them to our own purposes. Of nothing else, were anything else scientifically conceivable, is this true.

Once perceive the significance of this fundamental faith in the uniformity and dependability of nature, and it becomes evident that the scientist must regard man as a part of nature, and must hold that social relations, for all their seeming whimsicality and indeterminate complexity, function in complete accord with the universal law of cause and effect. Both man's organism [13] and his social organization and processes are simply parts of the natural mechanism of cause-and-effect correlations and sequences. As we more fully realize this fact, and as we attain more adequate analytical power and knowledge, we can investigate these psychological and social mechanisms and describe their operation—their correlations and sequences—and formulate these descriptions in the convenient form of scientific psychological and sociological generalizations or laws.

The mechanistic conception of the universe, including human activity and social relations, leaves no place for "explanation" of phenomena by reference to mystical or metaphysical entities, nor for the time-honored idea of the freedom of the will. Psychologists have practically ceased to have any interest in the old dispute over free will and determinism, partly, no doubt, because the phrase free will can be made to mean anything or nothing, but mainly because psychology, becoming scientific, necessarily becomes thoroughly deterministic. Those philosophers who still think that the free will tradition is worth saving, are compelled by the march of the scientific conception of life and our increasing specific knowledge of the mechanism of human behavior, either to state the libertarian doctrine in terms which deprive it of any practical significance, or to push it back into transcendental metaphysics where it takes on a wordy and scientifically meaningless nebulosity.

A very essential prerequisite to the scientific study of social relations and processes is a well-developed objective, scientific psychology. The lack of a mechanistic psychology, free from

---

[13] Whether analyzed and described in "psychic" or physical terms, or in some inconsistent but possibly convenient combination of the two.

à priori philosophical and metaphysical presuppositions, based upon prolonged and disciplined observation and inductive analysis of human behavior, which will utilize the fast accumulating knowledge of physiology, has probably been the chief obstacle to the development of an objective treatment of human affairs. Such a psychology—the mechanistic psychology of behavior [14]— is now in process of rapid development. Its methods and postulates aim to be scientific in the fundamental sense. It regards the human individual as a mechanism, and the key to its understanding an objective analysis of the mechanism of stimulus and response, from the simplest to the most complex aspects of that process. In a word, behavioristic or mechanistic psychology seeks the verifiable causes (sequences) of human activity. It aims to discover the facts as to the mechanism of human personality and the causation of the individual temperaments and attitudes.[15]

Already, although research in this field is still in its infancy, it is becoming clear that variations in temperament and "personality" and hence in the type of behavior to be expected of an individual, are to no small degree influenced by the secretions of the ductless glands. Knowledge in this field has gone far enough to have occasioned some important changes in the treatment of diseases and abnormalities.[16] This is in direct line with the faith that man is a part of nature, and that there is an observable mechanism of life and action, which if we are only at pains to investigate with sufficient scientific patience and accuracy will give us true knowledge of human nature and its work-

---

[14] It is needless to state that the term behavior as used in modern psychology carries no moral implications whatever.

[15] Many able men still, of course, either reject this mechanistic view on ethical grounds or hold it impracticable as a guide to method. Because every advance hitherto made in study of the "psycho-physical" mechanism reveals, as he thinks, ever greater complexities and more difficult problems calling for solution, Mr. J. S. Haldane, for example (*Mechanism, Life and Personality*, 1921), despairs of our ever reaching a thoroughgoing mechanistic—that it, scientific—explanation, and falls back on a mystical entity "personality," which really explains nothing.

[16] Although it is highly technical and somewhat daring in its inferences, the reader may consult S. W. Bandler's *The Endocrines*, 1921. See also W. B. Cannon, *Bodily Changes in Pain, Hunger, Fear and Rage*, 1920, and B. Harrow's *Glands in Health and Disease*, 1922. For other references see p. 145.

ings. The psychoanalysts, although they use a different method of approach, and a different terminology, are working along the same mechanistic lines.

We may be permitted to point out again that the more thoroughly we see the truth of this mechanistic theory of life, and the more we know about the causation of human conduct, the less room we have for personalistic praise-and-blame attitudes. The thoroughly scientific position leaves no room for praise, blame, or punishment, if by punishment we mean any element of revenge and not simply the sort of stimuli which act as deterrents on socially undesirable conduct. Praise and blame may be used as methods of influencing behavior, but for any other purpose or in any other sense science has no place for "moral responsibility" or "moral desert."

Not only, then, is the scientific mind deterministic; it does not limit its faith in cause and effect to the physical world, but extends it to include man; it regards man as a part of the mechanistic universe; it rejects the doctrine of freedom of the will as incompatible with scientific attitude; and finally, in its psychology it shows an increasing tendency to be thoroughly behavioristic.

But while the thorough scientific mind believes that nothing happens except as an effect of a complex of causes, and that every event has its train of effects, it does not hold that we can state causal laws with more than approximate truth or accuracy, although the inaccuracy may be found only "in the fourth decimal." The scientific mind is in this sense pragmatic. It regards scientific knowledge as a sort of calculus of probabilities.

With regard to mental processes, the scientific attitude is marked by certain characteristics which we can only mention, trusting that their importance will be recognized without discussion. In general, the scientist is what William James called "tough-minded," or empirical. His mind is inductive before it is deductive. It is keenly analytical. It is constructively, but critically, imaginative. It is highly skeptical and critical of all assumptions and hypotheses, and never accepts any one of them as established truth, suitable as other than tentative basis for deductive processes, until it has successfully withstood the test of the most exacting criticism and experience. It is severely critical of all logical processes and methods, whether of inductive or deductive inference.

Finally, the scientific spirit is characterized by certain distinctive attitudes toward facts. These include (1) scientific curiosity, that is, a certain breadth and intensity of interest in things, which is sustained and directed by a faculty for concentrated attention and power of penetrating, accurate, and extensive observation, (2) an unlimited respect for facts, combined with fearless honesty and the utmost attainable impersonality (freedom from interest-and-emotion-bias) in facing facts, however inconvenient and disagreeable they may be, (3) cautious skepticism with regard to alleged facts if their authenticity or reality has not been established by scientifically adequate objective testimony.

4. *Difficulties and Obstacles*

The difficulties in the way of applying the scientific method to the evaluation of conflicting interests and the solution of social issues may be treated in two groups, (1) difficulties due to subjective interests and biases, and (2) difficulties which would be encountered even if we were free from subjective biases and personal interests and were all of normal physical temperament.

We shall consider first the difficulties due to subjective biases, inasmuch as they involve a contrast, which it is needful to analyze at this point, between the scientific attitude, the elements of which we have just outlined, and the non-scientific or popular attitude.

This first group of difficulties must itself be divided into two classes; first, those which are encountered in the scientist's own mind, but which he consciously recognizes, and as far as possible guards against; second, the qualities of the average popular mind, which has little or no conception of the rigors of scientific method and makes no pretense of applying it.

The subjective difficulties in the scientist's own mind are difficulties more or less inherent in the scientific method, especially where it is used in the investigation of human affairs. They are in a sense intensive difficulties. The difficulties which lie in the characteristics of the popular mind are rather obstacles to the extension and acceptance of scientific method as the only sound basis for social construction. Here two considerations should be noted. Minds which come anywhere near the scientific ideal are scarce. There is a dearth of men and women who have at the same time the requisite intellectual power, the disinterested objectivity of attitude, and the rigid discipline in scientific method, essential to the investigation of social problems and issues in a non-partisan and non-temperamental manner. In the second place, it is necessary to get scientifically established truth, once it has been obtained, before the people in a way that will secure their attention and interest, their acceptance of it, and finally action upon it. The more partisan, dogmatic, self-interested, and in general subjective the people are, the harder this task will be.

The subjective difficulties in general, and in particular those inherent in popular-mindedness, are of exceedingly great importance, especially in a democracy, where scientific conclusions can have ready influence upon social practice only if the people can be induced to acquire the ability and the willingness to heed them and apply them. Unfortunately, it is the popular, unscientific mind which makes up the bulk of the voting public, which usually secures the active leadership in politics, and constitutes the great, and thus far, unsurmounted, obstacle to the rationalizing of social control and our handling of social and economic problems. Social efficiency, peace, and justice, and more specifically, the de-emotionalizing and de-personalizing of the conflict between conservative and radical, thus rest squarely upon our success in rationalizing and disciplining the popular mind.

Leaving for later discussion the subjective difficulties which the scientist finds in his own mental traits, let us first ask what are the significant traits of this popular mind, in so far as they constitute obstacles to the spread of the scientific attitude and method.

These traits are so important that we shall outline them with some fulness. They can be brought out most clearly, and the contrasting characteristics of the scientific mind indicated more fully, if we compare, in parallel columns, the characteristics of the two types of mind.

The Scientific Mind	The Popular Mind
1. Objective. Impersonal. Desire subordinated to intellect and reason.	1. Subjective. Personal. Intellect and reason subordinated to desire.
2. Observant. Sensitive. Curiosity impersonal and disciplined. Attention alert and pointed.	2. Unobservant. Insensitive. Curiosity personal or lacking. Attention diffuse and uncertain.
3. Significantly informed.	3. Insignificantly informed or ignorant.
4. Objectively skeptical, (factual skepticism).	4. Credulous, or subjectively skeptical.
5. Critical (a) of premises (b) of logical processes.	5. Uncritical, or critical only of logical processes.
6. Tolerant.	6. Intolerant.
7. Intellectually patient. (Can suspend judgment.)	7. Intellectually impatient. (Jumps at conclusions.)
9. Constructively imaginative.	9. Fanciful, or unimaginative.
10. Fearless in facing facts.	10. Fearful of disagreeable facts.
11. Courageous in defending its scientific convictions.	11. Lacking in the courage of its convictions, unless motivated by special interest, or backed by authority.
12. Unimpressionable by authority or prestige.	12. Reverential to authority, impressed by prestige.
13. Intellectually unconventional.	13. Intellectually conventional.
14. Unegotistic.	14. Egotistic.
15. Deterministic. Behavioristic. Not given to praising and blaming. Faith in law.	15. Libertarian. Given to praising and blaming. Faith in whim.

Some of these characteristics require elucidation; some perhaps do not. Taking them in order named, the traits first contrasted, objectivity versus subjectivity, determine, or include, all the rest. In other words, the traits which approximate a mind to the scientific ideal collectively amount to objectivity of attitude and method, while the further from the scientific standard a mind is the more its traits make for subjectivity. The content of the term "objective" is thus accurately indicated by the characteristics set down in the first column; that of "subjective" by those in the second column.

Put, inadequately, in terms of belief, the objective mind believes what it *has* to believe, the subjective what it *wants* to believe.[17] The objective mind senses reality, observes the world, without reference to its own personal desires; the subjective mind looks at things through the glass of desire. The scientific mind maintains an impersonal attitude toward the world—the attitude of an emotionally distinterested but intellectually curious onlooker. The non-scientific mind usually approaches the world with the thought, "How is this going to affect me?" The objective mind is intellective and relatively unsentimental. The subjective mind is always sentimental (though it may hide the fact); it may be intellective and rational, but only to a degree and within limits set by its emotional habits and predilections.

The popular mind is unobservant. It does not use its senses; they are relatively untrained and unalert. It perceives only that part of the world to which its routine of life habituates it, and the more it is habituated the less, even of that, it sees. In saying that the popular mind is unsensitive, we use the term in a literal, psychological (even physiological) sense. The average individual may be "thick-skinned" or he may be so "sensitive" that his feelings are hurt at every turn. This moral or emotional sensitiveness is not here under consideration. By sensitiveness we mean the delicacy, adaptability, and efficiency of the five senses and sense organs, as agencies which put us in contact with the world. At the same time it is worthy of remark that the scientist is not one whose feelings are easily hurt; he has to take as well as give criticism.

There is a close connection between the insensitivity of the

[17] Of course, in ultimate deterministic analysis, both believe what they have to believe.

popular mind and its lack of impersonal curiosity. The scientific mind is curious about phenomena, whether "natural" or social. The popular mind is curious about persons and their affairs—as persons, not as phenomena. Much of this personal curiosity flows from sympathy; not a little of it contributes to assuaging the pressure of inferiority complexes. Here subjective interests are potent. We revel in scandal and gossip, and enjoy other people's failures and defeats. They prove to us that we are not so inferior as our morbid complexes try to lead us to suppose.

Scientific attention must be alert, and concentrated upon the particular problems in hand. When the problem is solved, or in the interims necessary to relaxation and recreation, the attention may rove, but wherever it stops, if even but momentarily, it is likely to be penetrating. Here, it must be confessed, we are at the threshold of one of the most difficult and puzzling problems of the relation of science to culture. Specialization and concentration of attention are essential to scientific achievement. This is the day of the specialist, and in his own precinct he is master. Outside of it, however, he is often lost, and he not infrequently exhibits much subjectivity and superficiality. Scientific specialization does not necessarily produce thoroughly scientific minds. To relieve us in some measure of the narrowing effects of specialization, we need to insist upon a broader cultural training for our oncoming scientific specialists, and also to encourage a greater amount of synthetic scientific work.

If the scientific specialist is sometimes unobservant and distortedly attentive outside of his own field, the popular mind, a stranger to the scientific attitude in any field, usually exhibits much diffuseness, vagueness, and uncertainty of attention. This is often attributed to the touch-and-go character of our newspapers; but that is probably giving them more discredit than is their due. The popular mind, after all, bears a close analogy to the scientific specialist, in that it may be closely and sustainedly attentive to the matters which, so far as it is aware, concern it—usually matters of business and vocational interest. The difference lies in the fact that even in these fields, its attention is not objective, but subjectively selective, being guided by motives of personal profit.

The popular mind is either ignorant or insignificantly informed. When a committee of fifty expert engineers, after months of investigation, attribute over fifty per cent of the inefficiency of American industry to defective management,[18] there is basis for doubt as to whether the American business man is well-informed concerning even his own immediate interests—unless we are to assume that business prospers on inefficiency. The results of the army tests during the war do not give us room for satisfaction with regard to the mental equipment of the population at large. The ease with which demagogues control large portions of the electorate, the interest of the populace in the personalities of candidates, their comparative lack of interest in principles, their reluctance to consider real issues in anything like an open-minded, objective, and constructive way, their sectionalism and localism, their toleration of a controlled press—these and many other evidences might be cited to support this point. With a considerable proportion of our citizenry eager to join a secret and irresponsible organization to "uphold law and order" against the menaces of "bolshevism" and Catholicism—even in districts where there are no bolshevists and few Catholics,—with our leading automobile manufacturer spending good money to spread an absurd propaganda to warn us against impending domination by our Jewish fellow citizens, and with a large number of clergymen and congregations more absorbed in Sabbath observance and the immodesty of flappers' dress than in what shall be done to rehabilitate Europe or promote peace between labor and capital, there is perhaps cause for doubt about the functional quality of our education. Certainly a nation whose destinies depend upon the intelligence and informedness of its people, under a universal franchise, cannot reasonably look into the future with great confidence, if it squarely faces the facts with regard to the present mental equipment of its electorate.

Lacking in power of attention, and ill-informed (indeed, often grossly misinformed), the popular mind is credulous, sometimes to a ridiculous degree. This is one thing that makes the propaganda of special economic interests effective. But if the popular

---

[18] Federated American Engineering Societies, *Report on Waste in Industry*, 1921, Ch. 2.

mind is on the one hand adept at believing what it wants to believe, it has, on the other, the corresponding power of disbelief. It is often subjectively skeptical. This subjective skepticism—refusal to face facts—is at the bottom of our incorrigible American self-complacency, unreasoning, sentimental optimism, and our jingoistic pride. It is also in part cause why there is not a more productive and constructive give and take of ideas between conservative and radical.

To say that a person is credulous, or subjectively skeptical, is to say that he is uncritical. Let it be remembered that a critic is one who is able to discuss profitably, one who has judgment and discernment; and that criticism involves appreciation of good as well as bad points in the thing criticized. It follows that the objective, scientific mind should have the best critical capacity, and that the mind dominated by subjective biases and personal or class interests has the least. There are relatively few able critics in this country; there are a few criticasters— "knockers"—who, in the absence of fair critics, are not without value; and there is a host of people who never rouse themselves out of their habitual acceptance of the commonplace as the ideal, further than is necessary to damn somebody who is momentarily disturbing their intellectual vacuity and moral complacency.

Victor Cousin said that *"la critique est la vie de la science—*criticism is the soul of science." It is that and more—it is the salvation of democracy. And perhaps nowhere in the world is there more need of it than in America to-day—not the personalistic praise and blame and the trite dogmatisms which constitute the stock-in-trade of the ideo-motor conservatives and radicals, but the criticism which is a calm, informed, and objectively intelligent "sizing-up" of the various elements and issues in our national life.

The higher type of popular mind—common in the clergy and the bar—falls mainly in the dogmatic-emotional group. This type, as we saw,[19] is critical of logical processes, but not of premises. It is useless for a thoroughly objective and critical mind to attempt discussion on any but superficial matters with a dogmatic, emotional individual. When the latter's premises and postulates are questioned, he is unable, or unwilling, to meet

---

[19] See above, p. 177.

criticism. His dogmatism then asserts itself. His mind has reached its closed door, over which is written "thus far, and no farther." Between dogmatism and science there is no common meeting ground; between two· conflicting dogmatisms nothing but war.

That we are not only lacking in critical capacity but are grossly intolerant, in this country, as in other countries, is shown by many things, but most of all by the unwillingness or incapacity of the popular mind to stand for, or to consider, adverse criticism. With a certain section of our population, not to embrace unquestioningly all the dogmatic emotionalism and impatience of extreme radicalism is to be considered a willing vassal of reactionism; with a very large proportion of the populace, on the other hand, to be thoughtful, open minded, critical, and intellectually honest and courageous is to be "radical," and to be radical is to be a "bolshevik." Is it needful to suggest that out of such intolerance neither intellectual honesty, moral balance, nor democracy can emerge?

The tolerance of the objective mind is derived from, or at least intimately associated with, its intellectual patience—its scientific discipline and its ability to suspend judgment. The intolerance of the popular mind goes with its lack of intellectual discipline, its impatience, and its limited power of refraining from judgment when it has not the necessary data. The popular mind jumps at conclusions, and is restless if required to suspend judgment. It cannot bear to say "I do not know."

It follows that cases of the exercise of scientific caution are rare in the popular mind. While the nearer to the scientific ideal a mind is, the more cautious it is in drawing anything but hypothetical generalizations, unless it is in possession of all the essential data, the popular mind generalizes on evidence of the most unreliable kind, both as to amount and content, and often upon the most tenuous kind of hearsay. This lack of caution is merely a specific aspect or consequence of deficiency in critical capacity.

Imagination is a necessary qualification of the scientist as well as the inventor, because by its aid are formulated the working hypotheses which serve as guides to investigation. In the use of imagination and hypothesis, scientists differ; some exercise extreme care and will not allow themselves to range far beyond established fact; others are fertile in devising hypotheses —possible clues, explanations, and solutions—which may aid investigation through a process of elimination. Each hypothesis is tested. Many fail, but one may be found which points the way to the truth. Science thus profits by disciplined constructive imagination.

The imagination of the popular mind is more in the nature of fancy. This is perhaps truer of the dreaming type of idealistic radical, given to picturing utopias. The imagination of the conservative, as we saw, is more the product of fear. The amount of human suffering caused by unfounded fear and worry over fanciful dangers is beyond computation. At the same time it is not to be overlooked that a large proportion of the population is normally in a state of mental lethargy, in which neither fancy nor active fear-imagination is much in evidence. For this reason a great deal of propaganda is devoted to "rousing the people" to this or that impending danger. Frequently the thing is overdone, so that when a real danger appears, it is difficult to get people to see it.

Another result of fear complexes is the popular attitude toward facts. The subjective skepticism, the uncritical quality of the popular mind, and to some extent its ignorance and intolerance, are geared to its fear of facts. We saw that the scientific attitude is marked by respect for fact, and that scientific caution is motivated in part by fear that all the facts essential to the solution of a given problem have not been taken into account. The scientist's respect for facts is founded on his well-learned lesson that a "nasty little fact" may destroy a fine theory. The popular fear of facts has a similar basis; but whereas the scientist is afraid his theory is not sound and so wants to know the destructive fact if there is one, the popular mind is afraid of the destructive fact and tries to ignore it because it wants to keep the theory. So, again, we find fear and dogmatism associated.

If the scientist is fearless in facing facts, he is also courageous in defending his convictions. In contrast, the popular mind is often vacillating. It is only when backed by authority that it shows marked courage. When an individual not trained to the scientist's moral standard of truth-seeking has special interests of his own at stake, he may make rigorous defense of those principles which he believes necessary to his position; but quite as often special interest, as we saw in the discussion of interested conservatism, causes the soft pedal to be applied. Soft-pedalling may be tact, and it may be pusillanimity.

When we say that the popular mind has great respect for authority, we do not mean the authority of the various agencies of social control. In general the populace is law-abiding, but there are lawless elements enough in it to render untrue a too sweeping generalization as to popular respect for authority in either the legal or moral sense. What we have in mind may be called, for want of a better term, intellectual authority. The ideo-motor mind is frequently impressed, momentarily, by what it cannot understand. The dogmatic-emotional mind usually holds to a sort of authoritarianism which may be called an apostolic succession of intellectual dogmas. Join this succession, or get by hook or crook a spectacular prestige with the hero-worshipping public, and it will for a time take as gospel anything you choose to tell it—provided you are reasonably consistent and take care to make your statements with a sufficient air of finality.

The scientist has no particular respect for authority *as such,* and none for the extraneous elements of prestige which often lift a charlatan to the heights of authority in the minds of the untrained masses. But the scientist has respect for the real authority of scientific intellectual power and achievement. The scientist knows how to evaluate these things, at least in his own field. The opinions and conclusions of a savant are justly given more weight than those of a comparatively unknown man; but they are not accepted without verification. No scientist accepts the untested conclusions of another, no matter how prominent. And in spite of delays, and occasional failure of recognition, the work, if sound, of the obscure investigator is ultimately incorporated into the body of scientific data which form the basis of further research. The fact that scientists sometimes exhibit too great conservatism—sometimes even disregard and contempt, without hearing—with regard to new theories advanced by relatively obscure newcomers should not blind us to the general truth that the scientific attitude involves a *critical* and discriminative respect for scientific authority. This is inevitable. Otherwise each new scientific investigator would have to begin at the beginning, taking nothing—even the principles of elementary mathematics—as established.

Now it is just this critical and discriminative respect which we find lacking in the popular mind. On the one hand the populace may be emotionally loyal to dogmas and prestige; it usually has a profound desire to conform to standards of "respectability"; and because of its ignorant and undiscriminating respect for impressiveness, it falls prey to much foolishness masquerading as "science." On the other hand, it is characterized by a sort of Jacksonian contempt for real scientific capacity and expert advice, a fact which bodes ill for the future honesty and efficiency of democracy. Americans have been victims of this weakness, both in their political and economic policies, just as the Germans reaped at the other extreme the tragic fruits of a too implicit faith in the disinterestedness of their expert officials. Not until recently did the American populace manifest any willingness whatever to listen to the trained economist or political scientist. As this is being written, a commission is sitting in a town not far distant to revise its municipal charter. Of the twelve members of the commission, only two or three have any practical experience in municipal administration. One member is one of the country's recognized scientific students of municipal government, an expert authority on the subject, but he is a minority of one, and without practical influence on the commission.[20] Obviously not all of us can be experts on city government. The judgment of those who are should have weight. How to get the populace to accept, or at least to heed, the advice of experts is not the least difficult of the problems of political democracy.

The fact is that the popular mind is slavishly conservative and conventional, and deficient in intellectual originality and individuality. This again is partly the result of fear. The popular mind is afraid of revealing its ignorance. The scientist knows that only by frankly recognizing and admitting his ignorance, where he is ignorant, can he keep on the road to truth.

The reluctance of the average citizen to listen to expert advice on public affairs is also due in part to the egotistical quality of the popular mind. This quality is by no means the lowest in

---

[20] This member later resigned.

significance of the characteristics of the unscientific attitude. If one witnesses the quarrels among specialized scientists for "credit" and "priority of discovery," however, one may conclude that scientists, too, are not always characterized by a retiring modesty, and that the popular mind has no monopoly on egotism. That is true in a sense, but to the extent that an individual is egotistic it is fair to say that he falls short of the ideal scientific attitude.

At bottom the difference between the scientific mind and the unscientific lies in their respective attitudes toward the self and the world. The non-scientific person, no matter how timid and modest he may appear on the surface to be, is commonly an egotist. That is, his intellectual conception of the world is colored by a certain egotistical attachment to his own experience and his own ideas, sentiments, loyalties, etc., no matter how limited, as somehow more valid, truer, and more authoritative, than any one's else. This egotism may, of course, in some persons be a sort of vicarious self-esteem, reflected from their attachment to some authority, personal or traditional, which has impressive prestige. It may also to a certain extent be a combination of inferiority complexes with the "equality" idea fostered by our crude conception of democracy. With the subconscious knowledge that his own opinion, not being based on objective knowledge, is vulnerable, the individual attempts to compensate for his intellectual insecurity by personal bumptiousness.

This fact of attachment to one's own ideas, opinions, and beliefs, as better, by the simple fact that they are regarded as one's own (however completely the result of borrowing and imitation), than the next man's, brings us back to our starting point—the contrast between the objectivity of the scientific, and the subjectivity of the popular, mind. But we may now sense the fact that subjective bias is not based alone on material interests, but also on egotisms very deeply seated in human temperament.

The final proof and expression of the subjectivity of the popular mind is its belief in free will, in personalistic whim in nature, and its constant gravitation toward praise and blame of what it likes and dislikes. The popular mind may be in many respects a shrewd "judge of human nature," and consequently may be adept at political manipulation. But of that disinterested objectivity of observation which characterizes the scientific psychologist it has little.

If we turn back a moment to the characteristics of the conservative and the radical minds respectively, we shall now sense anew the significance of many of the subjective traits there noted. In the case of the disinterested conservative it is easy to see that his attachment to things-as-they-are (habituation), his fear of the new and the unfamiliar, his loyalties and pride, and his exaggerated valuation of the past can hardly fail to prevent his mental processes attaining to the scientific level. It is equally plain that the attitude and methods of interested conservatism are diametrically opposed to the scientific spirit, and thoroughly incompatible with it. Just as soon as science becomes the handmaiden to apologetics of any kind it stands in imminent peril of ceasing to be science and becoming propaganda. The impatience of the radical, his sentimentalizing, his proclivity for the new simply because it is new, his jumping to conclusions, and his espousal of programs without investigation of their probable unforeseen and complicated effects—these and other traits make it improbable that the scientific spirit will frequently be met with in radical ranks, though it is likely to be as common there as among conservatives. In both conservative and radical, traits like intolerance, combat attitudes, emotionalism, and the clinging to ideologies (like eighteenth century individualism or Marxian socialism), are distinctive factors.

Experience shows that a people may manage to survive and even attain a certain degree of cultural development without acquiring a great amount of objective knowledge of the world. Most of the history of the race, in fact, has been lived on a composite basis of instinct, sentiment, and illusion. The amount of illusion still prevalent is, from the objective scientific point of view, interesting, to say the least; from the moral point of view (if truth has anything to do with morality) it is appalling.

But of this you cannot readily convince the popular mind— any more than you could persuade a flounder that the sea has more than two dimensions. Popular-minded cocksureness in the validity of its ideologies and illusions rests upon the fallacy that "we know social reality because we live in it"—the idea that we have a right to generalize, without special and thorough investigation, on the basis of "common sense." The fallacy of this practice lies, as Thomas has pointed out, in the limitation and subjectively selective nature of any one individual's experience. "The individual's sphere of practical acquaintance with social reality . . . is always limited and constitutes only a small part of the whole complexity of social facts." In addition to this "exterior limitation" there is an interior one, "still more important, due to the fact that among all experiences which an individual meets . . . perhaps the larger part is left unheeded, never becoming a basis of common-sense generalizations."

The popular selection of experience for attention and generalizations, as Thomas goes on to state, is thus subjective—"valid only for this particular individual in this particular social position"—and therefore "quite different from, and incommensurable with the selection which a scientist would make in face of the same body of data from an objective, impersonal viewpoint." [21] The application of this analysis in estimating the probable objectivity of conservative or radical should be evident. The conservative's habituation to the *status quo* precludes the ability to observe objectively or to analyze critically the things he takes so completely for granted. On the other hand, the radical's consciousness of desire-obstruction causes him to select for criticism and attack only certain elements of a situation, which means that its complexity as a whole is likely to escape him.

This brings us to the question noted above [22] concerning possible subjective difficulties which may be encountered by the scientific investigator in his own mental makeup. While the characteristics of the popular mind are far and away the most extensive and troublesome of the obstacles to scientific method, they are not the only subjective factors which have to be taken into consideration.

No mind can be completely scientific, and no human individual has ever reached the ideal of the critically intellectual mind. But individuals do, and will, differ in the nearness of their approach to this ideal. What we call, for practical purposes, the scientific or the critically intellectual minds, approach it

---

[21] W. I. Thomas and F. Znaniecki, *The Polish Peasant in Europe and America*, 1918, Vol. I, *Methodological Note*, pp. 4, 5.

[22] Page 220.

more or less closely. Nevertheless, such a mind has tendencies of its own to bias and subjectivity which must also be guarded against. Even the astronomer has to make allowance for the "personal equation" in his own field—*e.g.*, for the reaction time of the observer in recording the time of the passage of a star over the wire of a transit telescope.

These subjective factors, from which the most objective actual mind is not entirely free, flow from a variety of sources. Where human relations are under investigation, the chief of these are interest conflicts, class association, sympathy and antipathy, ingrained moral habits, and egotism—pride in priority and desire for credit and personal prestige in the scientific field. The last-mentioned factor is by no means the least of the actual motives active in scientific work. Interest conflicts, and susceptibility to some influence from the prevalent conflict psychology, no one can entirely escape. Class bias also is exceedingly difficult to avoid—if not bias with respect to the industrial class conflict, at least that which results from the relative isolation of the intellectual, with others of his kind, from the much larger popular group.

As to the rôle played by sympathy, some difficult questions arise. In scientific investigation in the physical and biological sciences sympathy has no function. If it does creep in—as, for instance, in comparative psychology, where the investigator may be tempted to read his own reactions, emotional or otherwise, into those of the animal under observation—it can only vitiate the objectivity and the truth of the conclusions reached.[23] Such a slip is only a case of belated anthropomorphism.

In research having to do with social facts the matter stands on a different footing. Social facts are human facts, and to observe human facts most fruitfully the observer cannot confine himself to external indications.

There is scarcely a department of social science, economics, jurisprudence, social psychology or what not, in which investigation of social organization and social process does not involve, or at any rate ought not to involve, a study of motives. For motives are to be regarded both as immediate (though not sole)

---

[23] Cooley, *Principles of Science*, 1912, p. 60, says that it is "not improper to interpret animal intelligence by human when proper allowances are made,"—but what are the proper allowances?

causes of actions and as links in the stream or nexus of the general mechanistic causation of social phenomena. Hence it is important to get at the real motives, and observe them. The alleged motives, the motives which the "cold-blooded" investigator may infer from surface phenomena, or the motives which the actor conscientiously believes and asserts to be his real motives, may not be the real motives at all. However skeptical we may be of the method and specific findings of the psychoanalysts it will probably be generally conceded that they have thrown much light on the lack of correspondence between alleged and actual motives.

Now, as is abundantly illustrated in the methods and results of psychopathology, it is continuously necessary for an investigator to gain and keep the confidence of his patient, by convincing him of his disinterested sympathy, and through ability to put himself in the patient's place and reconstruct the patient's experience, both conscious and unconscious. If this is necessary in the study of abnormal cases, there is no reason to suppose that it is not equally essential to an understanding of the experience and the motivation of normal individuals.

Sympathy, in fact, far from being something to be eschewed, is an indispensable part of the investigational equipment of the truly objective student of social phenomena. In the first place, as just intimated, sympathy is a prerequisite to confidence, and confidence is essential to the securing of true evidence. And secondly, sympathy is necessary as an aid to understanding, through vicarious realization, the experiences of others perhaps situated very differently from ourselves in the economic, social, and intellectual scale. In this latter sense sympathy partakes somewhat of the functions of the constructive imagination of the natural scientist.

An infinite amount of misunderstanding between classes, races, and the sexes, and of illusion, error, misrepresentation, and fanaticism, would have been avoided, had persons who presumed to express opinions or to present conclusions on social problems and issues had the grace of this capacity—merely the gift to look at the situation from the standpoint of the other fellow as well as their own.

It might be objected at this point that what is here stated to be the function of sympathy in scientific social investigation, especially investigation involving evaluation of motives, is not in accord with the behavioristic or mechanistic trend of present-day psychology. Such objection would not be well taken, however, because the investigator who knows the most about the mechanism of human behavior and human attitudes is most likely to be able to put himself intelligently and interpretatively in the other fellow's place and to reach a true and objective understanding of his behavior. Behaviorism is strictly deterministic, as all true science must be, and determinism does rule out of court praise and blame and subjective or affectional sympathies and antipathies. On the other hand, it is a great aid to the objective sympathy of which we have been speaking.

As a tragic illustration of the failure which may result from the absence of this objective sympathy and from the presence of subjective, emotional antipathy, we may take the impossible Versailles treaty. From the array of geographical, economic, financial, and other experts gathered in Paris it was reasonable to suppose that the Peace Conference would result in a treaty' which would not only be enforceable but which would not exacerbate old antagonisms. But scientific objectivity went down under the pressure of ingrained emotional antipathies. On the other hand, an outstanding example of the clearing of the intellectual atmosphere resultant upon objective sympathy, or the capacity to look at the situation from the point of view of each of the interested parties, is to be found in the two well-known essays of John Maynard Keynes.[24]

It should go without saying that the sympathy which it is here held is an essential aid in understanding human motives has nothing in common with maudlin sentiment. Just as much as combative antipathy, must sympathy in the sense of pity be rigidly excluded from scientific method. It is perhaps a failure to distinguish between two types of sympathy, the intellectual or objective and the affectional, which accounts for the idea that sympathy cannot be an element in scientific procedure. It also explains why some social research falls short of truth—the investigator either did not put himself in the other fellow's place at all or, on the other hand, put himself there altogether too much, crediting him with what would have been his own

---

[24] *The Economic Consequences of the Peace*, 1920, and *A Revision of the Treaty*, 1922.

emotions and motives under the circumstances. It would be difficult to say which is more detrimental to objectivity, a total lack of sympathy, or the presence of sentimentalism. It is clear, however, that the social scientist is called upon to steer a careful, circumspect course between these two defects of attitude.

We come now to our second problem: Can a scientific inquiry be instituted with reform as its motive? Can ethical considerations be permitted to enter into the motivation of social research, if that research is to merit the name of science?

The answer to these questions depends upon what we agree to mean by them. It is entirely permissible to hold that ideally all scientific inquiry should be initiated and carried through in obedience to no other motive than the desire to know the truth. It should be a search for truth and nothing more. Truth, yes—but what truth? Had we no utilitarian needs, no social problems demanding early solution, and yet waiting for that solution upon the carrying out of the requisite scientific investigations, the answer would be "Any truth." One truth or scientific generalization, whatever its subject matter, would be as good as any other. But practically and actually, the solution of many pressing technological and social problems at the earliest possible moment is desirable, if not essential to the preservation of our civilization. These are the problems to which, it will hardly be questioned, the social scientist should devote his main efforts. This is not saying that he may not have to go far back in his investigation to fundamental determinants, which the popular mind would pronounce useless. Economy of effort and of utilization of our limited amount of developed scientific capacity demands that scientific research shall be directed in the main to lines of inquiry which give most promise of yielding results of value for the practical solution of actual problems and issues.

This does not mean that the decision as to what is important as a "practical problem" is to be left to the superficial popular mind. The objective scientist will have something to say as to the relative importance of the matters calling for investigation.

Most, if not all, of the social problems upon which we need scientific knowledge and judgment are problems involving conflicts of interest and viewpoint, of sentiment and popular judgment, and of norms of conduct. Different groups, which will be affected in diverse ways by a given reform or attempted solution of an issue, hold to quite different standards of conduct, of justice, and of expediency. Usually so intense is special interest that each group welcomes any investigation which takes as its starting point and premise the particular norm held high in the estimation of the group, and which accordingly will come out with the thing it started with—reasons for supporting the policy and attitude of the group. The W. C. T. U., for instance, has always been able to find "scientific" reasons why the sale of cigarettes should be forbidden.

Now it should be clear without extended argument that the scientist cannot lend himself to any such procedure in investigation. He can discover and state the existing objective facts (providing they do not entail classifications which cannot be made, because of lack of objective definition) and can say, in effect, "such and such results would probably flow from your proposed reform." Further than that he can go only in exceptional cases.

The approach to theoretical problems from the point of view of desirability and undesirability is criticized by Thomas,[25] in his able "Methodological Note." This approach, he thinks, is the usual one in "practical" sociology.

"The norm may be intrinsic to the reality, as when it is presumed that the actually prevailing or customary state of things is normal [e.g., the conservative's habituation to things-as-they are?]; or it may be extrinsic, as when moral, religious, or æsthetic standards are applied to social reality and the prevailing state of things is found in disaccord with the norm, and in so far abnormal."[26]

This procedure, as he shows, leads to biased and unscientific selection of some of the facts and deprives us of opportunity to study all the facts in connection with one another, which is the only connection in which their study can be scientifically valid. Moreover, it is patent that "when the norm is not the result but the starting-point of the investigation, . . . every practical custom or habit, every moral, political, religious view, claims

---

[25] W. I. Thomas and F. Znaniecki, *The Polish Peasant in Europe and America*, 1918, Vol. I, pp. 7-10.
[26] *Op. cit.*, p. 8.

to be *the* norm and to treat as abnormal whatever does not agree with it."[27]

From these considerations Thomas concludes (1) that "from the method of the study itself all practical considerations must be excluded if we want the results to be valid," and (2) that "as soon as the investigation is started both indignation and idealism should be put aside."[28]

All this is clear and sound, and we can have no quarrel with it. The results of starting with norms and of measuring everything by them during the investigation have been abundantly indicated in our analysis of the conservative and radical attitudes. *When an investigation is once started*, scientific objectivity—mere honesty—demands that we "hew to the line, let the chips fall where they will." But this is not saying that the *initiation* of a piece of social investigation may not legitimately be made from motives of ethical interest. Nor it is saying that a scientific psychology cannot enable us to distinguish between good and bad norms.[29]

Let us take just one illustration. For a hundred years or more economists have been writing about the distribution of wealth, but among the hundreds of volumes written on this subject, only a mere handful have made any attempt to discuss the actual distribution of wealth—that is, to present the facts before proceeding to theoretical generalization as to the forces which determine distribution. Then came the advent of the early socialist doctrine of increasing misery (the assertion that the rich were getting richer and the poor poorer). When that theory was shown to be too little in accord with facts so far as the poor were concerned, and it was replaced by the introduction of the later doctrine of "comparative poverty" (the assertion that while the poor are gradually becoming a little better off, the rich are getting richer so fast that the gulf between the two is rapidly widening), the whole question of distribution ceased to be merely academic and became a real issue. The patent massing of large fortunes, with their power in finance and politics, made it a very important issue. Nevertheless, practically all the economic theorists continued to publish elabo-

[27] *Ibid.*, p. 9.
[28] *Ibid.*, pp. 7, 8.
[29] See Chapter X.

rate deductive disquisitions on why distribution must be thus and so, and ought to be either thus and so or so and thus. The few statistical studies or indications undertaken, mostly by foreign students and based on foreign data, received scant attention from American economists. It is only fair to state that this neglect was due mainly, perhaps, to the fact that in the United States we had no ready data for anything more than the roughest guesses as to the distribution of income, until the Federal government, pursuant to the income tax law of 1913, began to require reports of incomes from all persons receiving over $4000 if married and $2000 if single.[30] The returns threw a flood of light on the distribution of income in this country. Still it remained true that there were no direct, and but one outstanding attempt [31] to analyze the indirect, data bearing on the amount of our national income going to wages, profits, interest, and rent respectively. Recently, however, there has been a growing tendency to factual investigation of income distribution in the United States. Objective research, as scientifically accurate as the available statistical data permit, has been carried through by the Bureau of Economic Research,[32] so that we now have much needed, if not yet wholly adequate, information as to the actual distribution of income in this country.

For this we have to thank the scientific objectivity and expertness of certain investigators; for their impulse to undertake this difficult task, we have to thank, mainly, the circumstances that made the whole matter a real ethical and political issue. In other words, the motive to the investigation was doubtless an ethical impulse—the desire to give to the thinking public essential information with regard to the *facts* of distribution, to the end that discussion and policies in regard to it could be taken out of the realm of surmise and dogmatic assertion.

---

[30] In 1917, the limits were made $2,000 and $1,000.

[31] W. I. King, *The Wealth and Income of the People of the United States*, 1915. See also G. P. Watkins, "Growth of Large Fortunes," *Publications of the American Economic Association*, 3d Series, Vol. VIII, No. 4, 1907; David Friday, *Profits, Wages and Prices*, 1920.

[32] Wesley C. Mitchell, Frederick R. Macaulay, Wilford I. King, and Oswald W. Knauth, *Income in the United States, Its Amount and Distribution*, 1909-1919, Vol. I, Summary, 1921. See also Walter R. Ingalls, *Wealth and Income of the American People*, 1922.

This example is sufficient to illustrate, though not to prove, our point that scientific social research is now chiefly motivated by some initial ethical interest. It also illustrates what should be the function of science in relation to the solution, or at least the rationalization, of conflicts of social interests, economic or other. The economists and statisticians who carried through this investigation into the actual distribution of income in the United States doubtless had some opinions as to the desirability or undesirability of an alteration in income distribution, but they have kept their opinions to themselves. They say in effect: "Here are the facts; after considering them fairly and frankly, take what measures you deem necessary or advisable; but don't neglect the facts." In this way, they avoid the assumption of a specific "norm"—to which assumption Thomas rightly objects.

In summary. We have tried to establish the proposition that from the nature of the data he has to work with, the social scientist, and we should say especially the social psychologist, cannot dispense with objective sympathy as an aid to observation and interpretation. He must be careful, however, to distinguish clearly between the type of sympathy which enables him to understand the motivation of other people, and the sentimental type of sympathy which will lead him to substitute his own reactions for those of the persons under investigation and bring it to pass that he does not get their motives and point of view. With regard to the permissibility of ethical motivation to social research we arrive at substantially the following conclusion: in practice, ethical interest is properly a prime motive in the initiation of scientific inquiry; but while the social scientist may be motivated by an ethical interest, e.g., desire to see what valid objective evidence there may be both for and against a given proposed reform, he must lay aside, during the investigation, any leanings of this kind which he may have had. If he cannot do this he is not a scientist, and his conclusions will probably be defective in objectivity. Lacking in that, they will be deficient in practical applicability to the rationalization of interest conflicts.

We must now turn from the dangers of subjective bias to which the actual (not the ideal) scientific mind is exposed, to a consideration of the difficulties scientific investigation of social phenomena would encounter even if every investigator were totally free from subjective interests and biases of any kind. This subject is an extensive one, and we can here consider only its main outlines.

The first difficulty lies in the magnitude and complexity of almost any task of social investigation that we may undertake. All social problems hang together, because all human phenomena are interdependent. This means that the basic task of observation and record is enormous, and full of pitfalls. The factual data are complex, often obscure, frequently unattainable.

Among the essential facts are those pertaining to the motives of individuals. Perhaps nothing in the world is harder to get at, let behavioristic psychology and psychoanalysis give us all the aid they can. People are rarely honest with themselves, let alone others, especially with prying investigators. Real motives are encrusted in layer upon layer of "rationalization"—*i.e.*, casuistry—and hidden or camouflaged in a great variety of ways.

The scientist can proceed not otherwise than on the assumption that human life, like the rest of nature, is completely and dependably mechanistic. But human life is also shot through and through with the purposes of human individuals. These purposes are but a part of the mechanism. Consequently the social scientist cannot dodge, if he would, the necessity of including motives in his factual data. If he cannot get at motives directly, he must do the second best thing, and infer them from such evidence as he can get. It goes without saying that these inferences must not be made on the basis of any such *à priori* norm as the economic man, innate depravity, consciousness of kind, or inherent racial psychology.

It is well known that observers of the same event will often give most diverse accounts of it. The courts have to contend not only against wilful perjury but against the precarious ability of human beings to see a thing as it is and to state accurately what they saw.[33] If actual observers prove so unreliable, what is to be said of evidence which is at a further remove from

---

[33] "Thirty-eight witnesses positively identified a man in Chicago the other day as an accomplice in a swindle. He was lodged in jail to await trial. There, in the usual course, fingerprints were taken, and found to vary entirely from those of the real culprit, which fortunately for the prisoner were on file."—*The Nation*, Feb. 15, 1922, p. 181.

the event? If even external, physical characters cannot be reported correctly, what is to be said of the usual sort of evidence about motives?

These difficulties are very prominent in historical research. It must be remembered that a full understanding of a particular situation or event is not to be had until we know the real history of the events leading up to it—among which are the motives of men, long since dead, who left either no records, imperfect records, or records purposely falsified to put themselves in a favorable light. The historical or genetic method of research is indispensable to social science, but its use must always be hampered by its own inherent difficulties and defects. The historian is confronted with the question of the authenticity of documents, and with the absence of record of many essential objective facts of which the documents give no hint.[34] Is it strange that two able historians of the administration of Andrew Jackson, for instance, both using the same material, and both without any conscious bias, arrive at diametrically opposite conclusions as to Jackson's character and motives?

But the genetico-historical method is not the only one open to us. We must have recourse also to statistics, and the statistical method, as is well recognized, has also difficulties of its own. The difficulties here referred to are entirely distinct from those subjective frailties and conscious chicaneries often in evidence in the statistical work of the hired experts of special interests. The popular cynicism, "liars, damn liars, and statisticians," doubtless has some correspondence to reality when applied to the dishonest uses to which the statistical method is occasionally put. But the same could be said of the historical method. Histories have been written with conscious bias, if not with definite propaganda purpose, perhaps with a frequency indeed quite as great as that with which statistics are "doctored" to bolster up a doubtful cause.

The difficulties here referred to are inherent in the statistical method even when it is honestly and expertly handled. They fall into two classes, those relating, respectively, to the gathering and to the analysis of data. In practice, the most elementary

---

[34] For an illuminating brief presentation of the tasks and difficulties of scientific history, see Henry Johnson, *Teaching of History*, 195, Ch. 1.

statistical generalizations can usually be made only after the collection of a vast mass of statistical data, *i.e.*, facts which can be counted, classified, tabulated, averaged, summarized—in short handled by mathematical methods. This laborious but necessary collection of the primary data involves the maintenance of expensive statistical bureaus and offices, both governmental and private. A newspaper item tells, for instance, that the general price level has gone up or down so many points. Few people have any conception of the enormous amount of labor required in the collection of individual commodity prices before that apparently simple statement could be made. Not only the collection of the primary data, but their "reduction"—their classification, tabulation, co-ordination, summarizing, averaging, and correlation—entails great labor and expense.

If the very massiveness of the data makes the statistical method laborious and expensive on the one hand, the impossibility of securing full statistical record of social phenomena entails, on the other, the necessity of employing intricate technical methods of calculation and inference. Even with the most extensive possible collection of primary data—*e.g.*, registration of births and deaths—statistical summaries, averages, and "rates" can usually be arrived at only through the employment of assumptions and calculations which may contain more or less error. For instance, the death rate for a given year is stated as the number of deaths per each 1000 of the population *that year*. If it happens to be an intercensal year the population has to be estimated. While this can usually be done with a fair degree of accuracy, it is nevertheless an inferential element in the calculation of the death rate. The same is of course true of nearly all *per capita* statements.

Great as is the mass of published statistical material—even assuming it all to be even passably reliable—hardly an inquiry involving the use of statistical data can be carried through without encountering lacunæ and uncertainties in the data which drive the investigator to the use of roundabout inference and calculation. Of course the more of this indirection there is, the less near the truth his conclusions are likely to be, however conscientiously and skillfully he may try to avoid ill-founded generalizations.

The use of statistics does not give us absolute knowledge. It is only a method of dealing quantitatively, with a degree of accuracy, with masses of facts which otherwise could not be handled.

Notwithstanding its expensiveness and laboriousness, and the many difficulties, both subjective and objective, to which it is heir, the statistical method is undergoing a wide and rapid expansion as an instrument of scientific investigation. We have suggested only some leading difficulties, and not all of them. A full treatment would far exceed the limits of this book. Of the desirability of extended use of the statistical method there can be no question, if only adequate technical training in the use of such methods be provided.

The statistical and the genetico-historical methods are the only fundamental scientific methods of social investigation. The so-called "comparative" method is only a variation of the one or the other, or a combination of the two. In fact, the genetico-historical method is dependent in no small degree upon the employment of statistics.

Given a body of facts capable of statistical classification and summarization, the statistical method is really the application of mathematics; and mathematics is symbolic logic. Statistics is therefore a logical method. But it is what Pareto[35] calls a "logico-experiential" method—i.e., its logical processes have to do with objectively observed data and are continually checked up by them. In this it differs radically from the older deductive methods which started from a few supposedly universally valid postulates, and proceeded to long trains of deductive reasoning, rarely if ever tested by reference to actual facts.

Whatever method or combination of methods may be used in scientific social investigation, there are certain problems and difficulties which remain to be mentioned.

The first of these is the problem of definition and classification. We noted above that natural science has got beyond the taxonomic state. It is doubtful if social science has. It may be questioned, in fact, whether social science will not always be greatly troubled by difficulties and disputes as to definition and classification.

There are few social science concepts which do not involve

---

[35] *Traité de Sociologie Générale*, 1917, Vol. I, Ch. 1.

matters upon which interest conflicts may hinge, and to which, in consequence, the popular mind will not now and again attach a penumbra of ethical connotation. Aside from this, moreover, is the fact that a large proportion of social inquiries are motivated by the desire to give scientific aid toward the solution of practical problems and issues. And these issues involve dispute as to facts where the bearing, and even the observing of these facts, hinge upon the practicability of securing objective definition in matters where definition is exceedingly difficult.

This can best be understood by illustration. It has been, and still is, a live issue as to whether the railroads can afford to pay wages at the present level and at the same time reduce transportation rates. The economic experts of the Railway Brotherhoods claim, with an impressive marshalling of statistics, that they can. With equally impressive array of accounts, the railway executives claim they cannot. How determine the truth? The whole question is one of scientific accounting. No matter how full the railway accounting may be, judgment on the issue must depend largely upon accurate definition of accounting concepts, as well as upon the accuracy and honesty with which the railroads have classified under the proper concepts ("accounts") their earnings and expenditures. Broadly speaking, just judgment must depend upon correct distinction —and adherence to it—between expenditures which should be charged to capital account, i.e., investment, and those properly chargeable to operating expenses. If, as is the case, even scientific accountants cannot agree where some important items should be placed, or if, as is alleged, the railroads, even under the control of the Interstate Commerce Commision, classify many large items as capital investment, which should be charged to operating costs, a definitive settlement of the issue on objective evidence is impossible—in the first case because of lack of standardized concepts, in the second because of public inability to compel the companies to keep their books scientifically and with due regard to the public interest.

The court decisions are crammed with attempts on the part of presumably capable and unbiased judges to find and apply a reasonable rule for the regulation of public utility rates, based upon fair return upon "value" of the property. Just as soon as attempt to define value of the property is made, however, insurmountable difficulties arise. It is impossible to determine a valuation which is fair to the consuming public, the investor, and the employees of the company.[36]

Take another question. What proportion of the workers are getting a "living wage"? Here it is obvious that the answer depends not only on the results of extended statistical research into money wages, commodity prices, and amount of unemployment, but upon the definition of "living wage."

Other pertinent illustrations will readily occur to the reader. Is the negro naturally inferior in mental capacity to the white? What do you mean by "natural"? Are high wages a cause of high prices? What is your criterion in measuring "high" wages? Is there a tendency toward undue extension of the powers of the Federal Government? What is the dividing line between "due" and "undue"? Could the state justly take a part of the increment of land values on the ground that such increment is unearned by the owners? What is the dividing line between "earned" and "unearned"? Are rising prices conducive to prosperity? What do you mean by "prosperity"? and *whose* prosperity? . . . What are "entangling alliances"? What is "normalcy"? Overpopulation? Woman's sphere? Double taxation? Confiscatory taxation?

It may be said, with truth, that these are questions involving standards of equity of which no exact objective definition can be made. Yet they are the type of question upon which legislatures and the courts and the general public are constantly passing judgment, and toward the solution of which the scientific student of social matters should be expected to contribute objective data, if not formulated conclusions. It may be said that the scientific investigator should avoid problems involving such difficulties. But the patent fact remains that if the scientist does not grapple with them the non-scientist will, with results that can scarcely be expected to be as well founded in objective fact or as free from subjective defects of logic as those the scientist will arrive at. If we cannot be objective, we must be as objective as we can.

---

[36] For an informing article on the impossibility of valuation (whether based on cost of production or cost of reproduction), as a basis of rate making, see Donald R. Richberg, "A permanent Basis for Rate Regulation," *Yale Law Journal*, Vol. XXXI, No. 3, pp. 263-282.

The difficulties inherent in such quasi-ethical problems are *sui generis*. But even in problems in which subjective valuation does not enter, and in which scientific definition and classification can be attained, the social scientist has difficulties enough.

The extreme complexity of the data he has to deal with renders some provisional simplification imperative. An omnipotent mind could handle any number and complexity of variables, but ours cannot. Consequently we have to resort to one of three devices: (1) plough a line straight through the complexity and interrelatedness of phenomena, ignoring everything not closely contiguous to the central march of our inquiry, (2) try to explain everything as manifestation of a few "fundamental social facts," or (3) pursue the method of approximation; considering in the first survey only the larger and more obvious factors, and then, in successive surveys over the same ground, bringing under observation and calculation as many of the hitherto neglected or minor factors as we can. The trouble with the first method is that it does not give us a true view of reality, any more than looking along a railroad cut gives us a view of the surrounding landscape. The second method we have already criticized, because it tends to be too deductive and too analogical, and in the past has been pseudo-scientific, in that the "postulates" were inadequate to the heavy load placed upon them. Nevertheless, this second device is valid within limits. Just as the physicist, for instance, may safely take the law of gravitation as a datum, so may the sociologist take the mechanism of stimulus and response. But to explain the instability of a given type of aeroplane by reference only to the law of gravitation, or the spread of an epidemic of hatred through a whole population by reference only to stimulus and response, would tell us little in either case. The third method is the safest and best. In fact, it is the method by which science has developed from the start.

The trial-and-error method, or research by hypothesis, should perhaps be included here, but it is in practice an aid in each of the three mentioned, especially in the third, rather than a distinct method.

What the chief dangers due to complexity are should be fairly clear upon a little consideration. They include the presence of unproved hypotheses taken as established; undetected assumptions; important, perhaps signally important, facts left unobserved and hence not taken into calculation; the temptation to use false analyses and to take analogy for proof; and, above all, the lazy habit of recoiling from the enormous labor of inductive research and trying to substitute for it long trains of deductive logic.

This last we may call the fallacy of linear reasoning. It is the besetting sin of "one-track" minds. Examples of it are all too common in the social sciences. All of classical political economy, from the economic man and Ricardo's theory of value to the frictionless static state and Clark's specific productivity, is full of fine examples. In sociology, the biological or selectionist school is a pertinent example. In fact, practically every sociological treatise (other than the "patched-together," eclectic, elementary texts) affords illustration. Eugenics literature is shot through and through with linear reasoning. Less than formerly, but still, to all intents and purposes, the eugenists, like their precursors the selectionists, are so keen to trace out the influence of heredity that they constantly take for heredity much that non-linear observation would show to be due to ontogenetic variation under environmental influence. If human life is ever reduced to a mathematical equation it is safe to say it will not be a simple linear equation. Causation does not work in lines. That is the reason we have spoken of the "nexus" rather than of a "stream" of causation.

From the complexity of social phenomena results another fundamental difficulty which cannot be avoided, and which is a growing menace to scientific realism. The field of investigation has to be divided and subdivided, until there are a dozen more or less distinct and disparate social sciences, in no one of which can the investigator cover more than a small part of the total ground, and of the whole content of which he can have but imperfect knowledge. Furthermore, ramifications of many, if not most, of the question the investigator is called upon to study in any special field are so numerous and extensive that it is practically impossible for any one individual to carry out the necessary research.

The more specialization—the more minute the division of intellectual labor—the greater probability that an investigator objective and scientific in his own field, will in other matters betray much the same subjectivity and sentimentalism as so unfortunately characterize the popular mind. The specialist, moreover, is likely greatly to overestimate the importance of his own particular knowledge, and of the type of phenomena which he studies. Specialism thus makes both for subjectivism in the general sense and for a distorted perspective in scientific attention and valuation. The necessity for so much close detailed work in a restricted area puts us in a position where we cannot see the forest for the trees.

For the present there does not seem much remedy for this situation. No surely grounded reform or achievement, not the product of wasteful conflict or of trial and error, can or will be made in the absence of a tolerably well-balanced view of social organization and the social process as a whole—not merely its political, its economic, and its biological aspects, respectively, and still less any partial sector of any one of these main phases. But it is equally true that the broad view necessary cannot be had without a previous study of the main details. An accurate map of the outlines of a country can be made only after a detailed survey of bearings and distances, contour, and cultural features. It is the same with society. And neither in geography nor in society can we know where we are or how to get where we want to go without a reasonably accurate map to tell us.

This means that we shall have to have an enormous amount of specialized research done and recorded in published reports and monographs. But it means also that this study of details and partial phases will be without much avail unless there be coupled with it the work of other scientific students, who take the results of the monographic surveys and synthesize them into as full and as tenable an objective, scientific theory of social causation as the available knowledge at the time makes possible.[37]

The task of necessary research, even as a basis for the solution of specific social questions, is so burdensome that it can be accomplished only through organized co-operation. The independent investigator has his place, but it will probably be a

---

[37] Cf. L. L. Bernard, "The Function of Generalization," *Monist*, Oct., 1920, pp. 623-630.

diminishing one as time goes on. The effectiveness of scientific objectivity and induction will be greatly increased when the research activities of individuals and groups are co-ordinated and focused by scientific steering committees.[38]

It may be noted in passing that while most scientific investigators in the social field as yet work independently, for the most part, with only such contacts and suggestive stimulus as they derive incidentally from the annual meetings of their various "learned societies," there is a very noteworthy tendency for the development of adequately financed organized research. This is particularly true in the field of economics.

The reader may conclude that our treatment of scientific method and attitude has been rather a setting forth of difficulties and obstacles than a constructive exposition. But if these difficulties exist—and they have not been unduly emphasized—the first step toward a constructive attitude is to recognize them. "Happily foreknowing may avoid." Nor should we be intimidated by them. Let the difficulties to the attainment of the scientific attitude and in the use of scientific method be ever so great, that is not saying that the scientific method, used even imperfectly, will not give better, more economical, and more permanent results than the method of blundering through, or of sentimental praise and blame and ignorant combat psychology.

---

[38] Will Durant, *Philosophy and the Social Problem*, 1917, Ch. 4.

CHAPTER X

1. *Individualism of Ends*

GIVEN an end to be accomplished, science can be called upon to suggest the best procedure, regardless of the value or morality of the end. Science can be the handmaiden of conservatism or radicalism, aristocracy or democracy, production or predatory acquisition, construction or destruction. But can science have anything to say in drawing the distinction between good and bad purposes? Can it help us to decide between alternative ends as well as between methods or means?

The most fundamental social issues hinge far more upon conflicts of ends than upon divergencies of opinion as to method. The fundamental conflict between conservative and radical sentiments results from incompatability of ends. The capitalist conservative, for example, regards his own class as an end and the workers as means, while the labor radical looks upon the workers as ends and the capitalist as a parasite. This in a nutshell is the explanation of the bitter opposition between the aristocratic, or plutocratic, tradition and the sentiment of democracy.

Now has ethics anything to say on this age-old conflict? Is it merely a matter of taste whether one should prefer a society composed of one set of people who regard themselves as ends and another to be treated as mere means, or a society in which all are recognized as real ends and in which all are expected to be serviceable units in a complex co-operative organization of means? Or is it possible that we may formulate, at least as a working hypothesis, some objective, scientifically justifiable, standard of "right" and "good" by which we can judge the two points of view?

If an objective standard is possible, it is fairly evident that it must be based upon a scientific, and that is to say, a mechanistic psychology. Metaphysics and figures of speech will have to be ruled out of court. Ethics is essentially a calculus of ends and means. Ends are things or states desired. In other words, they are motives. A valuation of ends not founded on an objective analysis of human nature can lay no claim to scientific status. This does not mean that we must join the extreme behaviorists in denying recognition to "consciousness" and in refusing scientific status to any psychological observation or generalization not stated in terms of neurons and glandular secretion. But it does mean that we have to get rid of such vagaries as "social mind," "social consciousness," "social value" and the like. These conceptions are objectionable, as mere figures of speech, the result of analogical reasoning, but the fatal objection to them is that they are responsible for an unconscionable amount of loose thinking in regard to the ethics of means and ends. They should be made to walk the plank along with soul stuff and innate ideas.

An ethics grounded in a hard headed objective psychology will have to regard the individual as the only possible end. The moment some metaphysical absolute (like God, or the "race") or some figurative thing like "social" welfare is set up as end, ethics gets into logical difficulties with the known facts of motivation and breaks company with scientific psychology. Whatever be the various types of motives (whether unconscious reflexes, sub-conscious "complexes," or conscious desires and interests), these motives have psychological reality and significance only as they determine the activity of *individuals;* and they have ethical significance only as they involve problems of individual conduct in a society of individuals.

When we say that the individual is the only possible end, we must define our terms with some care. What is an individual? What do we mean by "end"? And what makes the individual an end?

By an "individual" we do not mean an independent, self-contained, and self-determining entity, an entirely distinct and discrete something set up out of nothing and sharply outlined against the rest of the universe. So far as physical structure is concerned, the individual is a discrete and definite unit. Functionally he is not so. Functionally he becomes an individual, gets his growth and development, and lives, only by virtue of a host of symbiotic relations with other individuals. Theoretically it would be possible for a new born child to be fed and protected without ever hearing a human voice or being subject to stimuli of any kind from human beings. Such a child would get physical development. But of any mental development it would have very little, if any. It would not, and could not, develop into a human being. Actually, every child is born into a social environment. The child comes with an hereditary equipment of reflexes and instincts which give it the initial capacity to make such reactions to its environment as are essential to its existence and growth, first physical, then mental. Through the learning process the functioning of this hereditary equipment is modified and directed and developed to meet the child's need in his own specific surroundings. In the final analysis the whole process of learning and habituation is simply the adjustment of a neuro-glandular-muscular mechanism to function in a particular environment, and to function in such a way that it can survive and live to go through the normal cycle of life. Because of his helplessness, the child has to make, or rather have made in him, those adjustments imposed and required by his environmental, and especially his social, situation.

Somewhere in this process of adjustment, development, and learning, what we call consciousness, or conscious experience, begins. How consciousness develops and what it is we need not stop to consider. Certainly it is a form of behavior, and has a physical basis in the physical states and responses of the whole organism; indeed it is doubtless fair to say that it *is* those states and responses. Whatever it is and however it develops, consciousness is what defines the human individual. It is a social product in that it is response of a physical organism to stimuli from a social environment. But as no two of us have, or ever could have, exactly the same stimuli from our environment, so the systems of responses we develop, while similar, are never the same. We know our own stream of experience as we cannot know that of another person.

It is precisely this fact of differential consciousness or experience that not only defines the individual but constitutes the individual an end, so far as the concept of end has any ethical significance.

An end, regarded from a slightly different angle, is something in the literal sense idealized, imagined. It is a design—something marked out to be accomplished—a *purpose*. Purpose involves an intellective process, memory, imagination, association, and attention. A simple unideated reflex, or a reaction which is purely instinctive can have no purpose, though it may fulfil very essential functions. Hence when we attribute "purpose" to the behavior of lower organisms or to the organization of the universe we simply pursue the method of primitive man in judging everything by himself, and read our own consciousness into the organism or into the universe.

Now the behaviorist will say that the ideational, *planned* reactions of the cultured human being are different from those of the amoeba only in degree. Both are wholly mechanistic. Both are determined. The actions of a human being are more intricate, that is all. With this we need have no quarrel. For if we accept the fundamental faith of science that every effect has its cause and every cause its effect, we are bound to hold that an individual's behavior, however complex and "purposive," is in the final analysis the mechanistic response of his organism to the stimuli of its environment. But the difference of degree, in complexity, in directness *vs.* indirectness, and in subordination of the impulse of the moment to the real or supposed whole-life interests of the organism capable, through memory and imagination, of a *continuum* of experience, is signally important. The physiological processes of the amoeba or of a cow enable the amoeba or the cow to exist. Both will avoid danger and seek subsistence, just as I do. Neither is aware of what it is doing. Neither thinks. Now when I think, my thinking itself is a mechanistic neuro-muscular stimulus-and-response process, but it is a process through which I am aware (more or less) of what I am doing, and what I shall aim (prepare) to do next week or next year. To the extent that I think, I am conscious. Thinking, I live not only in the present, with some wisps of the past sticking to it, but in the future as well. Thinking, I form purposes, and these purposes—imagined future states or situations—play a part in determining my present actions. In other words, I am an end because I think.

We define the term end, therefore, with reference to consciousness. If an organism is not conscious of being an end it is difficult to see in what ethical sense it can be one. Unconscious activity may serve some functional "end" in the biological or physiological sense—which is merely in the sense that certain results flow from it—but hardly in the ethical sense unless its results ultimately in some way become presented in consciousness.

This admittance of consciousness into the discussion is of course not in accordance with the views of the most extreme behaviorists. In the first flush of their determination to construct an objectively scientific psychology, and their resultant rejection of all conclusions arrived at through the method of introspection, they have convinced themselves that they can have nothing to do with "consciousness." Taking consciousness to mean a distinct entity of some sort—the "soul," the "self"—something existent "above" and in a measure apart from the mechanistic functioning of the neuro-muscular organism, they hold that it can be observed only through introspection, which is to say that objective, verifiable observation of it is impossible. In thus accepting the transcendental, quasi-mystical conception of consciousness from the older, introspective psychology, they are themselves guilty of an unscientific attitude. For the fact remains that some kinds of mechanistic responses give rise to (or are) what we call consciousness, while other kinds do not (or are not); and consciousness is not obliterated by saying that the introspective method of observation is unscientific, whether that assertion be true or not.

Whatever the mechanism of consciousness is, we are using the term consciousness simply to denote that mechanism, and say that in its absence there may be function but not purpose, or in our nomenclature, end.

It cannot be expected that a doctrine of individualism of ends will rapidly gain acceptance in formal codes, however universally it may correspond to the facts of human motivation and conduct, or however "ethical" and "social" and in accord with what is glibly and superficially called altruism it may be shown to be. To say that the individual is the only possible end amounts to saying, if our thought be confined to ends, that there is no such thing, in the last analysis, as altruism, and that all the paraphernalia of discourse on duty and the elements of "good" character (including truthfulness, loyalty, industry, conscientiousness, self-control, sympathy, charity, honor, etc.) are matters having to do primarily with means, rather than ends. It is saying, also, that in the last analysis there is no such thing as self-sacrifice; or rather that all that any man can sacrifice is one or more of his many conceivably possible selves (whether "lower" or "higher") for the self that *must*, from all the forces of the universe, be the one which at the moment obtains realization.[1]

We always act in obedience to the strongest urge or combination of urges—using the term to include unconscious as well as conscious processes—and the strongest urge is, if conscious, the one obedience to which we believe or feel will give us the greatest happiness or the least unhappiness under the circumstances; and if unconscious, the one which is the natural and logical expression of our organism and its needs at the time.

It makes little or no difference whether we consider the strongest motive in terms of happiness (utilitarianism) or in terms of self-expression (energism). Whatever an individual does, in a given situation and under given environmental stimuli, whether of freedom or of repression, is the response of a particular organism to a particular set of stimuli. Given the stimuli, the nature of the response is determined by the individual's hereditary traits and by all his past experience, that is, by all his past responses. Whatever he does is an expression of self, as conditioned by the environmental situation.

In one case, he may kill a man to save his own life; in another, he may give his own life to save another man, or to fulfill his conception of duty, *e.g.*, as to patriotism. In either case the action is self-expression. In the first case the act may be merely instinctive or it may be premeditated. In the second case the act may also be instinctive or it may be the result of compulsions, external (the draft) or internal (fear of regarding himself as a slacker), or of what are ordinarily called self-sacrifice and altruism. In either case the action, if premeditated, is the one which, "all things considered," the individual thinks will contribute most to his happiness.

---

[1] This is not saying, of course, that better selves, in uncounted myriads, may not be sacrificed by the stupidities of narrow selfishness, and of class, nationalistic, and racial rivalries stimulated by commercial materialism.

If we could consider the individual as an independent functional entity, happiness could be regarded as that psychophysical tone resultant upon, and accompanying, the full, free, and healthy functioning of those of his powers and capacities which have been trained to function, and also, it may be, of powers and capacities, hitherto repressed, but now released.[2]

But the individual is never alone. As he is a social product, so also is he always a member of society—which means that he never can be "free." An act which, in itself, for him alone, might give happiness, may result in great unhappiness for him because of its effect on other individuals. If he should do certain things he knows other persons would punish him. If he should do certain other things he knows that his sympathetic appreciation of the unhappiness caused others would make him himself unhappy. Hence the idea of happiness must be stated in a way which takes full account of the fact that every individual is a member of a society of individuals. Happiness, then, is that psycho-physical state or tone which results from, and accompanies, the full, free, and healthy functioning of the individual's powers and capacities, to whatever extent and intensity and in whatsoever directions do not interfere with a like functioning of the powers of other individuals.

It is desirable, indeed essential, here to make a distinction between what have been called respectively "the narrower selfishness" and "the broader selfishness." The narrow egotist, pursuing happiness by direct means, acts, so far as he can, as if he himself were the only end. He pursues the satisfaction of his own desires and interests with little reference to the happiness of others and with no thought that they too are ends in themselves. It must be admitted that he often succeeds in acquiring certain pachydermous characteristics—the unhappiness of others does not affect his spirits. But it should also be obvious that such an individual also narrows his own capacity for experience, and in limiting that, narrows his own personality; with the result that many types and sources of happiness, available only through sensitive sympathy and co-operation, are closed to him. The broader egotist, on the contrary, may, be-

---

[2] A sort of vicarious release and functioning may take place through day-dreaming, dream symbolization, and anticipation; but into this intricate psychoanalytic aspect of the question we need not enter.

cause of his quick sympathies, suffer all the miseries he sees others suffer,[3] but he also vicariously enjoys the happiness of others, and by entering into their experience may live an infinitely larger life than the narrow egotist ever has the capacity to conceive.

We must go even further. The limitation of the principle of happiness necessitated by the fact that we are all members of society must be put positively as well as negatively. Not only am I in my own self-interest bound not to use you as a door-mat, but also positively I am bound to co-operate in your happiness. Without this positive qualification, I may go my own sweet way and let you go yours. There is perhaps something to be said for this policy in a world in which so many persons are ready to mind everybody's business but their own —so quick to prescribe for you how you shall live your own life. Nevertheless, from a larger point of view, it will not do. So social is the nature of man—so much is happiness and even "self" expression the product of a social process—so much is our life widened by sympathy, and so happy a field for the satisfaction of gregariousness and workmanship do mutual aid and "altruistic" co-operation afford, that my life should be broadened, my self-expression multiplied, and my happiness increased in the proportion that I not only refuse to live at your expense (equally refusing to let you live at mine) but equally in the proportion that I co-operate with you to widen your sphere of self-expression and to increase your happiness. To illustrate a broad principle by specific and perhaps trivial examples: I may enjoy perfect physical health, but I shall certainly enjoy it more if you too are healthy and can play and work with me. I may get a certain pleasure of prestige in possessing a fine and costly library, but I shall get more enjoyment out of it if you have had such opportunities that you can enjoy with me the literature it contains. I may enjoy living in a million dollar palace, but it would have taken, perhaps, but slight change in my past experience, to lead me to enjoy much more living in a ten thousand dollar cottage and devoting the

---

[3]In cases of hypertrophied sympathy, he suffers miseries that others, less sensitive than he is, do not suffer, because he reads his own personality into their experience and vicariously suffers what he would feel were he in their place.

other $990,000 to facilities which the whole community could enjoy.

Whichever avenue to self-expression and happiness—the narrower or the broader—men have chosen, or have been driven into by their environment and inherited temperaments, and however much they have tried to convince themselves that something other than the individual is end, the chief end of man has always been happiness through self-expression.[4] Where temperament and environment were such that self-expression was acquired through head-hunting or gladiatorial combats, those were the activities in which the men of that region found that functional satisfaction which may properly be thought of, generically, as happiness. If, on the other hand, training and environment had puritanized men into beings who could find self-expression only in the stern pursuit of disagreeable duty or in escaping hell-fire, a man in that part of the world could not be happy unless he were thus active.

If only conscious individuals are to be regarded as ends, it is evident that no group, society, or institution, regarded as distinct from the several individuals who compose it, can be an end. Consciousness has never been observed in disconnection from a nervous system, nor self-consciousness apart from a highly developed nervous system—probably in none below man is it present. There is organic functional activity in plants and animals below man, but it is not conscious, thought-of activity—at least it is not conscious in any sense comparable to that in which human conduct is so. It is for this reason that we do not think of animals below man as ends in themselves. No group, society, or institution can be an end, because it has no nervous system and no consciousness. To speak of group consciousness, social mind, and the like, or even of public opinion and public sentiment, is to speak in elliptical figures of speech. The only consciousness, mind, opinion, or sentiment there is in any group is the consciousness, mind, opinion, or sentiment, of the individual members of the group. Likewise the happiness of the group is the happiness of its individual members.

It should be clear now, therefore, that those who set up the state, the family, the race, or any process or attitude, such as

---

[4] A utilitarian suggestion crept into even the Westminster Catechism. "The chief end of man is to glorify God and *enjoy Him forever*."

parenthood[5] or loyalty,[6] as end are putting the cart before the horse—confusing means and ends. No institution can be other than a means, however much its devotees and beneficiaries may talk and act as if it were an end in itself.

The direction in which we should hope, then, to find the trail to a scientific ethics would lead us through psychology to a utilitarian doctrine of *individualism of ends*—but not, let us hasten to add, to an individualism of means, such as is exemplified in our social inheritance of economic *laissez faire* from the political revolt of the eighteenth century.

The individual is end because he only is capable of experience, and, specifically, of what makes life worth living—happiness through conscious functional activity. But the individual is a social product, has a social nature, and must cease to function if taken out of the social medium in which he lives and moves and has his being. His happiness, and the self-expression of which it is the product, are really a locus of social (*i.e.,* inter-individual) "forces," stimuli, and opportunities. The individual may be regarded as a sort of dynamo, in which center a multitude of lines of social influence, which are there transformed into currents of energy and personality that, then, flow out from him to the external world. The amount and character of his self-expression and happiness depend on two things, (1) the amount and kind of energy of which he is the locus, and (2) the outlets for this energy as transformed and re-co-ordinated by his personality. The first we may summarize under the term *opportunity*, the second under *service*.[7]

2. *Society as Means*

What now is the means through which the individual realizes himself, lives his life? Whence comes the opportunity for happiness and self-expression?

The amount of opportunity available to the individual, and hence the amplitude of his life, depend very largely upon the efficiency of the social organization of which he is a part. Whether we take it on the ground of psychology—the nature

---

[5] Cf. C. W. Saleeby, *Parenthood and Race Culture*, 1909.

[6] Cf. Royce's "Loyalty to loyalty," in his *Philosophy of Loyalty*, 1908.

[7] Avoiding, however, any narrow or sentimental connotations of the term.

and variety of stimulation and outlet for self-expression—or upon economic grounds—the production and distribution of the material goods,—the character of the individual's self-expression, the degree of his happiness, depends upon the co-operative creation of opportunity.

It is true that an individual motivated by the narrower egotism, as we saw above, may take no part in this co-operative creative workmanship and yet be what is ordinarily regarded as happy. He may take the position that he is not to blame for his own existence, and that the world consequently owes him a living. In obedience to this idea one person may become a thief, or a profiteer, always actuated by the acquisitive motive, always scheming how he may get something for nothing. Another may become an idle society woman without a thought as to who pays for her privileges or to her moral right to support in idleness. In the history of the race millions have acted this way and "prospered." They have "played the game and won," finding the joy of self-expression in the sense of power, of guile, or of charm.

But one may perhaps be permitted to aver without becoming homiletic that they have also lost. To say nothing of sympathy and vicarious experience, they have missed the joy of workmanship. One instinct has been atrophied and smothered in the overgrowth of another. Creativeness has been subordinated to acquisitiveness.

This is not saying that creativeness is necessarily "higher" than acquisitiveness. It is, however, more essential. For if none created, there would be nothing to acquire. Hence without resorting to "moral" postulates, we can easily see that a productive sharing in the co-operative activities of society, if not undertaken voluntarily by the individual, out of joy in work and from a sense of self-respect, will be required of him by other individuals in protection of their own interests. Productively we stand, acquisitively we fall.

A very large part of the individual's life is a vicarious living of the lives of others. For this reason we can rely to a certain extent upon sympathy for the co-operative creation of opportunity. But it is sadly evident that such motivation, in our present degree of culture, is inadequate to our dire need of social peace and co-operation. We are neither sensitive enough nor intelligent enough to understand the truth intuitively expressed by Jesus in his query, What shall it profit a man though he gain the whole earth, if he lose his soul? We are still too near our rough ancestors of the German forests, still too much under the spell of the acquisitive individualism of Manchesterism and the frontier scramble for spoils. Yet there is a real scientific foundation for this doctrine of "super-individualism."

That society is a co-operative organization for the production of opportunity may be a truism as a theory. It would be so in fact with a race adequately rationalized and socialized, one that had no holdover characteristics of barbarism and had recovered from the *laissez faire* individualism of means of the eighteenth and nineteenth centuries. It is noticeable that the nearer one gets to geographical or racial frontiers and perhaps also to the frontier of business, the more people talk of their "rights" and the less of their duties. Considering the hold that narrow acquisitiveness and predatory greed still have on us, we will risk emphasizing what might otherwise be regarded as a platitude.

While a scientific ethics would thus seem to point unmistakably to an individualism of ends, it points with equal sureness to a *co-operation or sociality of means*. Put in another way, individuals (society) are means in their co-operative power to create opportunity, but opportunity serves an end only for individuals.

All this, however, while fundamental and necessary, does not throw direct light on the ethics of the interest conflict between conservative and radical. Merely to show that the individual is end and society means does not solve the class conflict.

3. *Democracy*

In the present alignment of conservatism and radicalism, it happens, as has been common throughout history, that the radicals, broadly speaking, stand for the democratic principle and the conservatives on the whole for the aristocratic. The democrat and the aristocrat hold very different theories both of ends and of social means. We are thus compelled to touch upon the meaning of democracy, if we are to get much light on the ethics of the interest conflict between conservative and radical.

Most of what has thus far been written on democracy reveals little understanding that democracy can mean anything but a type of political machinery and control. According to this conception, democracy has to do with means, hardly at all with ends.

Political democracy may or may not be the best conceivable form of organization and control. It is probably, however, the form that will come nearest to insuring that which we shall shortly define as the essence of real democracy. But it will be effective toward the attainment of a real democracy only with a people educated to its use. It is easy to have the form without the content, for what looks like political democracy, in external form and process, may be in reality, as is well known, a veiled plutocracy.

If, then, we direct our attention to the more fundamental question of ends, the answer we get will go far to direct the solution of the problem of means—machinery and control. If we say that only individuals are ends, we must immediately be confronted with the query, "What individuals?" Most radicals will at once answer, "All individuals," while most conservatives will forthwith object, "No, only some!"

Here, consequently, we come to the real test of the practical value of the principle of individualism of ends and socialism [8] of means. What ground is there for regarding all individuals as ends, or on the contrary, only some? And if all individuals are to be regarded as ends, are they all equal ends?

Every individual, because he has power of conscious self-expression and happiness, is not only an end, but he is at the same time a means, because he can live fully only to the extent that he contributes his services and capacities to the general co-operative process of creating the opportunities under which self-expression and happiness are possible for any one.

But neither as ends nor as means are individuals of equal worth or importance. Actually and potentially, individuals dif-

---

[8] It is needful to repeat that this term, as here used, is in no sense meant to suggest any particular type of social organization. It is used merely as a somewhat more euphonious term than "sociality," or "mutualism," to denote the essential fact that all means to the fulfillment of individual ends are social and co-operative—that *society* is the means.

fer, both in capacity for self-expression and happiness and in their power to contribute to the co-operative production of opportunity. They differ actually, not only because their organic inheritances are diverse, but because the opportunities for development which they have had have been different. They differ potentially, "naturally," to the extent that their hereditary endowments differ.

How much strictly hereditary capacity differs in different individuals, families, or races, no one, as a matter of fact, knows, and we are not likely soon to know, for the reason that close discrimination between the hereditary and environmental factors which have made an individual what he is, is practically an impossible task.

The dead level theory of democracy maintains that individuals are equal in native capacity and hence in "rights." This theory, which few informed persons now hold, practically denies any influence to heredity, and is so contrary to the probabilities of the case that it need not detain us. Even yet, however, there are many polemics written against democracy by persons who assume that it means this dead level theory. Such arguments are simply waste labor.

While no reasonably informed person to-day would attempt to defend the thesis that all individuals are equal by hereditary endowment, there has been on the other hand an immense output of unwarranted conclusions as to natural inequality and the scarcity of hereditary capacity, drawn from investigations which have purported to isolate and measure hereditary capacity (mental as well as physical). In most cases such investigation can be shown to be grossly oblivious of the presence of probable environmental influences in the creation of talents or defects which it has taken as hereditary.

Whatever may be the truth about natural inheritance— whether we are as different in natural endowments as eugenists like Pearson and Davenport would have us believe, or are more nearly equal than any one now believes we are, this much should be clear: we cannot on scientific grounds condemn an individual to inferior status and deprive him of opportunity before he has been tried out for a time under opportunities equal to those granted others. There is much that goes for hereditary feeble-mindedness, for instance, which is due to mal-nutrition and adenoids.

Whatever the natural distribution of potential capacity is, opportunity should be distributed to individuals in proportion to that capacity. Distribution of opportunity is a matter of economy as well as of ethics—if indeed the two be not synony-mous. Opportunity is limited, and it should be dealt out where it will do the most good. To distribute opportunity according to the dead level democratic theory, as the Communists have attempted, would certainly fall short of ideal economy, and probably fall short by as wide a margin as does our present distribution by status.

Opportunity is restricted fundamentally by the limitation of natural resources, secondarily by our limited technological capacity to utilize economically the resources we have. It is not only business that needs talent of the first grade; society itself needs it, in self-protection against the headlong rush of modern business to squander our natural resources as rapidly as possible. From whatever angle the situation is viewed, we need not only to distribute opportunity (and the material wealth and income on which it is based) economically, but we need above all to discover, develop, conserve, and utilize every ounce of human capacity we can—barring, of course, those capacities which are wasteful and destructive rather than serviceable.

This means that those who have the greatest hereditary capa-city should be given the best education and the greatest oppor-tunity in every way to develop their talents. The only excep-tion to this rule may be where between two equal potential talents we may show preference for the one the services of which society stands in the most need at the time.

To each individual, opportunity in proportion to his capacity, within the limits of the total opportunity available for all; and from each individual, service in proportion to his developed capacity. This is the criterion of fundamental democracy. Democracy, instead of meaning *equality* of opportunity, means *equity* of opportunity, together with service proportionate not to reward but to capacity.

"Thus understood, democracy holds (1) that every individual is an end in himself; (2) that no individual is to be regarded primarily as a means to the fulfillment of the purposes or desires of any other individual; (3) that no class or group of individuals is to be regarded primarily as a means to the interest of another class as end; (4) that opportunity, and, so far as opportunity is dependent upon them, material wealth and income, should be distributed to individuals in proportion to capacity and willingness to use it for the collective good; (5) that the collective good will reach its highest mark when opportunity, which at best is limited in quantity and quality, is distributed so that each individual is enabled to develop his potential powers and capacities in like proportion to the development of these potentialities in every other individual; (6) that the means to the utilization of individual capacity and the development of individual happiness can be found only in the willing, fair-minded co-operative work of individuals and groups, all of whom accept and live up to the foregoing principles. Democracy, in other words, is the real recognition of each individual as an end, and an economy in which human powers and capacities for achievement, service, and happiness are symmetrically developed, wherever found, without deference to race, sex, language, birth, or nationality. As a philosophy of means, democracy denotes equity of opportunity and the co-operative use of human and natural resources to produce a worthy life for individuals."[9]

While we cannot give the matter the full consideration it ought to have, it should be distinctly pointed out that the problem of the distribution of opportunity and the population problem are very intimately related, not only from what is ordinarily known as the economic point of view but from the ethical as well. With the utmost industry and technological skill, our productive capacity is limited by the limited quantity and quality of our natural resources. We can for a time, it is true, and in spite of uneconomical distribution, consume and waste our material resources at an astounding rate, as we have been doing for a hundred years. But future generations will have to pay for our recklessness. An ethics and an economy not blindly limited to the interests of the existing generation would

---

[9] A. B. Wolfe, "Some Psychological Aspects of Industrial Reconstruction," *Publications of the American Sociological Society*, Vol. XIV, 1919, pp. 74, 75.

therefore extend the principle of equity of opportunity to include the oncoming peoples of the future.

Leaving the future out of account, and assuming an absence of waste in current production, distribution, and consumption, population movements still complicate the problem of democratic equity. Beyond a certain point, further increase in population cannot fail to reduce the average opportunity, per capita, available. Suppose, then, that the size of the population in relation to the available natural resources were such that further population increase would reduce average income; and suppose that distribution had attained approximate equity. Then if certain individuals ignorantly or imprudently cause a further increase in population, are those already here in duty bound to relinquish a part of the opportunities they have enjoyed in order to give the newcomers their proportionate share? If they are, and did there not arise from any quarter effective restrictions on multiplication, it is evident that democracy might lead, as Malthus argued of communism, to universal poverty or the virtual disappearance of all opportunity save that of unremitting toil to maintain physical existence. Nevertheless, there is no escaping the fact that no baby has ever yet been consulted as to whether it should be born or not. And if parents call into being hordes of new and unneeded lives, society has no moral right to make the involuntary newcomers suffer for its own remissness of control. It should be obvious that society—those of us already here—in self-protection, and in the interests of utilizing existing human capacity, indeed, to prevent its wholesale waste in a flood of numbers, must devise and enforce the rational limitation of procreation. Here is the fundamental ethical necessity and justification of birth control. The optimum relation between population and resources, once attained, must be protected and maintained. The whole principle of fundamental democracy demands it.[10]

Let us now glance at the position taken by aristocracy with regard to the problem of means and ends.

Practically, the aristocracy theory takes no account of the

---

[10] This position was explicitly taken by John Stuart Mill as early as 1848. See his *Principles of Economics*, Vol. I, Book XX, Ch. XII. (American edition, Vol. I, pp. 444-447.)

distinction between hereditary and environmental differences; when it pretends to do so, it merely jumps with dogmatic casuistry to the conclusion that those individuals who now enjoy the greatest opportunities are thereby proved to be from hereditarily superior stocks.

The aristocratic theory is one of *status*. The privileged aristocrat, to the manor born, simply takes it for granted that he is an end and the "lower orders" means. Essentially this modern master-class attitude is not different from the classical Greek's justification of slavery: My pursuit of happiness, self-expression, culture, requires leisure; if I have leisure, someone else must do the work; the barbarians were provided by the gods for that purpose, and they should be kept in that status.

This master-class attitude lasted almost unbrokenly down to the French Revolution, and underwent a new development with the rise of modern capitalism in the machine era. In the determination that some classes shall be ends and other classes means lies the real explanation of conservative and reactionary opposition to liberalism and radicalism. Under whatever vagary of idea as to the way it could be accomplished, liberalism and radicalism have fought for democracy, equity of opportunity, co-operation in social workmanship, freedom for the unfolding and expression of individual powers.

The privileged had freedom, at least as much freedom as they could appreciate. The "lower orders," on the other hand, condemned by hook or crook of historical processes—one is tempted to call them accident—to the servant status, and admonished by all the principles and ruses of master-and-servant ethics to be content with that status, naturally groped for liberty. More and more they are to-day insisting, in action if not in so many words, that they, individually, are ends, as well as means, and consequently that they are entitled to opportunity to realize themselves as ends.

While the political and economic trend toward individualism in the eighteenth century was fundamentally due to a widening conviction that all men are ends, the movement worked itself out as a philosophy of means. In effect, to free society from the master-and-servant ethics, the revolutionary philosophers took the extreme position that social control has no other political or economic function than to clear the track and prevent

fouling in the race of individual acquisitiveness. The old burden of special privilege, prescriptive rights, and restrictive regulation was so great that men were denied the opportunity to
help themselves by their own effort and initiative. The very
purpose of a very large amount of this old regulation had been
to prevent men from escaping from the quasi-servile status.
There were thus abundant reason and justification for the "system of natural liberty" developed by English philosophers from
Hobbes and Locke to Adam Smith, and in France by the brilliant pre-revolutionary encyclopædists and *économistes*.

Thus the eighteenth century revolt was an insistence upon
rights ("natural" rights) rather than functions, although it
would be truer to say that in its origins it grew out of insistence
upon the right of individuals to function freely.

In Germanic countries and generally on the Continent, outside of France, the state was made the end, and so much emphasis was placed on authoritatively imposed and enforced social
co-operation that the individual was lost sight of. In England,
France, and America, however, the individualistic revolt was
so complete that social co-operation was thought of only as a
by-product of individual acquisitiveness. Distributive economy,
the discovery and conservation of individual capacity, its utilization to the best social advantage, and the organization of social
functions for the positive service of the people, were frequently
dismissed in pious phrases about the "economic harmonies."
In America, they were smothered under a flood of ignorant
sentiment and rant about inexhaustible resources, boundless
opportunity, room at the top, and the American citizen's superior ability to look out for himself. Even the (relatively)
magnificent educational system in America was built up with
primary reference to the needs, not of social co-operation, but
of self-help.

All this was a natural and inevitable result of our geographical situation, our economic condition, and our political background here in America. All might have continued to be very
well if the Industrial Revolution had not transformed the entire
situation, if our free land and other "boundless" natural
resources had held out and not been handed over to the exploitative activities of private corporations, and if we had not grown
from a handful of squabbling but industrious colonists to a

population of a hundred million people, some not so industrious. Hardly, in fact, had Englishmen, Frenchmen, and Americans acquired the right of individual initiative and self-help, when changing technology and industrial organization largely nullified that right.

Political "democracy" was then thought of as the road of freedom, and adequate expression and evidence of it. Gradually, however, the fact that manhood, or even universal, suffrage might exist contemporaneously with economic vassalage became clear. The right to vote did not get one a job, though if one voted right one might retain a job already held. The right to work, to freedom of contract, to acquire superior income and property, did not seem to have the old real content after the Western World became thoroughly industrialized and individual entrepreneurship gave way to corporate organization and financial control, and the "boundless" resources of a new country had nearly all been appropriated by the first comers and handed down in the family. The process of change from "status to contract" seemed somehow to be reversing itself. Differential status was creeping back. Labor, as capital had done from the start, began to combine. Freedom of contract was no longer an unquestioned ideal. Discipline and class solidarity seemed necessary to the maintenance of any opportunity above a subsistence level. Trade unionism and then "radicalism" of every hue and color developed—all, with the exception of anarchism, calling for more co-operation and more control as the way to freedom and opportunity.

Traditional American "individualism" and "democracy" had proved in some essential respects a failure. The aim of true democracy of opportunity and an efficient organization of production is not freedom of acquisition but a symmetrical freedom for all men and full service from all men. A serious alteration must doubtless take place in the distribution of material income before we can approach the equity of opportunity which constitutes democracy, but if any one instinct is to be freed by democracy it is the instinct of workmanship and not that of acquisition.

Radicalism, and to a lesser degree liberalism, undoubtedly contemplate a reform of our social arrangements such as will gradually bring about this necessary redistribution of oppor-

tunity. In that sense the balked desires which produce radicalism belong in the class of acquisitive interests. But there are
reasons to believe, as we have seen, that the radical attack on
"privilege" goes deeper. Its underlying urge to social reform
is not so much to raise the dollar income for its own sake as it
is to secure a fuller measure of freedom for the functioning of
individual capacities now felt to be atrophied by the acquisitive,
commercial individualism of means inherited from earlier philosophies and earlier social conditions. The revolt is against the
unexpected results of the individualistic revolution of the
eighteenth century.

It is not strange that a remarkable re-alignment of sentiment
has taken place. The privileged aristocrats, who in the eighteenth century fought economic individualism of means (free
trade, *laissez faire,* etc.) and opposed the extension of political
democracy, now herald helf-help and freedom of contract as
the final embodiment of economic wisdom and social morality,
and exhibit surprise that the masses show a tendency to under-
value the democratic machinery of politics. Liberals and radicals, on the other hand, who forced through the program of
political democracy and compelled the striking off of many
(not all) of the mediæval prescriptive restrictions on self-help
and individual energy, now turn their backs on individualism
of means and demand new measures of collective control, sur-
passing in range and complexity anything to be found in the
period prior to the Industrial Revolution. This new demand
is made, of course, on the ground that changes in economic
technology and financial organization and control have, in fact,
rendered individualism of means—self-help—impossible in practice and dishonest as a theory. Continued attempt to keep up
the fiction of self-help individualism is held simply to cloud the
issue in a mist of cant phrases and specious reasoning, and to
throw industrial and political control into the hands of vested
interests still dominated by the master-and-servant ethics.

We have now developed four propositions which we believe
will stand the test of objective analysis, and which accordingly
can be used in estimating the ethics of the present attitudes
of conservatives and radicals. These propositions are: (1)
individuals, and only individuals, are ends; (2) individuals
differ in potential natural capacity and hence are not all ends

of equal magnitude; (3) economy of limited resources therefore demands that opportunity be distributed to individuals *pro rata* first to their potential, and later to their developed, capacities; (4) efficient production and economical distribution of opportunity cannot be obtained by any *laissez faire* system of individualistic acquisition; they can be obtained only by intelligently planned, rationally co-ordinated, social co-operation.

If the foregoing attempt to outline the foundations of an ethics with individualism of ends as its cornerstone be accepted as valid, it evidently carries some very direct implications as to the ethics of privilege and democracy; and hence as to the ethics of conservatism and radicalism.

From the standpoint of economy—development, conservation, and efficient utilization of human capacity—there can be no question that democracy as here defined, namely, equity of opportunity and service according to developed capacity, would give us the ideal distribution and the most productive society possible. To the extent that conservatism stands for untested privilege and a denial of equity of opportunity, and radicalism for the fundamental economy of democracy, ethical justification is on the side of radicalism and against conservatism. The staunch defender of everything-just-as-it-is would have to show, or at least to believe, that present distribution is substantially proportional to natural capacity. Few, when forced squarely to face the facts, will have the temerity to say that it is. Conversely, the fanatical egalitarian, if he could be brought to drop his fanaticism long enough to look calmly at evidence and probabilities, would be forced to admit the non-economy of dead-level democracy.

The problem of scientific ethics does not lie in a choice between these extremes. The problem lies in finding out, as nearly as is scientifically possible, what the natural capacities of individuals are, and how they are distributed between different individuals. Toward the solution of this problem we have scarcely made a beginning. The biologists can give us little aid, for they are not able to experiment with human heredity, and are handicapped by their inability to isolate the hereditary factors from those due to environment. Much aid may eventually come from the development of the art of psychological tests. But even here extreme care must be used not to attribute to hereditary talent or deficiency what may very well be due, in part at least, to training, education, and social stimulus in general. There is reason to think that in their enthusiasm over a new method of research many present-day psychologists are somewhat remiss in keeping this necessary caution in mind.

For a long time to come, a society which really wished to be fair and economical in its distribution of opportunity would have to proceed by a refined and orderly trial-and-error method. All individuals would have to be given as nearly equal environmental stimulus (education, etc.) as possible, clear through the formative years of childhood and adolescence. At the conclusion of such a period—or even earlier in cases of palpable mental deficiency or superiority—the psychological testers could be called in, vocational experts summoned for advice, and the sheep definitely separated from the goats.

Needless to say, it is not likely that society will soon adopt any such Platonic plan of procedure. Nevertheless every time we enforce a compulsory education law or add a new scholarship for "worthy and indigent" students, or take a child away from unfit parents, we are taking a step along the road which led Plato to his highly democratic suggestion that a child of "golden" constitution, wherever born, should have opportunities equal to the best.

It may be objected, of course, that inasmuch as we know so little, from actual, verifiable scientific observation and measurement, as to the part played by difference in hereditary endowment, and that played by environmental stimulus, we should let things go on as they are. It may even be argued, with considerable show of reason, that in many particulars we now have a sort of inverted democracy—in that we give to inferior hereditary endowment opportunity that could better be devoted to individuals of demonstrated capacity. There can be little question, of course, that many wealthy individuals of the type that cannot or will not use opportunity productively owe the opportunities now thrown away upon them to gambling luck or to the exercise of anti-social acquisitive talents which it would be undesirable to encourage.

Nevertheless, it would probably be the concensus of opinion, among those most entitled by scientific research and observation to hold opinions on the subject, that we do not come now anywhere as near as we could, even with our present limited knowledge of human heredity and social psychology, to distributing opportunity to individuals in proportion to their potential capacities. And whether we do or not, it is patent that the growing masses of radicals do not think we do. If they are wrong, the only proof that will still their clamor is a prolonged experiment under conditions in which special privilege, whether acquired by legal inheritance or otherwise, is reduced to a minimum.

CHAPTER XI

THE ETHICS OF CONSERVATISM AND RADICALISM

GENERALLY speaking, it follows from the analysis of the two preceding chapters that the ethics of conservatism and radicalism hinges, as to motivation and results, upon whether they aim at individualism and democracy of ends; as to method, whether they pursue their social diagnoses and analyses in a personalistic, praise-and-blame spirit or in accordance with impersonal, scientific investigation; and whether they attempt to carry out their purposes and designs by conflict or by co-operation. In suggesting the general norms of scientific method, individualism of ends, democracy of opportunity, and socialism [1] of means, we do not intend to lay down absolutes. That in itself would be a violation of the scientific spirit. Under certain conditions conflict is doubtless unavoidable. But unless the preceding analysis is scientifically ill-founded and logically confused, these are the standards by which social attitudes, purposes, and movements must be judged. Justification of any avoidable departure from them, if it is to be admitted, must have extraordinarily good grounds. It seems clear that the principle of economy would put opportunity where it will do the most good both in "service" and in happiness. It would seem, too, that the world had experimented with the conflict method long enough to begin to arrive at a strong suspicion that the co-operative, constructive method will produce better results. And, finally, unless there is some scientific reason for supposing that man is not a part of nature, and is therefore exempt from its laws, the scientific method of investigating and ordering human relations may be expected, when really applied, to yield results far preferable to those produced by the motor-habituations, the superstitious sentimentalism, the dogmatic loyalties, and the weddedness to rationalized illusions which

---

[1] See the caution, page 264, as to the sense in which this word is here used.

have thus far been man's chief guides in social organization and social process.[2]

But to point out general norms, however concrete and free from metaphysical abstraction and unreality they may be, is not sufficient. There should be a detailed consideration of conservatism and radicalism, as well as other social attitudes, in the light of these ideal standards. All we can attempt here is comment on certain salient points, in the hope that independent critical and constructive thought may be stimulated.

Let us take first disinterested conservatism. What is the ethics of its fundamental characteristics, habit and fear? The ethics of habit depends upon the extent, the intensity, and the incidence of habituation, that is, upon how much we are habituated, and to what. If we are habituated to the things which are inimical to democratic, co-operative individualism, and to scientific method, our habituation is unethical, at least from any constructive point of view, from the standpoint of "creative intelligence." In this regard the case for conservatism is not a strong one. The more conservative a man is, the more intensively and extensively he is habituated to things-as-they-are. That means that he is uncritically and quietistically content with a distant and equivocal approach to democracy, and that he probably shows slight interest in the application of scientific method to the settling of interest conflicts and the better ordering of social relations. Complete habituation would be destructive of conscious living because it would reduce all our acts to automatic reflexes. A certain amount of habituation is necessary and a matter of organic economy, but the habituation of the happily functioning and productive citizen should be like the repose of a Greek statue. The repose is there, but there is also readiness and poise for instant action.

The other psychological element of conservatism, as we saw, is fear, the impulse to avoidance. The ethics of fear, also, depends upon what one is afraid of, and upon the intensity of the fear and the extent to which it is objectively rational. Animals have instinctive fears and are not ashamed of them. Man has some remnants of instinctive fears and a whole regiment of fears acquired and institutionally inculcated. Man is

---

[2] Cf. J. H. Robinson, *The Mind in the Making*, 1922, Ch. **1**.

more or less ashamed of his fears; he has accordingly been fertile in casuistical justification of them; and he is intolerant of persons who put him to shame by not sharing them or by not accepting his rationalizations.

These rationalizations, illusional as many of them are, are highly respectable. Not to accept them at their face value, or at least not to appear to do so, is to run the risk of social disapprobation. Fear of social disapprobation is essentially motivation by respectability. The ethics of such motivation obviously depends upon the standards of respectability, as well as upon the amount of mental or verbal dishonesty, or more mildly put, disingenuousness, which desire to conform to canons of respectability involves. Did the norms of respectability always coincide with those of democratic individualism and scientific objectivity, respectability-motivation would not be obstructive of progress. In other words respectability would not be a device of conservatism and reactionism. To a great extent, however, the standards of respectability are those of unthinking habituation, and of the emulated prestiges and point of view of the privileged vested interests. To the extent that the conventions of respectability are set by those whose interest it is to oppose democracy of opportunity, co-operative efficiency in production, and the development of scientific rationalism, respectability-motivation must be set down as unethical.

The ethics of the conservative's fear of the new and unfamiliar depends (1) on whether he fears it because he thinks that it will (or will not) be conducive to democracy and scientific rationalism, and (2) on whether the fear is founded on objective analysis of available factual data. If the fear is based on a factually well-grounded conviction that a proposed innovation will impair irrational habituations or reduce special privilege, it is unethical. If it is a fear not factually supported that the innovation will be harmful to democracy and objectivity, it is scarcely less unethical. Fear, like habit, has legitimate and important social functions, but to function in accordance with the ethical standards which we have arrived at, it must be an objectively *informed* fear of those things which would not be conducive to an approach to democratic individualism, co-operative creation of opportunity, and diffusion of the scientific attitude and method.

The process of repression and sublimation instituted by the

fear motive may at times and in a measure be necessary to democracy and objectivity. But it is certain that repression and sublimation mean the loss of a vast amount of personal energy which would yield more productive results, both for the individual himself and for society at large, were the personality allowed greater freedom. Respectability-motivation is one of the chief sources of conservative repression and sublimation. It must be admitted, however, that its repressive influence is less than it would be were there a smaller amount of "make-believe" in our respectability.

From the standpoint of objective ethics, not a great deal can be said for other-worldliness and self-sacrifice, the favorite sublimative devices recommended by the leaders of certain institutions and established interests, nor for the more popular devices of gossip, scandal, and commercialized sensation (*e.g.*, the movies and baseball). Whether so designed or not, their actual effect is to distract attention from our deficiency in democracy and scientific rationalism, to relieve momentarily the tension of balked desire, without removing the causes of desire-obstruction, and to drain off intermittently the forces of popular unrest into innocuous but futile channels of dalliance. At the present time, it is true, when the world is still suffering from war psychoses, and unrest is likely to wreck itself in the futility of mob violence, these sublimative devices may serve a temporary good purpose. But as a settled, continuous policy for dealing with social discontent they have practical drawbacks as well as obvious ethical shortcomings.[3]

The motive to interested conservatism lies in the desire either for security or for privilege. Where the desire is for security, interested conservatism may not differ much from disinterested. Within limits, desire for security is justifiable. It is common to all men. So far as measurable security is an essential condition to life, liberty, and happiness, security is not only a right, but a duty. Desire for a competence of property, or steady and adequately remunerative employment, or provision against sickness and old age, makes for conservatism; and while such security may be gained by individuals at the expense of a development of the much-needed sense of social sympathy, that

---

[3] For a popular sketch of some of these sublimative devices, see Ross *Principles of Sociology*, 1920, pp. 201-205.

does not alter the basic fact that in the absence of security there would be little production of opportunity for anybody. Where individual security is not obtained, or maintained, at the cost of insecurity of others, or of uneconomical (non-democratic) distribution of opportunity, it would seem to be in accord with the demands of objective ethics.

When, however, the acquiring or maintaining of security involves insecurity for others, security becomes special privilege, and its ethical quality is not so clear. Were it not for the difficulty introduced by population growth, and the impossibility of providing security and opportunity for all the new individuals improvident folk, following their undisciplined instincts, may bring into the world, we might conclude that all privilege, in the sense of security maintained in the face of insecurity of others, is unethical. This position would be tenable, however, only in a society which succeeded in maintaining an informed and scientifically rational policy with regard to population increase. As between the living, special privilege may be defined as a right to enjoy an opportunity, or an exemption from service, which cannot be justified by the democratic criterion of distribution. In this sense, privilege is to be regarded as unethical.

There are probably many more interested conservatives who are motivated by a justifiable desire for security than those who are motivated by desire for privilege, but the latter are immensely the more powerful, energetic, and unscrupulous in defending and furthering their "rights." Their whole tone is likely to be formalistic, and the corporate organization and absentee ownership of modern industrial property tend to make them cynically legalistic. Not only do they go as far as the law allows, and not infrequently even a little further, but wherever they can, they make the laws to suit their own interests. The ruling moral code of the commercial vested interests is a code based upon a narrow and unscrupulous selfishness. The vested interests constantly dwell upon their rights, and upon the iniquity of any social change which would limit those rights, no matter how much nearer such change might bring us to an efficient economy of production and a democratic distribution of opportunity. Amid a welter of casuistic rationalization the clear fact emerges that the vested interests do not want social economy if it means equity of opportunity and curtailment of any of their differential privileges.

That this attitude toward life narrows the individual, however great his privileges may be, needs no further argument. Its main motive is acquisitiveness. Workmanship instincts, sensitiveness, and sympathy, tend to go by the board, except as they may be saved, through mental compartmentization, to function narrowly within limited circles, family, personal friends, etc. Moreover, such an attitude compels all to live the pig-trough life. It leaves little or no room for the spread and development of æsthetic taste and artistic activity. It is the chief positive force which prostitutes religion to formalism and cant. As a result, the cynical, privileged conservative defeats himself. He may gain the earth, but he loses his soul, through the atrophy of disuse.

In this conclusion, scientific ethics and Christian ethics will be at one, as indeed they are at many points. There is nothing in either to justify individualism of means under conditions in which all have not a fair start; or distribution of opportunity on the basis of privilege unsupported by tested capacity; or any form of exploitative acquisition. Yet, broadly speaking, these are the ethical norms and the proximate aims of the powerful privileged classes.

Turning to the ethics of the motivation of radicalism, which we have found mainly in obstructed interests, it does not appear that a balked desire is necessarily a good desire. Nor on the other hand, does it follow that it is bad simply because the existing standards and organization of society prevent its realization.

Insofar as the radical's desires are merely of the emulatively acquisitive order, a determination to get his feet into the trough where the interested conservative already has his, there is little to choose between the two, unless it can be shown that realization of the radical's acquisitive impulses would bring us nearer to the ideal of economical distribution of opportunity and service. Judgment on this point will doubtless vary according to specific cases and circumstances.

How much radical motivation is materialistically and narrowly selfish, we shall not attempt to say. In a society in which standards of respectability and prestige are currently set in terms of wealth and industrial exemption, it is not improbable that materialistic emulation plays no small part in the production of radical unrest. But there can be no question that an immense amount of radicalism is based on sympathy and on outraged sentiments of artistry and workmanship.[4] In any case we are estopped from preaching thrift and ambition and at the same time condemning the radical for demanding opportunity to enjoy a measure of the material blessings which we ourselves pursue with such whole-hearted abandon.

Barring the tendency to personalistic blame reactions, which is a matter of method rather than motive, it is probable that the motivation of radicalism more nearly conforms to the standards indicated by an objective ethics than does that of conservatism. If the radical demands, as he does, a higher material standard of living, that demand can be refused on ethical grounds only if it can be shown that its fulfillment would result in undemocratic and uneconomical inequity of distribution. If the conservative has surrounded himself, from fear, with a shell of sublimation and rationalization, and the radical refuses to shelter himself in a similar refuge, that refusal is no argument that the radical's insistent demand for freedom has not both theoretical and practical ethical foundation. And if the radical demands democracy because he lacks opportunity, and the conservative is luke-warm toward democracy because he has all the opportunity he wants or knows how to use, neither is that any very clear indication that the conservative is right and the radical wrong.

In other words, insofar as our present social organization fails to approximate to the ethical ideal "to each according to his capacity, within the scope of opportunity for all, and *from* each according to his capacity and according to the needs of socially co-operative production," and to the extent that it can be shown that the freedom and democracy of control desired by the radical would bring us nearer to this ideal economy, the balance of ethical justification, so far as motive goes, lies with the radical. But the radical has no more right to acquire an opportunity that he cannot use than the conservative has to maintain a privilege. The democratic criterion of distribu-

---

[2] See above, p. 136.

tion might be as disappointing to some radicals, if actually realized, as it is distasteful to the vested-interest conservative.

Turning from motive to method, the chief ethical interest attaches to the methods of vested-interest conservatism and of radicalism.

Of the ethics of certain methods, whether practiced by conservative or radical, it is unnecessary to speak. Claptrap and chicane, with their attendant tribe of disingenuous and worked-up sentimentalisms, bribery (if not patronage), and the emasculation of political democracy through vested-interest control of politico-business machines should all stand condemned in the judgment of fair-minded persons. The case for or against the other methods, force, intimidation, economic pressure, espionage, censorship, and propaganda is not so clear-cut, and no categorical answer can be given.

Resort to force or intimidation in an interest conflict is evidence that one or both of the parties to the issue have not reached the rational attitude required for the type of conduct demanded by objective ethics. Between two individuals, or two nations, which lived up to the principles of a thoroughly broad-minded and rational democracy there could be no resort either to force or to intimidation, any more than there could be between two genuine Christians.

Since, however, the complete Christian or the rational and socialized democrat, did either actually exist, would find himself, the world being what it is, ever and anon confronted with individuals bent on domination and exploitation, what would he do? Not to resist such aggression would be practically to turn the world over to their ilk and thus destroy any chance for the growth of justice and rational ethics. Both force and intimidation therefore find in practice some justification. We see here that judgment as to method, based on objective, factually-supported ethical grounds, is not a simple matter. Whatever may be the ultimate objective ethical ideal, a practical objective ethics has to work with and in the world as it is. Some compromise between what would be ideally permissible and what is practically expedient or possible must be made. The real problem is to make no compromise which departs further from ideal standards than is unavoidable. Neither force nor intimidation can be justified in practice further than is essential for the protection of such approximation to democratic individualism and social co-operation as we have already reached. Not all types of force and intimidation are to be countenanced even for this purpose. Nor have force and intimidation, ostensibly used for the protection of social order and democracy, but really to prevent nearer approach to democracy, any ethical sanction.

It is significant that even now the use of force, in civilized countries, is currently proclaimed justifiable only as a defensive measure. At least such was the case before the World War. Actually, of course, this is a sentiment which we are very far from living up to. Self-defense is the habitual pleading of those who either have a poor case or do not wish to show their hand. No small part of the chicane of vested interests is just this sort of sheep's clothing for wolfish designs.

Much the same considerations apply to economic pressure as apply to force and intimidation. Pressure is justifiable only when unavoidable, and then only in defense of rights or relations which are themselves proper on grounds of an objective, democratic ethics. From the point of view of psychological expediency, pressure can rarely be regarded as desirable. It is now well recognized that pressure and threats generate reprisal attitudes; in industrial relations, for example, in the form of withheld effort by the worker, and a frame of mind incompatible with good will and co-operation. Economic pressure as exerted by the great vested interests, to freeze out the small producer through unfair competition, or to starve labor into submission, can be justified neither upon grounds of expediency nor of fundamental ethical norms. It is in practice intimidation for the narrowest selfish ends, without even distant reference to any other principles than those of class power and acquisitiveness. It belongs to an ignorant ethics on the tooth-and-claw level.

Espionage and censorship come near to belonging in the same category. They can in extreme cases perhaps be justified as methods of self-defense, but their use is inexpedient if our care be to develop rational co-operation. Censorship rests upon fear—fear of the other fellow's arguments or sentiments. It thus betrays a lack of confidence in one's own case, or in the attitudes which the populace may assume. If the latter, it is a confession that the populace has not been educated to a plane where it ceases to be a prey to every shifting vagary of interested propaganda. This is perhaps true, but the way to rationalize and stabilize public sentiment nevertheless does not lie through censorship. Those who advocate or resort to censorship of the other party's propaganda would be the loudest in their objections to any curtailment of their own propagandizing. Those who desire interference with the freedom of teaching and preaching are usually interested, not in scientific objectivity or in intellectual honesty, but in maintaining inherited creeds, dogmatisms, and special interests by intimidation. Such persons cannot be influenced by evidence or argument.

Those who see the intellectual and moral necessity for freedom of thought and speech need no long disquisition upon its ethics. Let it suffice to say that to the extent that we desire good will, rational discussion on an impersonal plane, and objective attitudes, we will discourage all interference with expression, even the expression of foolishness.

That this desire is far from prevalent, however, is evidenced not only in industrial affairs and by the hue and cry against "radicalism," but by the great number of sectarian schools in which critical, objective teaching has only a precarious foothold and students are permitted to hear no teacher who does not, nominally at least, subscribe to the authoritarian creeds. In however good a cause it may be conceived to be, such censorship makes education the handmaid of propaganda. From such institutions liberally educated men and women cannot be looked for.

On a somewhat different footing, but still of doubtful ethics and expediency, is the closing of the supposedly "open" platforms of college and university student open forum clubs to speakers whose sentiments or whose mode of presentation the administrative officials disapprove. Doubtless much that is foolish and extreme would be said were entire freedom given for such addresses. But the plea that students must be "protected" from propaganda is, if not transparently thin, in any case ill-considered. For students will certainly go out into a world which is honeycombed with propagandas, and it would seem that a part of their scientific, objective training might well be to analyze the logic, sentiment, and methods of those who make a business of propagandizing. Moreover, if a detached objectivity is the purpose of these academic censorships, why do we never read that reactionaries and interested conservatives have been forbidden to present their views to "immature youth"? The plain fact is that the censorship net is so meshed that while it may catch radical propaganda, the conservative passes through with ease.

The essential difference between propaganda and education is that propaganda is *ex parte,* while education is, or should be, scrupulously objective. *Ex parte* education can hardly be distinguished from propaganda. And this is what many conservatives and dogmatic radicals want when they advocate "education." The less tolerant of fair opposition propaganda is, the less ethical justification it has. Disguised propaganda is to be unequivocally condemned. This includes propaganda masquerading as news, as nonpartisan information or "scientific" objective education, as well as propaganda under the disguise of amusement. To be condemned, also, is propaganda forced upon people, and that which takes advantage of ignorance and of ideo-motor and emotional temperaments. All such propaganda is tinctured with chicane.[5]

Much could be said, both on the mechanism of the control of public sentiment, and on the ethical questions raised by the exceedingly large rôle which propaganda, both overt and concealed, plays in such control.[6]

During war time, it seems now taken for granted that public sentiment is to be inspired and "molded" by every available device of official and irresponsible private censorship and propaganda. Americans knew that this was being done in Germany, and now the Germans know it themselves.[7] We were not so vividly conscious that the same thing was being done in Eng-

---

[5] Take as a small illustration the exploitation of the sentiments of children by the special interests which sometimes offer prizes to school children for the "best essay" on why one should be thus and so. It goes without saying that a child who wrote a critical essay on "One Hundred Per Cent Americanism" for the average patriotic society would stand small chance of landing the prize.

[6] For a recent discussion, rather diffuse, but concrete and suggestive, see Walter Lippmann, *Public Opinion,* 1922.

[7] See, for example, Hellmut von Gerlach, "The German Mind," *Atlantic Monthly,* Feb., 1922, pp. 246-258.

land and France, and are not yet fully cognizant of the extent to which it was done in the United States.[8]

It is not to be insinuated in any way that motives ulterior to those of national safety and honor actuated this control. But the student of the moral aspects of propaganda in relation to public sentiment and attitudes will learn much from a study of the methods used in war time, whether in Europe or in America. He will have much food for thought with regard to the intellectual and moral integrity, and the ability of a population long habituated to this kind of manipulation ever to take objective attitudes. He may set the results down as one of the necessary moral costs of war, but he should go on to inquire how far similar methods are common in peace time, and what are their probable psychological and moral results. It is safe to say that where news and "education" are carefully censored in the interest of propaganda, no matter how admirable the aim of the propaganda may be, any real democracy of control becomes an impossibility, and the development of an objectively informed and balanced public opinion is held in check by a mass of inspired subjective prejudices. The scientific spirit cannot flourish in a population in which primitive herd instincts are perpetually stimulated. If this is to be the process of "democratic" government, there is valid basis for all the cynicism prevalent about "democracy."

The ethics of radical method, fully treated, would involve consideration both of modes of diagnosis (blame-anger reactions vs. rational analysis) and of attack—the actual policy of radical movements.

We have tried to show that the blame impulse, while a natural one, must be ruled out of the ethics of the highly developed and rationalized state, except when consciously and premeditatedly used, in measured and dispassionate manner, as a device of social control—a stimulus to prevent the recurrence of unethical attitudes and conduct. Praise and blame as mere expression of likes and dislikes—in which case they are mere extrusions of the person's own ego—can have no place in an objective ethics.

If ethics be really an economy of means and ends, it follows

---

[8] Lippmann's book throws very interesting light on this matter.

that it is unethical as well as uneconomical to pursue desire-reinforcement against obstacles which may not be the real sources of obstruction. Correct analysis of these sources is a prerequisite to economical and effective attack, and correct analysis cannot be expected from the conventional and passionate blame-anger reaction. "Fixing of responsibility," in the sense of ascertaining causal sequences, is a different matter. It is true that the initial blame-anger reflex *may* in some cases cause scientific research to be pointed in the right direction, but the actual proof of responsibility is a scientific process, from which the disturbing factors of personal attachment and antipathy must be excluded. Blame, in the ordinary sense, then, as found in the attitudes of the rank-and-file radical (as well as conservative) is unethical because it is subjectively grounded and may be wrongly directed. It is also unethical in that it perpetuates and intensifies the conflict complexes of which we have inherited and acquired entirely too many for the smooth conduct of what now must necessarily be a highly organized co-operative society.

Of the ethics of the specific methods of radicalism it is unnecessary to add any extended discussion. The general basis of judgment in specific cases and for the various types of method has been indicated with sufficient clearness in the preceding consideration of the ethics of conservative method, as well as in the discussion of radical methods in Chapter VIII. Only on the use of force and intimidation will we risk tiring the reader with further suggestion.

The ethics of radical violence is not essentially different from the ethics of force when used by the conservative. If it is permissible to use force for the protection of rights, it would seem to be equally permissible to use it to acquire them where they are denied. In fact the radical will always say that he resorts to force only in protection of his rights—a variation of the familiar self-defense justification. Be that as it may, let us again emphasize the principle that appeal to force can be justified, if ever, only where it is a final and necessary resort in the interest of such rights and relations as are sanctioned by the principle of democratic equity of opportunity and service. Even in such case, it stands open to all the objections urged above, and especially to the objection that it perpetuates the conflict psychology, which is inimical to the rational settlement of interest conflicts.

As to intimidation, we have already seen that the radical is at a great disadvantage, except where a social revolution has upset society. All the main devices of intimidation are in the control of conservatives. The labor radical has left only the power of organized and concerted action in withholding labor, in short, the strike, or in extreme cases, the general strike.

The strike is an intimidative measure which may involve force, and is at best costly. Yet as long as we allow conservative capital to indulge in intimidation we cannot deny the same right to labor. At the same time we should emphatically regret that either side should feel compelled to resort to it. Here, of course, mere preaching or condemnation is worse than useless, as we should long since have learned from experience. The situation is one in which both contending parties may honestly believe that they are fighting for right and principle. And they may fight with all the spirit and abandon of fanatical loyalty, because no really objective norm or standard of rights has been appealed to. This is not meant to imply that in a given specific industrial conflict we can say to the combatants, with much hope that they will listen to us, ''Come, now, let's gather around a table and discuss the issue in terms of ethical democracy, a square deal, or Christian peace and good will!'' It is saying, however, that the more an objective, democratic ethics permeates the population, and especially the leaders, the less hair-trigger will be the appeal to force and intimidation, and the more the parties to interest conflicts will themselves try to find a common ground of equity.

It is worthy of note that the nearer radical leaders approach to the philosophical and scientific attitude, the more conservative they become with regard to method, the more reluctant to use force and intimidation. This is true of any growth of rationality, of course, whether in conservative or radical, but the world is much given to believing that rationality is confined to conservative circles, a conviction the truth of which is open to question.[9]

---

[9] Cf. Kegan Paul, *William Godwin, His Friends and Contemporaries*, 1876, Vol. I, pp. 104, 105.

The practical weakness in radical method lies in the fact that radicals have not been able to escape the conflict psychology, and that their attacks upon intrenched special interest have tended to increase the consciousness of interest conflicts and, perhaps, by that much, to retard the development of the co-operative good will and rationality necessary to democracy. Their answer to this is, of course, that they have been compelled to emphasize interest conflict and class struggle by the persistent hold which the ideals of autocratic control and the master-and-servant ethics have upon the ruling classes.

Another weakness results directly from the nature of radical motivation. So absorbed is the radical in removing obstructions that he generally has no time to fore-plan detailed constructive measures.[10] Could the spirit of constructive social co-operation gain ground, and the vested interests bring themselves to less pugnacious insistence upon their "rights," it is possible that constructive capacity, now concealed by the exigencies of the interest conflict, would prove to be quite as great in the radical as in the conservative.

If the weakness of radicalism lies, for all its idealism, in its deficiency in practical constructiveness, that of conservatism lies in its habituation, its fear, and its failure to conceive the meaning and ethics of democracy. If radicalism be thought destructive, conservatism can with equal truth be said to be obstructive. Leaving out of account the conservatism of vested interest, let us recall the salient characteristics of the disinterested conservative attitude: its exaggerated valuation of "order" (by which it always means the existing order), its worship of the past and the archaic, its uncritical conforming and clinging to tradition, its tendency to make institutions and "principles" or habits of thought ends in themselves, its inertia, mental laziness, and quietism, its propensity for custom-imitation instead of constructive originality, its uncritical bow-

---

[10] This criticism will probably diminish in force as time goes on. Much positive constructive imagination and hard-headed grappling with concrete problems marks such a work as Sidney and Beatrice Webb's *A Constitution for the Socialist Commonwealth of Great Britain*, 1920. The same is true in less degree of some of the literature of the guild socialism movement. And it should not be forgotten that many reforms which were first advocated in the platforms of radical parties have been taken up and adopted by one or the other of the old parties.

ing to authority, its high regard for uncritical and subservient loyalty, and its domination by fear rather than courage. It is easy to see, from these characteristics, that actual conservatism will tend to preserve everything, the good and the bad, the socially useful and the socially detrimental.

The functioning of the actual conservative is not unjustly, though somewhat caustically, described in John Morley's sketch of him "with his inexhaustible patience of abuses that only torment others; his apologetic word for beliefs that may not be so precisely true as one might wish, and institutions that are not altogether so useful as one might think possible; his cordiality toward progress and improvement in a general way, and his coldness or antipathy to each progressive proposal in particular; his pigmy hope that life will one day become somewhat better, punily shivering by the side of his gigantic conviction that it might well be infinitely worse." [11]

It is this lack of courage and the concomitant domination by habit that make actual conservatism so heavy a drag on the forces of progress. The result is that in the aggregate many times more effort has to be expended to accomplish a given step in progress than would be necessary had the mass of men and women less stolid indifferentisms, livelier constructive imagination, and more of the audacity which has always characterized progressive leaders.[12]

If the radical is less dominated by fear than the conservative, that is perhaps due to the fact that the very circumstances which have made him a radical compel him to have more courage. It is due also in part to the fact that radicalism has a nearer relation to scientific thought and is more given to rational reflection upon social relations and processes. Radicalism on its intellectual side is a logical historico-evolutionary result of the rationalistic development of modern scientific thought, and partakes to some extent of the scientific capacity to face facts courageously.

Thus radicalism of the better type attempts to substitute rational, even scientific, analysis for instinctive fear. But rea-

---

[11] *Voltaire*, 1st edition, 1872, p. 12, quoted by J. H. Robinson, *The New History*, 1912, p. 275.

[12] Even inexperience is sometimes a condition favorable to constructive progress. See T. H. Dickinson, *The Insurgent Theatre*, 1917, p. 128.

son functions effectively and justly only in proportion to the scope and accuracy of the knowledge with which it works. It is here that radicalism, like habitual conservatism, frequently fails, because the pressure of balked interests and ambitions and the prevalence of the inherited conflict psychology push it into blame-anger reactions and stimulate those personalistic recriminations and suspicions which may be regarded as by-products of fear.

It does not follow that fear should be totally eliminated. A supplanting of quasi-instinctive personalistic reactions by intelligent sympathy and informed rationalism involves the conscious recognition of the legitimate function of fear as a kind of moral governor or flywheel, which will both restrain the over-impetuosity of impulsive action, and on the other hand put fear under close limitations, by subjecting it to the control of knowledge and reason. Fear, alertness, knowledge of the country, and a quick and sure rational faculty, are the qualities of a good scout. A "fearless" scout would not last long; a man whose fear is not rationalized never becomes a scout. The same qualities are necessary in all able and progressive social leadership.

In driving out fear, in rationalism, the intellectual radical often goes too far. He fails or refuses to allow for the irrational element in our as yet imperfectly disciplined human nature. He discounts too much the fact that men have always thus far been more influenced by passion and narrow selfishness than by a courageous fact-facing reason.[13] Not until the scientific spirit, and a frankness and disinterestedness in analyzing personal and class interests—one's own included—are far more prevalent in thought about human affairs, will man have begun to approach the rationalistic character which the intellectual radical demands of the present and scorns the past for not evincing.

One-sided as it is, however, the radical's view of the past may contain a valuable antidote to too much pride and egotism

---

[13] Compare what Leslie Stephen says of Bentham: "Like many mechanical inventors, he took for granted that a process which was shown to be useful would therefore be at once adopted, and failed to anticipate the determined opposition of the great mass of 'vested interests' already in possession."—*The English Utilitarians*, 1900, Vol. I, p. 177.

about the present. We can fairly regard vast aspects of history in much the same light in which we can now understand the peoples of the future will regard the present; that is, as devoid of any very valuable lesson for us, because its people were crude barbarians, and its ideals as low as its knowledge, understanding, and rationality were infantile.

With a few exceptions, the past has never been able to rise above the personalistic praise-and-blame view of life, and the conflict method of providing for group-interests. But as long as the radical himself does not rise to a rational plane which is above personal blame-reactions and emphasis on the necessity of force and conflict, he is not in position to put forth in good grace over-much criticism of the past for its lack of impersonality and objectivity.

Progress may be had through conflict and cataclysmic revolution, but at terrific costs. The radical, if he realizes these costs, and yet advocates the conflict method, either counts these losses as less than those continuously but not so conspicuously inflicted upon the people by the non-democracy and the self-help individualism of the present, or he thinks that the conservative elements are so unreasonable and selfishly obstructive that they can be moved only by compulsion, not by reason. The practical leader of radical causes is doubtless, also, in a position where he has to recognize the lack of objective intellectuality among his rank and file. He is thus forced to utilize their emotional attitudes and reactions, even though to do so means further obstruction to the development and spread of objective rationalism. The conservative thinks the radical either a hare-brained dreamer or a materialist dominated quite as much by selfish acquisitiveness as is the most intrenched vested interest, and without the saving sense of caution, order, and continuity necessary to assurable progress.

Insofar as either conservative or radical fails to rise above these recriminative personalities; or falls short of the objective scientific attitude toward facts and investigational methods; or refuses to give up class ethics for the ethics of democracy, we must, according to the point of view we have developed, hold that he has not attained to the ethical attitude necessary as a prerequisite to economical social progress.

CHAPTER XII

1. *The Present Situation*

IF THE preceding chapters have in any measure accomplished their purpose, they will have suggested, again and again, and from a variety of angles, the great rôle played by sentiments and attitudes in the ordering or disordering of social relations. They will also have placed squarely before the reader the highly pertinent question as to what types of sentiments and attitudes—with regard to change versus stagnation; individualism (whether of ends or of means) versus socialism[1] (again whether of ends or of means); class versus democracy; and popular-mindedness versus scientific objectivity—are likely to prove most conducive, or least obstructive, to the development of a society rationally organized, peaceful, and co-operatively efficient in providing opportunity for the happiness and self-expression of its individual members.

That we have a very reasonable approach, judged by any but the most inexacting standards, to such a society to-day, few persons not characterized by the apologetic sentiments of conservatism will affirm. Scarcely any one will hold that the world has made progress toward such an ideal since July, 1914. If in normal times sentiments and attitudes play the fundamental rôle attributed to them in the preceding pages, no one can doubt that the abnormal stimulation and unsettling of sentiments by the war and the sequent years of comparative anarchy have had, and will have, a profound significance for the destinies of mankind during an indefinite period in the future.

There can be no doubt that the nine tragic years just passed have brought events, situations, and problems mightily provocative of thought—though hardly to a degree requisite to the needs of the time—and that it has been a period of most profound agitation and shock to habits, sentiments, attitudes, and

---

[1] Again see the caution, p. 264.

points of view. It would be an error, however, to overestimate the extent of this shake-up, or to suppose that it has been in the same direction or of the same intensity in all classes. There seems to be, in fact, considerable indication that large sections of the population in this country are virtually unaware that there has been a war. By this we mean to say that they have settled back into the habitual pre-war sentiments and pursuits, perforce devoting all their attention and energies to the day-by-day business of getting a living or of keeping up with the Joneses, and that they seem hardly more conscious of the world movements shaping their larger destinies, or at least those of their children, than they were, in June, 1914, aware of the impending world cataclysm. This is true more especially of the conventionalized masses of the rural and small town populations, including the well-to-do business men of the nation's 10,000 Gopher Prairies. It is scarcely less true of large sections of labor (despite all the unrest and alertness in labor circles), and of the common varieties of business men and respectable middle-class families in the urban centers. Our luncheon clubs, woman's clubs, State legislatures, and Congress are continually revealing how great is the shock-resisting capacity of set habits and traditionalized sentiments. Nor are the colleges and universities devoid of a discouraging capacity to proceed on the even tenor of their traditional ways. One could visit many classes in every department, from Greek to law, economics, and ethics, without catching more than a casual hint or two that the times are especially out of joint, though one might stumble into a chemistry lecture on the remarkable progress made since the war in the invention of more effectively lethal poison gases.

All this, however, is to be expected. The day's work has to be done; under present conditions we cannot look for the specialist, whether at the turret lathe or in the philosophical closet, to possess the mass of information, the complexity of attention and interest, and the multiple vision ideally requisite in a world, or a country, supposedly governed "democratically" by the people. In spite, however, of specialization, absorption in the affairs of the immediate moment, and the persistency of habit and socially inherited sentiments, it is probable that these nine years have made more people think, however ineffectively, than have ever thought before. In few junctures of history have thinking people been more distressed or more pessimistic over the social outlook—more especially the international political and economic outlook—than they are to-day.

The prevailing state of mind the world over, among those who think on social matters and those who have been more nearly touched by the destruction and anarchy of the war than has the average American, is one of disillusion. The new pessimistic attitude flows from an appreciation, not only of the material loss and disorganization resultant upon the war, but of the psychological consequences of five years of systematically stimulated and hypertrophied combativeness. Not since the Thirty Years' War; probably not since the fourteenth century when the Black Death scourged Europe; possibly not since the barbarian hordes swept out of the German forests to overrun the Roman world, has civilization been reduced to a more deplorable state of disorganization, distrust, intolerance, and of that futile obstructionism which comes from the hateful and passionate antagonisms of narrow class or nationalistic interests blindly pursued.

The briefest possible catalogue of post-war conditions will suffice to suggest how profound is this disorganization.

Beginning with the internal affairs of our own country, it is clear to us now that Armistice Day, 1918, dawned upon a world as unprepared for peace as we had ever been unready for war, even according to the statements of the militarists. The Day's delirium of popular joy was but the brief prelude to depression and paralysis. An eighteen months' orgy of extravagance (probably an emotional release from war strain), speculation, and profiteering ushered in the inevitable business depression, one of the most acute and persistent in history. A spectacular decline of prices and paralysis of credit marked the breakdown of production and the economic ruin of large sections of the population, especially the farmers; unsaleable goods meant locked factory gates, and chronic unemployment of unprecedented extent. All this, together with the foolhardy determination of employers to "show labor its place" and a dogged desire on the part of labor to yield no ground once gained, made inevitable a period of very acute labor disputes. The intensity of these disputes was, and is, at once an index of the extent of our economic disorganization, and a portent of danger to social peace. Economic disorganization and industrial strife led to an arbitrary and dangerous extension of administrative and judicial powers, to which the temporary destruction of civil liberty in England during and after the French Revolution furnishes a close historical parallel. This resulted in an unfortunate heightening of psychological tension and consciousness of class conflict.

What the economic consequences of the Peace have been abroad is well-known. Europe's economic life is paralyzed, partly due to war destruction, but in greater degree to the total derangement of international trade, and more specifically to the absence of an intelligent and courageous international economic statesmanship in the United States. The Peace Treaty violently tore asunder the world's economic fabric, and rejected the essential economic co-operation, for an illusory political self-determination. A debasement of national currencies which would have been criminal had it not probably been unavoidable —the United States alone having secured, to its own loss, half the world's total gold supply, and Europe having piled up war expenses beyond any conceivable ability to pay—evidenced the financial bankruptcy of Europe. Nationalistic selfishness, suicidal in its blindness, insisted upon the payment of impossible indemnities. In America popular ignorance of the most elementary principles of international trade and credit insisted on the impossible payment of the war loans which had been made to the Allies. Also in obedience to who shall say what promptings from vested interests or what domination by old economic illusions, a tariff wall was erected, designed to be impenetrable, at the time when the utmost freedom and encouragement of international trade was the essential basis and starting point of world reconstruction.

Politically, the world is at sea. Liberalism is without a definite program, radicalism has suffered some disillusionment and shows signs of fatigue, and reactionism, where not already in control, as in America, France, and Italy, is seeking favorable opportunity for violent resumption of power. And still there is no guarantee that the recklessness of reactionism[2] and the

---

[2] For example, militaristic nationalism in France, the royalists in Germany, the Fascisti in Italy, and the various "oil diplomacies" in the Near East.

constructive incapacity[3] of conservatism may not yet throw the direction of social reconstruction into the hands of well-meaning but inexperienced and undisciplined revolutionary radicals.

Political democracy, toward which, prior to 1914, the whole world was moving, now seems to many dangerous, to others futile, and to still others a hollow sham which must be replaced by a genuinely representative democracy of sovietism or guild socialism. The fountain-heads of public opinion and public sentiment are roiled, and poisoned by passionate propagandas and recriminations.

Our morale is badly shaken. We fought for democracy and got an amazing outburst of the old cynical, nationalistic, secret diplomacy, and a vigorous growth of administrative encroachment on constitutional rights. Setting up the ideal of self-determination, we have seen it turned into a forcing-bed of cynical insistence that to the victors belong the spoils. We fought to defend national honor (whatever that may be defined to be) and find that honor between nations is at a distinctly low ebb. Fondly persuading ourselves that we were fighting to end war, we are now not unreasonably fearful that we have only set the stage for an endless succession of wars. In the face of these conditions we are characterized by a deadly deficiency in tolerance and objectivity, a deplorable unwillingness or incapacity to face the facts, and a continued belief that issues must be settled by force rather than by scientific adjudication and adjustment. This does not mean that there is not, in the population at large, a deep desire for peace and co-operative good will. But the meagre results of the Disarmament Conference, as well as the one at Genoa and the preceding European conferences, and later, Lausanne, indicate either that such desire is far from universal or that the peoples of the various countries have insufficient organization to make their representatives carry out their will.

We have been brought to this pass because we sowed the wind; of narrow individualism, commercialism, nationalism, militarism, and capitalism—all, ironically enough, most highly developed in the ''Christian'' countries; and are now reaping the whirlwind.

---

[3] Ample illustrations are close at hand in the United States.

These were the characteristics, both institutional and ideological, of the society which grew to such astounding size and complexity, and with such unmanageable rapidity, between the fall of Napoleon and the fall of the Kaiser. This growth, which, after Graham Wallas, we may call the Great Society, was the inevitable resultant of the Industrial Revolution, business enterprise, modern applied science, machine industry, and the modern philosophy of power. It is no mere rhetorical indulgence to say that this mechanico-commercial and nationalistic society which we, Frankenstein-like, created during the nineteenth century, was a monstrous Thing, bound sooner or later to turn upon its maker and threaten his destruction.

The growth of this unmanageable social mechanism was the result neither of malevolent forethought nor of maleficent stupidity. It was the natural and inevitable result of powerful human instincts stimulated to unprecedented activity by the most remarkable outburst of intellectual development in history. The achievements of modern physical science opened the world to exploitation. They gave man a degree of utilitarian control over the forces of nature that he had never before dreamed of, and this control sent him over the whole face of the earth, bent on exploit and conquest. Thus instincts of acquisition and combat played in a world-wide arena for enormous stakes, and natural science supplied them with weapons.

These instincts were developed during the stages of biological evolution when the outfit of instincts most necessary to man was such as would assure survival in the struggle for existence. They were the result, and the expression, of a different type of life-process than man is called upon to-day to evolve, if civilization is to be much more than a transparent veneer for brutality. Instincts so developed, as a product of our biological past, especially the instincts of acquisition and combat, and the attitudes which we have absorbed from our historical past, are palpably unsuited to the moral, and even the biological, needs of men living in a society as complex as that we are now called upon to reconstruct upon a workable basis.

It should be remembered that compared to the long period of man's previous evolution, the duration of our present form of social organization—the nationalistic, capitalistic, machine-industry era—has been but a fleeting moment. Considering the discrepancy between our biologically created instincts and our socially inherited attitudes on the one hand and our present needs on the other, we may venture to think that the main cause of our failure to make the Great Society safe for human life and productive for human health and happiness—as safe and as productive, that is, as we can see it could be made—is not so much a deficiency in inherited intellectual capacity as it is a lack of will and the lack of an emotional inheritance suited to present needs.

We have not developed the motives and attitudes requisite to a worthy functioning of the great social mechanism to which, whether we like it or not, we are committed. In all our preceding biological and cultural evolution, man's instinctive nature has been developed and "set" under conditions infinitely more simple, on the whole more stable, and to the average mind more understandable, than those now existent. The exigencies of life, the struggle for survival, the hardened system of class statuses, required that the instincts of fear, pugnacity, self-assertion, self-abasement, and acquisitiveness should be developed to great strength and wide diffusion.[4] The social instincts of gregariousness and sympathy, while biological products with biological functions, were subordinated to combat impulses, as were the incipient instinct of workmanship, as well as other instincts of constructive self-expression.

To a significant extent, therefore, our inherited psychology is a conflict psychology instead of what we now need—a psychology of co-operative workmanship. The combative and acquisitive instincts, when the Great Society finally came into being, not only stood in the way of a lastingly effective organization and control for social safety and social welfare, but actually directed control to channels and methods which could only mean disorganization and relative failure in the end.

The unmanageableness of the Great Society results, therefore, primarily from the fact that our intellectual achievement in the field of physical science and technology has far outrun our moral development and our social-engineering capacity. Needing above all, control and directive capacity for social ends (that

---

[4] It must be remembered that in this book we make no attempt to use the term instinct in any technically exact sense.

is, for the life of individuals through a co-operative social organization); calling for the organization of thought and will for collective purposes; demanding widely concerted and intelligently planned action for its right handling; the situation has been met instead by populations ignorant of the forces shaping their destinies, and by leaders, not infrequently only less ignorant, dominated by instincts more suitable to a brute competition for survival and individual advantage than to the needs of a highly complex society of interdependent parts and functions.

Nor is it alone our inherited instinctive equipment which is, in part, inimical to the success of what must be, from its very size and functional specializations, a co-operative society. We are the victims, as has already been suggested, of a social inheritance from the individualistic political and economic philosophy of the eighteenth century, a philosophy which is still used, great as have been the modifications, with popular, apologetic effect by those who oppose the development of a new and a more social-minded liberalism. This philosophy, which was both cause and result of the eighteenth century revolt against political absolutism and economic mercantilism, was centrally insistent upon the rights of the individual, especially his rights of acquisition, rather than upon his social functions and duties. Its political expression was the night-watchman theory of the state; its economic, the doctrine of free competition and the devil take the hindmost. Both gave color to the belief that what is everybody's business is nobody's business. The Great Society was expected to run itself.[5]

The Great Society thus carries within itself, as matters now stand, psychological and cultural incompatabilities bound to strangle its functional powers and to plunge it, in the future as in the past, into chronic cycles of universal contention and disorganization, unless they are removed or at least very greatly mitigated.

Its theory of functional organization has been motivated by

---

[5] Even the Christian religion was able to make but little headway against this combat-and-acquisition theory of life. The church itself, in fact, in spite of its nominal social idealism, became something of an addict to it. See C. A. Ellwood, *The Reconstruction of Religion, a Sociological View*, 1922, Ch. 4.

an individualism of means rather than of ends. It should, however, by this time in our cultural experimentation be clear that through co-operation, and co-operation alone, can the Great Society be made to function productively and creatively to the full and healthful life of its individual members. Every conflict of industrial interests, every international war, every class conflict, however inevitable it may be under present conditions, is a violation of the principle of co-operation and of co-operative understanding and good will.

Inimical also to the proper functioning of the Great Society is the attempt to combine a system of industrial autocracy with a system of political democracy. A real political democracy and any sort of feudalism are incompatible. Autocratic refusal to extend to the workers any voice whatever in industrial management, bitter "open shop" opposition to the workers' ideal of collective bargaining, and the seeming failure of political democracy to guard industrial management and productive resources from the exploitative direction of men and classes believed by many penetrating and disinterested observers to be dominated quite as much by acquisitive as by constructive motives, perpetuate the feeling of class conflict and intensify the conviction that political democracy is an illusion. Curiously, this conviction flourishes at the extremes—with a considerable percentage of the academic intellectuals on one side and with the extreme left labor radicals on the other. To what extent it actually is an illusion will in the long run depend upon whether political democracy has the ability to devise an organization of economic processes devoted primarily to the interest of production rather than individual or corporate acquisitiveness.

Another survival incompatible with the efficient operation of the Great Society is the notion of class ascendancy and mass subservience. This notion is concretely embodied in our socially inherited master-and-servant ethics, itself an expression of the older, non-democratic attitude, according to which the privileged few are the end and the masses of the people frankly means. Such an attitude will always be in conflict with the democratic ideal and with the aspirations of the people. Where it is concealed by a cloak of chicanery which uses democratic slogans and shibboleths to cover differential privilege and exploitation,

it is probable that as time goes on the people will more prevalently and more intelligently see through the ruse.

So long as the gulf between leisure and toil is sufficiently wide,
and the workers are kept in a proper state of ignorance, the
master-and-servant ethics, however incompatible with democracy, need not be a very great obstacle to social peace and efficiency—as these are measured by the leisure classes; but as soon
as the masses have obtained some degree of education, and have
begun the emulative process of raising their standard of living,
the democratic ferment—some may prefer to call it a virus—
begins to work, and peace and efficiency are at a discount. For
no people which really senses the meaning of the democratic
ideal is going to abide indefinitely by the inherited master-and-
servant ethics. Such an ethics and democracy are utterly incompatible. Until one or the other gives way we cannot hope that
the Great Society will work smoothly.

Vigorous as is the fight now waged for the retention of the
master-and-servant ethics, the trend of the times indicates that
conservatism and reactionism are in this matter fighting a losing battle. There is no indication that the masses will recede in
their struggle against privilege, however deficient in organization and knowledge of the real lay of the land they may be.
A general attitude of class subservience is not to be expected
under a system of universal education. The more education,
even the more literacy, we have, the greater will be the spirit
of resentment at any form of autocracy or of arbitrary and
artificial restriction of opportunity.

Finally, it needs no argument to show that our traditional
policy of nationalistic selfishness and aggrandizement is now
suicidal. Modern engineering technique has brought the world
to such specialization of industry and such universal intercom-
munication and interdependence that merely exploitative attitudes and processes must either react, like a boomerang, upon
those who temporarily profit by them, or destroy civilization in
its present form once for all.

Out of these deep-seated incompatibilities, traceable to our
inheritance of instincts, attitudes, and philosophies tragically
unsuited to our present requirements, come the transcendent
task and duty of a profound psychological, and thence social,
readjustment.

2. *Is There a Way Out?*

Our task is to find a practical method of directing social evolution to some adequately rational aim or purpose. Negatively speaking, it is to put human life on a plane from which it will not drop back into the non-productive and destructive conflicts of special interests. Positively, it is to make life worth living to the individual from some point of view and motive other than that afforded by the blind instinct of existence and biological survival. It is to replace "drift" by "mastery"— captaincy of our own collective advance. It is to substitute what Lester F. Ward, in his somewhat ponderous terminology, called "collective telesis" for "social genesis."[6] It is to make human experience and knowledge constructively creative rather than imitatively conservative and argumentatively apologetic for established differential privilege.[7]

Obviously escape from the present situation, with the elements of anarchy inherent in it, can only land us in greater anarchy —more conflict of purposes and interests, greater dispersion of thought and effort—unless we can come to some rational and practical agreement as to the direction in which social evolution should consciously be guided. Otherwise it is hard to see how life will not continue indefinitely to be a congeries of conflicting and more or less irrational loyalties and mutually negating morales, as destructive as those which brought on the World War and fought it through to the kind of peace on earth, good will to men we enjoy to-day.

The needful common purpose is not to be thought of as a fixed and static something that we are to strive for, nor as an ideal state to be accomplished by sudden revolution or miraculous conversion. It must be a common purpose in reasonable conformity with human nature, or more properly speaking with what a scientific psychology shows that human nature, under adequate stimulus of education, can be brought to be. It must be something to which men in their reasonable mind, not torn by the emotional conflicts of narrowly self-seeking special interests, and not intellectually hypnotized by the metaphysical

---

[6] *Outlines of Sociology*, 1899, Chs. 10-12; *Pure Sociology*, 2d edition, 1907, Ch. 20.

[7] Cf. John Dewey, *Reconstruction in Philosophy*, 1920.

absolutes of apologetic philosophies, can be expected to grasp as a fair and reasonable purpose for humanity as a whole.

We have tried in these pages to suggest a purpose, or at least an attitude toward life, which corresponds with these requirements. We do not mean to imply for a moment that we have presented a theory that has not been set forth before, in substance if not in set terms, by other writers, both popular and academic. But perhaps a contribution of something constructive will be found in our attempt to base an objective ethics on the facts of behaviorism; to make a sharp distinction between individualism of ends and individualism of means;[8] to reveal concretely the bad consequences which flow from the popular blame-anger reaction in interest conflicts; and to insist, upon what we regard as scientific ground, upon a tolerant, willing, and rational social co-operation, without falling into the ineffective superficialities of "brotherhood," "service," "sacrifice," and other conventionalized ideals commonly and sentimentally associated with "Christian morals."

We attempted to show, in Chapter X, that the central moral or social function of science is to rationalize interest conflicts —to furnish the data and the spirit by which issues can be settled by appeal to fact rather than through praise-and-blame personalities, much less through force. The general conception in the popular mind in regard to ethical norms is that they are either a matter of taste or that they can find final sanction and authority only by appeal to absolute metaphysical and religious postulates. This is one reason why religion has thus far failed to overcome the wrong balance of our inherited instincts and proclivities sufficiently to bring the world a durable peace. Conflicting religious beliefs have worked hand in hand with nationalistic loyalties to perpetuate and intensify the conflict spirit. Both the notion that ethics is a matter of taste, without the possibility of a scientifically founded norm, and the opposed idea that ethics is by no means a matter of whim but that its norms must be found in authoritarian prescription, we are compelled to reject, on scientific as well as on practical grounds.

---

[8] Right here lies a very important difference between the individualism presented in this book and that set forth as the final ethical norm by Warner Fite in his *Individualism: Four Lectures on the Significance of Consciousness for Social Relations*, 1911.

Practically, if ethics is only a matter of taste, there is no reason to suppose that even distant agreement as to ends can be
reached; and if it is a matter contingent upon the sanctions of
metaphysical mysticism and religious dogma there seems no
greater probability of agreement, since in these fields of speculative thought we are beyond the limit of verifiable fact, and
every thinker is free to start from whatever speculative postulates he pleases. So that, in the last analysis, metaphysical and
theological ethics are in near accord with the popular notion;
they both reduce to a matter of taste. Moreover an ethics
grounded on transcendental authority is all too likely to be
conceived and interpreted in terms of protection to the authoritative institutions which claim the exclusive right of interpretation. At least it has been so in the past.[9]

It may be an act of philosophical temerity to hold that science
can have any such function as we hold it must have. Certainly
most scientists outside the field of the social sciences, and not
a few timid souls within that field, would aver that it is; but
that would be perhaps because they have not themselves
attained to a consistent scientific, that is, a deterministic, mechanistic, view of the domain of experience with which their
science has to do. If we have in the moral field some hold-over
instincts of little value in the Great Society, we have in the
intellectual perhaps some undetected wisps of animism and
magic attached to our mental processes. Human life has thus
far been lived and organized very largely on illusions, and these
illusions are continually getting into violent conflicts with one
another, with results not always beneficial to "the race," and
rarely to the defeated individuals. The only thing that can
dispel illusion is science. We can look nowhere else than to
science to dispel the mystical, metaphysical, nationalistic, class,
and narrow, hyper-egotistical illusions that still stand in the
way of our sensing a rational direction in which collectively to
guide human evolution.

It is our confidence in the scientific quality of the new psychology, with its inductive, experimental study of the organism, in part and in whole, as a mechanical organization and
process, and its ideal of complete divorcement from metaphysics,

---

[9] Cf. Dewey, *Reconstruction in Philosophy*, 1920, pp. 1-3.

which leads us to the conclusion that the ethical end is the life of the individual and not the supposed transcendent interests of any group or institution. In other words, his own life—healthy, functional, symmetrical, and happy living—is the only ultimate purpose to which any individual can rationally assent. That this does not mean to us that the individual is to be viewed as an isolated and independent thing, rather than a locus of biological and social forces, should be clear from our discussion of democracy and of the methods through which the life of the individual is subserved (Chapter X).

For if behavioristic psychology points to the individual as the only end, social psychology, which should be but an extension of behaviorism, with equal certainty points to social co-operation as the indispensable means to this end. It also indicates, with greater cogency than metaphysics or sentimentalism ever can, that the policy of direct individualism of means, the narrow selfishness, the insistence upon legalistic, crystallized, static, acquisitive "rights," does not pay.

In this way it should now be clear that we arrive, on scientific grounds, at very much the same conclusions as the Founder of Christian ethics attained through what we may regard, without irreverence, as a marvelous intuitive insight. But the concepts of duty and service will belong in the category of means, not ends, and they will have a rational, empirical appeal to the self-regarding elements in human nature, which has proved itself more or less refractory to sentiment with regard to the practice of self-sacrifice and "altruism."

To all this there will be two stock objections, from very different sources.

The first of these emanates from persons who have little faith in man's capacity to acquire a rational attitude. If they can be brought, for the sake of argument, to admit that the individual is end and social co-operation means, they still object that there is no possibility of erecting a workable social ethics upon a rational scientific foundation, even of the "broader selfishness." Some other sanction, they hold, has to be appealed to, and since it cannot be that one to which we think a scientific psychology will lead us, it must be a transcendental religious motive. Without quarrelling over terms, what this religious motive is, in final analysis, but an emotional appeal to the interests of the

larger self it is difficult to see. But into this purely logical
phase of the subject we need not go.

Where an appeal to some super-sanction actually works better
than a directly and frankly rational appeal to scientific insight, let it be used by all means. We cannot afford to discard
the help of any method which will promote social peace and
sanity, provided it is so accepted that it does not tend to promote
the continued deficiency in objective rationality, which is one
of the main grounds for its temporary use. In the long interim
which must elapse before humanity acquires in a requisite
degree the objective, scientific attitude, we may welcome, as a
working compromise, any agency which will reduce narrow
selfishness and strife, and decrease the retardation to a broad
and liberal living which they entail.[10]

But there is perhaps some room for question as to whether
nineteen centuries of admonishment to self-forgetfulness and
self-sacrifice, on the sanction of transcendental absolutes and
religious imperatives, have been sufficiently successful in developing peace, good will, and whole-hearted social co-operation to
warrant us in refusing to formulate and utilize an entirely
objective and scientific calculus of ends and means. It would
seem fair to raise the question whether socially-minded leaders,
in the church or out, should not see the desirability, if not the
necessity, of substituting for "militant" Christianity, militant
Mohammedanism, or militant what-not, a more objective and
constructive method.

The other objection comes from those who take no stock in
mysticism and emotional appeal, but on the contrary, pride
themselves on their hard-headedness. From this point of view
it is held that the broader selfishness is only a verbal quibble
for altruism and "service," and has no more chance of
appealing effectively to the average individual than have the
more traditionalized and conventionalized precepts of religious
authority. According to this view, Christian ethics has failed
because it is contrary to human nature, and by implication the
so-called objective, or scientific, ethics will fail for the self-same
reason. For, the argument runs, human nature is essentially

---

[10] Cf. C. A. Ellwood, *The Reconstruction of Religion, a Sociological
View*, 1922; V. Pareto, *Traité de Sociologie Générale*, 1914, Ch. 1.

and narrowly and directly selfish; the joy of life is in competition, struggle, and the exercise of power; human progress is
largely the result of war, conquest, and the violent elimination
of the "unfit"; your democratic, Christian, "neighbor morality," try to disguise it as you will by calling it "scientific" or
"objective" and appealing to the "new psychology," is bound
to fail because of the very inherited instinctive equipment which
has been dealt with in these pages—the instincts of fear, pugnacity, and acquisitiveness. This, in effect, is the argument, not
only of protesting rebels against romantic sentimentalism, like
Nietzsche, but of all the militarists and a large number of "hard-
headed" business men. It is also, unfortunately, pretty nearly
the position taken by not a few social scientists who, in their
overly-sensitive fear of any reference to "ought" and "should,"
would make social science, if they were consistent, a barren
intellectual pastime, the indoor sport of highbrows.

That there is, however, some cogency in this line of argument
may be admitted. That the narrowly self-seeking and combative tendencies in human nature are very strong we have
indeed emphasized; and we must re-emphasize that it is precisely
these traits which now stand in the way of the effective functioning of the Great Society. That these instincts, developed
during long ages of biological evolution, can at a turn of the
hand be eliminated no one will claim. But there is also no
scientific ground to suppose that they cannot by ontogenetic
adaptation be minimized and sublimated to a degree which will
gradually remove them as obstructions to the co-operative functioning of our individual capacities and our social organization.

It is certainly true that man's instinctive inheritance includes
narrow selfishness and conflict psychology, but it is equally true,
and quite as significant, that these characteristics have been systematically cultivated and reinforced by the nationalistic and
commercialistic rivalries of civilized times, by the self-help,
individualistic philosophy, and by militant religion itself.

Man's instinctive inheritance, however, also includes other
powerful tendencies, which are not directly and narrowly self-
regarding. Among these are sympathy, play, gregariousness,
desire for recognition, and impulses to self-expression through
curiosity, workmanship, æsthetic creation, and the like. Nor
must it be forgotten that in spite of apparent indications to

the contrary, man is a rational animal. He has always reasoned logically with regard to his interests, within the limits of his knowledge and intellectual capacity. With reasonable opportunity to secure objective knowledge, and with better intellectual discipline, we may look for him to arrive in the future at less illusory beliefs and attitudes than he has in the past. When direct individualism-of-means proves inimical to the best interests of the individual himself, it should not be regarded as a hopeless task to get him to see that fact.

It will not be questioned that the combat instincts have to some extent been sublimated by social controls and training, so that infra-group conflict has been reduced and regulated enough to enable the group to acquire, if not perfect peace and internal security, at least sufficient cohesion and capacity to meet the pressures of outside groups. In fact, what we call civilization and socialization have been accomplished, in no small measure, just by the process of enlarging the group within which conflict is prohibited or mitigated and refined. That there yet remains much work in reducing the amount and intensity of infra-group conflict is but too evident. It should be clear, also, that this reduction should not come about through oppression of the weaker by the stronger. So long as such a tendency persists, there will inevitably remain the seeds of potential conflict. But where, with the growth of democracy, the various social classes become somewhat more evenly balanced in power and organization, there is hope that the recognized necessity for tolerance will force the adoption of objective methods of resolving interest conflicts. Mere enlarging of the size of the group is not enough without this rational diminution of the causes of internal conflict. Frequently the process of group enlargement is too rapid, as in the case of the Alexandrine and Roman Empires, and the overgrown group breaks up. Such cases only emphasize the fact, however, that the unity of the group must be real, and that it is as difficult to base real unity on conquest and military power as it seems to many chimerical to attempt to base it on a developed sense of mutual interests.

Those who insist that the conflict ethics is more nearly in accord with human nature than co-operative ethics overlook or unduly minimize both the sympathetic and the rational aspects of human nature. Moreover, while they counsel loyalty within the group, and feel that there it is not contrary to the nature of man, they more or less consciously stimulate and cultivate combat attitudes between groups. The inter-group conflict which they declare inevitable is thus in a measure made so by artificial stimulation and unnecessary emphasis on interest differences. The same is true of those who insist that narrow, direct selfishness is an innate and ineradicable trait. They cultivate and encourage the very part of our nature which we should be modifying and sublimating in the direction of a broader and more rational selfishness.

Neither the theory that man is pre-eminently and unchangeably a combative animal, nor the theory that his selfishness is so inevitably narrow and direct, if he is left to his own guidance without the support of super-rational sanctions, is sufficiently near the whole truth to warrant in us pessimism as to the practicability and utility of establishing an objective, rational sanction.

If the Great Society is to be made to work at all satisfactorily, the world will have to be brought to a clear theoretical insight into the objective ethics of democracy and into the most economical and effective, that is, the most moral, methods of approximating democracy in practise. This means of course that the world will not only have to do much pointed thinking on ethics, but that it will have to have an immense body of knowledge on social relations and processes. Given requisite knowledge, we shall find it far easier to subordinate narrow selfishness and personal sentiments to the needs of social co-operation than we now think.

Reduced to their lowest terms, the prerequisites to making the Great Society safe and productive of life worth living for all its members are two: the requisite knowledge and the appropriate attitudes.

The knowledge which we must have, but as yet are sorely deficient in possessing, is objective, systematized, scientific knowledge of social relations and processes in all their aspects. That there are great difficulties in its acquirement, both in the nature and method of sociological research and in the obstacles put in the way by popular-mindedness, we have pointed out (Chapter IX). Yet without such knowledge, and, furthermore, persistent educational effort to diffuse the scientific attitude through the population at large, we shall continue to be at the mercy, relatively, of the combative, personalistic, and obstructive sentiments of conservatives and reactionaries on one side, and the militant sentiments of dogmatic radicals on the other.

Given this scientific knowledge of society, and its diffusion as well as may be among the men and women whose sentiments and opinions constitute the final court of appeal in a democratic society, is knowledge enough?

In itself, it is not.

For in default of a profound change in our attitudes, intellectual education and development alone will be inadequate to the great task before us. Only to the extent that we acquire the scientific attitude shall we be able to strike a just balance between fossilized stability and impatient volatility, and a capacity, unterrified by slogans, claptrap, and epithets, to choose wisely and magnanimously, after a survey of the divergent paths of conservatism and radicalism, the course we shall take.

We need more than scientific method and scientific attitude, as these are commonly understood by the physical scientist. As we tried to show, in Chapter X, an indispensable aid to scientific observation, where human beings and their motives are involved, is sympathy. Without sympathetic insight, a thorough and delicate study of the motives which dominate social processes cannot be made.

Moreover, without sympathy social co-operation must be tremendously hampered. Both from the standpoint of pure science and from that of a practical ethics, therefore, it is the part of wisdom to encourage the development and expression of rational sympathy in every possible way.

The world needs, in fact, to be converted to Christianity almost as much as it does to science. Needless to say, by Christiantiy is not here meant theology or ritual, ecclesiastical æsthetics or other-worldliness, much less sabbatarianism, heresy-hunting, conventional charity, and holier-than-thou attitudes. What is meant is precisely the human ethics of Jesus, the social point of view, the real, inner, ethical democracy which respects the personality of man, woman, and child, native and alien, black and white, manual toiler and brain-worker; which is dominated by that fundamental self-respect which forbids one either to be a parasite or to be subsidized by the toil of others;

which makes one recognize one's self as an end, but as an end whose fulfillment is not to be sought through using or regarding others primarily as means; which puts modern content into the organic conception "We are members one of another," and so leads us to see that the broader individualism of ends can be served only through sympathy, concerted volition, and constructive co-operation; in short, a socialism of means organized on the broadest mechanistic and humanistic basis.

It is because we believe that a general diffusion of social knowledge and of the scientific method and attitude would bring us to this self-respecting, co-operative, genuinely Christian spirit much sooner and much more effectively than the fears and special interests of conservatism, the headlong desire-reinforcement of emotional radicals, or the mystical absolutes and prescriptive imperatives of the theological ethicists, that we pin our faith in the possibility of social salvation—the transformation of the present chaotic Great Society into an efficient co-operative mechanism—to the scientific method and attitude.

Here, then, if the Great Society is not to become a grim and tragic travesty on human reason, are our specific tasks: (1) to develop all the intellectual capacity we potentially possess, and to apply it to the scientific rationalization of interest conflicts; (2) to free knowledge from censorship of any kind; (3) to secure in our leaders and in the general population as rapidly as possible a near approach to the scientific attitude; (4) to develop sympathy between nations and classes, and a spirit of tolerance and understanding; (5) to acquire a morality of self-respect, such that the privileged will be ashamed to cling, either by force or by casuistry, to the right of subsidy and parasitism, and the masses will refuse to be subservient means to any end not inclusive of themselves.

These tasks involve the toning down of the instincts of pugnacity, acquisitiveness, self-aggrandizement, and self-abasement, which have made possible the long reign of the master-and-servant ethics. They involve the upbuilding of a new social philosophy in the place of the eighteenth century natural-rights individualism which still dominates us. They involve the substitution of a co-operative psychology of production for the prevalent business psychology of acquisition.

It must be admitted that in a sense we have a choice between scientific Christianity (if the term may be permitted, and its meaning is clear from the preceding context) and cynical, combative commercialism. Content with drift, we can join the anti-intellectualists in their reliance upon competition and eliminative struggle to produce whatever social advance there is to be. Or we can entertain a more virile conviction that when human intellect and reasoning capacity appeared in the play of evolution a new character was given to social development, and that sooner or later the stage will have to be reset not only for rationally, but for scientifically, directed progress. Is it too much to hope, with John Dewey and others, that we have now arrived at the stage of creative intelligence and that we can develop a technique for directing our social destinies in a rational manner? No certain answer can be given to this question. The events of the past decade do not give over-much encouragement. How great our constructive capacity, and how creative our intelligence, can be determined only through greater opportunity for their discovery and development, a better organization of our productive and directive forces, and in general a much fuller application of science in the solution of social problems.   We have not been so successful in securing human safety and welfare, even ignoring the retrogression of the past decade, that we should shrink too much from social experiment. Even with much fuller development of social science than anything now in sight, a considerable use of the trial-and-error method will for a long time be necessary.[11]

If social evolution is to be directed, if it is to become in a measure a scientifically rationalized process, we must, to repeat, reach some agreement as to where we want to go. Unless the analysis in the preceding chapters has been grossly inaccurate and inadequate, the fair conclusion is that we shall take the road to democracy, if we are wise. It is perhaps equally clear that we shall not take it if the vested interests have their way; that our progress will be halting if we permit ourselves to be held back by the irrational fears of the disinterested conserva-

---

[11] Herein lies the shortsightedness, if it be not due to domination by special interests which do not desire the experiment tried for fear it may be successful, of the State Department's refusal, in violation of long-established precedent in international law, to recognize the *de facto* governments in Russia and Mexico.

tives; and that we shall be frequently drawn off the main road if we follow the leads of personalistic, praise-and-blame radicalism.

If we are to find a way out of the world's present comparative anarchy, if we are to be the masters and not the victims of the Great Society, it will be only under a leadership measurably adequate to the task. For all social tasks, whether of rehabilitation or of new construction, are co-operative, and no attempt at co-operation has ever yet succeeded without the co-ordinating services of leaders equipped at once with a clear conception of the purposes to be accomplished, and capacity to guide and understand the rank and file of the individuals and groups whose co-operative good will and labor is essential. The people, like a drowning man, may either aid in their own rescue, or under the influence of terrorizing fear, make rescue difficult or impossible. Fanatical loyalties, emotional intolerances, combat attitudes, paralyzing the rational centers, may produce a comparable result in society.

Enough, perhaps, has been said in the preceding pages concerning the obstacles which leadership must find a way to overcome. Without falling into the pessimism of certain intellectuals with regard to the alleged insurmountability of the obstacles presented by "human nature" and popular-mindedness, we yet have just grounds for fearing that the people, with their emotional attitudes and their comparative ignorance of social forces, are their own worst obstacle to a better and more rational ordering of their social life. All the more reason, then, for disinterested leadership, and for the kind of education that will help to produce it.

It should be the function of behavioristic psychology to analyze human nature, without fear or favor. The active leader of affairs, on his part, has to meet and manage human nature, with all its elements of fear, habit, sentimental valuations, narrow personal interests, casuistic rationalizations, and active combativeness, and to modify it or utilize it as best he can for constructive social purposes. There can be little question that the existing traits of human nature can be modified more effectively by leaders who, through wide knowledge of behavioristic psychology as well as practical experience, know their genetic causation, than by leaders who act wholly or in large part under the impulses of personalistic praise-and-blame philosophy and combat attitudes.

The clue to the way out of the present situation—if there is one—thus lies in the temperament and the education of the men and women chosen to lead. No one type of temperament and intellect can take us out. As was suggested in Chapter VIII, social leadership itself must be a co-operative process, with a tolerably clear division of labor between the active men of affairs and managers of ''movements'' and the critically intellectual, scientific men who refrain from much active participation in the settlement of social issues and, in particular, exercise caution in allying themselves with parties or sects of any kind.

The relation of the critically intellectual, scientific mind to constructive leadership may be indicated in a few paragraphs.

The purely critical, intellectual mind, did such a thing exist, would be devoid of any emotions save those attached to the functioning of curiosity, the pursuit of knowledge, and, perhaps, the instinct of workmanship. Actually, however, the only difference between the critically intellectual and the dogmatic-emotional mind is that while the former may have strong conflict emotions and impulses, they are kept in tolerably strict subordination to the critical reason, to the spirit of scientific objectivity and balance, and to the impulse to constructive workmanship. More especially, are the fear-anger complexes and combative impulses kept under strict control, in the interest of clearness of vision, true analysis of the causes of social obstruction, and a true evaluation of the interests obstructed.

The scientific reaction to an obstruction to wish-fulfillment, even though the obstruction be found to lie in the attitudes of human individuals or groups, is not personalistic. The obstruction, and the obstructors, are taken ''philosophically,'' and regarded with scientific interest. The true social scientist will reach a point where he can regard a human enemy of society, a secret diplomatist, a monopolistic profiteer, a corrupt labor leader, or a sadistic criminal imbecile, for instance, with the same scientific curiosity and objectivity with which an entomologist regards a boll weevil or gypsy moth, or a bacteriologist a congregation of staphylococci or colon bacilli. His first interest is to know the nature of the thing; knowing that, he will tell the rest of us what to do about it. It is not "up to" the laboratory bacteriologist to get out and conduct a public health campaign, any more than it is "up to" the sociologist to become a deputy marshal and chase down the insane criminal.

While as a man, with desires, emotions, passions, and interests like other men, the critically intellectual individual may be at times tempted to indulge in personalistic, blame-anger reactions, as a scientist he replaces personal blame with genetic explanation. His impulse, as a man, may be to damn the obstructive traits and persons; as a scientist his attitude is one of attentive curiosity. *Why* do these people assume this obstructionist attitude? And *is* the obstruction due wholly to personal attitudes and interests, or is the explanation to be sought further afield?

Having answered these questions to the best of his knowledge and research ability, having laid bare the real causes so far as he can, he may co-operate with the active leaders to the extent of passing on to them the results of his investigations, and of suggesting the probable best methods, first for the removal of the obstruction, personal or otherwise, and then for positive construction.

This is presumably as far as the typical scientific mind will, or should go. In the interest of scientific objectivity, and that means in the interest of truth, it must protect its intellectual processes from the emotional strains and stresses of field leadership.

It follows that the scientific mind fails to function socially unless the results of its work are taken up and applied by active leaders. The only exception to this rule is found in those comparatively rare individuals who can lend their active aid, and actively take sides on public issues and movements, without impairing their open-minded objectivity.

As a matter of fact, there can be little doubt that the open-minded scientist, when his thought and investigational ability are turned upon social organization and processes, in many cases does become something of a radical, in sentiment and conviction, if not in activity. He cannot take popularly accepted sentiments and principles uncritically at their face value. He is in position to see the irrationality and the scientific groundlessness of many popular superstitions, beliefs, and convictions. He notes a lack of correspondence between theory and practise.

He sees the make-believe, the chicane, and the claptrap of much of our public life and conventional posing. He may have balked interests of his own—perhaps, for instance, popular hue and cry against freedom of scientific research—and he naturally turns the light of scientific analysis upon the sources•and causes of these popular illusions. He may also, like others, be a man of wide and sensitive sympathies, with a keen perception of the unnecessary restrictions to which people less fortunately situated than himself are subject. If he be socially-minded, he will, under some complex of motives probably derived jointly from sympathy and something akin to an instinct of workmanship, survey and evaluate the possible methods by which these limitations can be lessened or removed. Social injustice and exploitation will stimulate both his sentiments and his intellectual processes, and social inefficiency will be offensive—and consequently stimulative—to his sense of good workmanship. Such a man, or woman, has to be constantly on his guard to keep a proper balance between his sympathies and his critical faculty. A deterministic philosophy and a mechanistic psychology, scientifically necessary, are the greatest aids in this task. Taking these standpoints, he knows, if he ''explodes'' occasionally in a tirade of objurgation of human obstinacy, selfishness, and ignorance, that such explosion is only a temporary catharsis for his over-charged sensibilities. He will countenance the use of blame or objurgation as a social goad to get people to recede from obstructive attitudes, but the logic or the utility of blame in any other sense he cannot see. ''Responsibility'' in the popular sense is replaced, in his view of things, simply by the stream or nexus of genetic causation. Responsibility for obstruction, in this sense, is attributed partly to personal characteristics (the causation of which is open to analysis), partly to the influence of institutions and mores (the ''system''), partly to historical evolution.

The main characteristics of the actual leader of radical movements were suggested with sufficient fullness in Chapter VIII. To state the ideal qualifications of the constructive leader (whether liberal or radical) is less easy. Perhaps it will suffice to say that the constructive leader must avoid the indecision popularly, and with some justification, attributed to the critically intellectual mind, but that at the same time he will respect the scientist's objectivity of spirit and equip himself with the knowledge which the scientist is able to hand on to him. This does not mean any desultory "keeping up with the advancement of science." It means, if the actual leader and the scientist are actually to be in touch with each other, that the actual leader will have a specialized organization the function of which will be to have at hand the scientifically established data upon which policy, if not aim, must be based. Nor will the scientist on his part refuse such information and advice as he has to give. He will refuse only to give categorical yes or no, favorable or unfavorable, answers where—as in most cases—categorical answers cannot truthfully be given.

The scientist may be without moral convictions or norms, although if the thesis we have attempted to set up as a working hypothesis with regard to the fundamental relation between ethics and science be true, the social scientist at least, to be thoroughly scientific, must have ethical norms, fundamental norms, of a quite definite and unequivocal character, in fact.

It is just at this point, and through a full knowledge and clear understanding of the significance of scientific determinism and mechanistic psychology, that the active leader and the research scientist will come into the closest contact and exhibit the closest co-operation. We need not fear that this contact will not be beneficial to both, as well as to society at large. For the "intellectualist" will gain an objectivity at once more sensitive to facts and less delicately liable to perversion by emotional strain. And the active leader, without losing, like Buridan's ass, his power of making decisions, will gain in capacity to see a situation as a whole in something like its true perspective. The ideal active leader will probably have a type of mind belonging to the highest dogmatic-emotional, but below the scientific, level. The essential difference is that the scientific man is extremely cautious in coming to a definite decision on policy before he is convinced that he has all the essential facts, while the leader of a movement—almost any executive, in fact—knows that he has to make definite, and perhaps signally important, decisions as to ways and means, in the absence of complete data. The scientist can find refuge in an hypothesis. The actual leader must act, and his act is a reality, with the consequences of reality. And it should be remarked in passing that the terms "higher" and "lower," when applied to the critically intellectual and the higher ranks of the dogmatic-emotional class, respectively, are not to be taken too literally or as implying an invidious comparison. For the tasks of the honest, intellectual, informed leader are certainly as difficult as those of the scientist, and obviously call for a type of courage in which the scientist may be totally deficient. The actual leader has to take many a chance of doing the wrong thing, at junctures where a wrong decision may have extremely bad consequences. All the more reason, therefore, why he should avail himself of all the knowledge and information he can get from the objective scientist.

It has been the underlying thought throughout this book, a thought definitely expressed in the present chapter, as well as in Chapters VIII and IX, that escape from the personalism and combativeness of the conservatism-radicalism conflict can be had only through a great development of scientific knowledge of social relations and a profound change in social attitudes.[12] A new spirit must come to at least three classes of people: to the scientists, especially the social scientists, who must take considerably more intelligent interest in the ethical function of science; to the active leaders, who must gain more of the scientific attitude; and to the general populace, who must be brought to less intolerance, personalism, and combativeness, and to something nearer an objective view of life.

If, as is certainly true, this new knowledge and this modification of attitudes can be had only under wise, disinterested, and broad-minded leadership, whence will come the leaders adequate to the task?

Mr. Slichter,[13] after a survey of the support, both intellectual

---

[12] People have always been demanding a "new spirit," of course. Such a demand is the central sentiment of evangelism of whatever type, whether ecclesiastical or "social." But the demand varies in intensity, in honesty, and conventionality. Even he who runs as he reads must feel the reality and the cogency of the demand as we have it today. No one has made it with more sincerity and greater freedom from tradition and conventionality, perhaps, and certainly with greater voluminousness, than H. G. Wells. It was strikingly expressed by Charles S. Slichter, in an address entitled "The New Philosophy," before the Phi Beta Kappa Society of the University of Wisconsin, 1922.

[13] *Op. cit.*, p. 14.

and financial, given by English men of wealth to science—the "new philosophy" of the time—from Francis Bacon on, and of the luke-warm attitude shown, to a late date, by the English universities, feels both skepticism and hope. To-day, he says, quoting an unnamed economist, "in the natural sciences the inventor and original thinker is rewarded and honored, but in the social sciences the inventive mind is more or less ostracised and new ideas that touch upon the key problems of modern life, namely, the control of human and economic activities, are at once branded as radical and dangerous." There is perhaps an element of exaggeration and undue pessimism in this conclusion, and Mr. Slichter forgets that the natural scientists themselves had to endure a long period of popular hostility. Certainly to-day the economists, if no others among the social scientists, are coming into their own, if by that we mean having one's advice sought. To be sure Main Street is not yet aware that they have anything to contribute, but the Federal Government and business corporations have drawn so many of these men away from academic chairs that university research and teaching in economics are temporarily impaired.[14]

Mr. Slichter is of the opinion that the universities in America may have little to do with the development of the new spirit needed in the coming century.

"They do not seem to be generating grounds for courage and virility. I expect, therefore, a reversal in the position of university influence. In England the spiritual growth may grow and thrive from the universities. In America I expect the hope of the New Philosophy to lie, not with university faculties, but with men of the world; with leaders in the industries; with engineers· and business men and lawyers and men close to affairs."

We may share, mildly, Mr. Slichter's pessimism with regard

---

[14] It is, of course, open to question whether the young economists who enter the service of business corporations and labor organizations become merely expert advocateš for special interests, or succeed in maintaining their scientific objectivity and their regard for the public interest. For some questioning as to the ability of the economists to carry with dignity their new rôle ᴬas public advisers and active leaders, see Jacob H. Hollander, "The Economist's Spiral," *American Economic Review*, March, 1922 (XII, No. 1), pp. 1-20, the presidential address at the thirty-fourth annual meeting of the American Economic Association, 1921.

to the universities,[15] and look, with Mr. Veblen, for a new type of social leadership on the part of the engineers, but we shall be warranted in considerable skepticism as to the part likely to be played, in the near future at least, by the business men and lawyers. If we must look to the business men for the new leadership toward the scientific attitude and the essentially democratic spirit, it is safe to say that it will be found only in limited measure among the lawyers and merchants of Main Street, and that it will not soon be inspired by the Boosters' Club of Zenith. It will come, if it comes from the business classes at all, from the cream of the big business men of the metropolitan centers—and the chances are that they will have gained their social point of view from their university training.

We cannot at present look, very confidently, for a new spiritual constructiveness, for disinterested and liberal progressivism, to the commercialized and intellectually straight-jacketed middle-classes, whatever we may hope for when their sons and daughters now in high school and university "get out into life." For the middle classes are the buttresses of "respectability," and the victims of their own subjective fears of new—"radical," "bolshevist"—ideas. Leaving aside the liberally and technically trained social scientists, the main hope lies in the men and women, in whatever vocational calling, of social position and liberal culture, who are free from the emotional pressures involved in keeping ahead of the neighbors, and in the intelligent working classes with their balked interests, their reaching out toward more liberal living, and their increasing number of broad-guage leaders.

Above all, the hope lies in the youth to whom we may succeed in giving a liberal education. And there's the rub.

Is our education of to-day liberal, in a socially functional sense?

A little education is traditionally a dangerous thing. It is in fact the more dangerous in proportion to the native mental capacity, the balked desires, and the emulative ambitions of the masses whom we insist on making "literate." Education not directed with wide vision and far sight to broad social and

---

[15] He may be suspected of having too assiduously and observantly attended faculty meetings.

ethical purposes is perhaps quite as dangerous. There is excellent reason for thinking that much of our education at the present time, despite all the popular interest in it and the expert service devoted to it, is grievously misdirected. This doubt—with the present writer it amounts to a conviction— as to the functional shortcomings of our educational processes applies to the whole system, from the lower grammar grades to the curriculum for the A.B. degree and the graduate and professional schools. From the standpoints of the needed specific knowledge, the tolerance, the objectivity, and the co-operative spirit essential to the safety and the success of the Great Society, they come far short of practical requirements. This is due in part to the magnitude and complexity of the task that must be accomplished by them, if it is accomplished at all. It is due more, however, to the fact that the direction of our education is so prevalently in the hands of men who are still under the impress of the older psychology; the political philosophy of self-help individualism; an uncritical educational tradition; and an inadequate subjective ethics; if not of an intolerant, superficial, and static religious formalism. These acting directors are thus seriously deficient in the scientific spirit and social attitude essential to constructive educational leadership. We bar from consideration the considerable percentage who must be regarded as politicians bent primarily on their own personal advancement.

It is unnecessary to single out the universities in the ungrateful task of adverse criticism. No part of the system is more culpable than another, and there is altogether too much "passing the buck" of responsibility among educational critics themselves. To the extent that the universities get a chance to train and influence prospective leaders, and are not so swamped with numbers, in proportion to financial resources, that their own educational processes come to look like a machine for producing endless duplicates from the same pattern—a mechanical going through with the motions,—they are to be held responsible in no small degree for the character of future leadership, both in the educational and other fields. But it must be remembered that comparatively few public school teachers ever see the inside of a university class room. No very great percentage, probably if we take the country as a whole, have even the benefits of a normal school training, and there is room for some question as to the amount of socially orienting value in such training when they do get it. Ask any thoughtful person who has been called upon to teach classes of middle western school ma'ams who drift into the summer schools from the small Main Streets, say of Kansas, Missouri, and Nebraska, spending their annual savings to obtain six or eight weeks of culture which will be of "practical value" in their teaching, or at least provide them with the certificate of attendance which may mean some slight salary increase. He will tell you that not a few of them appear to regard a new idea as a kind of social impropriety, and advise you not to entertain a too great confidence in the breadth, the social efficiency, or the moral adequacy of our public school education.

To be sure, there is a vigorous movement for "citizenship" training, but careful examination of its aims and methods will show that it is largely concerned with specific details and machinery, even where it does not spring from more or less sentimental "Americanization" impulses. It is debatable whether any very significant development of an objective attitude and a genuinely constructive spirit may be expected from it. Dependent as it is upon the temper of the community and the ability and attitudes of the teachers, its norms may or may not be consonant with a progressive liberalism, with encouragement to creative thinking, and with the more fundamental ethical needs of a Great Society, sick from too much dogmatism, intolerance, and disorganizing conflict.

Jared Sparks, once an instructor in mathematics and natural philosophy at Harvard, later a minister of the Gospel, and still later editor of the *North American Review*, in preparing his voluminous Life and Writings of George Washington, altered, in the interest of sentiment, some of the writings of Washington which gave indication that the Father of his Country was not on all occasions the model of conventional morality which the youth of the land have generally been led to suppose. Those educators whose enthusiasm for "safe" conformity and "patriotic" training in citizenship overcomes their historical objectivity and their intellectual honesty find this a good precedent for their wish to extend such emendation and expurgation to the lives of all our heroes. A committee of New York City school principals appointed officially to examine and report upon the history textbooks used in that city recommended the following rule:

"The textbook must contain no statement in derogation or in disparagement of the achievements of American heroes. It must not question the sincerity and purposes of the founders of the republic or of those who have guided its destinies." [16]

A superintendent in another city excluded an excellent high school text on social problems on the ground that it contained a chapter on evolution, and adopted an inferior but "safe" text.[17] A normal school president forbade his English department to use the *New Republic* in classes and transferred a live instructor of public speaking to work in elementary composition, because his students were getting so interested in social and economic problems, that the merchant residents of the town were objecting to his "teaching" of "radicalism." The librarian of a denominational college for women, in a city of a hundred thousand inhabitants, expostulated with the instructor of sociology for assigning Main Street to a class to read, because "the young women will lose their idealism if they read such a book." A professorial member of a university department refused to look into the qualifications of a possible appointee to a vacancy, because the candidate had a name that "sounds Russian Jew." A promising young economist was driven out of a western university, to a lucrative position, incidentally, with a metropolitan daily, because he wrote a monograph on taxation which did not meet with the approval of the copper company regnant in the State. A professor of sociology in another western State university was put through a humiliating doctrinal examination because a State senator was sure that he was a socialist, and the ground for his assurance was that he taught sociology and "sociology and socialism are the same thing." [18]

---

[16] *The Historical Outlook*, Oct., 1922, p. 251.

[17] This incident happened before the recent clerical and legislative hue and cry against the "teaching of evolution."

[18] These are all actual incidents, of comparatively recent occurence. A full list would be very long. Too recently in the public print to need comment are the dismissal, for "teaching evolution" and having his students read Robinson's "The Mind in the Making," of a professor in the University of Tennessee, and then of five others who came to his support; the successful (?) fight against the "radicalism" of President Meiklejohn at Amherst; and the widespread hue and cry against the "unpatriotic" history textbooks of Professors Hart, Robinson, Mussey, West, and others.

It is not mainly because of such vested-interest influence and such vagaries of the popular mind, however, that skepticism as to the liberal and functional character of our education finds justification. The attitudes revealed by such incidents do indicate that our education cannot be said to be liberal, taking liberal in the sense that teachers shall be free to give their students their best according to their light and capacity; for there is no doubt such freedom is essential to an education liberal in a broader and deeper sense of the term. But doubt as to this broader functional liberalism in education rests on other grounds.

In the first place must be emphasized the entirely inadequate financial support given education. Let it be said that in the aggregate the amount annually spent in this country on education, counting not only that which comes from taxation, gifts, and interest on endowment funds, but that spent directly by students, probably mounts into the hundreds of millions. Large in amount as this huge sum may be, however, its largeness does not count alongside the amount required to fill the need of the Great Society for a broad and genuinely liberal education which will produce an adequate supply of leaders and raise the masses above the level of mere "literacy" (an illusional fetish). The comparisons frequently made between the amount devoted to education and the amount spent on candy, cosmetics, tobacco, and pleasure cars are perhaps not entirely to the point. Barring automobiles, these are comparatively small expenditures made by all classes of our people. The per capita cost of these comforts or conventional necessities is relatively small; it must be remembered that we are a population of 110,000,000, and that a small per capita expenditure runs up into an enormous sum in the aggregate. The real wastes and extravagances lie elsewhere—in advertising, in the senselessly rapid changes of fashion, in emulative waste in dress and house furnishings, in the heavy costs of selling goods, in military expenditures, in inefficient government organization and service, in the inflated standards of living rendered possible by monopoly, vested interest, capitalization of intangible assets, and socially created land values. There can be no reasonable doubt that the American people—the productive adults—could spend, as soon as they care to do so, five times as much as they now do for the educa-

tion of their children. It is only a matter of a radical change
in the valuation which they now put on education. If they
prefer to spend their money on showy cars, bridge parties,
hotel bills, ornate churches, and sojourns at Palm Beach; or if
they spend more taxes on concrete speedways than on schools
and public libraries, all that is only an indication that they do
not sense the need of better education. Most individuals, in
fact, have but slight conception of the nature and requirements
of the complex society in which they live. Least of all do they
realize that a quintupling of the amount spent for education
would repay itself over and over again, not only in a direct
greater capacity for living, but in increased economic productive power. For many parts of the country are caught in a
vicious economic circle at present; poor educational facilities
mean inefficient labor; that means low economic productivity,
a poor community, low tax capacity, and thence again poor
schools. Nor can we overlook the patent fact that many persons—it is unnecessary to specify of what type and position—
do not want better educational facilities, for fear that it will
mean more "unrest," more demand for opportunity and democracy, and a working class more intelligent in looking out for
its own interests.

If these obstructors of democracy and national safety are not
to continue in a measure to have their way; if our educational
system is to serve the larger needs of co-operative democracy
and individual freedom; if it is to prepare the oncoming generations for a broader-minded and less make-believe citizenship
than the present generation can offer as an example; if it is to
contribute what it should to the personal and institutional foundations of peace and social efficiency; our education must be
adequately supported: and that means that where we now
grant a million dollars we must grant four or five fold that sum.

Conceivably, Americans might be induced to grant this larger
financial support, on the popular assumption that a thing must
be excellent because it is expensive. But they might also be
disillusioned. Mere spending of money is not enough, although
with more adequate financial support the educational system
would no doubt automatically lose some of its present shoddy
character. Until, however, not only the people but more especially the educational leaders—the persons whose satisfaction it

is to be known as "educators"—have much deeper and broader apprehension of the fundamental social functions of education in a society like ours, and until the teachers from primary up, upon whom devolves the real educational task, have a wider and more pointedly social interest than that implied in the technicalities and meticulous conscientiousness of "school management" and class room "methods," we need look for no rapid progress in functional educational, that is, in the fitting of our educational system to the larger, fundamental requirements of the Great Society. Presupposing something like adequate financial support, the main educational problems lie in personnel, in attitude, and in the content of curricula.

We have repeatedly touched upon the characteristics and functions of leadership. We have just seen that the way out of the present situation can be found only through leadership of the requisite intelligence, attitude, and vision. Now, briefly and pointedly, we have to emphasize the fact that the very kernel of the whole problem and task lies in the character of the educational leaders—in securing a leadership that will strive to develop an educational system which will insure a really functional and liberal education. Let us not lose sight of the fact that the two fundamental needs are the knowledge requisite, and the attitudes appropriate, to a complex society which we must make tolerantly, intelligently, and co-operatively democratic. Briefly put, a liberal education is that which provides the individual with his share (according to his capacity and natural talents) of this functional knowledge, and above all with the interests and attitudes—self-respect, tolerance, objective sympathy, the scientific spirit, and co-operative, progressive, democratic sentiments, rationally grounded on objective understanding—essential to good citizenship. Considered from the point of view of such a standard, the puny and perverted character of much of our so-called educational effort will be patent, at least to one passably familiar with it and at the same time able to look at it in a perspective detached from personal vested interest.

The task of democracy, the task of making the Great Society safe for humanity, is a task of construction, not of exhortation. An acquisitive society, possibly, can get along on advertising, wit, and oratory; a productive society has to know a great deal, and to work intelligently and constructively on the basis of its knowledge. The leadership capable of developing a liberal and functional education will not come from men and women whose chief equipment is comprised in a timid conservatism and conventional sentiments. It can be expected only from those whose attitudes are founded on an objective knowledge of what the Great Society means.

It is idle to look for such leadership to emerge in the absence of the universities. Here we are compelled to differ with Mr. Slichter. He does not look to the universities. He looks to far-seeing, public-spirited business men, probably also to the leaders of working class movements, and possibly he sees hope in the workers' education movement. There are those of much experience in "social work" who hold that the workers must lift themselves by their own boot-straps. But boots and boot-straps have gone out. Search through the list of your really public-spirited business men, through the roster of leaders, or at least of teachers, in the workers' "colleges" and see how many of them have come through the universities. Or take the experts, the accountants, the engineers, the economists, who are aiding the workers to find themselves, or are devoting their energies to co-operative social research and constructive work— they trace back directly or indirectly to the universities, in respect both to their special knowledge and to their attitudes. And the same is true in great measure of the educational leaders at large. If they hold the key to the future, the universities have been largely intrumental in the determination of which way they will turn it.

Much then depends on the universities. Where they are remiss or ineffective, the results are much worse for a society like ours than they would be for one such as our grandparents lived in. The attitudes of the general populace are in part derived from, or at least are influenced by, the public schools. The attitudes, the mental capacity, and the functional knowledge of the public school teachers, in turn, are greatly influenced by the training they have received in the higher educational institutions. Hence the universities, however aloof from the public school system they may appear to stand, really have a profound and lasting influence upon it. The universites and colleges constantly complain of the poor training given to the boys and girls sent on from the public schools. The schools, with equal force, might complain of the equivocal results of higher education on the men and women sent back to them as teachers. There is here, in fact, a dual difficulty, another vicious circle. With better expenditure of more money, with better teaching, less waste of time in conventional subjects, and some resistance to narrow commercialization and energy-scattering fads in the public schools, the colleges and universities can make a better showing in their product, because they will have better prepared students to work with. On the other hand, the reform of the public school curriculum, saving of time now wasted, and the necessary improvement of personnel in the public school staffs, depend upon the ability of the colleges and normal schools, and ultimately of the universities, to send out men and women with the needed qualifications. That they are wholly successful in this at present no informed person will assert.

The central trouble in higher education (barring lack of funds) lies in lack of functional purpose and co-ordination. The mid-nineteenth century college was very sure that it had a purpose, and it had a co-ordinated curriculum and point-of-view adapted to that purpose. But the purpose was not large enough, nor the curriculum elastic enough, for changing social needs. Then the elective system was introduced, later modified by certain "requirements" and "group systems." The old purpose was lost, or became extremely vague and diffuse. Chairs were multiplied and divided, and filled with specialists interested in subjects (or fractions of subjects) quite as often as by men with interest in liberal education or much conception of the purpose of education. With but slight hyperbole one may say that from the standpoint of an education liberal and functional to the larger moral needs and outlook of the Great Society, our universities have in great measure ceased to be educational institutions. Magnificent professional schools, yes; and an amazing array of courses open to undergraduates; libraries bursting their walls; finely equipped laboratories; student self-government with its training in ward politics; intercollegiate athletics as an advertising factor; and a flood of young men and women, some of whom become students. But if an occasional student gets a great deal that can rightly be called an education liberal and functional to the needs of leadership in the Great Society, it is a fortunate accident. For the general assumption is that somehow a liberal education will result from four years' attendance in courses chosen, as often as not, because they come at a convenient hour, or because they fulfill certain "group" requirements which have been enacted with due deference to the various "departments of knowledge," not to say departmental vested interests.

The great influx of students in recent years into the colleges and universities is a healthy sign, in spite of the suspicion that many of them are sent because it is "the thing" and others come attracted by the prospect of a good time socially and possible newspaper fame in athletics. The size of student bodies is now so great, however, that college education has become a mass process; we are going through the motions as best we may, and the results will be deficient until more funds and more real teachers are provided. But even the motions are in good part not functionally purposed; where there is a purpose, it is often some inherited academic ideal of gentlemanly culture or scholarship for its own sake—an arid ideal in this day and age, when we have such need of scholarship and capacity directed to real social purposes. A "reading knowledge (?) of two foreign languages" and "two courses in English" are deemed more basically important elements in a "liberal" education than any combination of psychology, economics, history, and government. To be sure, the great swing of student elections in the choice of subjects is toward the social sciences, but that does not mean necessarily that a given student gets much, even in these fields, of functional value. College catalogues are loaded down with specialized and semi-technical courses with extremely elastic prerequisites. It is unusual for a student to manage to get a consistent group of co-ordinated social science courses of a type to give him insight into the social world in which he is to live, rather than a disconnected aggregate of courses given because of the special interests of professors and instructors. There is no guarantee of a broad educational perspective in the social science departments. There are few universities in the country whose economics departments have not fallen in some degree prey to the craze for "business administration" and schools of "commerce." There is a distinct materialization and commercialization in process. And it is matched in the sociological departments by the trend toward "practical" courses in "social service," without always requiring the essential background of general orientive study.

These may seem technical professional matters, allusion to which should find no place in a book of this kind. It is not our intention to conclude this chapter with an educational essay, but if the colleges and universities are to be the main source of leadership, educational and otherwise, suited to the needs of the time, problems of curriculum-content, of faculty personnel, and of educational attitude and outlook, have a bearing and significance far beyond a mere professional interest.

There is fortunately indication, not only in the colleges and universities, but in the public schools, that lively interest is developing in the problem of readapting curricula and educational ideals to social needs. So long, however, as an influential number of teachers and educators regard a split infinitive as a greater offense than inability to take an objective attitude, or place vocational training above a more broadly functional social education, no very rapid progress may be looked for.

Taking the educational system as a whole, division of labor and of function is, of course, everywhere necessary, because it is necessary in all social and economic processes. The main attention of the vast bulk of the population must be directed to making a living. The "requisiteness" of the amount of knowledge any individual is to have is therefore a relative matter. Not all can be social engineers and leaders. Failure to sense this fact has been one important source of the pitiful shortcomings of what is popularly but erroneously regarded as democracy. Moreover, the amount of knowledge which the schools can impart is limited. What the public schools *can* do—when they secure the properly qualified teachers and reform their curricula—is to encourage the needed *attitudes.* Their task in this will not be easy, because they will be running counter to subtle influence elsewhere, in the home, for instance, and to powerful interests in business, and well-meaning but obstructive institutions. And apart from quasi-professional and technical knowledge, the development of social *intelligence,* interests, and attitudes is about all that the colleges can undertake.

The attitudinal reform requisite to the efficiency and safety of the Great Society can come only through education, education adequately supported and properly directed. Educational reform must come first. Always, wherever we start, we come back to education. The eugenists and selectionists, it is true, demur, and say "yes, we need education, of course, but it is of secondary import; the primary task is to secure a better human stock." They forget that in the absence of a socially educated populace no serious eugenics program (even granting that we are in position to propose one based on secure scientific conclusions) has much chance of adoption.

It is not our hope that the undesirable habits and sentiments of conservatism, radicalism, and popular-mindedness can be eliminated over night; that a near approach to, and diffusion of, the scientific attitude is soon to be looked for. But insofar as we secure the needed attitudinal modification at all, it will not be through segregating a few feeble-minded or exhorting the well-to-do to have larger families. It will come through functional, courageous, progressive education.

When history placed industrialism and political democracy in one side of the scales, it called for ethical democracy, objective sympathy, social knowledge, and the scientific spirit in the other. It is the function of the teachers, wherever they may be working, to put them there.

Is it possible that the Great Society will ever come to an equilibrium of peace and productiveness for human living, if the educators fail in their primary function?

They have the tutelage, the guidance, and the stimulation of youth in their hands. The way out of the present situation— if there is a way out—lies in the youth of the land and in their attitudes, their points of view, their functional knowledge, their courage, and their freedom from the heavy impediments of precedent. Well may we say to them, Ye are the salt of the earth, the light of the world! But we owe it to them to provide an education which will not dim the light; which will not rob the salt of its savor.

BIBLIOGRAPHY

The following books and articles have in one way or another been helpfully suggestive in connection with the matters considered in this volume. No attempt, of course, can be made at anything like a full bibliography. The list of books bearing on conservatism and radicalism alone would be endless, although curiously enough, with the exception of the writings of Professor Veblen, especially his "Theory of the Leisure Class," there seems to have been no direct and serious attempt, in English at least, to work out a consistent theory of the nature and causes of conservatism and radicalism. So far as concerns individualism and democracy, the greater part of what has been written is beside the point, if judged from the viewpoint of the present book; for we are concerned with individualism and democracy less as theories of social means than as theories of ends. On the scientific method, especially in its application in the so-called social sciences, there is a growing literature in English, but it is mostly buried in the philosophical journals. The French and Germans have an extensive literature on scientific method, but we have deemed it best to confine the references, with one or two exceptions, to English and American books.

Only a rough attempt is made to classify the references. Many of them bear on matters appropriate to groups other than those under which they are placed.

I. CONSERVATISM AND RADICALISM

ALBERT, A. D.—"The Tents of the Conservative," *Scribner's Magazine*, July, 1922.

ANDERSON, MAXWELL—"Modern Casuists," *The Freeman*, August 25, 1920.

BAGEHOT, WALTER—Physics and Politics, 1873.

BEARD, C. A.—The Economic Interpretation of the Constitution of the United States, 1913.

BRYCE, JAMES—Modern Democracies, 2 vols., 1921.

CHAPMAN, J. J.—Practical Agitation, 1900.

DUNLAP, K.—Mysticism, Freudianism, and Scientific Psychology, 1920.

EDMAN, IRWIN—Human Traits and Their Social Significance, 1920.

ELLIS, H.—The Philosophy of Conflict and Other Essays in Wartime, 1919, Ch. 6.

EMERSON, R. W.—Nature, Addresses, and Lectures (Works, Vol. I), the essay on "The Conservative," 1841.

FRINK, H. W.—Morbid Fears and Compulsions, 1918.

HUNTER, ROBERT—Violence and the Labor Movement, 1914.

INTERCHURCH WORLD MOVEMENT—Report on the Steel Strike of 1919, 1920. Public Opinion and the Steel Strike, 1921.

KELLAR, A. G.—Social Evolution, 1915.

KROPOTKIN, P.—Mutual Aid a Factor of Evolution, 1902.

LAPOUGE, G. V.—Les Sélections Sociales, 1896.

LEOPOLD, LEWIS—Prestige, A Psychological Study of Social Estimates, 1913.

LEWIS, SINCLAIR—Main Street, 1920. Babbitt, 1922.

MILL, J. S.—Dissertations and Discussions, 1859 (the essays on Bentham and Coleridge).

NEARING, SCOTT—"Who's Who on Our Boards of Education," *School and Society*, January 20, 1917.

NEW YORK, JOINT LEGISLATIVE COMMITTEE OF THE STATE OF NEW YORK INVESTIGATING SEDITIOUS ACTIVITIES—Revolutionary Radicalism, Its History, Purpose and Tactics, With an Exposition and Discussion of the Steps Being Taken to Curb It. 4 vols., 1920. (The Lusk Committee Report.)

PARKER, C. H.—The Casual Laborer and Other Essays, 1920.

PATON, S.—"The Psychology of the Radical," *Yale Review*, October, 1921.

PAUL, KEGAN—William Godwin, His Friends and Acquaintances, 2 vols., 1876.

PUJO COMMITTEE REPORT, 1913 (Committee Appointed Pursuant to House Resolutions 429 and 504 to Investigate the Concentration of the Control of Money and Credit).

ROBINSON, J. H.—The New History, 1912, Ch. 8. The Mind in the Making, 1921.

ROSS, E. A.—Social Control, 1904. Sin and Society, 1907. Social Psychology, 1908. Principles of Sociology, 1920.

SHAPIRO, J. S.—"The Revolutionary Intellectual," *Atlantic Monthly*, June, 1920.

SCHROEDER, T.—"Conservatisms, Liberalisms, and Radicalisms," *Psychoanalytical Review*, 1920, pp. 376-384.

SMITH, J. H.—The Spirit of American Government, 1907.

STEPHEN, LESLIE—The English Utilitarians, 3 vols., 1900.

TAYLOR, L. A.—Revolutionary Types, 1904.

THORNDIKE, E. L.—The Original Nature of Man (Educational Psychology, Vol. I), 1913.

TROTTER, W.—The Instincts of the Herd in Peace and War, 1916.

VEBLEN, T.—The Theory of the Leisure Class, 1899. The Theory of Business Enterprise, 1904. Imperial Germany and the Industrial Revolution, 1915. The Vested Interests, 1919.

WARREN, H. C.—Elements of Human Psychology, 1922.

WATSON, J. B.—Psychology from the Standpoint of a Behaviorist, 1919.

WELLS, H. G.—Discovery of the Future, 1913. The Outline of History, 3d edition revised, 1921.

WEYL, WALTER—Tired Radicals and Other Essays, 1921, Ch. 1.

WILLIAMS, J. M.—Principles of Social Psychology, as Developed in a Study of Economic and Social Conflict, 1922.

WOODWORTH, R. S.—Dynamic Psychology, 1918. Psychology, A Study of Mental Life, 1921.

YARROS, V. F.—"Induction and Radical Psychology," *Psychological Review*, May, 1922.

On the conflict between youth and age, see—

BELL, B. I.—"The Church and the Civilian Young Man," *Atlantic Monthly*, September, 1919.

BRIARLY, MARY—"The Man, the Woman, and the University," *Scribner's Magazine*, November, 1922.

BUTLER, SAMUEL—The Way of All Flesh, 1903.

ELLIS, H.—The Task of Social Hygiene, 1912, the chapter on "Religion and the Child."

LASKER, B.—"The Youth Movement," *Survey*, December 31, 1921.

PARSONS, E. C.—Social Rule, a Study of the Will to Power, 1916. Social Freedom, a Study of the Conflicts Between Social Classifications and Personality, 1915.

SHAW, B.—Misalliance, 1914 (the Preface, on "Parents and Children").

STEVENSON, R. L.—Virginibus Puerisque (the chapter on "Crabbed Age and Youth").

TURGUENIEV, IVAN—Fathers and Sons, 1862.

See also the series of articles, by various writers, in the *Atlantic Monthly*, 1920, cited in note, page 58, of this volume.

On censorship, etc., see—

AMERICAN ASSOCIATION OF UNIVERSITY PROFESSORS, *Bulletins*.

BLEYER, S. H.—The Profession of Journalism, 1918.

CHAFEE, Z.—Freedom of Speech, 1920.

CUSHMAN, R. E.—"National Police Power Under the Postal Clause of the Constitution," *Minnesota Law Review*, March and May, 1920.

LIPPMANN, W.—Liberty and the News, 1920. Public Opinion, 1922.

SCHROEDER, T.—Free Speech Bibliography, 1922.

SINCLAIR, U.—The Brass Check, 1920.

VEBLEN, T.—The Higher Learning in America, 1918.

WHITE, A. D.—History of the Warfare Between Science and Theology, 2 vols., 1896. Autobiography, 1905, Vol. I, Ch. 24.

On the ductless glands in relation to temperament, see—

BANDLER, S. W.—The Endocrines, 1921.

BERMAN, L.—The Glands Regulating Personality, 1922.

CANNON, W. B.—Bodily Changes in Pain, Hunger, Fear and Rage, 1920.

HARROW, B.—Glands in Health and Disease, 1922.

KEMPF, E. J.—Psychopathology, 1920.

II. SCIENTIFIC METHOD AND SCIENTIFIC ATTITUDE

BERNARD, L. L.—"The Function of Generalization," *Monist*, October, 1920.

COOLEY, W. H.—The Principles of Science, 1912.

CURTIS, W. C.—Science and Human Affairs, from the Viewpoint of Biology, 1922.

CREIGHTON, J. E.—An Introductory Logic, 4th edition, 1920,, Part II.

FISKE, JOHN—Outlines of Cosmic Philosophy, 1874, Vol. I, Part I, Chs. 1, 3, 5, 6, Vol. II, Part II, Ch. 17.

GIDDINGS, F. H.—"A Provisional Distribution of the Population of the United States Into Psychological Classes," *Psychological Review*, July, 1901.

HALDANE, J. S.—Mechanism, Life, and Personality, 2d edition, 1921.

JEVONS, W. S.—The Principles of Science. A Treatise on Logic and Scientific Method, 2 vols., 1874.

LILLY, W.—An Introduction to the History of Science, 1917.

MILL, J. S.—A System of Logic, 2 vols., 1862.

PARETO, V.—Traité de Sociologie Générale, 2 vols., 1917, especially Vol. I, Ch. 1.

PEARSON, K.—A Grammar of Science, 2d edition, 1900.

RUSSELL, B.—The Problems of Philosophy (Home University Library), Chs. 4-7, 12-14. Scientific Method in Philosophy, 1913. Mysticism and Logic, 1918, Chs. 2, 6, 9.

THOMAS, W. I., and ZNANIECKI, F.—The Polish Peasant in Europe and America, Vol. I (Methodological Note, pp. 1-66), 1918.

III. INDIVIDUALISM AND DEMOCRACY

CARVER, T. N.—The Religion Worth Having, 1912.

CLAPPERTON, J. H.—Scientific Meliorism, 1885, Ch. 24.

COOLEY, C. H.—Social Organization, 1909. Social Process, 1918.

DEWEY, JOHN—Reconstruction in Philosophy, 1920. Human Nature and Conduct, An Introduction to Social Psychology, 1922.

DEWEY, JOHN, and Others—Creative Intelligence, 1917.

DICKINSON, Z. C.—Economic Motives, A Study in the Psychological Foundations of Economic Theory, 1922.

DURANT, WILL—Philosophy and the Social Problem, 1917.

ELLWOOD, C. A.—The Reconstruction of Religion, a Sociological View, 1922.

FITE, W.—Individualism: Four Lectures on the Significance of Consciousness for Social Relations, 1911.

FOLLETT, M. P.—The New State, 1920.

HOBSON, J. A.—Problems of a New World, 1921.

LUMLEY, F. E.—Slogans as a Means of Social Control, *Publications of the American Sociological Society*, Vol. XVI, 1922.

OPPENHEIMER, F.—The State, 1914, Ch. 6.

PAULSEN, F.—A System of Ethics, 1899, Book III, Ch. 1, on "Veracity."

TAWNEY, R. H.—The Acquisitive Society, 1921.

VEBLEN, T.—The Instinct of Workmanship and the State of the Industrial Arts, 1914. The Engineers and the Price System, 1921.

WALLAS, G.—The Great Society, 1914. Our Social Inheritance, 1921.

WARD, L. F.—Outlines of Sociology, 1899, Ch. 12. Pure Sociology, 2d edition, 1907, Ch. 20.

WILSON, W.—The New Freedom, 1913.

WOLFE, A. B.—"Some Psychological Aspects of Industrial Reconstruction," *Publications of the American Sociological Society*, Vol. XIV. 1919.

INDEX

Absentee ownership, 143, 280.
Absolutism, ecclesiastical, 165, 305, 313; metaphysical, 214, 304, 305.
Academic freedom, interference with, 92, 93, 184, 324-326. *See also* teaching, censorship of.
Accounting, 246.
Acquiescence, 146.
Asquisitiveness, 262, 263, 270-272, 281, 299-301, 313.
Adams, John Couch, 207.
Adaptation, 23, 42, 43, 78, 79, 81, 141; ontogenetic, 43, 44, 46, 47, 140, 142-144, 249, 309; phylogenetic, 43, 142.
Addams, Jane, 184.
Adrenal glands, 144, 145.
Advertisers, power of, 94.
Advertising, 197, 326; in relation to standard of living, 149.
Age, conservatism of, 56-59; prestige of, 56, 57, 105.
Agents provocateurs, 91.
Aggressiveness, 146.
Agitators, 112, 114, 137, 176.
Agricultural bloc, 135.
Alexandrine Empire, 310.
Allen, A. N., 58.
Altruism, 256, 257, 259, 307, 308.
Ambition, 72, 73, 114, 133, 138, 149, 187; parental, 57.
American Association for Labor Legislation, 114.
American Association of University Professors, 93.
American Bar Association, 73.
American Economic Association, 321.
American Federation of Labor, 141, 192.
American Legion, 187.
American Public Health Association, 114.

Americanism, 101, 114, 115, 286.
Americanization, 101, 324.
Amusement, disguised propaganda in, 286.
Analogy, 203, 207, 208, 214, 248, 249, 253.
Analysis, 204, 205, 207, 209, 211-213, 215, 216, 218, 243.
Anarchism, 15, 102, 114, 130, 155, 168, 271.
Anarchy, 80, 150, 304, 315.
Ancestor worship, 171.
Anderson, Maxwell, 76.
Anger, 121-123, 128, 135, 152, 153, 170, 172, 173, 175, 176, 180, 186, 187, 189, 216, 288.
Animism, 306.
Anthropological parallels, 214.
Anthropology, 176, 213, 214.
Anthropomorphism, 234.
Anti-intellectualism, 314.
Apprenticeship, 65.
Approximation, method of, 248.
Aptitudes, 23, 24, 27, 44.
Aristocracy, 139, 143, 268, 269, 272.
Arizona, 191.
Armament manufacturers, 101.
Association, 255.
Associative emotionalism, 16.
Astronomy, 213.
Attachment, 157, 183, 189, 201, 231, 232. *See also* Egotism, Habituation.
Attention, 122, 123, 128, 130, 220, 221, 255; scientific, 222, 224, 250.
Attitudes, 2, 3, 10, 47, 202, 294, 300, 303, 311, 320, 329, 332; defined, 9, 201; distinction between generalized and specialized, 6; scale of, 11, 12, 17, 18.
Authoritarianism, 35, 49, 148, 209, 285, 305.

Authority, respect for, 228, 229.
See also Authoritarianism.
Autonomic nervous system, 145.
Avoidance, 122, 146, 182, 184, 228, 277.

Bacon, Francis, 321.
Bagehot, Walter, 11, 141.
Bakounin, Michael, 188, 191.
Balked desire, 120-123, 126-133, 136, 138, 139, 143-145, 150, 152, 153, 163, 170, 173-175, 178, 180, 185, 186, 189, 233, 272, 279, 318, 322.
Balked disposition, 37, 120, 121. See also Balked desire.
Balked interest. See Balked desire.
Bandler, S. W., 145, 218.
Banks, 86, 87, 165, 194, 197.
Beard, Charles A., 106, 157.
Behavior, 217-219, 255.
Behavior-pattern, 9, 45.
Behaviorism, 45, 124, 171, 173, 217-219, 236, 242, 253, 305-307, 315, 318, 319.
Bell; Bernard Iddings, 53.
Bell, Graham, 18.
Benn, A. W., 4.
Bentham, 292.
Berman, L., 145.
Bernard, L. L., 251.
Big business, 70, 71, 85, 86.
Bio-chemistry, 213.
Biological analogy, 140.
Biological origin of conservatism, 23, 42-46.
Biology, 208, 213, 214.
Birth control, 152, 171, 268.
Birth registration, 244.
Blacklist, 85.
Blame, 121, 122, 128, 135, 152, 153, 170-178, 180, 187, 190, 198, 202, 209, 219, 231, 236, 251, 282, 293, 305, 317; ethics of, 287, 288.
Bleyer, W. G., 96.
Bolshevism, 16, 17, 90, 91, 114, 225.
Bonar, James, 182.
Boosting, 109.
Boycott, 85, 191; Chinese, 193.
Brailsford, H. N., 101.
Brain-patterns, 45.

Briarly, Mary, 58.
Bribery, 96.
Brissenden, Paul F., 188.
British Labor Party, 198.
Bryce, James, 14.
Buridan's ass, 179, 319.
Burkholder, A. C., 87.
Business control of government, 106, 107.
Business enterprise, 171.
Business ethics, 69.
Business inefficiency, 225.
Business men, conservatism of, 69, social leadership among, 321, 322.
Butler, Samuel, 58.
Byron, 137.

Cabot Fund for Industrial Research, 91.
Cannon, W. B., 145, 218.
Capital, 208, 209.
Capitalism, 156, 171, 269, 298.
Carlyle, Thomas, 152.
Carter, J. F., Jr., 58.
Cartoons, 114, 176, 199.
Catchwords, 101. See also Claptrap, Slogans.
Catharsis, 318.
Catholic Church, 162, 225.
Cattlemen, 135.
Causation, 180, 205, 208-211, 219, 235, 318.
Cause, 208-210, 216-219; final, 209.
Caveat emptor, 119.
Censor, 123, 124, 126.
Censorship, 83, 90-96, 184, 313, 324-326; ethics of, 283-286; of teaching, 91-93; of the press, 93-96. See also Press, censorship of.
Chafee, Zechariah, 90.
Chance, 216. See also Whim.
Charlatanism, 229.
Chicane, 83, 96, 97, 100, 102, 110, 113, 115, 116, 183, 198, 200, 203, 243, 283, 284, 286, 302, 318.
Child labor legislation, 107, 109.
Child welfare, 147.
China, 4, 142, 171, 191, 193.
Christian ethics, 281, 283, 307-309, 312, 313.
Christian morals, 305. See also Christian ethics.

Christians, early, 161.
Church Influence, 48, 49, 52, 53, 129, 301.
Citizenship, Prussian ideal of, 166; training for, 52, 81, 101, 324.
Civics, 53.
Civil liberty, 91, 297.
Claptrap, 83, 100-116, 118, 198, 283, 318; business, 105-115; legalistic, 102; nationalistic, 103, 115; political, 104, 105; types of, 102.
Clark, John B., 249.
Clarke, William, 14.
Class, 52, 55, 143, 148.
Class conflict, 2, 16, 71, 72, 82, 172, 173, 180, 263, 297, 302. See also Class struggle.
Class consciousness, 72, 166, 190, 252.
Class interest, 6, 61, 97, 118, 172, 173, 296.
Class solidarity, 72, 135,. 162, 181, 190, 271.
Class struggle, 158, 166, 214, 290. See also Class conflict.
Classes, incidence of social chance upon, 143, 144.
Classical political economy, 249.
Classification, 174, 204, 205, 208, 216, 238, 244-246.
Clayton Anti-trust Act, 116.
Clergymen, conservatism of, 74-76.
Clericalism, 28, 166.
Climate, 140.
Clinical laboratories, 169.
Closed shop, 65, 66.
Coal strike of 1919, 192.
Cobdenism, 16.
Collective bargaining, 66, 84, 85, 111, 113, 192, 302.
Collective telesis, 304.
Collectivism, 16.
College students, mental traits of, 33, 35, 79.
Colleges, denominational, 75, 184, 285; trade union, 184, 195.
Combativeness, 122, 296, 299, 310, 311. See also Pugnacity.
Committee of Forty-eight, 193.
Commons, John R., 156.
Commune, 189.
Communism, 16, 114, 266, 268.

Comparative poverty, doctrine of, 149, 239.
Compensation, 127, 231.
Complex, 125, 253.
Compromise, 76, 77, 193, 202, 283.
Concept, 205, 208.
Concerted volition, 5, 155, 313.
Conduct, result of strongest motive, 257.
Conflict, 5, 11, 16, 172-174, 180, 310; between youth and age, 57-59.
Conflict complex. See Conflict psychology.
Conflict psychology, 172, 180, 234, 251, 288-290, 300, 309; intensified by certain religious attitudes, 305.
Conformity, 77.
Consciousness, a form of behavior, 254; correlated with nervous system, 260; in relation to purpose, 255, 256; in relation to thinking, 255; social, 253.
Conservation, 147.
Conservatism, biological origin of, 23, 42-46; casuistic, 76-78; characteristic, 24; defined, 12; disinterested, 21-60 (see also Disinterested conservatism); emulative, 62; interested, 61-118 (see also Interested conservatism); lackadaisical, 31; methods of, (see Disinterested conservatism, Interested conservatism); motivation of (see Disinterested conservatism, Interested conservatism); of age, 56-59; protective, 24; symbolical, 127; temperamental, 24; vested-interest, 62, 65-73.
Conspiracy of silence, 184.
Constabularies, 84.
Constitution, the Federal, 41, 90, 104-106, 190.
Constitutional mythology, 104, 105.
Constitutional rights, invasion of, 90, 188, 298.
Constructive imagination, conservative lack of, 38; element in scientific method, 207, 219, 227, (see also Imagination, scientific); radical's deficiency in, 158.

Control, based on scientific knowledge, 211, 212.
Convention, 62, 80, 88, 133.
Cooley, C. H., 26, 46, 149, 163.
Cooley, W. F., 208, 234.
Cooperative research, 224, 250, 251.
Corruption, 117, 199.
Cost of production, 108.
Courage, 6, 163, 320, 321, 333; scientific, 222, 228.
Court decisions in labor cases, 192.
Cousin, Victor, 226.
Creative intelligence, 202, 304.
Credit, 86, 87, 231, 296.
Credulity, 93, 98, 222, 225, 226.
Creighton, J. E., 208.
Criminal syndicalism statutes, 90.
Crises, historical, 4.
Critical faculty, 49, 54, 97, 115, 150, 165, 219, 222, 226, 227, 233.
Critically intellectual mind, 175, 176, 178-180, 233; in relation to leadership, 316-320.
Criticism, 34-36, 39, 60, 100, 219, 220, 223, 226, 227, 229; conservative aversion to, 183, 184; restriction of, 183, 184.
Cross fertilization of ideas, 40, 41.
Crowd psychology, 108.
Curiosity, 122, 132, 133, 141, 146, 151, 220-224, 309, 316.
Custom, 62, 238; shell of, 11, 13, 62, 142.
Cuvier, 204.
Cynicism, 178, 179.

Dallas Open Shop Association, 112.
Dante, 137.
Darwin, Charles, 42, 209.
Dawson, W. H., 89.
Davenport, C. B., 265.
Day dreams, 153, 258.
Death rate, 244.
Deduction, 206, 213, 245, 249.
Defection of radical leaders, 96.
Definition, 208, 209, 238, 245.
Democracy, 28, 40, 70, 101, 116, 148, 149, 185, 221, 230, 231, 263-275, 277, 279, 282, 283, 303, 311, 312; as equity of opportunity, 266, 267; dead level theory of, 265, 266, 273; need of criticism

in a, 226; political, 264, 271, 298, 302; relation to radicalism, 263; vested-interest opposition to, 88, 89.
Demography, 209.
Demonstrations, 196.
Dennison, Henry S., 111.
Denominational colleges, conservatism of, 75, 184, 285.
Deportation of radicals, 91, 176, 188.
Desire, balked (see Balked desire); for distinction, 54, 55, 309; for recognition, 54, 55, 309; nature of, 120; sources of obstruction to, 152-155, 180; subordination to reason, 222, 223.
Detectives, 187.
Determinism, 125, 173, 216, 219, 223, 236, 257, 306, 318, 319.
Dewey, John, 50, 198, 208, 306, 314.
Diagnosis, 169, 170.
Dickinson, Z. C., 8, 29.
Dictatorship of the proletariat, 168.
Dilettantism, 127, 130.
Diminishing utility, 215.
Diplomacy, 173, 183; "oil," 297; secret, 59, 115, 298.
Direct action, 90, 188-190, 192.
Direct election of senators, 89.
Direct primary, 89.
Disarmament, 70; Conference, 298.
Discussion, 96; appeal to prejudice in, 100; personal-interest bias in, 100, restriction upon, 60, 99, 100, 183, 184, 285 (see also Censorship.)
Disillusion, 296.
Disinterested Conservatism, 21-60; a matter of sentiment, 22, a product of adjustment, 23, 24; a safety-first attitude, 21; characteristics of, 31-42, 290; ethics of, 277-279; methods of, 60, 181-184; motivation of, 21-31; sources of, 42-59 (see also Biological origins of conservatism); weakness of, 290, 291.
Disloyalty, 114, 116.
Disorder, radical's sense of, 164.
Displacement, 126. See also Substitution, Sublimation.

Dogmatic-emotional mind, 175-178, 181, 226, 229, 316, 319.

Dogmatism, 160, 165, 226, 227, 229, 306.

Douglas, Paul H., 146.

Drainage, 126. *See also* Substitution, Sublimation.

Dream symbolization, 258.

Due process of law, 103.

Dunlap, Knight, 124.

Durant, Will, 251.

Duty, 263; belongs to category of means, 256, 257, 307.

East Africa, 191.

Economic disorganization, 296, 297.

Economic harmonies, 270.

Economic man, 214.

Economic motive, 214.

Economic pressure, 83-88, 91, 135, 143, 144, 191, 192; ethics of, 283, 284, through control of patronage and credit, 86, 87; through hiring and firing, 84, 85; in relation to feminine character, 88; in rural communities, 87; in the professions, 87, 88.

Economics, 213, 214, 234; courses in, 113, 331; interested in function, 208; organized research in, 250; teaching of, 321, 331.

Economistes, 270.

Edison, Thomas A., 18.

Education, 46, 174, 180, 203, 274, 303, 304, 312, 316; conservative influence of, 49, 50; deficiency of, in functional purpose, 225, 330-333; financial support of, 326-328; leadership in, 323, 328-333; liberal, 151, 322-338; religious, 52, 53; stimulus to unrest, 148, 149; vested-interest control in, 184.

Educational administration, vested-interest influence in, 92, 93.

Egotism, 28, 37, 55, 138, 222, 234, 258, 262; of the popular mind, 230, 231.

Eighteenth Amendment, 17, 28, 155.

Einstein, 211.

Elders, conservative influence of, in public affairs, 59. *See also*

Age, conservation of.
conservation of.

Elective system, 330.

Ellis, Havelock, 49, 184.

Ellwood, C. A., 301, 308.

Emotion, 7, 47, 144, 175; defined, 8.

Emotional tone, 8, 144.

Emotionalism, associative, 16.

Empiricism, 219.

Employers' associations, 197.

Emulation, 55, 56, 62, 66, 72, 73, 132, 133, 149, 214, 281, 282.

Emulative conservatism, 62.

Encyclopædists, 270.

Ends, 252-256, 260; conflict of, 252; in biological sense, 256.

Energism, 257.

Engels, Friederick, 176.

Engineers, social function of, 133, 173, 321, 322.

England, 89, 101, 111, 193, 286.

Environment, changeableness of, 140-144; influence of, 46, 47, 139-143, 265, 269, 273-275.

Equality, before the law, 103; of opportunity. (*See Opportunity*).

Equity of opportunity. See Opportunity.

Espionage, 83, 84, 90, 91, 194; ethics of, 283-286; private, 91.

Espionage acts, 90.

Ethical norms, danger of, in scientific research, 237-239.

Ethical training, 53.

Ethics, 213; as taste, 305, 306; based on behavioristic psychology, 253; a calculus of means and ends, 253; Christian, 281, 283, 307; master-and-servant (*see* Master-and-servant ethics) objective, 283, 305, 308; sex, 53, 184; synonymous with economy, 266.

Eugenics, 249, 333.

Eugenists, 153, 177, 333.

Evidence, 202, 220, 242, 243.

Evolution, 42-46, 139, 140, 209, 299, 300, 309; teaching of, 92, 184, 325.

Exact sciences, 213, 215.

Excess profits tax, 116.

Expansibility of human wants, 147,

Experience, 206, 211, 212, 233, 235, 254, 255, 257, 258, 261, 304; dread of, 150, 151; expansion of, 145-150; vicarious, 259, 262.
Experiment, 207.
Exploitation, 102, 103, 117, 135, 148, 153, 158, 171, 189, 270, 299, 302.

Factual data, 206, 207, 209, 214, 242-244.
Fairchild, H. P., 146.
Faith, radical's, 166; scientific (*see* Scientific faith).
Fallacy, of familiarity, 232, 233; *ost hoc propter hoc*, 210.
Family, 128, 204; conservative influence of the, 48, 49, 51, 57; not an end, 260, 261; training, 48, 49, 51.
Fancy, 222, 228.
Farm tenants, 87, 107.
Farmers, 68, 106, 135, 190.
Fascisti, 297.
Fashions, 214.
Fear, 13, 19, 21, 24-26, 27, 29, 32, 36, 38, 39, 41, 61, 63, 64, 66, 68, 70, 71, 122, 123, 128, 129, 133, 146, 150-154, 162, 175, 176, 186, 202, 212, 222, 228, 230, 257, 282, 290, 300, 309, 314, 315, 322; a main element in conservatism, 21, 24-31; ethics of, 277-279, 291, 292; in relation to radicalism, 165, 166; of living, 150, 151; of social disapprobation, 29; of the familiar, 28, 29; of the unknown and unfamiliar, 27, 28, 232.
Fecundity, 214. *See also* Birth control.
Federal Trade Commission Act, 116.
Federated American Engineering Societies, 147, 225.
Federated Press, 176, 196, 199.
Feeblemindedness, 266.
Feeling, 7.
Feelings, the, 7, 8.
Ferrer, Francisco, 138.
First Amendment, 90.
Fiske, John, 208.
Fite, Warner, 305.
Follett, M. P., 14.

Force, 173, 180, 189, 202, 298; as method of conservative control, 83; ethics of, 283, 284, 288, 289, 305.
Foreign language press, 90.
Forty-eight, Committee of, 193.
France, 101, 141, 270, 287, 297.
Franchise reform, 89.
Free competition, 14, 101, 214, 301.
Free silver issue, 92, 135.
Free will, 175, 217, 219, 231.
Freedom, 269, 271, 272, 279; desire for, 145-152, 163, 180, 282; obstacles to, 151, 153, 154; of assemblage, 90, 91, 148; of contract, 101, 112, 113, 271, 272; of press, 76, 83, 90, 148; of speech, 75, 76, 83, 90, 91, 148, 285; of teaching, 75, 83; why demand for grows, 146-151.
Freeman, The, 195.
French Revolution, 3, 46, 269, 297.
Friday, David, 240.
Frink, H. W., 126, 145.
Frontier, 116, 263.
Full dinner pail, 115.
Fundamental sociological postulates, 214, 248.

Genera, 139, 204, 205, 208.
General strike, 190, 192, 193, 289.
Generalization, 204-207, 213-216, 227, 232, 233, 244.
Genetics, 213.
Genius, 145.
Genoa, 298.
Gentleman's agreements, 136.
Geography, 210.
Gerlach, Hellmut von, 286.
German Social Democracy, 194.
German universities, 92.
Germany, 101, 286, 297.
Gerould, K. F., 58.
Giddings, F. H., 37, 175, 181.
Ghandi, 193
Glands, 144, 145, 218, 253.
Government, business control of, 106, 107, 283.
Government subsidies, 165.
Gowin, E. B., 59.
Graft, 96, 98.
Granger movement, 68, 135.
Gray, Asa, 204.

Great Society, 300-302, 306, 309, 311, 313, 315, 323, 326, 328-333; sources of, 299; disharmony between attitude and function in, 300-303.
Greenbackism, 68, 135.
Gregariousness, 259, 300, 309.
Group cohesion, 310.
Group consciousness, 260.
Group egotism, 37.
Guild self-interest, 66.
Guild socialism, 90. See also Socialism.
Gunmen, 188.

Habit, 24, 25, 27, 122, 125, 133, 144, 155, 183, 223, 238; ethics of, 277.
Habituation, 23, 24, 31, 36, 39, 43, 44, 47, 79, 81, 119, 127, 131, 133, 142, 149, 151, 157, 174, 223, 226, 232, 233, 238, 254, 276-278, 290.
Haiti, 191.
Haldane, J. S., 218.
Hamilton, Alexander, 105.
Happiness, 142, 257-261, 265, 307; defined, 258.
Harrow, Benjamin, 145, 218.
Hart, Albert Bushnell, 325.
Hatred, 172, 176, 180, 248.
Hedonism, 20, 214.
Herd instinct, 34, 35, 162, 186, 287.
Hereditary differences, overemphasis upon, 273-275.
Heredity, 43-45, 249, 254, 257, 265, 269, 273-275.
Hero worship, 161, 229.
Higher criticism, 36.
Higher learning, 56.
Hiring and firing, 63, 84, 85, 88.
Historical parallels, 51.
Historical method. See Scientific research.
Historical research, 243.
History, study of, 38, 50, 51.
Hobbes, 270.
Hobson, J. A., 101.
Hollander, Jacob H., 321.
Hoover, Herbert, 164.
Human capacity, need of discovering and developing, 266.
Human nature, 155, 315.
Human wants, expansion of, 148-150.

Hunter, Robert, 185, 188.
Huntington, Elsworth, 141.
Hutchins, William J., 53.
Hypocrisy, 76, 93.
Hypothesis, 206, 207, 219, 227, 228, 248, 249, 319.
Hysteria, 115, 119, 187.

Idealism, 150, 160, 239.
Idealization, 183.
Ideo-emotional mind, 175, 181, 286.
Ideo-motor mind, 175, 181, 186, 226, 229, 286.
Illusion, 28, 203, 212, 232, 235, 276, 277, 302, 306.
Imagination, 27, 31, 38, 154, 157, 158, 161, 164, 183, 255; scientific, 207, 219, 222, 227, 228, 235.
Imitation, 27, 78, 132, 133, 146, 149, 163, 231.
Immigration, 140.
Imperialism, 156, 191.
Impression, 28, 54, 182.
Income, distribution of, 239, 240, 266, 271.
Income tax, 116, 240.
Increasing misery, doctrine of, 158, 239.
India, Nationalist Movement in, 4, 193.
Indifference, 146, 182.
Individual, the, a social product, 261; as end, 253-261; defined, 253, 254, 307. See also Individualism.
Individual differences, 264, 265, 273, 274.
Individualism, 5, 148, 162, 163, 189, 193; eighteenth century, 269-272 (see also Individualism, self-help); of ends, 252-261, 275, 305; of means (see Individualism, self-help; self-help, 69, 99, 116, 119, 165, 261, 263, 270, 271, 293, 301, 305, 307, 309, 310, 323.
Induction, 136, 204, 205, 213, 218, 249.
Industrial exemption, 143, 282.
Industrial Revolution, 3, 116, 140, 143, 147, 187, 189, 270, 272, 299.
Industrial unrest, 113, 148, 295.
Inefficiency, business, 225.
Infant mortality, 209, 212.

Inference, 207, 210, 213, 216, 220, 244.
Inferiority complex, 224, 231.
Ingalls, Walter R., 240.
Inhibition, 124.
Initiative and referendum, 89.
Injunctions, 85, 192.
Innate depravity, 102.
Innate ideas, 253.
Innovation, 17, 18, 39, 40, 41, 56, 132, 133, 139, 146, 187, 212, 248; relation to radicalism, 18, 132, 133.
Inquisition, the, 45.
Insecurity, a source of radicalism, 156, 157.
Insensitiveness, 222, 223.
Instinct, herd (see Herd instinct); of contrivance (see Workmanship, instinct of); take-a-lead, 161; of workmanship (see Workmanship, instinct of). See also Instincts.
Instincts, 24, 25, 44, 46, 124, 125, 132, 144, 232, 299, 300, 309; and purpose, 255; maladjustment of, to social needs, 299-301, 303.
Institutions, 172; cannot be ends, 260, 307; conservative control of, 187; conservative influence of, 47-53; tend to be regarded as ends, 163.
Intangible assets, 89, 326.
Intellectual radicals, 138, 158.
Interchurch World Movement, 91, 110, 114, 185.
Interest, 121, 122, 126, 131, 132, 133, 146, 151-153, 209, 220, 221, 224, 310; vicarious, 128.
Interest conflicts, 16, 153, 200-204, 220, 234, 237, 241, 246, 263, 277, 283, 289, 290, 304, 305, 310, 313.
Interested conservatism, 61-118; among skilled workers, 65-67; ethics of, 279-281, 283-287; in the different social classes, 63-76; methods of, 82-118, 182, 183; motivation of, 61-63; of active business men, 69-72; of big business, 70; of clergymen, 74, 75; of lawyers, 73, 74; of small property holders, 65; of necessitous condition, 62-64, 75, 119; of physi-

cians, 74; of rentiers, 67-69; of teachers, 74, 75; of vested interests, 62, 65-73; of white-collared workers, 72, 73; product of the social system, 81; types of, 61, 62.
International Workers of the World, 64-66, 130, 166, 185, 188.
Internationalism, 16, 17, 70.
Interstate Commerce Act, 109.
Interstate Commerce Commission, 246.
Intimidation, 75, 83-88, 112, 188, 191; ethics of, 282-285, 289.
Intolerance, 17, 44, 222, 227, 228, 232, 296, 298.
Introspection, 10, 129, 256.
Ions, 211.
Irwin, Inez Haynes, 196.
Isolation, 151, 162, 163, 234.
Italy, 297.

Jackson, Andrew, 243.
James, William, 219.
Japan, 59, 101, 198.
Jastrow, Joseph, 175.
Java, 191.
Jazz, 214.
Jesuits, 49.
Jesus, 263, 307, 312.
Jevons, W. Stanley, 208.
Jingoism, 226.
ones, F. W., 146.
Journalism, 151, 199; class viewpoint in, 94, 95.
Junkers, 89, 141.

Kautsky, Karl, 148.
Kempf, E. J., 145.
Keynes, John Maynard, 236.
Kidd, Benjamin, 42.
King, W. I., 240.
Kingsley, Mary H., 176.
Knauth, Oswald W., 240.
Knights of Labor, 85.
Knockers, 226.
Kropotkin, P., 44, 137.
Ku Klux Klan, 28, 103, 187, 191, 225.

Labor legislation, 83, 107, 108.
Labor press, 67, 95.
Laidler, Harry W., 188.

Lamberson, Frances, 146.
Landed aristocracy, 106.
Language habits, 158, 165. *See also* Claptrap, Slogans.
Lankester, E. Ray, 216.
Lapouge, G., 45.
Lasker, Bruno, 58.
Lassalle, Ferdinand, 161.
Lausanne, 298.
Law, 62, 80, 88, 96, 104, 211; scientific, 206, 207, 213, 214, 216, 217.
Law and order, 155, 188, 190.
Lawyers, as judges, 89; conservatism of, 78; predominant in Congress, 89; social leadership among, 321, 322.
Leaders, radical, defection of, 96.
Leadership, 28, 174-181, 189, 196, 221, 293, 315, 316-333.
Learning process, 46, 254.
Le Bon, G., 134.
Left Wing Manifesto, 189.
Legislative lobbies, 106.
Leisure, 152, 269.
Leisure class, 56, 98, 99, 303.
Lenine, 15.
Leopold, Lewis, 55, 59.
Leverrier, U. J. J., 207.
Levine, Louis, 188.
Lewis, Sinclair, 86.
Liberalism, 12, 14, 172, 183, 271, 324.
Libertarianism. *See* Free will.
Limitation of output, 65, 81, 112, 113, 284.
Linear logic, 249.
Linnaeus, 204.
Lippman, Walter, 96, 286, 287.
Literacy, 148, 303, 326.
Living wage, 108, 247.
Locke, John, 270.
Lockwood Committee, 199.
Loria, Achille, 137.
Lovett, Sir Verner, 193.
Loyalty, 16, 31, 33-37, 39, 44, 72, 101, 115, 160, 161, 177, 182, 189, 201, 230-232, 276, 289, 304; not an end, 260, 261.
Lusk Committee, 188, 189, 195.
Lynching, 83, 104, 187.

Macaulay, Fred R., 240.

Macdonald, Ramsay, 188.
Macdougall, William, 25.
Machine smashers, 187.
McKinley, A. S., 89.
Madison, James, 105.
Magic, 306.
Main Street, 325.
Maladjustment, basis of social unrest, 119, 120, 136, 137, 144.
Malnutrition, 266.
Malthus, Thomas Robert, 268.
Manchesterism, 263. *See also* Individualism, self-help.
Manners, influence of youth upon, 58.
Manual labor, a taint of servile status in, 98, 99.
Manufacturers' associations, 111.
Marginal productivity, 215, 249.
Mark Twain, 210.
Marx, Karl, 35, 137, 161, 176.
Marxism, 194.
Master-and-servant ethics, 71, 269, 272, 290, 302, 303, 313.
Mathematics, 213, 245.
May, T. E., 139.
Means and ends, 202, 252-263, 302.
Mechanism, 216, 218, 219, 235, 236, 242, 255, 256.
Meiklejohn, Alexander, 325.
Memory, 205, 255.
Mental astigmatism, 203.
Mental compartmentization, 40, 124, 174.
Mental flexibility, 159.
Mental tests, 225, 273, 274.
Mental types, in relation to conservatism, 38, 39; in relation to radicalism, 174-181.
Mercantilism, 165, 301.
Metabolism, 144.
Metaphysics, 214, 217, 253, 307.
Methods of radicalism, phases of, 169; psychology of, 168-181; specific, 181-199.
Mexico, 103, 104, 314.
Middle classes, the, 97, 98, 322.
Militancy, 178, 181; shortcomings of, 173, 174.
Militarism, 191, 298.
Militia, 83.
Mill, John Stuart, 208, 268.
Mind in the Making, The, 325.

Minimum wage legislation, 108, 109.
Mitchell, Wesley C., 240.
Mob violence, 104, 119, 187.
Modesty, 231.
Monographic research, necessity for, 250.
Moody, John, 87.
Moral philosophy, 214.
Moral responsibility, 219, 318.
Morale, 194, 298, 304.
Mores, 318.
Morley, John, 291.
Morocco, 191.
Morrow, Prince, 184.
Motivation, 253, 257, 262; of disinterested conservatism, 21-31; of interested conservatism, 61-81; of radicalism, 119-138.
Motives, necessity for studying, 234-236, 242, 243; to scientific research, 237-241.
Motor activity, 121.
Motor set, 120, 121.
Muck rakers, 114.
Municipal government, 230.
Mussey, H. R., 325.
Mutation, 140.
ıtual aid, 5, 43, 44, 259.
Mutualism, 264.
Mysticism, 32, 129, 165, 217, 306, 308.

Name-calling, 100, 114, 117, 198.
Nation, The, 195.
National Birth Control Conference, 197.
National Bureau of Economic Research, 240.
National Civic Federation, 114.
National Educational Association, 74.
National honor, 103, 298.
National Institution for Moral Instruction, 53.
National Woman's Party, 42, 196.
Nationalism, 4, 16, 17, 37, 115, 297, 298, 303, 309; and religion, 305.
Natural liberty, 214.
Natural rights, 270.
Natural selection, 42, 43, 46, 139.
Nearing, Scott, 198.
Necessitous condition, conservatism of, 62.

Nechayeff, 188.
Negro problem, 29-31.
Neptune, 207.
Neuroses, 126, 145.
Neurotics, 145.
New Republic, The, 195; barred from classes, 91, 325.
News "doctoring," 93-95.
Newspapers, concentration of ownership of, 94; policies of, 94; psychological influence of, 224; vested-interest control of, 94.
Newton, Isaac, 211.
Nietzsche, 309.
Nihilism, 168, 188.
Nineteenth Amendment, 196.
Nominating machinery, 89.
Non-Partisan League, 68, 135, 187.
Non-scientific mind, characteristics of, 220, 232.
Normalcy, 115, 247.
Norms, ethical, 238, 252, 305, 319.
North American Review, 324.
North Dakota, 103.
Nourse, E. G., 68.

Oath of fidelity, German, 166.
Objectivity, 6, 182, 203, 209, 211, 218, 220-223, 231-235, 237, 239, 240, 247, 279, 285, 308, 317, 318, 321, 323.
Observation, 204-210, 212, 213, 215-218, 220, 242, 249, 256.
O'Hare, Kate, 198.
Oil diplomacy, 297.
Open forums, 99, 100, 195, 285.
Open shop, 84, 85, 101, 102, 166, 302.
Opportunism, 164.
Opportunity, 30, 52, 98, 142, 151, 165, 261, 263, 271, 277, 278, 280; cooperation creation of, 262, 264, 267; democratic criterion of distribution of, 266, 282; equality of, 148, 266; equity of, 266-269, 271, 281, 288; limitation of, 152, 153, 266, 303.
Optimism, 6, 39, 152, 181, 226.
Order, 163, 164; sense of, 38, 136.
Organism as a whole, the, 254, 256, 306.
Ossification, 59.

Package libraries, 197.
Parades, 196; armistice day, 176.
Parasitism, 313.
Parenthood, not an end, 260, 261.
Parents, demands of, on children, 57.
Pareto, V., 208, 245, 308.
Parker, Carleton H., 65, 130, 185, 188.
Parsons, Elsie Clews, 59.
Party discipline, 159, 162, 193.
Passive resistance, 193.
Past, the, radical's attitude toward, 164, 165; reverence for, 51, 164, 183, 232.
Paton, Stewart, 140.
Patriotism, 16, 101, 115, 257, 324; prostitution of, 116, 117.
Patronage, 86, 96, 282.
Patten, Simon N., 25.
Paul, Alice, 196.
Paul, Kegan, 289.
Peace Conference, 59, 236, 297.
Pearson, Karl, 208, 213, 215, 265.
Peasants, conservatism of, 65.
Peonage, 87.
Persecution, 197.
Personal equation, 234. See also Subjective bias.
Personal liberty, 155, 156.
Personalism, 320.
Personality, 218, 258, 259, 261.
Personification, 176, 190.
Perspective, social, 1.
Pessimism, 6, 38, 178, 179, 296, 315.
Petition, right of, 90.
Phillips, Adele N., 166.
Phillips, Russell, 166.
Philosophy, 206, 214.
Physicians, conservatism among, 74.
Picketing, 191, 196.
Pittsburgh, 191.
Physiology, 218.
Plato, 274.
Play, 309.
Plutocracy, 264.
Police power, 83, 186, 187, 192.
Politics, in the schools, 74, 75.
Political democracy. See Democracy, political.
Political philosophy, 214, 301.
Political pressure, 196.

Political science, 213, 214.
Poole, Ernest, 137.
Popular uprisings, 189.
Population, 141, 147, 171, 209, 213, 214, 280; optimum, 268; in relation to distribution of opportunity, 267, 268.
Populism, 68, 135.
Postivity, 213.
Post Office Department, 90.
Postgraduate mother, 128.
Postal savings, 110.
Poverty, 63, 64, 75, 87, 98, 135, 268; personal and impersonal causes of, 170, 171.
Praestigiae, 98.
Pragmatism, 219.
Precedent, 183, 203.
Prediction, 211-213, 215.
President's Mediation Commission, 185.
Press bureaus, 94.
Press, censorship of, by advertisers, 94; through news "doctoring," 93, 94; through owner's control, 94.
Prestige, 28, 31, 54-60, 62, 67, 82, 83, 109, 166, 169, 182, 190, 222, 229, 230, 234, 259, 278; as agency of social control 96-98; bases of, 54-56; basis of desire for recognition, 54, 55; defined, 54; of age, 57-59; of leisure, 98, 99; of wealth, 56, 97.
Prevision. See Prediction.
Price fixation, 135.
Prices, 244, 296.
Pride, 36, 37, 72, 232, 234.
Principles, settled, conservative craving for, 32, 33.
Privilege, 58, 67, 80, 81, 83, 89, 98, 102, 105, 109, 116, 151, 185, 270, 272, 273, 281, 282, 302; ethics of, 279, 280.
Probability, science as, 219.
Professional men, conservatism among, 73-76.
Profits, 106, 108, 111, 113.
Progress, acceleration of, 159; liberal's sense of, 164; mutation theory of, 164; radical's sense of, 164; rationally directed, 304.

Progressivism, 13, 18, 67, 71, 119, 163, 183.

Prohibition, 115, 147, 155.

Proletariat, 189, dictatorship of, 168.

Proof, burden of, 182.

Propaganda, 60, 63, 83, 96, 97, 100, 101, 110, 117, 118, 137, 148, 158, 169, 173, 180, 184, 195, 197, 225, 228, 232, 243, 285-287, 298; anti-Jewish, 225; ethics of, 283, 286, 287; of the deed, 188, 190, 191; oral, 195.

Proscriptions, 45.

Prosperity, business man's concept of, 106.

Protective tariff, 85, 165, 297.

Protestantism, 162.

Psychoanalysis, 124, 125, 127, 136, 219, 235, 242.

Psychology, 213, 214, 217, 218, 236, 239, 253, 256; comparative, 234; scientific, the basis of ethics, 252, 253, 261; social, 234, 307.

Psychopathology, 125, 235.

Public Affairs Information Service, 197.

Public apathy, 117.

Public charity, right to, 63.

Public interest, 68, 101, 109, 117, 246, 321.

Public opinion, 83, 90, 196, 260, 298.

Public sentiment, 62, 75, 83, 107, 108, 111, 117, 260, 286, 287, 298.

Public utility commissions, 116.

Public utility rates, 246.

Public welfare, 106, 107.

Publicity, 95, 197; antagonistic, 197; radical, 196.

Pugnacity, 121, 127, 166, 180, 189, 192, 300, 301, 309, 313.

Pujo Committee, 87.

Punishment, 186, 219.

Puritanism, 148.

Purpose, 242, 252, 255, 304.

Radical leaders (see Leadership); defection of, 96.

Radical periodicals, 95, 184, 195, 196, 199; circulation of, 195.

Radical publishing houses, 196.

Radicalism ad hoc, 135, 136; as impulse to freedom, 145-157; characteristics of, 157-167; defined, 15; disinterested vs. interested, 133-138; ethics of, 281, 282, 287-289, 291-293; limited, 17; methods of, 168-199, 288, 289 (see also Methods of radicalism); motivation of, 119-138, 290; onhangers of, 134; opprobrious use of term, 16, 17; origin of, in social evolution, 139-145; partial, 17; product of discomfort, 119; relation to democracy, 15; result of balked interests, 120; symbolical, 127; temperamental, 144, 145; weakness of, 290.

Railroad strike of 1922, 192.

Railroad wages, 246.

Railway Brotherhoods, 246.

Rationalism, 150, 278, 279.

Rationalization, psychoanalytical, 19, 39, 60, 76, 77, 242, 276, 278, 280, 282, 315.

Reactionism, 12, 13, 15, 16, 46, 64, 84, 101, 119, 172, 187, 297.

Readjustment, 122, 303 (see also Reconstruction); psychological, methods of, 121-131; required by social evolution, 139-145.

Real estate dealers, 110.

Reconstruction, 297, 299.

Record, 204, 205, 209, 215, 242, 243.

Reform, as motive to scientific research, 237-241.

Reform Bill of 1832, 16, 139.

Reformation, the, 3.

Reinforcement of desire, 122, 130-132, 136, 145, 151, 154, 169, 174, 175, 178, 179, 186, 190, 203, 288, 313.

Relativity, 211, 213, 214, 216.

Religion, relation of, to attitudes, 305, 309.

Religious belief, 305.

Religious motive, 307.

Religious observance, 116, 129.

Rentiers, 67, conservatism of, 68, 69, 73.

Renunciation, 129.

Repression, 24, 122, 124, 125, 129, 130, 142, 150, 151, 154, 186, 187, 190, 278, 279.

Requisites for survival, 139.
Resignation, 152.
Respectability, 29, 69, 83, 97, 98, 128, 138, 179, 188, 279, 322; norms of, 278, 281.
Revisionists, 161.
Revolution, 83, 96, 98, 134, 142, 156, 173, 189, 293.
Ricardo, David, 249.
Richberg, Donald R., 247.
Right to work, 101, 111-113, 156, 271.
Robinson, J. H., 51, 277, 325.
Roman Empire, 51, 310.
Rome, 191.
Ross, E. A., 48, 53, 54, 55, 59, 66, 98, 110, 214, 279.
Rousseau, 105.
Royce, Josiah, 261.
Rubinow, I. M., 146.
Russell, Bertrand, 14, 15, 188, 208, 216.
Russia, 15, 91, 95, 189, 314.
Russian Revolution, 46.

Sabbatarianism, 225, 312.
Sabotage, 188.
Sadism, 186.
Saleeby, C. W., 261.
Salvation, 129.
Scape-goats, 176.
School boards, 88, 184.
Schools, conservative influence of, 49-53; curricula of, 49-52.
Schroeder, Theodore, 90.
Science, as measurement, 215; social function of, 241, 248, 305, 306, 318, 319; types of, 204.
Scientific attitude, 203; characteristics of, 215-220; obstacles to, 203, 215; relation to scientific method, 203, 215.
Scientific caution, 212, 227, 228.
Scientific courage, 222, 228.
Scientific description, 209.
Scientific faith, 215-218, 222, 255.
Scientific method, 141; difficulties in, 220-251; general features of, 203-215; moral function of, 203, 313; obstacles to, 215, 220-251; relation to interest-conflicts, 200-203.

Scientific mind, characteristics of, 219-231.
Scientific patience, 218, 222, 227.
Scientific research, historical method in, 243; interested in function, 208; motivation of, 211, 212, 237-241, 246, 247.
Seattle, 191.
Secret diplomacy, 59, 115, 298.
Sectarianism, 37, 42, 151, 162.
Sectionalism, 37, 104, 117, 225.
Security, desire for, 21, 22, 23, 38, 61, 69, 156, 176, 279; ethics of, 279-281.
Seductive prestige, 96, 194, 195.
Selection. See Natural selection, Social selection.
Self-abasement, 146, 300.
Self-assertion, 146, 155, 300.
Self-expression, 257, 259, 260-262, 265, 300.
Self-interest, 20, 78; guild, 66.
Self-sacrifice, 137, 179, 307; no such thing as, 257; ethics of, 279.
Selfishness; narrow, 136, 151, 257, 258, 262, 280, 292, 307, 311; the broader, 258, 307, 308, 311.
Sensitiveness, 150, 222, 223, 281; of the radical, 157.
Sentiment, 7, 9, 21, 22, 47, 100, 102, 175, 182-184, 201, 202, 231, 236, 260, 294; defined, 8, 201.
Sentimentalism, 6, 236, 237, 250, 276, 309.
Serial transference, 130.
Servant status, revolt from, 270-272.
Service, 261, 305, 307, 308; democratic standard of, 266, 271, 288.
Sex ethics, 53, 184.
Sex hygiene, 184.
Shand, A. F., 9.
Shapiro, J. S., 138, 195.
Shaw, Bernard, 58.
Sheppard-Towner Maternity Act, 147.
Shibboleths, 83, 96, 100-103, 111, 115, 117, 198, 302.
Shogunate, 59.
Siberia, 191.
Sienkiewicz, Henryk, 185.
Sinclair, Upton, 96.
Sin, sense of, 129.

Skepticism, 101; factual, 222; scientific, 220, 222; selective, 182, 226, 228.

Skilled workers, conservatism of, 65, 66.

Slave insurrections, 189.

Slave trade, 4.

Slavery, 99; classical justification of, 269.

Slichter, Charles G., 320, 329.

Slogans, 96, 100, 103, 105, 106, 109, 111, 115, 117, 198, 302.

Smith, Adam, 66, 83, 105, 270.

Smith, J. H., 106.

Social change, incidence on different classes, 143, 144; relation to conservatism and radicalism, 139-144.

Social consciousness, 253.

Social contract, sense of, 79, 214.

Social control, 26, 47, 80, 97, 155, 168, 203, 229, 264, 310; as aim of vested-interest conservatism, 83; struggle for, 168, 169.

Social cooperation, 150, 156, 172, 173, 252, 259, 276, 278, 305, 307, 312.

Social diagnosis, 169, 170, 172, 180, 275.

Social disapprobation, 29, 278.

Social equality, 29-31.

Social evolution, 42, 140-142, 164, 304, 314.

Social experiment, 159, 165, 314.

Social genesis, 304.

Social group, cannot be an end, 260, 307.

Social heredity, 300, 301.

Social institutions. See Institutions.

Social investigation, complexity of, 242, 248.

Social mind, 253, 260.

Social perspective, 1.

Social safety, conservative solicitude for, 29-31.

Social science teachers, attacks on, 92.

Social sciences, 213-215, 234, 245, 309, 331; linear reasoning in, 249.

Social selection, 25, 44, 45, 139.

Social service, 332.

Social stratification, 141; in relation to interested conservatism, 61, 62, 63.

Social value, 253.

Social welfare, 155, 253, 300.

Social work, as sublimation, 127.

Socialism, 5, 15, 16, 51, 70, 114, 152, 155, 156, 158, 171, 176, 188, 194, 198, 214, 232, 264; guild, 155, 194, 298.

Socialists, expulsion of, from New York State Legislature, 197.

Sociality, 264.

Socialization, 310.

Society, as means, 261-263; dynamic quality of, 140-143, 147; not an end, 260.

Sociological postulates, 214, 248.

Sociology, 213, 214, 249.

Sorel, Georges, 185.

Soul stuff, 253.

Sovietism, 90, 106, 298.

Sparks, Jared, 324.

Special creation, 209.

Specialization, 41, 151, 154, 224, 249, 250.

Species, 139, 204, 208, 209; origin of, 209.

Spectrum, attitudinal, 11, 12, 133.

Speculation, 165, 306.

Spencer, Anna Garlin, 128.

Spencer, Herbert, 141.

Spies, 91, 194.

Standard of living, 56, 63, 65, 66, 71, 133, 134, 136, 144, 146, 147, 152, 156, 164, 170, 282, 303, 326.

State, the, regarded as end, 165; static, 249.

State universities attacks on, 92.

States' rights, 103.

Statistical bureaus, 244.

Statistical method, 213, 215, 243-245.

Statistics, 210, 213, 243-246.

Stephen, Leslie, 16, 292.

Stevens, Doris, 196.

Stevenson, Robert Louis, 58.

Stoddard, Lothrop, 4.

Strike, 85, 191; Chinese students', 193; general, 190, 192, 193, 289.

Strike breakers, 187.

Struggle for existence, 63-65, 98, 299.

Sub-conscious, the, 123, 124.
Subjective bias, 206, 209, 220, 224, 226, 231, 233, 234, 241-243.
Subjectivity, 222-233, 250. *See also* Subjective bias.
Sublimation, 79, 122, 124, 125, 129, 130, 150, 151, 154, 278, 279, 282, 309-311.
Substitution, 122, 138, 186; in relation to conservatism and radicalism, 125-130.
Success, 57, 83, 128, 139, 141, 151.
Suffragettes, 42, 196.
Suggestion, 55, 96.
Suicide 209; spiritual, 154.
Sumner, W. G., 59.
Sumptuary legislation, 66.
Sunday schools, 52, 53.
Super-individualism, 263.
Superman complex, 71.
Supernaturalism, 176.
Superstition, 27, 98, 151, 165.
Suppression, 122-125, 130, 142, 154, 155.
Supreme Court, 85, 89.
Surplus value, 158, 214.
Survey, The, 195.
Survival of the fittest, 42, 43, 140, 309.
Suspicion, 166, 172, 180.
Symbiosis, 253.
Symbolical conservatism, 127, 128.
Symbolical radicalism, 127, 129, 130, 138.
Symbolization, 124, 126, 127, 129, 130, 176.
Sympathy, 118, 132, 133, 135, 157, 158, 178, 177, 224, 234, 258, 259, 262, 279, 281, 282, 300, 309, 312, 213, 318, 333; as source of radicalism 136-138; function in scientific research, 234-237; objective, 236, 241; subjective, 236, 241.
Syndicalism, 64, 166, 168, 188, 192, 194.
Synoptic sciences, 213.

Take-a-lead instinct, 161.
Talent, limited supply of, 266.
Taste, 128.
Taxes, school, 87.
Taxonomy, 204, 208, 245.

Teachers, attitudes of, 49-51, 74, 75, 323, 324, 327-329; conservatism of, 74-76, 324; restrictions on private life of, 88; "safe," 60, 91, 285, 325; salaries of, 75.
Teaching, censorship of, 91-93.
Temperament, 150, 154, 174, 218, 220, 231, 316; combative, 179, 180; physiological basis of, 144, 145.
Terrorism, 188. *See also* Propaganda of the deed.
Textbook commissions, 184.
Theorists, 114, 182.
Thinking, nature of, 255.
Thomas, W. I., 233, 238, 239, 241.
Thought, 207.
Thrift, 113, 119.
Thyroid gland, 120, 144, 145.
Timidity, 146, 150, 151.
Tolerance, 202, 237, 310, 313, 323.
Tolstoi, 137.
Trade union colleges, 184, 195.
Trade unions, 65, 66, 84, 188, 191, 271.
Transference, (*see* Substitution); serial, 130.
Trial and error method, 248, 250, 314.
Tridon, Andre, 188.
Trotsky, 15.
Trust movement, 70, 86.
Truth, test, of 206, 211, 212, 219, 229. *See also* Criticism, Pragmatism.
Tyndall, John, 216.

Unconscious, the, 122-125, 127, 235.
Under-cover men, 91.
Unemployment, 85, 111, 143, 156, 296.
Unfair list, 85, 191.
United States Senate, 89.
Universal military service, 84.
Universities, 295, 321-323, 329; German, 92; State, attacks on, 92.
University governing boards, personnel of, 93.
University of Oklahoma, 198.
University of Tennessee, 325.
University of Wisconsin, 198.
Unrest, 131, 133, 142-144, 149, 158.

Uranus, 207.
Utilitarianism, 257, 261.
Utopianism, 157.

Valuation, 9, 22, 38, 177, 201, 202, 215, 246, 247; radical's scale of, 163.
Value, 23, 163, 201, 246; surplus, 158, 214.
Value-reaction, 9.
Veblen, Thorstein, 22, 31, 43, 44, 56, 68, 69, 98, 143, 144, 322.
Vested interests, 58, 61-63, 65-67, 70, 80, 83, 84, 86, 88-97, 101, 103, 105-108, 111, 114-117, 135, 181, 184, 187, 188, 190-192, 194, 201, 272, 278, 280, 290, 314, 326; nature of, 62.
Vested-interest conservatism, 62, 65-74, 81, 83, 99, 105, 114, 116.
Viewpoint, 1, 2.
Villard, Oswald Garrison, 198.
Violence, 174, 181, 185-191; ethics of, 283, 284, 288, 289; in labor disputes, 83, 102, 103, 187, 191.
Vocational education, 51, 52.
Volstead Act, 17.
Voltaire, 137.

Wallas, Graham, 299.
Wanderlust, 130.
War, 83, 103, 147, 156, 187, 302, 309; aftermath of, 294-298.
Ward, Lester F., 304.
Warren, H. C., 8, 9.
Washington, George, 324.
Waste, 110, 136, 147-149, 164, 225, 267, 326.
Watkins, G. P., 240.
Watson, John B., 121, 125, 145.
Wealth, 151, 152, 208; conservative influence of, 56; distribution of, 239, 240, 262, 266; prestige of, 56.

Webb, Beatrice, 149, 290.
Webb, Sidney, 149, 290.
Weisman, August, 42.
Wells, H. G., 320.
West Virginia, 77, 191
West, W. M., 325
Westinghouse, George, 18.
Westminster Catechism, 260.
Wharton, Edith, 58.
Whigs, 139.
Whim, 216, 222, 231, 305. See also Chance.
White, Andrew D., 92.
White-collared class, conservatism of, 62, 67, 72, 73.
Williams, J. M., 3, 201.
Williams, Roger A., 77.
Wilson, Woodrow, 14, 89.
Wisconsin, 193; University of, 198.
Woman movement, 128.
Woman suffrage, 28, 40, 42, 89, 161, 196, 197.
Woman's Christian Temperance Union, 238.
Women, conservatism of, 63, 88, 127, 128; economic dependence of, 57, 88; teachers, 75; unrest of, 128.
Woodworth, R. S., 7.
Workers' education, 184, 329.
Workmanship, instinct of, 22, 128, 132, 133, 141, 146, 151, 262, 271 281, 300, 318.

Yarros, Victor F., 136.
Young, Art, 176.
Youth, 48-59, 78, 322, 333; conservatism of, 33; emotional radicalism of, 159, 160.
Youth Movement, 58, 198

Znaniecki, F., 233, 238.